Perspectives on Contemporary
Ethnic Conflict

Perspectives on Contemporary Ethnic Conflict

Primal Violence or the Politics of Conviction?

Edited by Santosh C. Saha

LEXINGTON BOOKS

A division of
ROWMAN & LITTLEFIELD PUBLISHERS, INC.
Lanham • Boulder • New York • Toronto • Oxford

LEXINGTON BOOKS

A division of Rowman & Littlefield Publishers, Inc.
A wholly owned subsidiary of The Rowman & Littlefield Publishing Group, Inc.
4501 Forbes Boulevard, Suite 200
Lanham, MD 20706

PO Box 317
Oxford
OX2 9RU, UK

British Library Cataloguing in Publication Information Available

Library of Congress Cataloging-in-Publication Data

Perspectives on contemporary ethnic conflict : primal violence or the politics of
conviction? / Edited by Santosh C. Saha.
    p. cm.
Includes bibliographical references and index.
ISBN-13: 978-0-7391-1085-0 (cloth : alk. paper)
ISBN-10: 0-7391-1085-3 (cloth : alk. paper)
1. Ethnic conflict. 2. Ethnic conflict—Case studies. 3. History, Modern—20th century.
4. History, Modern—21st century. I. Saha, Santosh C. HM1121.P46 2006
305.8009'04—dc22   2006003955

Printed in the United States of America

⊖™ The paper used in this publication meets the minimum requirements of American
National Standard for Information Sciences—Permanence of Paper for Printed Library
Materials, ANSI/NISO Z39.48–1992.

For

Professor Gouri Shankar Raychowdhuri

*a principled wholesome personality having a deep sense of ancient
Indian traditions and values*

Contents

Introduction   Toward Contexts More Intricate and Subtle   1
              Mark Lewis Taylor

Part I: Explaining Ethnic Violence

Chapter 1:   Third-Party Intervention in Ethno-Religious Conflict: 17
              Role Theory and the Major Powers in South Asia
              Gaurav Ghose and Patrick James

Chapter 2:   Ethnic Violence and the Loss of State Legitimacy: 47
              Burma and Indonesia in a Context of Post-Colonial
              Developmentalism
              Vivienne Wee and Graeme Lang

Chapter 3:   Not Ethnicity, but Race: Unity and Conflict in Rwanda 77
              Since the Genocide
              Helen M. Hintjens and David E. Kiwuwa

Chapter 4:   The Hutu-Tutsi Conflict in Rwanda   107
              Paul J. Magnarella

Chapter 5:   Politico-Psychological Dimensions of the Ethnic and   133
              Political Conflicts in India: Conflicting Paradigms at Work
              Santosh C. Saha

Part II: Contemporary Regional Ethnic Conflict

Chapter 6:   Multifaceted Ethnic Conflicts and Conflict Resolution   173
                in Nigeria
                Abdul Karim Bangura

Chapter 7:   Georgetown Shuffle: Ethnic Politics of Afro-Guyanese,   197
                Amerindians, and Indo-Guyanese in Postcolonial Guyana
                Sabita Manian

Chapter 8:   Sudan's Identity Wars and Democratic Route to Peace   225
                Rita Kiki Edozie

Chapter 9:   Ethnic Conflict in Mexico: The Zapatistas   251
                Michael R. Hall

Chapter 10:   Kurdish Ethnonationalism: A Concise Overview   269
                Mir Zohair Husain and Stephen Shumock

Chapter 11:   The Roots of Contemporary Ethnic Conflict and   295
                Violence in Burundi
                Johnson W. Makoba and Elavie Ndura

Bibliography   311

Index   327

About the Contributors   339

Introduction

Toward Contexts More Intricate and Subtle

Mark Lewis Taylor

> We need to embrace, in the place of mere realism, a more robust and
> complex view of the world, what we might call meta-realism, which
> recognizes a context more intricate and subtle than we had hoped
> would be necessary, that also takes into account some values, beliefs,
> wishes and hopes that are completely unrealistic.
>
> Charles L. Mee, Jr.

The above quotation is set at the conclusion of Branimir Anzulovic's *Heavenly
Serbia: From Myth to Genocide,* and fittingly describes the kind of thought and
action necessary for approaching contexts where ethnic differences become violent. The book you hold in your hands, *Perspectives on Contemporary Ethnic
Conflict,* helps give birth to the "meta-realism" so needed, an approach to ethnic
conflict that refuses the simplifications built of easy polarities, of mono-causal
theories, or from characterizations of human groups formed on centuries of
stereotype. It looks at some of the most conflictive sites in the world, where ethnic violence has been created and played out: Burma, Indonesia, India, Rwanda,
Burundi, Nigeria, the Sudan, Mexico, Guyana. As contributors to this volume

make abundantly clear, when careful analysis is made of these settings, the many forms of "mere realism" built from received analytic distinctions and categories about international reality fall away, just as do the simplifying ideals about "the nature of the human" or about "the nature" of this or that group.

A Call for a Meta-Realism

Western powers today need especially to hear this call to a meta-realism, still steeped as they are in the legacies of their colonizations abroad, evidenced by the way British and French empires still structure their relations to the present global developments, and by their histories of repression regarding those within their borders thought to be ethnically different. The several centuries of discrimination and oppression of non-white groups in the United States, also pull its leaders and scholars into the ranks of those who need this book, who would benefit from the greater complexity of its meta-realistic context.

Note that Mee suggests that such a meta-realism involves also a study of the *un*realistic values and beliefs of people, and the power those can hold. A complex analysis is one that honors the power of the *un*realistic myths as they often work to deadly effect amid the play of many other factors –economic, political, social. So it is that for understanding the strife of the Balkans in the late 20th century, we needed studies like Anzulovic's on the national myth of "Greater Serbia," as well as those that throw focus on the way economic matters drove the conflict.[1] Moreover, these myths exist not just between those who are studied by Western leaders and scholars – the "primordial others" caught up in cycles of violence. No, they exist also among those who claim to stand back and do the analyzing in the name of an allegedly more civilized way.

British Prime Minister John Major, for example, uttered these words about the conflict in the Balkans of the 1980s and 1990s.

> The biggest single element behind what has happened in Bosnia is the collapse of the Soviet Union and of the discipline that that exerted over *the ancient hatreds* in the old Yugoslavia. Once that discipline had disappeared, those ancient hatreds reappeared, and we began to see their consequences when the fighting occurred.[2]

Just as simplistic myths often drive the actual perpetrators of violence, so they drive observers of it like Major, who revealed also his myth, especially in his discourse of "the ancient hatreds." Major is not a lone example. Especially when talking about the Balkans, a host of political leaders and media pundits made recourse to the "ancient ethnic hatreds" interpretation of conflict in ethnically conflicted settings. Such interpretation often serves as a way to rationalize the presence of conflict stemming from past external interventions and dominance by great powers (colonialism, foreign invasion), and throws the fault back onto those who suffer it directly.

Not just national leaders like Prime Minister Major are steeped in this mythic tendency to project mythic violence outward and away from the "civilized" group, onto others who use myth for violence. Against the backdrop of a still prevalent white racism in the United States, the popular culture of that nation's people frequently show similar tendencies. In the wake of the social trauma resulting from Hurricane Katrina, for example, the urban poor who suffered the brunt of displacement were often referred to, as on a popular radio station in New Jersey, as "those people," groups who don't know how to get out of the way, or who "only know how to be served by the welfare state, unable to help themselves." Many other potential examples are legion, especially if we were to examine the values and beliefs of other nations, too.

Complexity and Care

If we attain to a more complex "meta-realism," this is not driven only by a scholastic worship of complexity and intricacy. The careful attentiveness to the complexity of diverse factors carries and expresses also a moral concern. Among many scholars, especially those who wish to mask or bracket the moral quandaries that attend their own socially-located knowledge, there is a kind of fetishizing of complexity that ever defers questions of moral care and discernment. That is not the approach of contributors to this collection. True, there are no quick moral judgments, and moral reflection is not brought to the fore. Nevertheless, navigating the complexities of the political traumas examined here suggests in numerous ways that a care for the well-being of the sufferers—as they strive for peace, justice, human rights, and democracy—is always close at hand. At times, too, the contributors will reflect on what might move parties in conflict toward redress or alleviation.

The connection to moral concern is evident in Mee's and Anzulovic's way of developing the call to complexity: "This meta-realism might finally be indistinguishable from the elusive and contradictory tenets of ethics, which are, finally no more nor less than the accumulated practical folk wisdom of millennia of human experience."[3] In other words, the meta-realist approach is no hiding from the decisions and expressions of moral perspective that conflict often generates. We might say that the study of the complexity of how worlds of conflicts are formed, aids in the study of how worlds of conflict ought to be redressed, mitigated. In other terms, an all too rare, careful attentiveness to complexity is a way to care for the trauma, injustice, wrenching and extensive pain generated by what is so frequently rendered "ethnic conflict." Meta-realism, to recall the words of Mee above, enables the forming of not just esoteric scholarly jargon, but the emergence of a practical human ("folk") wisdom, a knowledge of complexity that might serve justice and peace.

At the outset here, it is no doubt important to stress that in this book's study, a moral concern to care and redress is rooted in the extensive waste and loss of humanity that forms the backdrop of these studies. The nearly 1 million killed and 2 million uprooted in Rwanda of 1994 is one dramatic case. This book also attends to the 300,000 (mostly Hutus) killed in Burundi; the 500,000 refugees of the military regime of Burma, and the 600,000 internally displaced there as well; the one million lives lost in the Biafran war with Nigeria, the genocide that the U.S. congress has named as ongoing in Darfur of the Sudan, and more. These, though, are large numbers and broad terms for designating the human terror of this violence. The contributors here press beyond the statistics and overviews, and often engage the stories and details, the individual struggles of those who face the impoverishment, the vulnerability to rape, the unrelenting travail of war, the routine torture, and the indignities of occupation. A human care, a moral concern asking about the good of those in suffering, depends on the caring attention to detail.

Critical Exercises in Meta-Realism

The careful analyses of each essayist in this volume offer the surest route into the meta-realism we need deploy for studying the trauma named "ethnic violence." The essays are grouped into two major Parts, one focusing on explaining the sources and dynamics of ethnic violence, the other focusing primarily on descriptions of regional ethnic conflict across the globe. Readers should be prepared, though, to find this boundary between explanation and description not to be a firm one; for along the way of explaining the cases of violence in Part 1, there are discussions rich in the texture of description, and amid the portraits given in the Part 2 readers will also find gems to aid in scholars' work of explanation.

Even though the readers' journey through these essays, singly and collectively, is the surest route for grasping this book's contribution to meta-realist complexity, I suggest that we can fill out this Introduction with a series of critical exercises through which readers will journey as they confront the essays. Each of the critical exercises I present here involve key distinctions between two terms or ideas, which this book's writers both acknowledge but then render more complex. In presenting these critical exercises as I do, I presume that not all binary thinking is problematic; rather, the challenge is to enable a multiplicity of binary perspectives to prompt analysis that transcends the confines of binaristic thinking, perhaps to the point of shaking free from the chains of binarism that have structured so much academic and popular discourse about "ethnic violence." I stress that no one, or even only several, of the critical exercises I name below constitute a meta-realist approach to study of social conflict involving ethnic identity. Instead, all of them together, along with still other blurred distinctions made by scholars of violence, will be needed.

1. Contesting "Primordial" and "Constructionist" Explanations

With this first distinction, we can see that the explanatory structure of social science inquiries into ethnic violence, has often been embedded in the very problematic of "ancient ethnic heritages" that we discussed at the outset of this Introduction. The mythic simplifications of political leaders and popular writers about the Balkans conflict have been reformulated in traditions of scholarly analysis. The "primordialists," for example, approximate the process of mythic projection when they interpret group tendencies toward conflict as rooted in the make-up or character of a group. In this way of explanation, the group is often "essentialized" as problematic when it is seen in conflict with others, i.e. it is interpreted as having an essence that is conflict prone in some way.

The "constructivists" tend to reject scholars' primordialist explanations as no explanation at all. Saha, in his essay here, for example, sees it only as a kind of labeling. Other writers in this text would seem to agree. Constructivists place the emphasis on the creations of history, society, economy and politics, as at work in the agency of specific groups and individuals as the material for explaining violence between groups. These creations also are the material from which the very category of "ethnicity" itself is derived, and from which different kinds of ethnic identity are forged. In short, constructivists begin with an assumption that not only is "ethnic conflict" an activity constructed from the particularities and vicissitudes of history, also the very notions of "ethnic" and "ethnicity" are interpreted as constructions.

While most of the contributors here lean toward the constructivist side of this distinction, in keeping with the meta-realism we broached at the beginning of this Introduction, scholars here are hardly satisfied with defining the field of analysis only in those two terms. They go beyond it in two ways. First, and most obviously, they insist on considering other approaches to studies of ethnic violence: "instrumentalist," "consociational," and so on. The study of ethnic violence, in other words, is not just a matter of positioning constructivist studies over against primordialist ones. There are other types of study as well. Second, these scholars also respect the point made by Anzulovic and Mee that there is a seed of insight in the primordialist sensibility, in that overtime some groups have projected certain myths (about other groups and about themselves) and then have sought to live into them. This is to say, for all those myths' constructedness, those who live into them give them a certain power that shapes history and enables scholars to anticipate certain probabilities. It is just this that the primordialists often seize upon in their stereotypes and labeling. This insight, however, can be accommodated within a meta-realist perspective that factors it in as but one dynamic element within the fuller and more complex set of constructivist approaches. Most writers here, for example, will study the way certain groups, such as the Hutus of Rwanda, have internalized certain myths about themselves and others from the colonial past which when routinized and lived out over time yield some predictive patterns of violence. But that potential for gauging future probabilities does not fall back into primordialist theory. The emphasis in the meta-realist approach falls on the process of creating and internalizing the myths that come to have power. Readers do well to watch how these scholars work the primordialist/constructivist distinction in their treatments.

2. Moving Beyond Multi-causal and Mono-causal Analyses

From the foregoing it should be obvious that readers should also expect contributors to be bringing to bear a multiplicity of factors and causes that create and shape conflict and violence. A meta-realist perspective entails a multi-causal analysis. The complexities of constructed conditions that yield violence also predispose these scholars to multi-causal treatments.

This being acknowledged, readers will find it important to track the particular trajectories of explanation that the various authors tend to privilege in presenting their material. In other terms, we might say this: granted that there are a multiplicity of causes, the various situations examined by these writers lead them to raise certain analytic strategies of analysis to prominence. Some writers, for example, will highlight material conditions (realities of draught, scarcity of food, and so on), while others will throw a spotlight on the function of religious ideologies for defining who is within an approved group or entity, and who is not. Some writers, such as Magnarella in chapter 4 on Rwanda, will seek to sort out ultimate causes from proximate causes of ethnic conflict. The specificities of context, as probed by the book's contributors, do not ever yield a mono-causal treatment, but nor is the range of analyses simply a multi-causal free for all. Analytic decisions are made and certain factors among many are developed to explain and describe the scene at hand. Readers will be invited to gauge how writers limit multi-causality without resorting to mono-casual explanations.

3. Fusing Present and Past Horizons of Analysis (a Postcolonial Sensibility)

Nearly all of these contributors work with a sense of history. Indeed, to explore with any adequacy the strife and trauma at their sites, this is inevitable. The majority of these sites are hotbeds traceable to the tumult of their colonized pasts. Rwanda and Burundi are treated in relation to French and Belgian colonizers, Nigeria and India in relation to British rule, the Sudan in relation to Arabized, Islamized, as well as British rule. Even though not many of the writers style their analyses as "postcolonial" (Manian writes of "postcolonial Guyana, Wee and Lang of "post-colonial developmentalism"), they all are analyzing strife in the burned-over districts of empire's colonial projects.

The result is that the temporal horizons of these analyses float back and forth between past and present horizons. I deploy the notion of "fusion" for this interplay of horizons, in the sense of the hermeutical writings of H.G. Gadamer. This fusion is not a merger, in which the difference between past and present is lost, but an interplay of perspective, where a shuttling between past and present paradigms for viewing, is allowed to create more nuanced treatments of the contexts of violence. There is not here the kind of ethnography that abstracts society and groups from the flow of history, nor is there a historical plotting of events that ignores social forces and dynamics of present groups and their relations. No, nearly all contributors view their contacts through the lens of a historical analysis as well as through more sociological and political ones. The need to look at present ethnic violence, say in Nigeria and the Sudan, in relation to the past is especially evident given the way past decisions by colonizing powers, to carve up and draw new boundaries for "independent" nations, still haunt the attempts of so many cultural groups to live together today.

Since so many of these sites are previously colonized ones, this means that the analyses here dwell in that curious state of "the postcolonial"—a time and space "after" the colonial regime, "after" decolonization and independence, hence "post"-colonial, and yet not really "post-" in the sense of being free from the past conditions that are carried in groups and beliefs of the present. Add in various forms of neocolonialism and contemporary militarist and imperialist moves of powerful nations like the United States, and the "post-" in postcolonial does not seem "post-" at all, except in the less temporal sense of a quality or intention to struggle against, so as to move beyond, the constraints of colonial legacies. So, even if those famous rituals and events of "independence" did occur—in the 1940s through 1960s for African and Asian nations (and much earlier in the "decolonization" of Latin America in the eighteenth and nineteenth centuries)—the influence of the colonial past fuses itself into the social politics of the present. Given the prominence of the colonial heritage in making for conflict, and remembering Jürgen Osterhammel's insight that European and U.S. racism was "the ultimate version of the difference axiom" for the colonizing neocolonizing empires,[4] one might even interpret the violence stemming from legacies of the colonizer's policies as another form of "ethnic violence." From a full historical perspective on the present, it is not quite right to characterize as "ethnic violence" what occurs within small, newly independent states. Ethnic violence can also name the colonizing violence of epochs and empires, past and present.

4. Distinguishing Ethnic Differentiation and Ethnic Violence

We come here to another distinction, which is preserved, but then complexified and transcended in the meta-realist analyses of this book. Again, as with the previous pairs of terms, the contributors are careful not to collapse these two notions into one another. Not all ethnic differentiation leads on to ethnic violence. Groups with long constructed and nurtured identities have often lived together in zones that today are often depicted as predominantly conflictual. In the Balkan regions, for example, there was the impressive degree of toleration, indeed celebration, of different ethnic identities in Sarajevo and Belgrade.

Both notions, though—ethnic differentiation and ethnic violence—interact in this volume. As Vivienne Wee and Graeme Lang make clear, the research on ethnic violence brings together two others in the social sciences, "two largely non-intersecting literatures—studies of ethnic conflict and studies of political violence."[5] It is another example of the working of the perspective of the book, its meta-realism, it's taking on of complexity that engages a surplus of perspectives beyond what before has been taken as "real" about violence, conflict and ethnicity. Indeed, readers will begin to unravel much of the richness of the book's offerings simply by tracing the many ways authors here theoretically relate ethnic differentiation to ethnic violence. What *are* the differences at work and how have they been constructed? Is the construction of the relevant ethnicity itself a condition for the violence? Is construction of ethnic identity itself a kind of violence of its own? If it is not itself a violence, is it just "a difference" of human culture or practice? What factors lead differentiated ethnic groups to transition into violent conflict? These are all questions that emerge and are addressed for readers as contributors here explore the intersections between ethnic differentiation and ethnic violence.

5. Examining Ethnic Identity and the Politics of Race

Readers coming from outside the social science literature, but with a strong interest in the study of ethnic differentiation and violence, may need to be reminded of what for some time has become an axiom of studies of ethnicity. Ethnicity is not race. Ethnic differences, to be studied in all their fullness, need to break free from the strictures of the notion of race/races. Social science's freedom from scientific racism, a hard won and at times still continuing struggle, has meant establishing this difference between ethnicity and race. Human groups' genetic features and social existence do not correspond to the differentiations projected as races by racist standpoints, whether the crass hierarchies set out by scholars like Johann Blumenbach in 1795 ("Caucasian, Mongolian, Ethiopian, American and Malayan")[6] or other political projections that have occurred since then.

Exemplary of the difference between ethnicity and race, is Hintjens' and Kiwuwa's treatment of conflict between Hutu and Tutsi in Rwanda since the 1994 genocide. They portray "ethnic identity" (recall, always a complexly constructed notion) as different from "the politics of race." Racialized politics is defined by them as a "reading people's identities and social status off their position," a position in post-genocidal Rwanda usually set by people's experience of the 1994 events of genocide. The "post-" in post-genocidal is as ambiguous, if also as necessary, as the notion of the "post-colonial." The major point to observe here is that the scholar of the complexity that is Rwanda must navigate both the dynamics of ethnic differentiation and of the politics of race. However interconnected – and they are in a sundry and multileveled ways – they are not to be confused. In fact, as Hintjens and Kiwuwa suggest toward the end of their essay, peace and democratic growth in Rwanda will depend on the extent to which its citizens are able to forge ethnic and political identities that are free from the politics of race (free from, for example, the categorization of one's identity as "Hutu," as "Tutsi"). They point to some hopeful signs in the form of "more complex perspectives on political identity" that move beyond the Hutu-Tutsi divide. Even in some of the official categories used by national authorities since the genocide ("survivors and *genocidaires,* new and old caseload refugees, rural and urban Rwandans, Anglophone and Francophone") there is a cross-cutting of the binaristic racial politics. When one factors in, as Hintjens and Ki-wuwa do, other dynamics stemming from class, region, politics and religion, then the potential for constructing ethnic identity outside the politics of race, and so creating a more livable and democratic politics, becomes greater. With these complexities the "meta-realist" analytic comes to full flower. At the same time, the meta-realist's dimension of care, which laces the meta-realist care-full attention to complexity with moral interest, suggests the ethical aspect of meta-realist analyses of sites like that of Rwanda.

6. Linking ethnicity and politics

In the previous section we raised the question of politics, though largely in relation to the politics of race. This, though, is just one way in which the notions of ethnicity in these articles on ethnic violence will intersect with politics. Readers should prepare to examine the many complexities of the book's meta-realist analysis, in so far as they link ethnicity and politics as determinative forces in situations of violence.

What is meant by these two terms? It might be helpful to suggest at the outset here that "ethnicity" can be seen more as a marking term, a way to designate groups and persons that are in some way different from others with whom they relate. "Politics," on the other hand, designates the way power is dispersed between marked groups, by way of either the more positive practices of power-sharing, compromise and mutual support, or through more negative practices of dominance, repression, marginalization and exclusion. Often the political options are very complex amalgams ranging between these positive and negative political options.

There is an added complication, however, which will be brought to light by the following studies. Even though it is true that ethnically marked groups can be studied with a view to the play of powers in their contexts, the very marking process that produces the ethnic group's political experience is itself a process that is political. This need not be lamented as a vicious theoretical circle. It simply calls attention to the fact that ethnicity, and the ways ethnicity is marked in different settings, is not only studied as having present and future political consequences but also as always already a consequence of past political conditions. The marking of ethnic identity shapes politics, even as ethnic marking is shaped by politics. Nearly all the essays of the volume are cognizant of this complexity and readers are invited to compare the various ways this complex circle between ethnicity and politics is played out across the different contributions.

7. Focusing Material Conditions and Ethnic Conflict

This dynamic of interaction in the book concerns perhaps another way that politics intersects ethnicity. If politics is about the dispersal of power (shared, dominative, exclusive, et al) the question of material conditions raises the question of power in a more specific way. Here, the focus falls on infrastructural considerations of geography, ecological habitat, availability of resources, and the way the production of life-sustaining resources are made available (or not) to the various groups that share, or are contingent to, specific material ecospheres or bioregional sets of circumstances.

Nearly all the authors acknowledge the importance of material conditions, if only in their tracing the locations of the groups they study, describing habitat and climate of the worlds involved. This remains true even for those whose primary interest falls on other factors, i.e. myths and beliefs projected onto groups that cause conflict, or an "oppression psychosis" borne by certain groups. Some, such as Magnarella, will make a comparatively stronger case for the determinative role of material conditions in ethnic conflict. After acknowledging the many interpretations of what caused the Rwandan genocidal conflict between Hutus and Tutsis, he lists most of these as "proximate causes," with the "ultimate cause" proposed as "the increasing imbalance in land, food, and people that led to malnutrition, hunger, periodic amine, and fierce competition for land to farm." Magnarella sees this as not just a problem in Rwanda, but of the wider area of East Africa of which Rwanda is one part. This regional focus prompts one to consider, again, the legacy of colonialism in helping to create the shortages and conflicts that arise over so wide an area. The impact of colonialism on material conditions of ethnic conflict are also evident in Nigeria, as Bangura makes clear in chapter 6 when summarizing how the British colonizers' arbitrary drawing of lines across African land and space, making these into boundaries of national power, threw multifaceted ethnic groups into sudden and problematic proximity so that nation-building was a struggle, if not, often, an impossibility.

Readers should not expect to find here a material determinism with respect to ethnic violence, one that always and only privileges dynamics leading from theories of material conditions to ethnic conflict. Even Magnarella's strong case for material conditions as ultimate cause in Rwanda, situates that causality in relation to a set of important proximate causes. When reading the other contributors as well, one can attend to the role that is given to material determinants in the meta-realist perspective of writers and in the meta-realist perspective set in place by the book as a whole.

8. Considering Ethnic Violence and State Legitimacy
Beginning with this point and concluding with the next, I highlight two conjunctions within meta-realist analysis that lean a bit more toward the ethical dimension of that analysis. That is to say, without losing their analytic value, analyses here also carry a moral interest, if only in the care they signal when contemplating improvement of situations of trauma, whether this is Nigeria, the Sudan, Indonesia, Burma, India, Kurdistan, southern Mexico (Chiapas), or elsewhere. That care, this moral interest, is not quite an "emancipatory interest" that the early Jürgen Habermas and others often find nestled in the tangled interstices

of scientific inquiry's *a priori* assumptions,[7] but it is an "alleviatory interest," a concern constituting an ethical dimension of meta-realist analysis, a concern to mitigate and redress the trauma of violence contexts fraught with dynamics of ethnicity. This moral or alleviatory interest often seems to function as a final cause or lure as analysts unfold their descriptions and explanations.

The first conjunction of this sort lies in the occasional but steady interest of writers to examine the relationship between ethnic violence and state legitimacy. State legitimacy refers to the presence of a strong state that invites and commands the consent of groups in potential or actual conflict. Wee and Lang lay out the connection early on with their discussions of how ethnic violence tends to break out when "state legitimacy is fragile." So intimate for them are the connections between ethnic differentiation and political conflict, on the one hand, and state legitimacy on the other hand, that they plea that we "understand ethnic differentiation and nation-making as social phenomena situated at different points of the same political spectrum."[8] Again, there is no reduction of ethnic differentiation to nation-building, nor of nation-building to mere managing of ethnic differences, but the two major processes are intricately connected.

Readers will see contributors considering this relation in various national contexts—in the search for a state to prevent future replays of genocide in Rwanda and Burundi, in the struggle for power-sharing and compromises necessary for a legitimate state to emerge in the Sudan, or in the quest for a less corrupted leadership in state functions of Nigeria. The contributors' interests in state formation to alleviate ethnic violence is evident among the book, whether they focus on the development-states working within the dominant globalization paradigm (G7 nations implementing and enforcing agendas of the International Monetary Fund and the World Bank),[9] or they focus on more innovative nation-building aims by way of postcolonial people's movements that cut against the grain of current globalization structures, as in the Zapatista struggle of Chiapas that Hall explores, in the Nigerian women's movements challenging oil corporations, or in the movements of postcolonial Guyana that Manian analyzes.

One result of this attention to nation-building as site for potentially alleviating or redressing ethnic conflict is that readers are given a diversity of viewpoints on the nation-building process, and may even be led to consider new notions of just what a "nation" is. This, in turn, may be preparatory for considering the challenge laid down by Michael Hardt and Antonio Negri, in their books *Empire* and *Multitude*, in which they argue that the very notion of nation, and the nationalism that goes with it, are often so problematic that the nation-state cannot really function as a lasting remedy to emancipate peoples from trauma and group conflict.[10] Both the variety of nation-building operations and dissatisfaction with nation-state politics and nationalism, may turn the ethical interests of meta-realist analysis toward more expansive regional and global polities for redressing ethnic violence.

9. Studying Third-Party and Other Intervention and Ethnic Violence

The turning of attention to regional and global matrices of analysis, mentioned just above, is also evident in this book's attentiveness to "third-party" or other external interventions into given sites of ethnic conflict. The most sustained example of this is in the opening essay by Ghose and James, which offers a systemic framework for examining third-party intervention in ethnic conflict. Indeed, the intricate conceptual structure of this first essay may make the most demands upon readers, but it is exemplary of the complexity that this entire Introduction has attributed to the meta-realist approach to ethnic differentiation and conflict, which becomes all the more complex when one adds the study of intervention strategies and impact. Ghose and James test their framework in relation to Pakistan's intervention into Kashmir in 1965, and then to India's intervention in Sri Lanka.

The interest in intervention is evident in a number of other essays. It is taken up by Bangura in analyzing Nigerian conflict, is implied in Magnarella's focusing on the material need of the whole area of East Africa that calls for regional and global organizations' work of economic relief, and in Edozie's considerations of UN and U.S. failures to intervene forthrightly in the unfolding genocide of Darfur in the Sudan. Intervention is not the only mode of alleviation considered by the book's contributors, but it is a recurring motif that most contributors point to, regarding the many sites of postcolonial experiment they analyze, enabling them to express what Edozie refers to in her essay title as a "democratic route to peace." The book may hold lessons on intervention especially for the powerful G7 countries that have powers to intervene. It may clarify what genuine alleviative intervention is, as distinct from interference rooted in powerful nation's self-interests, or it may suggest models for bridging between effective alleviative intervention and nationally self-interested intervention. The record of intervention by powerful nation-states, especially by the United States, is not good. As Samantha Fox wrote after her journalistic experience in the Balkans and from the perspective of her work and studies at the Carr Center for Human Rights Policy at Harvard University, "The United States had never in its history intervened to stop genocide and had in fact rarely even made a point of condemning it as it occurred," until it made its belated response to the Bosnia genocide in the 1990s.[11]

The moral interest provoked by genocide and by other political traumas born from group interaction, and also the knowledge interests that become so exceedingly complex when we turn to what is called "ethnic violence" – both the moral interests and the knowledge interests, I suggest, call forward the kind of meta-realist perspective and analysis forged by this volume. The book's contributors and editors would be among the first to admit that not all the complexities surface in their works. Many necessary issues and complexities, however, are indeed broached in this volume, even if this Introduction has been only able to scratch the surface. The nine "critical exercises" discussed briefly in this section of the Introduction are offered more as portals through which readers might look out onto the complex sea of many more distinctions and arguments awaiting attention. The book's greater richness lies before them.

Notes

1. On the role of economics in the Balkans crisis, see Misha Glenny, "So Milosevic Leaves Serbia—and Goes Where? *The New York Times*, Friday, June 23, 2000, A23, Noel Malcolm, *Bosnia: A Short History.* New, Updated Edition (New York: New York University Press, 1994/1996), xxi. Also Scott Anderson, "The Curse of Blood and Vengeance," *The New York Times Magazine,* December 29, 1999, 29–30. Anderson insists on challenging the frequent talk of "centuries-old ethnic and religious hatreds" with a study of the economic and social conditions of rural groups in relation to urban ones.

2. Cited in Malcolm, xx (emphasis added).

3. Branimir Ansulovic, *Heavenly Serbia: From Myths to Genocide* (New York: New York University Press, 1999), 179.

4. Jürgen Osterhammel, *Colonialism: A Theoretical Overview* (Princeton: Markus Wiener Publishers, 1995/2002), 108.

5. Vivienne Wee and Graeme Lang, "Ethnic Violence and the Loss of State Legitimacy: Burma and Indonesia in a Context of Postcolonial Developmentalism," below [first page of their essay].

6. See Stephen Gregory and Roger Sanjek, "The Enduring Inequalities of Race," in Gregory and Sanjek, editors, *Race* (New Brunswick, NJ: Rutgers University Press, 1994), 5.

7. Jürgen Habermas, *Knowledge and Human Interests.* Trans. Jeremy Shapiro (Boston: Beacon Press, 1972).

8. Wee and Lang, [sentence immediately following section title: "Ethnic violence in two problematic..."]

9. For a helpful description of the "development" pattern of globalization, see Rebecca Todd Peters, *In Search of the Good Life: The Ethics of Globalization* (New York: Continuum, 2004), 70–100. For a critique of the development model, see Arturo Escobar, *Encountering Development* (Princeton: Princeton University Press, 1994).

10. Michael Hardt and Antonio Negri, *Empire* (Cambridge, MA: Harvard University Press, 2000), 109–13.

11. Samantha Power, *"A Problem from Hell: America and the Age of Genocide* (New York: Basic Books, 2002), xv.

Part I

Explaining Ethnic Violence

Chapter 1

Third-Party Intervention in Ethno-Religious Conflict: Role Theory and the Major Powers in South Asia

Gaurav Ghose and Patrick James

This study has used role theory in its explanatory form to account for third-party intervention in ethno-linguistic conflict. A theoretical framework, built in terms recommended by systemism, organizes instrumental and affective variables from the international environment, regional subsystem and within the state as actor toward that end. Two case studies from South Asia—Pakistan's invasion of Kashmir in 1965 and India's halting intervention in Sri Lanka from the 1980s —are used to assess the value of the preceding framework.

Introduction: Third-Party Intervention in Ethnic Conflict

Third-party intervention in ethnic conflicts is an old phenomenon, although scholarly attention with a general range of application is relatively new and un-common.[1] This study focuses on foreign policy decisions about intervention in ethnic conflict as an outcome resulting from the interplay of variables at multiple levels. Two dissimilar cases within the same geographic sub region—one in which intervention appears essentially to be an irredentist claim based on eth-noreligious considerations and the other an intervention primarily based on eth-nic affinity are assessed to gain understanding of (a) the interplay of the vari-ables in total and (b) how ethnic factors fit into the broader picture.

This study is divided into *five* additional sections: The second section intro-duces *systemism*, a framework that brings together unit- and system-level vari-ables. The theory of role analysis in foreign policy and its usefulness in explain-ing third-party, ethnic intervention is covered in the third section. Section four brings together systemism and role theory and elaborates linkages for variables at the external, macro and micro levels, respectively. The fifth section takes up two case studies, namely, Pakistan's intervention in India in 1965 and India's intervention in Sri Lanka in 1987. Finally, section six looks at the findings from the two case studies in terms of role analysis and comparative ethnic foreign policy.

Systemism: A Framework for Analysis

How can variables at multiple levels be connected to create an overall framework for analysis? *Systemism* provides the answer through a commitment to understanding a system in terms of a comprehensive set of functional rela-tionships.[2] In International Relations, the set of relationships reveals the connec-tions between and among international (system-) and domestic (unit-level) vari-ables.[3] Figure 1 presents Bunge's[4] framework of systemism; specifically, it shows the functional relations in a social system.[5] The figure traces the full range of effects that might be encountered in any such system, which includes both micro- and macro-variables. (Upper- and lower-case letters refer to macro- and micro-level variables, respectively.) The logically possible connections are micro-micro (m-m), micro-macro (m-M), macro-macro (M-M) and macro-micro (M-m). Macro variables may impact upon each other, as in the case of X affect-ing Y, with the functional form represented by F. The same is true at the micro-level, as in the case of x impacting upon y through function f. Systemism there-fore allows for *both* micro-micro and macro-macro connections. Furthermore, systemism recognizes that effects also can move *across* levels. Thus the macro-micro linkage of X to x through function g also appears in the figure, as does the micro-macro connection from y to Y on the basis of function h. Systemism de-mands that a theory tell the 'full tale' of units and systems, which includes the four kinds of linkages, along with the effects of the external environment.[6] Thus, by utilizing systemism, this study seeks to unify unit- and system-level variables with those at the external level to account for third-party ethnic interventionism as a foreign policy decision.

Figure 1: Systemism's Functional Relations in a Social System

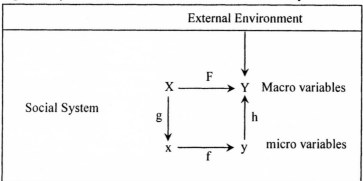

Source: Adapted from Bunge (1996), 149

Value of Role Theory in Explaining Ethnic Interventionism

Role theory can be used to explain foreign policy decisions and outcomes by connecting different levels and units and, in the process, providing a unified analysis. Such movement across levels and units consists of a:

> judicious mix of three elements: first, a richly multidimensional delineation of *role*...; second, self-conscious, flexibility in assigning alternating functions to independent, dependent and intervening variables...; and third, key determinants of decision making... that are so defined so as to generate linkages between familiar abstract categories of factors—for example, personal, organizational, social, cultural traits; ... the nature of the political system; and the external environment.[7]

Walker identifies three reasons for utilizing role analysis in understanding foreign policy: descriptive, organizational and explanatory. Descriptively, role theory provides varied images of foreign policy behavior that depend on the focus of analysis: systemic, national or individual. Besides this multilevel advantage, role theory extends the scope of analysis by moving beyond the narrow confines of looking at a "continuum of cooperative and conflictual behavior."[8] Organizationally, it can help explain behavior either in terms of structure or process. Finally, the explanatory value of role analysis depends on whether "its concepts are theoretically informed (a) by appropriate set of self-contained propositions and methods, or (b) by the specification of an appropriate set of auxiliary limiting conditions and rules linking these conditions with the role concepts."[9]

This study of ethnic interventionism as a foreign policy decision is informed by role theory, which offers a wide range of advantages.[10] The goal is to account for the decision by one state to intervene in an ongoing ethnic or ethnic conflict of another state—generally speaking, in neighboring countries or those in close geographical proximity—in support of either co-ethnics *or* the state trying to suppress the insurgent group. A part of Holsti's (1987) concept of "role performance", which encompasses the attitudes, decisions and actions the national government takes to implement its self-defined "national role conceptions" or "role prescriptions" that emanate from external environment, can be used to explain foreign policy decisions and actions. Thus, instead of defining role performance as way to implement role conception or role prescription,[11] we utilize Rosenau's concept of "role expectation", which can encompass variables from both domestic and external levels. Role expectation, which can emanate in a contradictory way from respective levels, is a concept that helps to bridge the gap between national role conception and role prescription.

Conflicting role expectations have source variables—internal and external—that produce role performance. Rosenau refers specifically to the number of roles in the range of systems that decision-maker(s) occupy. These leaders thereby become subject to conflicting role expectations:

> those that derive from the private systems in which they are or previously were members, from the government institutions in which their policy making is located, from the society in which they make policy, and from the international systems in which their society is a subsystem *as well as* [italics in original] the expectations to which they are exposed in their top-level, face to face decision making unit.[12]

Thus, in the context of role theory, an effective foreign policy "is one that not only protects or achieves its goals but also meets the expectations and demands of others in the situation. Although this set of criteria is *ipso facto* more difficult to satisfy, it is our contention that these norms are precisely what participants in foreign policy essentially strive to meet."[13] It almost goes without saying that the anticipated range of expectations for different levels is consistent with the frame of reference put forward via systemism in the preceding section.

National decision-makers are faced with multiple role expectations that come simultaneously from the macro- and micro-levels and also the external environment. Depending on the nature of domestic politics and influence from subsystem-level factors, either ordering or merging of role expectations can be expected to take place.[14] Thus role performance with regard to involvement as a third party in an ethnic conflict will reflect interaction of external, macro and micro variables.

Given the nature of international politics, with interactions between and among variables at different levels influencing foreign policy decisions and actions, the role performance of an intervener should be judged in terms of resolving role differences arising out of conflicting role expectations, which refer to the cues that emerge from various levels a la systemism.

Systemism and Role Theory

Systemism, as noted previously, entails four types of linkage between macro and micro variables: micro-micro (m-m), Macro-micro (M-m), micro-Macro (m-M) and Macro-Macro (M-M) and also the effects of variables from the external environment.

In this section, a framework is developed to account for the effects of respective variables in generating role expectations for the national government.

Influence could range from very high to almost non-existent, leading to varying role expectations. Furthermore, the framework includes variables that reflect *instrumental* and *affective* motivations (Carment and James 1996, 1997). Systemism, as applied through Figure 2, begins with the effects of the external environment. At this level, the first variable is *international structure and hierarchy*. In the international system, relations between and among major powers and their effective presence generate expectations for other states (James 2002).[15] Structural attributes of the international system and alterations in them are important in accounting for changes in role expectations of states. This becomes evident if we compare the Cold War and post-Cold war periods. With the 'teaching' a set of norms and thereby helping to revise states' conceptions of power. In particular, Russett and Oneal argue that a multilateral rather than unilateral approach to global issues on the part of the US would be more beneficial and better for world peace. In this case, where the virtues of multilateralism are being emphasized, we can cite the example of the United Nations, whose members are expected to adhere to the Charter and principles therein. Thus, in cases of conflict, the UN could call for restraint and even vote against third-party in cues sent by the UN can be expected to influence smaller states more than larger management and resolution of conflict.[16] Intervention, leading to a different role ones and its presence provides at least some hope for an amicable and a peaceful Linkages between variables within the *external environment* also are worth noting. The most salient link, immediately following our discussion of the role expectations generated by an international organization like the UN, is the one between the *international structure/hierarchy and the functioning of international organizations* (i.e., the arrow points from international structure toward international organization). Cooperation with, or opposition to, a UN resolution is affected by power 'equations' and existing structure of the international system, which consists of the great powers with, again, a notable difference between the Cold War and post-Cold War periods. Thus we should not consider the influence of an international organization on a state's role expectation in isolation from existing international structure.

Figure 2: National Role Performance and Ethnic Intervention

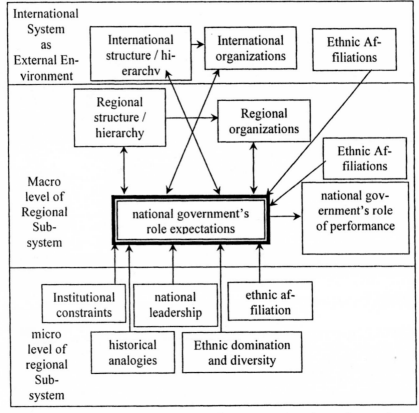

National role performance is not static. As the government carries out intervention, there is a feedback from role performance back into the variables at the external, Macro and micro levels. In fact, whether or not intervention is sustained, and in turn role performance, are influenced by the revised positions of the affected variables. Given the limited scope of our chapter, we do not go into the feedback effects. This is a dimension we intend to take up in future research.

Ethnic affiliations from the external environment can be anticipated to shape the national government's role expectations.[17] If one or more external actors should happen to share the ethnicity of the presumed target of intervention, that might cause the potential intervening state from within the region to give pause for one of two reasons. First, if the possible intervention by a great power from outside the region is expected to be in a preferred direction (i.e., in favor of ethnic brethren), it could cause a "free rider" effect.[18] Action by the great power would be preferred because of greater resources and a higher probability of success, along with removing the need by the present state to absorb any costs from involvement. If, by contrast, the outside intervener would be coming in against ethnic brethren, that also could serve to discourage intervention because then the conflict would include a high-capability and even overwhelming adversary. Either way, indifference from the external environment would tend, all other things being equal, to encourage role expectations that entail intervention.

With regard to the macro level regional subsystem, the variables parallel those from the external environment—but with a regional rather than global/international dimension. The *regional structure/hierarchy* variable is expected to elicit one kind of role expectation that would assume significance in an emerging scenario of third-party ethnic intervention. In fact, a dominant state at the top of a regional hierarchy can assume much more importance than interactions among great powers in the external environment. Lemke's "multiple hierarchy model" entails multiple, smaller 'pyramids' within the international hierarchy of power: "They are local/regional systems or sub-hierarchies.... These local hierarchies are often geographically small. They encapsulate local relations between geographically proximate states."[19] In addition, "structure in a subsystem would... be defined by the distribution of power between its parts and the relations that subsist between them."[20] The structure of the regional subsystem and interaction of its units will influence role expectations of states within that structure.[21]

Next come *regional organizations*, a variable with a different effect on a state's role expectations. Regional organizations are formed with a view toward cooperation in the interests (mostly toward economic and cultural integration but in some cases strategic) of the participating states of the region concerned while respecting the sovereignty of the member countries.[22] On issues of conflict and intervention, strategies and tactics of regional organizations like NATO (during the Cold War) have reflected superpower rivalry. NATO's involvement and continuous dialogue and negotiation with Turkey on the issue of Cyprus throughout the decade of the 1960s represent a significant instance of a regional organization's role in preventing overt intervention.

As pointed out at the level of the external environment (i.e., the case of the United Nations), here also the effectiveness of the regional grouping is constrained by the *regional power structure/hierarchy*. The region's dominant power would seem to have leeway on many of the controversial decisions, such as intervention. India in South Asia is acknowledged as a hegemonic power for its sheer size and economic and military power; it dwarfs the other countries that comprise the regional grouping. So, when India decides to intervene, a regional organization such as SAARC generally will have to watch as a bystander.[23]

The variable *ethnic affiliations* within the regional subsystem would be anticipated to follow the same logic as it did at the external level with respect to other states that are friendly to ethnic brethren, but with a reversal of effect otherwise. If another state in the region might intervene on behalf of ethnic breth-

SAARC = South Asian Association for Regional Cooperation

ren, the above-noted idea of the free rider once again becomes relevant. In other words, why make the effort if another government might do so instead? Possible intervention against ethnic brethren, however, does not automatically discourage action by the national government because interveners from within the region are not necessarily great powers. Instead, power balancing might be anticipated to take place, with the national government responding to—or possibly even seeking to head off—an intervention against those who share its ethnicity.

It should be pointed out that the variables discussed so far in the external environment and the macro-level sub-system is primarily instrumental in nature. We now proceed to discussion of the micro variables that include affective motivations. Some of these variables are hybrids, i.e., affective/instrumental.

Micro-micro linkages include those that connect the role expectation variable to its source variables at the same level. Figure 2 shows five source variables impacting upon the state's role expectation. While *institutional constraint*[24] is an instrumental variable, *ethnic domination and diversity* and *ethnic affiliations* are affective variables. The remaining two variables are hybrids that contain both instrumental and effective elements: *national leadership*[25] and *historical analogies.*[26] These micro variables influence the national government's forming of role expectations, a micro variable that determines its role performance.

Institutional constraints refer to the underlying patterns of domestic institutions, namely, the political and constitutional structure of the state, which are major determinants of elite policy making. Thus institutionalization can be considered in terms of low constraints whereby the power of the elites does not depend on support from the population at large. States in which elite decision-making is unconstrained by popular opinion or constituent interests include military dictatorships, one-party totalitarian and authoritarian regimes and revolutionary republics and monarchies. By contrast, high constraint states are those with where leaders are directly accountable to the people and their fate depends on regular elections. Legislative and electoral politics are the arenas in a federal system that form the basis of a relationship between elites and masses and constrain elites. Role expectations will vary with the degree of institutional constraint imposed on the leadership.[27]

Historical analogies refer to the policy makers' developing role expectations based on understanding the present by looking at the past. Analogies with the past "(1) help define the nature of the situation confronting the policy maker, (2) help assess the stakes, and (3) provide prescriptions. They help evaluate alternative options by (4) predicting their chances of success, (5) evaluating their moral rightness, and (6) warning about dangers associated with the options."[28] Analogies, of course, also can be used poorly, resulting in harmful role expectations.

National leadership refers to the personal characteristics of political leaders and a few other high-level policy-makers who affect foreign policy. Role expectations are formed out of the leadership's worldviews and personal preferences (and sometimes even whims), all of which influence foreign policy choices.[29] It is possible that, depending on the quality of the national leadership, conflicting role expectations can be reconciled favorably. Decisiveness and aggressive style can result in a more interventionist policy. The cultural background of policy maker(s) can influence resolution in favor of one over others. Similarly, relations among the top leaders are crucial in decision making—one domineering individual can set the tone and others can simply follow.

Ethnic composition in terms of whether the state is dominated by a single ethnic group or diverse ethnic groups is a crucial source variable in generating one kind of role expectation. Whether a single ethnic group enjoys political control over the state or various ethnic groups are equally important will affect how elites behave in framing policies. In the former case, elites appeal to their ethnic constituency and virtually all policies are made in favor of the dominant ethnic group, even when the issues are of marginal interest to them. In ethnically diverse states, leaders appeal to more than one ethnic group and see support from both ethnic and cross-cutting identities. Policies, in this case, reflect inter-ethnic compromise.[30]

Finally, *ethnic affiliations* within a state can be expected to influence its propensity toward intervention. If a conflict includes ethnic differences, and there is an affiliation with one or more the groups involved, intervention becomes more likely. Free rider effects, as noted above, are less relevant because pressure to act comes from within society and cannot be satisfied in the same way by actions from another state. In other words, ethnic mobilization in favor on interventionism concentrates on what the national government itself is doing —it must be seen as acting in some way and cannot risk inaction when the pressure becomes very intense.[31]

Case Studies of Ethnic Intervention in South Asia

Two case studies will be used to make a preliminary assessment of the viability of the framework from Figure 2. The first case refers to Pakistan's irredentist intervention in Kashmir in 1965, while the second one pertains to India's involvement and consequent intervention in Sri Lanka's Tamil secessionist conflict. These cases are used to illustrate the range of possibilities with regard to the interplay of micro and macro variables, along with external effects, as depicted by Figure 2. The two relatively dissimilar case studies are used to show how ethnic issues play out in foreign policy decisions. Foreign policy action as role performance is born out of conflicting role expectations. Thus, in cases of intervention, each of the expectations play themselves out to arrive at a role scenario where the state decides to intervene. The basic question is this one: Does ethnicity or, for that matter, any particular source variable, play a principal role in determining role performance?

The case studies will proceed in the same way as the theoretical discussion: After a basic case summary, the analysis will focus on (a) look first at the external environment and its linkages with other variables at the lower levels; (b) the macro level and assess linkages of those variables with both external and micro-level variables; and (c) how the micro-level variables link up with those at other levels.

Pakistan's Intervention in Kashmir, 1965: Case Summary

Like the first war over Kashmir in 1947–48, the second, in August–September 1965 and code named "Operation Gibraltar," involved a fully armed and militarily trained force of infiltrators that, according to the plan, would enter clandestinely into the Valley in small groups, cross the border in the first week of August and stir up a popular uprising among the presumably disaffected Kashmiri people.[32] Pakistan's planning reflected confidence derived from a relatively successful show of strength against Indian forces during a clash in April 1965 in the Rann of Kutch, a barren area bordering the western state of Gujarat. This led Pakistani policy-makers and military strategists to conclude that time was ripe to strike Kashmir and resolve the dispute once and for all—a calculation based on Pakistan's "fundamentally flawed inference" that India, still believed to be reeling under the disastrous impact of the 1962 Sino-Indian clash, would be unprepared and therefore unable to fight a full-fledged war.[33]

Pakistan's leaders also believed that Kashmiris were clamoring for an end to their subjugation under Indian rule. Several developments supported that belief: (a) continuous unrest in the Valley, which broke out for various reasons (including the arrest of their ruler, Sheikh Abdullah); (b) theft of a sacred relic, the hair of the Prophet, from the Hazaratbal shrine in Srinagar; and (c) attempts by the central government of India to erode the autonomy of Kashmir, which had been granted earlier by a special provision under the constitution, by integrating it within the Indian union (like any other Indian state) through certain constitutional measures. Anti-India demonstrations by the Kashmiris because of the preceding reasons caused Pakistan's leaders to infer, again incorrectly, that these events showed support for Pakistan and even Pakistani intervention.[34] Finally, Pakistan did not see anything coming out of attempts by the US and UK to pressure India to resolve the dispute. Karachi saw the Indian leadership as adamant because it steadfastly resisted suggestions coming from the western powers. Pakistan also looked upon the United Nations as ineffective. The world body had hoped to use a plebiscite to force India into a settlement at the end of the hostilities that broke out immediately after independence and partition in 1947–48. This did not succeed.

Things did not turn out as Pakistan had hoped. The military conflict ended inconclusively, only to be followed by a United Nations' call for an end to hostilities. By September 22, both sides accepted a ceasefire and the war came to an end. The United States showed no interest in helping the two adversaries reach an amicable post-war settlement, but the Soviet Union stepped in and, on 10 January 1966 in Tashkent, Pakistan and India agreed to withdraw their forces to the *status quo ante*, i.e., to positions held prior to 5 August 1965. Both sides also agreed to abstain from using force in settling outstanding disputes. Finally, India gave up certain strategic areas—Haji Pir and Tithwal significant among them—and Pakistan did the same, giving up some of the territories it had gained in the conflict.[35] The conflict over Kashmir, however, continues to this day and includes a terrorist element.[36]

Application of the Model

We can move on to Pakistan's policy of intervention in terms of the components from Figure 2—external, macro and mirco. All three types of factor, as it turns out, are useful in generating Pakistan's role expectations and subsequent involvement in Kashmir for second time after 1947–48. Thus this analysis begins at the highest level of aggregation and moves downward to completion.

In the external environment, the changing behavior of the major powers in the international system affected Pakistan's attitude and, in turn, the course of the intervention. US policy toward India in the 1950s and early 1960s affected Pakistan's foreign policy behavior. In the immediate context of the regional subsystem, great powers like India and China also influenced the role expectations and role performance of Pakistan. Some details follow.

The *international structure/hierarchy* seemed to move in a favorable direction when Ayub Khan came to power. He immediately assured the western allies, the US and UK in particular, that Pakistan remained committed to the SEATO and CENTO regional pacts. In March 1959, Pakistan and the US signed an agreement of cooperation for security and defense.

Things began to change in the 1960s as Ziring points out:

> Pakistan's relevance to United States policy began to erode in the sixties due to a number of developments in the international system which included the advent of reconnaissance satellite and ICBMs that reduced the importance of American bases in Pakistan and elsewhere, the Sino-Soviet split, and the Sino-Indian border conflict, 1962. The United States began to manifest some fascination for nonalignment and decided to strengthen India's security to counterbalance China. This was bound to evoke the displeasure of, and protest from, Pakistan which felt the United States was pursuing policies which adversely affected an ally, i.e. Pakistan.[37]

More specifically, with John F. Kennedy's election as President of the US in 1960, things took a new turn affecting Pakistan's relations with the US, China and, of course, India. Kennedy's election ushered a new era in Indo-US relations. To cement closer ties with India, the United States brought in a series of amendments to the United States Mutual Security Act to facilitate the flow of arms to neutrals like India, causing anxiety and heartburn in Pakistan.[38] By 1962, India had signed the first of what became a series of military agreements with the Soviet Union. Moreover, the Sino-Indian conflict of 1962 saw the United States rush huge arms aid to India.[39]

Amidst these changes in the external environment, the US and UK tried to resolve the Kashmir dispute by prodding the adversaries into a dialogue. In December 1962, an Anglo-American mission led by Duncan Sandys of Britain and Averell Harriman of United States visited New Delhi and then Islamabad. These visits persuaded the governments to start talking to each other about Kashmir. A series of talks, held subsequently held in various cities of both countries, produced inconclusive results.[40]

With respect to *international organizations*, the United Nations remained deadlocked on the issue. In fact Ayub vented his frustration over the UN's inability to conduct the plebiscite as promised after the first war in 1947–48 and saw no point in appealing to the world body. This factor later influences his calculations about intervening in Kashmir.

Ethnic affiliations at the external environment level, or the influence of the great powers sharing the ethnic of the presumed target of intervention, might lead the intervening state to pause and reconsider its decision. No such factor based on ethnic affiliations operated in this case; the great powers did not have any ethnic interest in the Indo-Pakistani conflict. Instead, the Christian great powers witnessed a Muslim state targeting a Hindu state's Muslim population in an irredentist conflict.

At the macro regional subsystem level, the two major powers are India and Pakistan. The *regional structure/hierarchy* does not present a clear picture in 1965, just 15–18 years after both countries achieved independence. Although India could be placed on top because of its sheer size, the Indo-China War of 1962 had dented India's reputation as the dominant regional power. In fact, defeat in that war, as noted above, formed the fundamental basis of Ayub's "flawed inference," that is, underestimating India's defense preparations.[41]

No *international organization*, such as SAARC, existed as a potential influence on both India and Pakistan. Hence no role expectations emerged from this direction. *Ethnic affiliations* at the regional subsystem level did not influence events; a single state, Pakistan, identified along ethno-religious lines with the Muslims of Kashmir. Hence the free rider aspect for other states in South Asia (e.g. Sri Lanka, Bhutan, Nepal, Maldives, etc.) does not play a part here.[42]

With regard to micro level in the regional subsystem, all of the source variables, leading to what might be termed 'domestic' role expectations, seem to have important effects.

Pakistan had low *institutional constraints* during the Ayub era, fallout from developments a few years after Pakistan was born. The Muslim League, the vanguard party that led the freedom struggle, failed to develop into a national party like Congress in India. Internal dissension, along with a national and federal leadership unwilling to hold elections, led to fragmentation and a decline in the political institutions. Leaders showed scant respect for democratic institutions and parliamentary principles and conventions; they compromised their positions in asserting a leadership role. In the process, the bureaucratic-military elite came to dominate policy-making and gained the upper hand, leading finally to the bloodless coup of 1958 when Ayub Khan, the Commander-in-chief of the army, captured power. Ayub promulgated a new Constitution in 1962, which at first did not allow political parties to come into being. As pressure mounted for the revival of political parties, he enacted the Political Parties Act in July 1962, "which legalized the formation and functioning of the political parties with a proviso that these could neither advocate anything prejudicial to the Islamic ideology, integrity and security of Pakistan nor accept financial assistance from, or affiliate with, any foreign government or foreign agency." The system that functioned under him, however, remained top-heavy, with a concentration of power in the hands of the president. The *bureaucracy* served as the linchpin of the new setup. Ayub employed a 'carrot and stick' policy to dissuade political opponents from undermining political arrangements and imposed strong pressures on the dissenting press. The "organizational weaknesses and internal feuds" of opposition parties helped Ayub in the aggrandizement of his powers, which saw him sweep the presidential polls at both the national and provincial levels in 1965. Thus, under such low institutional constraints, the bureaucratic-military elite had virtually complete freedom to decide on an intervention.[43]

Except for harking back to the previous failed attempt of 1947-48 to annex Kashmir, Pakistan, being a young state, had no obvious *historical analogies* to fall back upon. This variable as a source of role expectations is more significant for states with histories that include interventions, both failed and successful. Interestingly enough, however, we might see the strategy adopted the second time to be very similar to the one in the first instance, although at this time it had not been designed consciously by the Pakistani foreign and defense establishment. The strategy once again involved clandestine entry into the Valley in small groups, with a shift to fully armed and militarily trained infiltrators.

National leadership, confined mainly to Ayub Khan and his foreign minister Zulfikar Ali Bhutto, assumes considerable significance as a source variable. The importance of Ayub Khan in Pakistan's politics during this period led many commentators to term it as the "Ayub Khan era." Both subjective and objective factors are involved in determining leadership.

While not denying the role Islam had played in the founding of Pakistan as a separate state, Mohammad Ali Jinnah, the founder, favored a secular state. Jinnah's successors, however, failed to implement his vision and saw Pakistan's identity as an Islamic state, although not a theocracy.[44] As a modernist, Ayub tried to distance himself from orthodox Muslims. However, following the model of his Muslim League predecessors, he could not avoid upholding "the Islamic heritage of the Pakistani state."[45] At the beginning of his rule, Ayub tried to be

secular, but it became difficult to keep the religious forces at bay. The Constitution of 1962 had dropped "Islamic" from the "Republic of Pakistan", which had
been there since the 1956 Constitution. Within a year, however, fundamentalists
forced Ayub Khan to reinstate that word. However Ayub never entered into an
alliance with religious leaders and tried to maintain some distance from orthodox elements.

Ayub, in a sense, did engage in limited political use of Islam. For example,
he "seldom used the expression 'Holy Quran and Sunna' and preferred to use
instead expressions such as 'basic principles of Islam' or 'the essence of Islam."[46] During Ayub's era, the practical impact of Pakistani nationalism, based
on an Islamic ideology, became multifaceted and significant.[47]

The views of Zulfiquar Ali Bhutto, Foreign Minister during the Ayub regime, are informative here and points to the zeal of Bhutto in particular to pursue an aggressive foreign policy.

> If a Muslim majority can remain a part of India, then the *raison d'*
> *etre* of Pakistan collapses. These are the reasons why India, to con-
> tinue her domination of Jammu and Kashmir, defies international
> opinion and violates her pledges. For the same reasons, Pakistan must
> unremittingly continue her struggle for the right of self-determination
> of this subject people. *Pakistan is incomplete without Jammu and*
> *Kashmir both territorially and ideologically* [emphasis added by
> Ganguly]. It would be fatal if, in sheer exhaustion or intimidation,
> Pakistan were to abandon the struggle, and a bad compromise would
> be tantamount to abandonment; which might be in turn lead to the
> collapse of Pakistan.[48]   *aggressive language*

Bhutto's words—then as part of the national leadership and later as prime minister of Pakistan—show a depth of commitment. Standard scholarly treatments
also connect the survival of Pakistan to Islamic identity.[49]

If not Ayub, Bhutto saw the unfinished task of adding Kashmir to Pakistan
as a through the prism of religion. Here religion is seen to be used by the leaders
as the basis of Pakistani nationalist identity.[50] The national leadership thus generates role expectations that derive from their values and interaction with societal forces.

Ethnic domination and diversity is not as significant as ethno-religious affiliation as a source variable for role expectations. Kashmiris did not share the
same ethnicity as the majority Pakistanis. Ethnicity had a tangential effect; the
decision to intervene in 1965 was aided by a single ethnic group-dominated bureaucracy. During the initial years of Pakistan, Mohajirs (refugees who came
from India) predominated in the government and bureaucratic leadership. Within
a decade, however, the domination of a single ethnic group, the Punjabis, came
to be the defining feature of Pakistani politics, and also bureaucracy and military
leadership. Thus decision-making bodies comprised overwhelmingly of a single

ethnic group made the task of formulating and implementing policies of intervention easier, with no significant opposition.

With regard to the *ethno-religious affiliations* variable, the propensity to intervene in Kashmir was based on Pakistan having an affiliation with the Kashmiris, specifically, the majority Muslims of the state, based on a shared ethno-religious identity.[51] Geographic and demographic realities caused Pakistan to view its claim on Kashmir—a Muslim-majority province—as legitimate. The claim became more vehement because of its irredentist nature.[52] Thus we need to look, if only briefly, at the role of religion, that is, Islam, in Pakistani politics. This will underscore the importance of religious affiliations in Pakistan's foreign policy, most notably as related to Kashmir.

Although religion served as an overarching factor in defining Pakistan's nature and foreign policy, in particular on the question of Kashmir, multiethnic identities within Pakistan threatened its would-be Islamic unity. As noted above, the Pathans bordering Afghanistan clamored for an independent Pakhtunistan on one side and the eastern wing of Pakistan also posed a threat to the very integrity of Pakistan and, in 1971, became Bangladesh.[53]

Ethno-religious identification played a role in Pakistan's foreign policy, especially with regard to its policy on Kashmir. The free rider concept, as pointed out in theorizing about the impact of ethno-religious affiliation at the micro level, does not seem to be relevant. Here the pressure comes from within and the national government's (in) action becomes crucial in ethno-religious mobilization in favor of intervention. As discussed above, the very identity of Pakistan remains incomplete unless Kashmir, a Muslim majority province contiguous to the Pakistan's border, is incorporated. However, the more proximate causes of a particular intervention, in this case the one which Pakistan carried out unsuccessfully in 1965, derive from the evolving situation of the regional environment along with the changing attitudes of the major Western powers toward the conflict. The failure of the United Nations also became a significant factor in pushing Pakistan to obtain a solution on its own. At the domestic level, because of low institutional constraints, it became possible for a military ruler to go ahead with the decision to intervene. This factor is significant, but the impact of Islamic ideology brings out the overriding importance of ethno-religious identification in both domestic politics and in foreign policy for Pakistan.

India's Intervention in Sri Lanka

Case Summary

Anti-Tamil riots in 1983 led to the outbreak of full-fledged Tamil militancy in Sri Lanka. Sri Lankan army reprisals against Tamil militants, under orders of then-President J.R. Jayewardene, became brutal; several hundred Tamils were killed and injured in what some called a pogrom.[54] This response only served to ignite both the people of Tamil Nadu and their political parties, namely, the ruling AIADMK and the opposition DMK. The latter called for the issue to be taken up with national leaders in New Delhi, with action to follow. The Tamil Nadu State Chief Minister M. G. Ramachandran demanded that the Prime Minister raise the issue in the United Nations. Even more outspoken was the leader of the state opposition party, DMK, K. Karunanidhi, who demanded a Cyprus-like solution "in order to prevent the extermination of the Tamil race.[55] The DMK asserted that India should support openly the separation demanded by the Tamil parties in Sri Lanka and asked the Indian Government to make arrangements to immediately send an international peacekeeping force.

The Indian Government's subsequent decision to get involved in Sri Lanka reflected both affective and instrumental considerations. First, Indian Tamils had expressed outrage at the treatment being meted out by the Sinhalese majority to their co-ethnics in the neighboring state of Sri Lanka and wanted the Indian Government to stop it. Indian leaders worried that the prevailing situation, which seemed to be getting worse by the day, would threaten both internal and external security in terms of spill-over effects.[56] Internally speaking, India had to heed the sentiments of its own Tamil population, which numbered around 50 million, as well as the Dravidian parties of the state.[57] Based on a shared language, culture and religion, the people of Tamil Nadu had a natural affinity with the Sri Lankan Tamils. In essence, both peoples had the same ethnic identity. A constant exchange of visits between the co-ethnic Tamils and the Dravidian parties, from the 1970s onward, confirmed the identification of Indian Tamils with Sri Lankan Tamils.

Second, electoral compulsions forced Congress Party ruling at the center to enter into an alliance with the regional party in Tamil Nadu, AIADMK. The Congress Party perceived that betraying the sentiments of the Tamil population would have adverse electoral consequences for both parties and also "would have been taken as a sign of betrayal of the Tamils by the government, thus leading to a possible domestic instability.[58]

Third, with the ethnic violence against the Tamils getting worse, a massive refugee influx of Tamils came from Sri Lanka. They brought stories of the ruthlessness of the Sri Lankan Government and army against them, stoking the already incensed sentiments of the people of Tamil Nadu. From a security standpoint, this was considered volatile. Amidst this situation, there were intelligence reports that the Sri Lankan Government hired British, Rhodesian, Israeli and South African mercenaries. It was reported that Israel "set up an interests section in the U.S. embassy in Colombo and the Mossad... and Shin Beth... became active in Sri Lanka in the training of government forces to counter the Tamil militants." China, Pakistan, Malaysia and Singapore supplied arms to Sri Lanka. These geostrategic and security reasons compelled India to abandon its non-interventionist policy in Sri Lanka and become actively involved in Sri Lankan affairs by enunciating the "Indian Doctrine of Regional Security." This doctrine forced Sri Lanka to heed India's latest posture and seek its assistance to tackle Tamil insurgency.[59]

Indian involvement took three forms: initially, it supplied covert military assistance, a training base and arms to various Tamil insurgent groups. The next move took the form of diplomatic involvement, where the Indian Prime Minister, Indira Gandhi, not only internationalized the fate of the Sri Lankan Tamils but also earnestly tried to bring the antagonists into a compromise. G. Parthasarthy, Mrs Gandhi's envoy, tried a formula to establish elected regional councils in the northern and eastern provinces, but failed to find support from prominent Sinhalese groups, including the ruling and opposition parties. The failure of the Parthasarathy formula came about because of the absence of the main Tamil militant groups in the conference called to discuss it. Unfortunately, Mrs Indira Gandhi was assassinated before any other diplomatic initiative.[60]

Rajiv Gandhi succeeded his mother as the prime minister of India. Ethnic violence escalated in Sri Lanka and the government of the day reacted by massive arms acquisition. Simultaneously, the Tamil militant groups stepped up their terrorist activities. President Jayawardene sought India's help to counter violence in his country. The two premiers met at New Delhi in June 1985 and, based on their discussions, representatives of the Sri Lankan Government and four major militant groups, LTTE, TELOS, EROS, and EPRLF met at Thimpu in July–August. The meetings failed, however. Seeking a military solution, increasing violence from both sides alerted India to the fact that a fresh initiative would be necessary to prevent the situation from getting out of hand. In December 1986, under Indian pressure, President Jayawardene met the Indian Prime Minister Rajiv Gandhi, the Tamil Nadu chief minister M. G. Ramachandran and the LTTE leader, V. Prabhakaran. The meeting resulted in the "19 December Proposals" which also fell through. The failure saw a similar reaction from the Sri Lankan Government as on the last occasion, but on an unprecedented scale formally called "Operation Liberation Two", which saw the bombing of Jaffna and embargoing of food and fuel in the Jaffna peninsula. Pressured by Tamil Nadu leaders, India announced that it would send relief supplies to the beleaguered peninsula and, despite warnings from Sri Lanka, went ahead and para-dropped food and relief supplies.[61]

Thereafter President Jayawardene initiated diplomatic channels to resolve the problem politically, which finally culminated in the Indo-Sri Lankan Accord of July 1987. The proposals included commitment of Indian troops on Sri Lankan soil for the first time to guarantee and enforce the cessation of hostilities.

Application of the Model

Variables from the external environment create both opportunities and constraints with respect to foreign policy role expectations. The *international structure/hierarchy*, at that time in the form of the superpowers, had manifestations in regional rivalries. In the context of South Asia in general and Indo-Sri Lankan relations in particular, superpower rivalry in the Indian Ocean added to tensions between the two countries. This rivalry affected India's role expectations. India increasingly became concerned with external security interests, with Sri Lankan actions adding to those worries.[62]

Opportunities can mean direct support, but in most cases of interventionism, aloofness or indifference to the ongoing conflict serve as permissive conditions that frame role expectations accordingly. In terms of the overall influence of the external environment, however, leading Western states saw no compelling reason to get involved in the Sri Lankan ethnic war— "at least not enough to jeopardize their relations with India.[63] Later, when India did go ahead with the peacekeeping force agreement, the superpowers, in particular, hardly showed any interest, which made things easier for India in its resolving the conflicting role expectations which had arisen from the earlier postures of the big powers vis-à-vis the Indian Ocean.

As far as *international organizations* are concerned, the UN did not see itself as a player in the ongoing interaction of Sri Lanka and India. Neither country referred the issue to international bodies in an effort to discourage India from intervention. Both countries looked upon it, despite recriminations hurled at each other prior to the agreement, as a bilateral issue (although in the negotiations to resolve the matter, the good offices of SAARC were used, albeit without significant effect). *Ethno-religious affiliations* emanating from the external environment did not play a role.

At the macro level, the *regional structure/ hierarchy* had a significant impact on how India formed its role expectations. India's predominant position as a regional hegemony or superpower[64] on the subcontinent affected the positions taken by her neighbors. As Kandian wryly observes, India thought herself to be the security manager of the region. Especially after the Bangladesh War of 1971, and blasting a nuclear device (although reportedly for peaceful purposes) in 1974, India emerged as the regional superpower in a military sense.[65] As a result, South Asian states in general did not see themselves to be of much individual relevance either to the ongoing civil war in Sri Lanka or India's role in it. Pakistan, however, had priorities determined more by full-fledged involvement on her Afghan borders and the war in Afghanistan than by a lack of interest in the Indo-Sri Lankan imbroglio.

Regional organizations had minimal impact; India did not have to contend with any such role expectations. SAARC, the nascent regional organization, which had come into being only in 1983, had yet to take off. India's hegemonic image within the sub-system did not and still does not augur well for an efficient working of SAARC (i.e., the arrow going from regional hierarchy to the regional organization in Figure 2—we do not discuss this link in detail in the present chapter). However, SAARC did serve as a platform to hold meeting as an attempt to resolve the ongoing crisis. Thimpu, the capital of Bhutan, served as a venue for Indo-Sri Lankan parleys. The talks there, however, proved to be disappointing.

Ethno-religious affiliations emanating from the macro level regional sub-system are at the center of the strife. Sri Lanka's Tamil problem is looked upon most accurately as a strictly ethnic issue, although we still should keep in mind that the two groups in conflict, Tamils and Sri Lankans, are predominantly Hindus and Buddhists, respectively. (Tamil Muslims as well as Sri Lankan Muslims and Christians also are present in Sri Lanka.) Ethnic identity derived from language in particular; discrimination against Tamils took the form of making Sinhala the official language and removing recognition from Tamil as one of the languages of Sri Lanka.

Thus, among the various external and macro source variables for India's role expectations as a third-party intervener, two are significant. First, the regional distribution of power was highly skewed in favor of India. Status as a regional superpower served as a determining factor in resolving conflicting role expectations, if any at all. This quasi-hegemony remains constant and more so in the specific instance of India's dealings with Sri Lanka because of the deliberate aloofness and indifference of the great powers, alluded to above. This factor provided a positive cue to India to assert itself further and carve out a role performance that suited its domestic compulsions more than anything else. The second important source variable from the macro level, as is made obvious by the connection with Indian Tamils, is ethno-religious affiliation.

At the micro level, India is diverse in ethnic composition, with high *institutional constraints* on its leaders, which generated a role expectation favorable to an interventionist policy in Sri Lanka. However intervention as a policy came at the end, after going through mediation and compliance.[66] In fear of being replaced as an effective actor in South Indian politics, Indira Gandhi, the Congress Party leader and Prime Minister of India for most part of 1970s until her death in 1984 (and her son Rajiv Gandhi, who succeeded her), initially had forged alliances with DMK and then with the AIADMK parties of Tamil Nadu. This creation of alliances by Congress with respective parties at various times brought with it support from them at the national level. Indian decision makers' role expectations responded to considerations of domestic electoral politics.[67] To stay in power, the decision-makers in a multi-party and multi-ethnic democracy must make electoral calculations relative to supporting partners in the government, which can produce an ethnic foreign policy. Foreign policy decisions about third-party involvement are particularly acute in democratic societies with internal constraints that derive from party formation, electoral politics, and cabinet composition.[68] In high constraint situations the interplay between ethnicity and politics is important. When class and other bases of mobilization are weak, ethnic elites depend on direct support from their constituency and, in turn, seek to control and influence these groups. In the context of India, political competition increasingly manifested itself in terms of multi-party ethnic factionalism, which leads to an ethnic foreign policy from national leaders to outflank other political groupings and remain in power.[69]

Indian decision-makers can be understood as representatives of a party in power that had entered into an electoral understanding with the AIADMK in the early 1980s. In the specific context of the national parliamentary elections in 1985, the Indian Government had to do something concrete with regard to the situation prevailing in Sri Lanka. It started with covert military assistance[70] training and base facilities for the various Tamil secessionist groups In extending full cover to these organization, the Indian intelligence department under the central government (Research and Analytical Wing (RAW)), played a key role.[71] The Indian Government then internationalized the issue by raising the issue of the plight of Sri Lankan Tamils through various diplomatic channels.[72] India also tried the path of mediation to bring about a compromise between the warring sides and finally intervened as a peacekeeper, meaning to disarm Tamil militants and bring peace to the island. However, to understand the links in the chain of India's role performance, it is important to bear in mind that it

> Was not predisposed to using force; it could easily have taken formal control of Sri Lanka. Perhaps it would have if it was faced with fewer domestic constraints. Instead it initiated covert support for Tamil rebels. Supporting these rebels had important domestic ramifications for India's leaders. Yet India's decision makers were also concerned about the conflict spreading and hence their mixed motives and resulting strategy. [73]

Ethnic intervention and a role expectation favoring it, in whatever form, can originate from reference to *historical analogies*. Lessons 'learned' from previous operations helped decision-makers to arrive at a policy and played a key part in explaining India's supposed role in the Sri Lankan imbroglio. India's support for the Bangladesh war of independence in 1971, essentially an ethnic crisis based on linguistic nationalism, succeeded completely. The later ethnic crisis in Sri Lanka presented an opportunity for India to play the same kind of role, short of dismembering Sri Lanka. This self-perceived role can be attributed to India's emergence as a regional hegemonic power after the 1970 war with Pakistan. Especially during the era of Mrs. Gandhi—who was well aware of the part India successfully played in 1971—this led to a greater perceived role in the region. After she came back to power in 1980, Gandhi asserted that the Janata interlude (i.e., a brief period that saw her out of power) had squandered the Indian quasi-hegemony acquired with so much effort in 1971.[74] Since then, India's role expectations emanating from such instances of historical intervention influence either directly or indirectly latter-day role performance, such as the decision and action to compel, mediate and then intervene (but with a difference) in the Sri Lankan case.

National leadership, which pertains to values and inclinations of leaders and their associates, influence the trajectory of India's Sri Lanka policy. The personal inclinations of a national leader can create a perceived role, but in a democratic society that also is influenced by cross-currents of domestic as well as international political opinion. Indira Gandhi had an assertive style, as exemplified in the Bangladesh crisis and later on in dealing with President Jayewardene of Sri Lanka. Gandhi mixed diplomacy with threat.[75] At times there were veiled warnings to Sri Lanka, but the openly stated options never included military intervention.[76] Ms Gandhi's choice of G. Parthasarathy as the emissary to work out a solution for the ethnic crisis in Sri Lanka turned out to be disastrous; as an Indian Tamil, he either would show bias or lack credibility anyway.

Rajiv Gandhi, the son of Mrs. Gandhi who succeeded her in power and inherited the unresolved crisis, on the other hand, was perceived as a personality more oriented toward negotiation. Although assisted by high-profile ministers Natwar Singh and P. V. Narasimha Rao, Rajiv Gandhi personally took over the formulation of foreign policy for Sri Lanka after he became the prime minister. Entering into a compromise with the Sri Lankan government of the day was in tune with his approach toward Indian domestic politics. He tried to accommodate disparate elements within other parts of India where there were ethnic conflicts. For example, he entered into various peace agreements with India's ethnic nationalities in Punjab and Assam while trying to gain peace and resolve the problems at hand. For Sri Lanka, he ruled out the use of force and insisted on direct negotiations between the militant groups and the Sri Lankan Government.[77] As will become apparent, one of the role expectations emanating from his mode of operation gave a twist to India's involvement in Sri Lanka via a peacekeeping force.

Nevertheless, the importance of *ethnic domination and diversity* in many political decisions must not be overlooked. In terms of the national government's composition, India mostly has reflected diversity rather than domination of a particular ethnic group. However, as pointed out above when discussing institutional constraints, India's ethnic foreign policy, as in the case of Sri Lanka in 1987, was oriented toward fulfilling demands from an ethnic constituency. This role expectation for the national decision-maker is born out of the presumed supporting coalition's desire to rescue ethnic co-nationals. This, however, is but one of the various role expectations that compete with each other to influence the national government's role performance—that is, the decision about whether to intervene in an ethnic conflict and subsequent action, if any.

Finally, *ethno-religious affiliation* via Tamils in India and Sri Lanka played an obvious role in how the conflict played out over a number of years. India's role expectation reflected this primarily ethnic affiliation across the Straits.

Conclusion

This study has used role theory in its explanatory form to account for third-party intervention in ethno-linguistic conflict. A theoretical framework, built in terms recommended by systemism, organizes instrumental and affective vari-

ables from the international environment, regional subsystem and within the
state as actor toward that end. Two case studies from South Asia—Pakistan's
invasion of Kashmir in 1965 and India's halting intervention in Sri Lanka from
the 1980s—are used to assess the value of the preceding framework. Pakistan's
interest in Kashmir was (and is still) born out of ethno-religious affinity with the
Kashmiris, the majority of whom are Muslims. This factor is a given; it cannot
explain why Pakistan attempted military annexation of Kashmir more than once
(if Kargil episode is included, four times) because each intervention was preceded by unique conditions that made Pakistan perceive for herself different
roles. For 1965, among the factors that explain role expectations as perceived by
Pakistan are the changing positions of the great powers vis-à-vis Pakistan and
Bhutto's emergence as an aggressive leader. Ethno-religious affinity provided
motivation, but situational factors from the changing external, macro and micro
environments created a role performance in the form of military intervention.
     The framework also does well in explaining India's intervention in Sri
Lanka. The international structure/hierarchy, along with the regional structure
hierarchy, impacted upon Sri Lanka's role expectations. Even more factors
emerged from the micro level, such as the varying effects of institutional constraints, a historical analogy with the events of 1971, leadership in the form of
the 'two Gandhis' and ethnic diversity. Thus many components of the framework come into play in explaining India's Sri Lankan intervention.
     Finally, with regard to ethno-religious identification as related to foreign
policy, the two cases of intervention suggest the significance of context in determining which aspects will matter the most in respective cases. For Kashmir,
Islam took center stage in determining its role as a foreign policy actor. India, by
contrast, responded to primarily ethnic imperatives in taking on its role vis-à-vis
Sri Lanka.

Notes

1. David Carment and Patrick James, "Third-party States in Ethnic Conflicts: Identifying the Domestic Determinants of Intervention" (paper presented at the Annual Meeting of the American Political Science Association, San Francisco, August 2001); Carment and James, eds., *Wars in the Midst of Peace: The International Politics of Ethnic
Conflict* (Pittsburg, PA: University of Pittsburgh Press, 1997); Carment and James, "Toward a Model of Interstate Ethnic Conflict: Evidence from the Balkan War and the Indo-
Sri Lankan Conflict," Canadian Journal of Political Science 29 (1996): 521–554; Stephen
M. Saideman, The Ties that Divide: Ethnic Politics, Foreign Policy, and International
Conflict (Columbia: Columbia University Press, 2001); Stephen M. Saideman, "Explain-
ing the International Relations of Secessionist Conflicts: Vulnerability Versus Ethnic
Ties," International Organization 51 (1997): 4:721–53; Stuart J. Kaufman, Modern Ha-
treds: The Symbolic Politics of Ethnic War (Ithaca, NY: Cornell University Press, 2001).

2. The choice between unit and system is viewed as a "flawed dichotomy." See Patrick James, *International Relations and Scientific Progress: Structural Realism Reconsidered* (Columbus, OH: Ohio State University Press, 2002); Patrick James, "Systemism in International Relations: Toward a Reassessment of Realism," in Michael Brecher and Frank Harvey (eds.), *Millennial Reflections on International Studies* (Ann Arbor, MI: University of Michigan Press, 2002), 131–144; Systemism "accounts for both individual and system and, in particular, for individual agency and social structure," so it becomes the preferred alternative to both individualism and holism. See Mario Bunge, *Finding Philosophy in Social Science* (New Haven, CT: Yale University Press, 1996), 264.

3. As mentioned above, systemism expresses the linkages in a functional form to establish whether they are monotonic or step-level; this task, however, is left for future research.

4. Mario Bunge, *Finding Philosophy in Social Science* (New Haven, CT: Yale University Press, 1996), 149; Patrick James, *International Relations and Scientific Progress: Structural Realism Reconsidered* (Columbus, OH: Ohio State University Press, 2002); James, "Systemism in International Relations: Toward a Reassessment of Realism," in Michael Brecher and Frank Harvey, eds. *Millennial Reflections on International Studies* (Ann Arbor, MI: University of Michigan Press, 2002), 131–44.

5. This presentation of systemism is based primarily on Patrick James, *International Relations and Scientific Progress: Structural Realism Reconsidered* (Columbus, OH: Ohio State University Press, 2002); James, "Systemism in International Relations: Toward a Reassessment of Realism," in Michael Brecher and Frank Harvey, eds., *Millennial Reflections on International Studies* (Ann Arbor, MI: University of Michigan Press, 2002): 131–44.

6. Bunge, Finding Philosophy in Social Science, 149.

7. Synder 1987, xiii

8. Stephen G. Walker, "Introduction," and "Conclusion" in *Role Theory and Foreign Policy Analysis*, ed., Stephen G. Walker (Durham, NC: Duke University Press, 1987), 1–4, 241–59.

9. Walker, in *Role Theory*, 3.

10. K. J. Holsti, "National Role Conceptions in the Study of Foreign Policy," in *Role Theory*, Walker, 5–43; James N. Rosenau, "Roles and Role Scenarios in Foreign Policy," in *Role Theory*, Walker, 44–45; *Role* Theory, Walker, "Introduction" and "Conclusion."

11. The idea of "national role conceptions" has its limits. These conceptions include the policymakers' "definitions of the general kinds of decisions, commitments, rules and actions suitable to their state, and of the functions, if any, their state should perform on a continuing basis in the international system or in the subordinate regional system." See K. J. Holsti,, "National Role Conceptions in the Study of Foreign Policy," in *Role Theory*, Walker, 12, 36. Furthermore, national role conceptions may be more influential than role prescriptions, although the former concept is static and offers no ideas about sources.

Static role conceptions cannot explain the very peculiarity of ethno-religious politics in relation to foreign policy decisions and actions resulting from them. The nature of ethno-religious conflict is such that, as an internal conflict unfolds in a neighboring or proximate country – in turn, leading to its internationalization – the role of the third party can be set into motion. Various factors at the domestic level come into play when a third party decides to become involved. This role, in most cases, shifts from one kind of involvement to another. Involvement can come in the form of mediation, intervention and even compellence. In understanding such twists and turns in a third party's actions, static conceptions, such as national role, do not add much.

12. Rosenau, "Roles and Roles Scenarios," 46.

13. Walker and Simon, "Role Sets and Foreign Policy Analysis in Southeast Asia." *Role Theory*, Walker, 142.

14. Walker and Simon, "Role Sets and Foreign," 142.

15. In a classic exposition, Waltz asserts that "the structure of a system is generated by the interactions of its principal parts" and the "units of greatest capability set the scene of action for others as well as for themselves" (emphasis added). In other words, the great powers of the time determine international politics at the system-level: "The fates of all the states and of all the firms in a system are affected much more by the acts and the interactions of the major ones than of the minor ones.... To focus on great powers is not to lose sight of lesser ones. Concern with the latter's fate requires paying most attention to the former.... A general theory of international politics is necessarily based on the great powers," Kenneth N. Waltz, *Theory of International Politics* (Reading, Mass: Addison-Wesley Publishing Co, 1979). 72–73. Gilpin reinforces that point in observing that equilibrium of the international system is maintained "if the more powerful states are satisfied with the existing territorial, political and economic arrangements," Robert Gilpin, *War and Change in World Politics* (Cambridge: Cambridge University Press, 1981), 11.

16. Bruce M. Russett and John R. Oneal, *Triangulating Peace: Democracy, Interdependence, and International Organizations* (New York: W.W. Norton, 2001).

17. Religion is investigated as a featured element of ethnicity vis-à-vis intervention. Studies of religion and international conflict include the theoretical essays and cases from K. R. Dark., ed., *Religion and International Relations* (New York: St Martin's Press, 2000), and data analysis by Jonathan Fox. Jonathan Fox. "Towards a Dynamic Theory of Ethno-Religious Conflict," *Nations and Nationalism* 5(4) (1999): 431–463; Jonathan Fox, "Clash of Civilizations or Clash of Religions: Which is A More Important Determinant of Ethnic Conflict?" *Ethnicities* 1(3) (2001a): 295–320; Jonathan Fox, "Two Civilizations and Ethnic Conflict: Islam and the West," *Journal of Peace Research* 38(4) (2001b): 459–472; Jonathan Fox, "Religion As An Overlooked Element of International Relations," *International Studies Review* 3(3) (2001c): 53–73; Jonathan Fox, "Civilizational, Religious, and National Explanations for Ethnic Rebellion in Post-Cold War Middle East," *Jewish Political Studies Review* 13(1–2) (2001): 177–204; Jonathan Fox, "Are Middle East Conflicts More Religious?" *Middle East Quarterly* 8(4) (2001e): 31–40; Jonathan Fox, "Religious Causes of International Intervention in Ethnic Conflicts," *International Politics* 38 (2001f): 515–532; Jonathan Fox, "International Intervention in Middle Eastern and Islamic Conflicts from 1990 to 1995: A Large-N Study" (unpublished paper prepared for the Israeli International Studies Association Convention, February 2002); Jonathan Fox, *Ethnoreligious Conflict in the Late Twentieth Century: A General Theory* (Lanham, MD: Lexington Books, 2002); Jonathan Fox and Josephine Squires, "Threats to Primal Identities: A Comparison of Nationalism and Religion as Impacts on Ethnic Protest and Rebellion," *Terrorism and Political Violence* 13(1) (2001): 87–102.

18. Mancur Olsen, Jr., *The Logic of Collective Action: Public Goods and the Theory of Groups* (Cambridge, MA.: Harvard University Press, 1965); Todd, Collective Action: Theory and Applications (Ann Arbor, MI: University of Michigan Press, 1992).

19. Douglas Lemke, *Regions of War and Peace* (Cambridge: Cambridge University Press, 2002), 49.

20. Sheton U. Kodikara, ed., *The External Compulsions of South Asian Politics* (New Delhi: Sage Publications, 1993), 18.

21. Although not within the scope of this chapter, there are linkages between the international and regional power hierarchies in terms of generating different role expectations for a state: "When the dominant power or another great power feels strongly about the issues at stake in a dispute within a local hierarchy, interference might be expected. However in the absence of such strong interest by external great powers, the local hierarchies are expected to function in a manner parallel to the overall international power hierarchy." Within the regional hierarchy, however, the dominant power might extend its influence upward to reach the global power hierarchy; China outgrowing East Asia would seem to be an obvious example, Douglas Lemke, *Regions of War and Peace* (Cambridge: Cambridge University Press, 2002), 51, 53.

22. Pevaiz Iqbal Cheema, "SAARC Needs Revamping," in *The Dynamics of South Asia*, ed. Eric Gonsalves and Nancy Jetley (New Delhi: Sage Publications, 1999).

23. Lemke, *Regions of War and Peace*, 51, 53. While not a part of our chapter (i.e. for future research), links between the external and macro levels also are important. One is whether there is any interaction between the international or great power hierarchy and the regional/local hierarchy to explore in the future. Although we will not explore the linkages between the international and regional power hierarchies in terms of how they affect the role expectations of the units at the local level, we can touch on how the two interact. Lemke provides some answers: "When the dominant power or another great power feels strongly about the issues at stake in a dispute within a local hierarchy, interference might be expected. However, in the absence of such strong interest by external great powers, the local hierarchies are expected to function in a manner parallel to the overall international power hierarchy." However there have been a few exceptions to the common fact that great powers never generally interfere in overt military interventions as far as local hierarchy relations are concerned. Within the regional hierarchy, it might and, in fact, does happen, as in case of the US when its influence when it expanded beyond North American interstate relations and China outgrowing East Asia: "... as states move from minor power to great power status, their control over local relations become solidified to such an extent, or their fears and worries about their local neighbors do diminishes to such an extent, that they can largely overlook the interactions of their neighbors." This "moving up" no doubt will have an impact on the role expectations of the other powers within the changed circumstances of the regional hierarchy.

Another example of a connection between the two levels is to look at the relations between the international organization and a regional organization. An example that comes to mind immediately is Turkey's involvement with Cyprus in the 1960s. This case reflects how the dealings between an international organization (the UN) and a regional organization (NATO) had an effect on the on the generation of a role expectation for Turkey. There could be a scenario in which the relationship is one of cooperation. The international and regional organizations jointly could produce significant influence in directing the behavior of the third party. As the situation unfolds, one organization might assume more importance and responsibilities than the other. One taking over for the other, at the latter's request, is a feasible scenario, as with NATO and the UN in Turkey's case. They also could combine to influence the role expectation for Turkey. In scenarios with disagreement, it is observed that one organization will try to override the other in influencing the third party and thereby resolving the ethnic conflict.

24. David Carment and Patrick James, "Third-party States in Ethnic Conflicts: Identifying the Domestic Determinants of Intervention" (paper presented at the Annual Meeting of the American Political Science Association, San Francisco, CA, August 2001, 2002).

25. This variable focuses exclusively on the leadership involved in foreign policy decision-making, that is, the body that includes the head of the state and cabinet colleagues and advisors, foreign secretary and defense secretary, ambassador(s), along with the armed forces heads, each of whom is expected to play a highly significant role in any interventionist strategy implementation.

26. Yuen Foong Khong, *Analogies at War: Korea, Munich, Dien Bien Phu and Vietnam Decisions of 1965* (Princeton: Princeton University Press, 1992).

27. Carment, "Third-party States in Ethnic Conflits."

28. Khong, *Analogies at War*, 10.

29. Hermann 1978, 68.

30. Carment, "Third-party States in Ethnic Conflict,"13–14.

31. Fox and Sandler, 2003.

32. Harbaks Singh, in Rajesh Kadian, *The Kashmir Tangle: Issues and Opinions* (New Delhi: Vision Books, 1992), 130.

33. Sumit Ganguly, *Conflict Unending: India-Pakistan Tensions Since 1947* (New York: Columbia University Press, 2001), 41.

34. Ganguly, *Conflict Unending*, 41.

35. Ganguly, *Conflict Unending*, 45–47; Shahid Amin, *Pakistan's Foreign Policy: A Reappraisal* (Karachi: Oxford University Press, 2000), 52–56.

36. Paul Wallace, "Globalizations of Civil Civil-Military Relations: Democratization, Reform and Security" (paper presented at the International Political Studies Association, Bucharest, Romania, 27 June – 3 July 2003).

37. Lawrence Ziring, *The Ayub Khan Era: Politics in Pakistan, 1958–69* (New York: Syracuse University Press, 1971), 85.

38. It should be noted, however, that the US might be seen as tilting toward Pakistan throughout the 1960s and 1970s, with assistance in the 1971 war over Bangladesh as one example.

39. G. W. Choudhury, *Pakistan's Relations with India, 1947–1966* (New York:: Frederick A. Praeger Publishers, 1968), 252–66, 273.

Pakistan reacted by voicing genuine concerns about a military imbalance in the region that had tilted the scales substantially in favor of India. Appalled at the behavior of its western allies, Pakistan moved closer to China and hoped to receive its assistance in the event of any act of aggression against her. Consider the notable trends in Pakistan's foreign policy: "continued friendship towards aid-giving West, with political reservation; normalization of relations with the Soviet Union and friendly attitude toward China; and cultivating friendship with Afro-Asian countries."

40. Ganguly, *Conflict Unending*, 32–35.

41. Ayub and Nehru previously had resolved a number of issues, such as signing the Indus water treaty. Ayub had tried to settle differences with India in 1959 when he suggested a joint defense regime for the subcontinent. Nehru turned down that offer.

42. However, Islam's relationship to foreign policy, in general terms, came through most directly in Pakistan's efforts toward forging close ties with Muslim states, which existed beyond South Asia. At least in principle, Pakistan extended support to the cause of Muslims anywhere in the world, including the anti-colonial struggles of Indonesia, Tunisia, Morocco, and Algeria. In the 1950s, Pakistan tried to form a platform bringing all Muslim nations together but became discouraged because other Muslim states (a) did not see Islam playing such a strategic role in their nationalist movements and (b) suspected that Pakistan aspired to leadership of the Muslim world.

43. Hasan-Askari Rizvi, *Military, State and Society in Pakistan* (New York: St. Martin's Press, 2000), 4,5, 113–17.

44. Ganguly, *Conflict Unending*, 5; Norman D. Palmer, *Pakistan: The Long Search for Foreign Policy* (Durham, NC: Duke University, Press, 1977), 418. All of Pakistan's constitutions, in varying degrees, have enshrined Islamic ideology as the basis of the state.

45. Partha S. Ghosh, *Conflict and Cooperation in South Asia* (New Delhi: Manohar, 1995), 22.

46. Mohammad Ayub Khan, *Friends Not Master* (London: Oxford University Press, 1966), Sangat Singh, *Pakistan's Foreign Policy: An Appraisal* (New York: Asia Publishing House, 1970), 12; Freeland Abbot, *Islam and Pakistan* (Ithaca: Cornell University Press, 1968), 223–26.

In fact, the theme of Islamic nationalism is writ large in President Ayub Khan's autobiography, Friends Not Masters (1966) (Singh 1970: 12). "'There are,' he [Ayub] had once told a Pakistani audience, 'other Muslim countries, if they leave Islam they can still exist, but if we leave Islam, we cannot exist. Our foundation is Islam,'" Abbot, in Ghosh, *Conflict and Cooperation*, 223–26.

47. Singh, *Pakistan's Foreign Policy*, 13–14. Singh notes that at least three components are in evidence. One in consonance with ideology, the sovereignty of the state rests with Allah, God, rather than with the people. As the minorities are not members of Millat (Islamic brotherhood) they cannot be entrusted with the power to propound and execute state policy at the highest level.

Two, conversely, the Muslims inside Pakistan and across the border in India, in view of Pakistani leaders, form one nation, though citizens of two states, Pakistan and India. Pakistan, therefore, still considers the Muslims across the borders as her special responsibility and preserve. To deny that is to deny the two-nation theory and the need to create Pakistan itself. It is here that the attitude towards India crystallises itself.

Three, because of its ideology, the fibre of Pakistani nationalism is very weak and Pakistan still feels psychologically insecure. The existence of a strong, powerful India in the neighbourhood further accentuates this sense of insecurity. Hence the security of Pakistan constitutes one of the chief motivating factors in the formulation of Pakistan.

48. Bhutto, in Ghosh, *Conflict and Cooperation*, 32.

49. Stephen Philip Cohen, "Identity, Survival and Security: Pakistan's Defence Policy," in *Perspectives on Pakistan's Foreign Policy*, ed., Surendra Chopra (Amritsar, Punjab: Guru Nanak University Press, 1983).

50. Fox and Sindler 2003.

51. Pakistan's very birth was based on a 'two-nation' theory, which put forward the view that Hindus and Muslims constitute two separate nations and hence need to be divided from each other. The Muslim League, the party formed during the freedom struggle to realize such a goal, voiced fears of being crushed under the domination of the Hindu majority and, based on Islamic nationalism, demanded a separate 'Pakistan' at the time of independence from Britain. The League's rival, the Congress Party, opposed that view and saw India as a secular entity. Thus, from the moment the two nations achieved their independence after partition of India, they became rivals in terms of ideological moorings, which provided an identity to each.

52. Sumit Ganguly, *The Origins of War in South Asia: Indo-Pakistani Conflicts since 1947* (Boulder, Colo: Westview Press, 1986), 11.

Based on Weiner's (1971) definition of irredentism, which is "the desire on the part of a state to revise some portion of its international boundaries to incorporate the ethnic/religious/linguistic minority of a contiguous state and the territory that it occupies," Gaguly regards Pakistan's claim as that type. The territory of Kashmir was not merely contiguous to Pakistan; it also had a Muslim majority population. From Pakistan's point of view, "Kashmir needed to be incorporated into Pakistan to ensure its 'completeness.'" See also Myron Weiner, "The Macedonian Syndrom," *World Politics* 23 (1971): 4: 665–83.

53. Singh, *Pakistan's Foreign Policy*, 19–20. Muslims of East Pakistan, separated from the West by 1000 miles of Indian territory, were not considered as 'good' Muslims or a safe bet for the ideology of the state coming into being as Pakistan. It was thought that Bengalis remained under the Hindu cultural and linguistic influence (most of all being converts from Hinduism). Ayub's military coup in 1958 eliminated the Bengalis from the ruling hierarchy of Pakistan.

54. Stasnley J. Tambiah, *Leveling Crowds: Ethnonationalist Conflicts and Collective Violence in South Asia* (New Delhi: Vistaar Publications, 1996).

55. In Ganguly *Origins of War*, 205.

56. S.D. Muni, *Pangs of Proximity: India and Sri Lanka's Ethnic Crisis* (New Delhi; Sage Publications, 1993); Maya Chadha, *Ethnicity, Separatism, and Security* (New York: Columbia University Press, 1997); Ganguly, *Origins of War*, 1998.

57. Rajat Ganguly, *Kin State Intervention in Ethnic Conflicts: Lessons from South Asia* (New Delhi: Sage Publications, 1998), 203.

58. Ganguly, *Kin State*, 206.

59. Ganguly, *Kin State*, 207–08.

60. Ganguly, *Kin State*, 210.

61. Ganguly, *Kin State*, 211–12.

62. Sheton U. Kodikara, ed., *The External Compulsions of South Asian Politics* (New Delhi: Sage Publications, 1993); Kodikara, "Internationalization of Sri Lanka's Ethnic Conflict: The Tamil Nadu factor," in *Internationalization of Ethnic Conflict*, ed., K.M. de Silva and R.J. May (New York: St. Martin's Press, 1991).

China and the US have had cordial relations with Sri Lanka since the mid-1960s; in fact, Sri Lanka's foreign policy could be described as essentially pro-US and pro-Chinese. This orientation in foreign policy became all the more entrenched with the Soviet invasion of Afghanistan in 1980 and resulting renewal of the Cold War in South

Asia. Sri Lanka openly criticized Soviet occupation of Afghanistan, which India did not take well. Around the same time, Indian intelligence reported the granting of oil storage facilities by Colombo to US companies and possible creation of a US naval-military base at the strategic eastern port of Trincomalee. On multilateral issues, such as the problem of managing the Indian Ocean and of a nuclear weapons-free zone in South Asia, India saw its role in the emerging ethnic conflict as one that would allow it to press its point of view upon Sri Lanka.

63. Chadha, *Ethnicity, Separatism*, 150.

64. Alfred Jeyaratnam Wilson, *The Break-Up of Sri Lanka: The Sinhalese-Tamil Conflict* (London: Christphrer Hurst and Co., 1988); Rajesh Kadian, *India's Sri Lanka Fiasco* (New Delhi, Vision Books, 1990); Sheton U. Kadikara, ed., *The External Compulsions of Siuth Asian Politics* (New Delhi: Sage Publications, 1993); de Silva, *Internationalization of Ethnic Conflicts*.

65. Rajesh Kandian, *The Kashmir Tangle: Issues and Options* (Boulder, Westview Press, 1993).

66. Carment, "Third-party States in Ethnic Conflicts."

67. Muni, *Pangs of Proximity*, 1991; James 1996; Ganguly, *Kin State*.

68. Bueno de Mesquita and Lalman 1992).

69. Carment, "Third-party States in Ethnic Conflicts."

70. P. Rao Venkateshwar, "Ethnic Conflict in Sri Lanka: India's Role and Perception," *Asian Survey* 28 (1988): 419–36.

71. Rohan Gunaratna, *Indian Intervention in Sri Lanka* (Colombo, Sri Lanka: South Asian Network on Conflict Research, 1993).

72. Ganguly, *Kin State*, 1998.

73. David Carment and Patrick James, "Toward a Model of Interstate Ethnic Conflict: Evidence from the Balkan War and the Indo-Sri Lankan Conflict," *Canadian Journal of Political Science* 29 (1996): 547–48.

74. Sankaran Krishna, *Postcolonial Insecurities: India, Sri Lanka and the Question of Nationhood* (Minneapolis, MN: University of Minnesota Press, 1999), 106.

75. Y.K. Malik and D.K. Vajpeyi, eds., *India: The Years of Indira Gandhi* (Lieden and New York: E.J. Brill, 1988); Sankaran Krishna, *Postcolonial Insecurities: India, Sri Lanka and the Question of Nationhood* (Minneapolis, MN: University of Minnesota Press, 1999).

76. Chadha, *Ethnicity and Separatism*, 152.

77. Chadha, *Ethnicity and Separatism*, 154.

Chapter 2

Ethnic Violence and the Loss of State Legitimacy: Burma[1] and Indonesia in a Context of Post-Colonial Developmentalism

Vivienne Wee and Graeme Lang

"Ethnicity," Conflict and Violence along a Cline of Social Differentiation

In recent years, ethnic violence has visibly increased in several parts of the world, including Southeast Asia. As noted by Brubaker and Laitin,[2] research on ethnic violence brings together two largely non-intersecting literatures—studies of ethnic conflict and studies of political violence. Two questions arise from this intersection: (1) under what conditions do ethnic conflicts manifest themselves violently? (2) Under what conditions does political violence become ethicised?

However, prior to answering these two questions, we need to address a basic conceptual question concerning ethnicity as a social phenomenon—that is, what is "ethnicity"? Much has been written about this. We discern two opposing approaches to this matter. The difference between these two approaches may be couched in the form of this question: is "ethnicity" born or made?

Van der Berghe[3] exemplifies those who espouse the former approach. He sees "ethnicity" as derived from the supposedly factual existence of "ethnies": "The prototypical ethny is…a descent group bounded socially by inbreeding and spatially by territory." In other words, "ethnicity" is a mosaic made up of the various "ethnies" that are primordial.

At the other end of the theoretical spectrum is Barth[4] who has pioneered the approach that "ethnicity" is made, not born: "To think of ethnicity in relation to one group and its culture is like trying to clap with one hand. The contrast between "us" and "others" is what is embedded in the organization of ethnicity."

Thus, for Barth and others in this camp, "ethnicity" is basically a process of social differentiation between Self and Other. Differences between Self and Other are thus not intrinsic but socially constructed to maintain the boundary between them... Ethnic groups that are formed through this process of social differentiation are thus situational, not primordial.

How are we to reconcile these two opposing approaches? We argue that there is an important developmental dimension that must be taken into consideration. In the first phase, social differentiation occurs between Self and Other, as shown by Barth and others arguing in this vein. Such social differentiation occurs as a result of particular interactions—historical, economic, and political. Once such differentiation begins, three options for further development are possible. It should be noted that, as with the first phase of social differentiation, the path of further development that follows, is contingent on specific historical, economic and political interactions, which must therefore be identified. The three options are:

(1) Stabilization of the differentiation, which is institutionalized in social behavior (such as clothing, rituals, speech, cuisine): The anthropological literature is replete with ethnographic examples of such institutionalized differences, which may be maintained for centuries.

(2) Reduction of the differentiation through countervailing processes of non-ethnic social solidarity: Research on the inverse relationship between ethnic conflict and non-ethnic or inter-ethnic associational forms of engagement provides evidence of this effect. (See, for example, Varshney[5]). This option is more likely to occur in a de-ethnicised society, where social differentiation occurs in terms of class, rather than ethnicity. Class linkages are potentially inter-local, inter-ethnic and inter-national, whereas ethnic linkages tend to be local, ascriptive and bounded. Therefore, even though class differentiation and ethnic differentiation may both arise out of competition for scarce resources, class formation is potentially inclusive, whereas ethnic group formation tends to be exclusive.[6]

(3) Increasing hardening of the boundary into a rigid barrier between the differentiating groups, such that they become increasingly distanced from each other: more will be said about this below; as this is the option we are most interested in for this paper.

This third option can lead progressively to conflict and violence. To develop another question beyond Brubaker and Laitin's two questions above, we can ask: under what conditions does ethnic differentiation become politicized, conflictual and violent? For this progressive hardening of differentiation to occur, the construction of differences must be naturalized, so that the construction process itself is disguised and the experience of difference comes to be felt as "authentic" and "real." As Wee[7] has argued, this naturalization of ethnic difference is effected through atavism and indigenism. "Atavism roots the imagination in time, indigenism roots it in space."[8] As a result, social differentiation is naturalized into unchanging ethnic categories that are presented as spatially fixed, unchanging traditions. At this point, if we chance upon these post-naturalized groups, they would seem to be "primordial" groups, for that is how they have come to look upon themselves. Therefore, what we are dealing with is not primordiality as a "fact." Rather, we argue that seemingly primordial ethnies are an ideological outcome of naturalization as a social process.

This analysis enables us to locate conflict and violence even further along this cline of social differentiation. Horowitz[9] argues that all conflicts based on ascriptive group identities can be called "ethnic." Significantly, his discussion focuses on conflict in particular, not just social differentiation in general. We would argue that ascription is the other side of the coin of primordialism. Therefore, not only are the socially differentiated groups construed as unchanging ethnies from time immemorial, membership in such groups comes to be acquired only through birth. The construction of "ethnicity" as being "born" thus entails the definition of the "ethnics" themselves as members by birth. Relinquishing one's membership by birth in such groups can be interpreted, from within those groups, as apostasy and treason.

It is also in this context that gender politics takes a vicious turn, as the women in the closely guarded group become defined as the reproducers of the collective political future, with their chastity and fertility used as the sole means of recruitment. In situations of ethnic conflict and violence, women are pushed to the front-lines of ethnic battles, because the ethnic enemy also comes to regard the women as the reproducers of the political future for the other side. This has motivated the use of organized systematic rape as a weapon of war. This has been inflicted, for example, on Shan women in Burma and in Indonesia, on women in former East Timor (now Timor-Leste), West Papua and Aceh.[10]

Varshney[11] points out that much of the existing literature does not distinguish between ethnic conflict and ethnic violence. He notes the significance of this differentiation: while not all conflicts are violent, all violence expresses conflict. He argues that the issue is whether conflicts can be expressed through the polity's institutionalized-channels, such as parliament, assembly and bureaucracy. As we shall see below, the validity of such channels rests in turn on state legitimacy.

For the moment, however, suffice it to note that the use of institutionalized channels as means of resolving ethnic conflict implies the presence of a neutral third party—that is, the state—to arbitrate between two contending ethnic groups. In the absence of such a neutral third party, extreme conflict between such groups becomes a zero-sum equation, where the naturalization of Self is concomitant with the deionization of Other. In its most violent form, the existence of Self becomes contingent upon the defeat and perhaps even the demise of Other. Thus, non-violent conflict can mutate into violence, which can, in turn, mutate into genocide.

In this paper, we examine a particular set of conditions that has the tendency to intensify non-violent ethnic differentiation until it becomes ethnic violence. We argue that this happens when state legitimacy is lost among certain sectors of the population, who are already ethnically differentiated, though hitherto in non-violent ways. Crawford and Lipschutz[12] have made a similar argument. They point out that a state's legitimacy relates directly to its ethnic policies: when the central government's policies in the form of entitlements are seen as benefiting ethnic majorities, this induces ethnic minorities to respond by organising themselves for political action. In other words, the violent conflict that ensues between these groups derives not from intrinsic social and cultural differences, but rather, from progressively hardened differentiations, brought about by a specific type of state-society relationship.

KEY POINT

Ethnic Violence in the Context of State Legitimacy

This dimension of violence is highly significant with regards to the integrity of the nation-state. Weber defined the state as the institutionalised monopoly of violence:

> "Every state is founded on force," said Trotsky.... That is indeed right. If no social institutions existed which knew the use of violence, then the concept of 'state' would be eliminated, and a condition would emerge that could be designated as 'anarchy,' in the specific sense of this word.... Today the relation between the state and violence is an especially intimate one.... Today... we have to say that a state is a human community that (successfully) claims the monopoly of the legitimate use of physical force within a given territory.[13]

INTERESTING!

In this regard, ethnic violence within a state could be taken as symptomatic of the inability of the state to monopolise violence and thereby establish itself as a legitimate state in the full Weberian sense of the term. In other words, ethnic violence indicates a fragmenting state.

Brubaker and Laitin[14] identify this "decay of the Weberian state" as a general feature of the "late modern, post-Cold War world," by which they refer to the (unevenly) declining capacity of states to "maintain order by monopolising the legitimate use of violence in their territories." In this paper, however, we argue that a lack of state monopoly over violence may arise from a lack of legitimacy of the state in question. In other words, it could be a problem endemic to the formation of a particular state, rather than being a quantifiable condition that waxes and wanes in different geo-political moments.

Legitimacy bestows governments with the right to rule. Without legitimacy, there are only relations of power, not authority. Legitimacy lowers the costs of governance—social, political and economic. Without legitimacy, much of a government's resources will be consumed for its survival—e.g. military, police, secret police, surveillance, and prisons—not for governance of the country.

Alagappa[15] notes that legitimacy is crucial to state-society relations. However, none of the three main approaches to the study politics of developing countries—political development, Marxism, world-system theories—pay attention to this issue, even though state legitimacy is central to political stability and change. One reason for this neglect is the assumption that the state is a given political norm and that the only area of research that needs attention is the trajectory of the state. However, the current phenomena of failed states, fragmented states and seceded states indicate that the state cannot simply be assumed as a given political norm.

As noted by Benjamin,

> The nation-state is problematical. Viewed as part of the grand sweep
> of human history, it is a late starter in the race between competing
> ways of trading off individual and local autonomy against higher-
> level organisational integration. The nation-state is, of course, not the
> only such form of higher-level integration, for there have existed in
> the past ten thousand years not only a plethora of pre-modern states
> and empires but also an extensive range of ranked and stratified non-
> centralized polities too. Nor was the nation-state the last in the line,
> for while nation-states are still being created in some parts of the
> world they are being dissolved away in others, and we cannot predict
> the nature of the sociocultural forms that will replace them.[16]

Weber[17] discussed legitimacy as a characteristic of the type of relations established between leaders and followers, and not just an attribute of the leader alone. He identified four "pure types" of legitimacy, out of which various combinations may emerge:

1. Traditional authority—based on the sanctity of tradition, of "the eternal yesterday"

2. Charismatic authority—based on the appeal of leaders who claim allegiance because of their extraordinary virtuosity, whether ethical, heroic, or religious   i e. Hitler ?

3. Rational-legal authority—based on rational grounds and anchored in impersonal rules that have been legally enacted or contractually established

4. Goal-rational authority—based on a supposedly rational relationship between the ultimate goal and the leaders.

We would like to develop Weber's typology further by noting that there is an important temporal dimension implied in these different types of legitimacy. Traditional authority is oriented towards the *past*—a golden age of perfection which legitimates a present quest to recover such perfection. Charismatic authority is oriented towards the *present*—specifically, the life-span of the charismatic leader who achieved perfection. Rational-legal authority is similarly oriented towards the *present*—a structure of legal rationality that has been established. Goal-rational authority is, however, oriented towards the *future*—a utopia that is yet to be achieved.

We focus on post-colonial states in this paper because state legitimacy is fragile in many such states. A major structural flaw found in most post-colonial states is that they did not exist as such prior to European colonisation. As a result, many such states come to be viewed as a historical product that is contingent upon earlier European colonization.

However, not all post-colonial states are wracked by violence, ethnic or non-ethnic. We argue that, in the absence of legitimacy based on the traditional authority of a pre-colonial past, post-colonial states typically try instead to legitimate their political existence through future-oriented, goal-rational authority. This has been articulated as "developmentalism"—the promise to bring economic development to the people once they are free of the colonial yoke. We hypothesize that the emergence of ethnic violence in a number of Southeast Asian states is closely related to the failure of developmentalism as goal-rational legitimacy. Without a functional role of the state as an effective agent of economic development, there is no primordial rationale for these historically contingent states to exist. In other words, the existence of these post-colonial states is legitimated by their functional role as agents of economic development.

Significantly, the political project of developmentalism implicates not just a temporal orientation towards the future, but also a particular social production of space, as defined by an institutionalised centre of state power. Over the last four decades, the Southeast Asian region has seen a centralisation of state power, coupled with an equally important attempt to (re)make the space of the nation-state in cultural nationalist terms. However, this production of national space is often layered on top of earlier pre-capitalist spatial structures, such that the more abstract space of cultural nationalism lies on top of multiple layers of different "ethnic" productions of space. These diverse "ethnic" productions of space are not just residual categories awaiting absorption into the cultural nationalist rubric. On the contrary, these draw on alternative sources of authority for spatial definition and thereby constitute alternatives to the cultural nationalist production of space. These alternative sources include, in particular, temporal imaginaries that may variously be construed as "history" (an event-filled past that defines the present) or "culture" (a meaning-filled present that reproduces the values and beliefs of the past).

In contrast, the temporal imaginary of national space is "development" (time that progresses from a traditional past to a modern future). Without this temporal dimension, there is no "developmentalism." The developmentalist production of space is inextricably coupled with the developmentalist production of time. The state's production of national cultural space is legitimated by the developmentalist project's temporal future. This temporal orientation rejects any aspect of past and present that is seen as incongruent with the imagined developmentalist future. This temporal-spatial imagining has the effect of standardising all national space as potential resources to be harnessed and accumulated for state development.[18]

When this political production of time and space is motivated by a regime of accumulation that clearly favours centres of state power, those in peripheral territories may become sceptical of the legitimacy of the temporal and spatial units that are produced—for example, 5 year plans, electoral boundaries, administrative units. These come to be seen not as objective "facts" but as subjective artefacts of certain expropriating interests. The failure of a developmentalist project in winning hearts and minds is countered by alternative productions of space justified, not by an imagined developmentalist future, but by an imagined pre-capitalist golden age. The goal-rational claim of developmentalism is thus challenged by the traditional authority of ethnic origins—a claim to ascriptive legitimacy derived from a socially produced past.

Wee and Jayasuriya[19] note that this social production of the past traces an alternative trajectory of the future—that is, a future defined as continuous with a supposedly inherited past and not a future defined in terms of a developmentalist present. These counter-productions of time are also plotted out in space, leading to counter-claims to resources and constituencies. We thus argue that ethnic conflicts are manifestations of clashes between competing productions of time, space, resources and constituency.

In this context, we can analyse ethnic conflicts as political battles between contending constituencies on two levels: the first is between a nation-state and an ethnically based nation-of-intent, while the second is between two nations-of-intent. The former is an asymmetrical type of violence –between a majority-dominated state and a minority-based non-state, even if the latter is an aspiring nation-of-intent. The latter, however, is a symmetrical type of violence between two minorities who are political peers, so to speak.

Tønnesson and Antlöv utilise the term "nation-of-intent"[20] to refer to the imagination of intended statehood, based on "a vision of a territorial entity, a set of institutions, an ideal-type citizen and an identity profile."[21] Tønnesson and Antlöv argue that a nation-of-intent differs from Anderson's "imagined community"[22] in that the former is envisioned by a relatively small group of activist advocates, but not yet involving the majority of its potential constituents, whereas "the latter has to be imagined by those who are part of it before it can be said to exist."[23] What is significant here is the distinction between the ideational domain and the institutional domain, between "those who imagine" and "those who are part of." What links these two domains is the transformative flow of power. On the one hand, those who imagine seek to realise their imagination in political institutions—namely, the institutionalised nation-state—and in so doing, make others part of this political reality. On the other hand, however, those who are made part of an institutionalised political reality need to re-imagine their existing reality, and to accommodate the new reality in their imagination of a legitimate state. Without their ideational engagement, political institutions including the nation-state become mere shells.

This has serious consequences for the exacerbation of ethnic conflict into ethnic violence. Varshney[24] has demonstrated from his research in India that ethnic violence is reduced when ethnic conflicts can be expressed through the state's institutionalized channels, such as parliament, assembly, and bureaucracy. The converse would also tend to be the case. Ethnic violence intensifies when institutions lose legitimacy. This situation may also be described by the term "social fragmentation." Narayan[25] see social fragmentation as arising from inequities in institutions, the state, civil society, and the household. Such inequities cause people to distrust society's institutions, motivating them to seek security within the group, rather than within society. This, in turn, creates conditions for a cycle of insecurity, social exclusion, and increased levels of conflict and violence. According to this logic, inter-ethnic violence is a response by certain sectors of the population to their distrust of the state and its institutions.

In this context, Gramsci's[26] analysis of subaltern classes is relevant. He argues that as a result of being marginalised by a regime of power, the subaltern classes could only be unified and united when they are able to become a state. We argue that if ethnic differentiation were to become polarised and rigid, in the way we have described above, the ethnic community becomes progressively politicized into, first, an ethnic constituency, then into an ethnic nation. As implied by Gramsci above, the aim of having/becoming a "state" would signify the highest degree of unity of an ethicized subaltern class, which would simultaneously have its identity most sharply crystallised.

This analysis of ethnic differentiation as a process of potential polarisation runs contrary to the assumption of "ethnicity" as a mosaic of statically formed "ethnic groups" that are located beneath the rubric of a state. Rather, such an analysis allows us to see how ethnic differentiation rests on the same continuum as nation-making. So when the legitimate existence of a state is challenged by contending communities, who reject its claim to rule over them and who counter-claim their right to independent statehood, then what they assert, in their own terms, is not ethnic identity but rather, *national* identity. Therefore, in this context, it is perhaps more appropriate to speak of ethno-nationalism, ethno-nations and ethno-nationalist conflicts. An ethno-nation is thus a nation-of-intent or, to borrow Guibernau's phrase, a nation without a state.[27]

This mode of analysis also enables us to see that underlying the term "ethnicity" is an assumption that this is a sub-state phenomenon that exists beneath the rubric of the state. So when a minority-based nation-of-intent achieves independent statehood—for example, in the case of former East Timor (now Timor-Leste)—then the discourse shifts from talking about inter-ethnic relations to inter-state relations. Yet the achievement of independent statehood does not necessarily change the socio-cultural content of the former sub-state "ethnic" group. Therefore, it is more valid to understand ethnic differentiation and nation-making as social phenomena situated at different points of the same political continuum.

Ethnic Violence in Two Problematic Post-colonial States: Burma and Indonesia

The current nation-states of Southeast Asia are, without exception, the historical results of European colonialisation. Their territorial extent, the ethnic make-up of their constituencies and sometimes their very names are colonial residues, which still constitute sites of contestation. For example, in a seminal paper, Leach[28] noted that prior to British colonization, there was no pre-colonial state called "Burma" sited on this post-colonial territory. As noted by Yawnghwe,[29] present-day "Burma" is derived from the territories that the British colonized and made into a political entity, then called "Ministerial Burma."

The same processes were at work in other post-colonial states:

• Indonesia—a territorial successor to *Netherlands-Indie* (Netherlands East Indies),[30] with a name coined by a German geographer in 1884, derived from *Indos Nesos* (Greek: "Indian Islands").[31]

• Malaysia—a territorial successor to British Malaya and British North Borneo, with a name combining the English word "Malay" (for a major ethnic group) and "-sia" (as in "Asia").

• The Philippines—a territorial successor to the Spanish colony of *Las Islas Felipinas* (Philip's Islands), named after King Philip II of Spain[32]

• Thailand—a territorial survivor that escaped direct European colonization because the British and French agreed to make it a buffer state, which nevertheless had its territory altered to make it a clearly demarcated buffer, with a name that combines "Thai" (the ethnic majority) with the English word "land."

• Singapore—a territorial successor to one of the three Straits Settlements (the other two being Malacca and Penang) that together constituted a British Crown Colony, with a name that is an Anglicized version of its original Malay name "Singapura".

Pre-colonial Southeast Asia was politically organized as loose networks of kingdoms and chiefdoms with shifting relations.[33] Some cultural elements were shared by these polities—for example, religion, while other cultural elements were unique—for example, the royal regalia. These pre-colonial polities were not tightly bounded territorial units. Rather, they focussed on control over people rather than control over territory, based on the assumption that if the rulers had the loyalty of their subjects, their territory automatically became part of the rulers' domain.[34]

This pre-colonial priority given to control over people contrasts sharply with post-colonial nation-states, which focused on control over territory more than control over people. The assumption is that if the state has jurisdiction over a particular territory, its inhabitants are obliged to give their allegiance to this state. Arguably, this post-colonial focus on territorial control is derived from the aims of the colonial state. For example, the Dutch colonial government stated in its regulations of 1802: "Colonies are there to serve the mother country, not the other way around."[35] The impetus for colonisation is to obtain the resources located in the territories of the colonies. Therefore, insofar as post-colonial states follow colonial states in adhering to this territorial focus, they too may come to be seen as using the controlled territories to serve the interests of the political centre.

As Paribatra and Samudavanija have noted:

> In post-colonial Southeast Asia...it has been conveniently forgotten by central governments that the constructing of what is more accurately a state-nation, merely means that external or western imperialism had been replaced by an internalized one, which is potentially more brutal and enduring.[36]

In this paper, we discuss two problematic post-colonial states—Burma and Indonesia—to demonstrate how ethnic violence arises from the loss of state legitimacy, which is thereby symptomised by the lack of state monopoly over violence. Of the two, Burma is probably the one that is more problematic. There is a historical process that has led to this. As noted by Yawnghwe[37], the British directly colonized the territories that were most useful to them. This was "Ministerial Burma," consisting of the Irrawaddy lowland, inhabited by Burmans.

> The remote, not easily accessible areas or frontier lands, whose resources were not easily workable..., were left more or less alone, with local chiefs and princes in charge, but under loose British supervision. The areas that were not easily exploitable were designated as Frontier Areas, which also included the Federated Shan States.[38]

As argued by Yawnghwe,[39] contrary to Burman nation-making myths, the British did not conquer a pre-existing unified Burmese kingdom and then partitioned it into separate parts in order to divide and rule. Yet, in the 1930s, prior to independence, Burman nationalist-imperialists (to coin a term) claimed that there are no ethnic differences between Burman, Shan, Karen and so on, that all are Burman, that the British created differences where none existed, and that the Frontier Areas and Federated Shan States should be (re)unified with Ministerial Burma to form a "Burma" that supposedly pre-dated British colonization. Following Yawnghwe[40] and Rajah[41], among others, we argue that it is this Burman nationalist-imperialist claim on non-Burman territory that lies at the crux of the ethnic violence in Burma. The clash is between a nation-state dominated by a

Burman majority and the nations-of-intent found among certain ethnic minorities.

However, before such violence erupted, during the 1940s, a more accommodating and equitable Burman approach was pioneered by U Aung San (father of Aung San Suu Kyi), who successfully persuaded the non-Burmans to cooperate politically. In 1947, prior to independence, an agreement called the Panglong Accord was signed between Burmans and non-Burmans laying out the structure of the state-to-be as a federal union of equal states based on different nationalities. The existence of this Accord shows that there was a real possibility for peaceful co-existence and even cooperation among the diverse ethnic groups in what was to become "Burma."[42]

Therefore, as we have argued above, ethnic differentiation by itself does not necessarily degenerate into conflict and eventual violence. Existing historical evidence of the pre-colonial situation in the territory that became "Burma" indicates that ethnicity did not figure significantly in major political events.[43] So while ethnic differentiation was of long standing, it had been stabilized and institutionalized in various forms of behavior, including ecological adaptations, cultural expressions and political formations.[44] Therefore, based on the paradigm that we have presented above, while the current ethnic violence rests on the same continuum of differentiation as earlier pre-colonial forms of ethnic differentiation, the degree of polarization and politicization that the current violence represents is historically unprecedented. Also, following Barth,[45] we argue that progressive differentiation is not automatic, but is brought about by specific historical, political and economic conditions.

The specific conditions that destroyed the multi-ethnic accord achieved in 1947 and led to increasing ethnic violence are well known. U Aung San was assassinated four months after the signing of the Panglong Accord. The Burmese constitution that emerged later that same year ignored the Panglong Accord and established instead a Burman-dominated centralized state, not a federal union of Burmans and non-Burmans, as previously agreed. [46] But even this constitution made provisions for non-Burmans to form states in their own right. In particular, it included a clause giving the Karenni state, the Shan state and the Kachin state the right to secede from the Union of Burma after ten years, if they were to choose to do so.[47] This clause was a concession meant to assure the non-Burmans that their inclusion in the Union of Burma would be a voluntary act which they could rescind.[48] Unfortunately, this clause became an impetus for military intervention, which sought to prevent such secession from occurring. This led to a military *coup d'état* in 1962 that brought the country under a yoke of political oppression and economic stagnation from which it has yet to emerge.[49]

The illegitimacy of majoritarian authoritarianism has been compounded by the military government's isolationist policy called the "Burmese Way to Socialism," under which military expenditure accounts for 40 percent of public sector spending, with the Burmese currency (*kyat*) overvalued by 8000 per cent. Urban inflation runs as high as 40 percent per year. Farmers are forced to sell fixed quotas of their harvest to the state at prices far below market par, causing them to grow two or three crops a year. The government then exports the rice at world market prices and keeps the profit. This colossal failure of economic development is compounded by economic sanctions and boycotts imposed by the United States, the European Union and multilateral organisations (including the International Monetary Fund and World Bank), as well as civic organisations and consumers, in response to the human rights abuses inflicted by the military regime.[50] Burma is now one of the world's ten poorest countries. The country is the world's largest producer of opium and has one of Asia's most alarming HIV/AIDS crises. The universities have been closed for years. The National League for Democracy (NLD), which won a landslide victory with 80 percent of the vote in the general election of 1990, has been prevented by the military from taking office. Many of the NLD's leaders and members are imprisoned or killed. The NLD's secretary-general, Aung San Suu Kyi (daughter of U Aung San of the Panglong Accord) has been under house arrest from 1989 to 1995, from 2000 to 2002, and from 30 May 2003 to the time of writing (May, 2005).[51]

The ethnic violence that has raged in Burma in the last five decades stems from this massive state failure. The United Nations notes that ethnic minorities are suffering from human rights abuses, including "torture, arbitrary executions, deliberate killings, indiscriminate use of landmines, pressure to join military forces exerted by both the government troops and armed opposition groups."[52] The Burmese military uses the "Four Cuts" (*Pya Ley Pya*) strategy against non-Burman minorities. This strategy is so called for the following reason:

> Its aim is to cut off food, funds, intelligence and recruits to the insurgents. This entails forced relocations of entire communities into "strategic villages," confiscation of food which is then re-issued as rations, destruction of crops, "taxes," and a shoot-on-sight policy during curfew hours. Civilian villagers have also been press-ganged as porters carrying military supplies and often made to walk in front of Tatamadaw troops acting as human "mine detectors."[53]

More than 500,000 are refugees in Thailand, India, Bangladesh and Malaysia, while 600,000 to 1,000,000 have been internally displaced inside Burma.[54] "In a survey of ethnic Shan women, 25% of rapes perpetrated by the Burmese military resulted in the death of the victims; 60% of the rapes were gang-rapes."[55] Human rights abuses committed by the Burmese military have worsened recently. According to a news report that they have started using chemical weapons against the Karen ethnic minority.[56]

In the face of these atrocities, it is not surprising that the majority of non-Burman minorities have been involved in protracted armed resistance. From their perspective, their armed conflicts are nationalist struggles against the imperialism of an illegitimate Burman-dominated failed state. These uprisings occurred first among the Karens, followed by the Mons, Karennis, Paos, Kachins,

Rakhines and Muslim *Mujahids*.[57] By 1989, there were 23 armed ethno-nationalist groups in Burma.[58] This means that most of the non-Burman populations are in armed conflict with the Burman-dominated *Tatmadaw* (Burmese Armed Forces). Indeed, Burma has the largest number of armed ethnic insurgencies in Southeast Asia.[59]

In the absence of a reliable census in Burma, the population and ethnic composition can only be estimated. The Burma Project estimates a population of about 47 million, with Burmans making up two-thirds. Karens and Shans are estimated as each constituting about 10 percent of the population, while Akha, Chin, Chinese, Danu, Indian, Kachin, Karenni, Kayan, Kokang, Lahu, Mon, Naga, Palaung, Pao, Rakhine, Rohingya, Tavoyan and Wa peoples each constitute 5 percent or less.[60] Including the Burmans, this would make a total of 21 ethnic groups. In contrast to the estimates above, there are two opposing extreme claims, with the military government currently ruling Burma claiming that 67–70 percent of the population is Burman (a claim that is said to be based on skewed data from an old census in which anyone with a Burmese-language name was listed as Burman), while non-Burmans counter-claim that 70 percent of the population are non-Burman, with only 30 percent Burman.[61] Since even the population of Burma is not definitively known, it is difficult, if not impossible, to record the number of people who have been killed as a result of the decades of ethnic violence and human rights violations.

Our analysis of the nexus between ethnic violence and the loss of state legitimacy indicates that the most effective way to break the gridlock of ethnic violence in Burma would be for the state to regain legitimacy. To achieve this, as of 2005, it would be necessary for the illegal military government (that is, illegal according to Burma's own laws) to step down and for the elected National League for Democracy (NLD) to form the government. Concomitantly, the NLD's leaders, including Aung San Suu Kyi, must be freed from imprisonment or house arrest so that they can take office.

While the military government seeks legitimacy through external endorsement, such as its recent admission into the Association of Southeast Asian Nations (ASEAN), this has not made it more legitimate in the eyes of its own citizens, because all of its structural failures, political bad faith and human rights abuses still remain. Indeed, ASEAN's policy of non-interference in the internal affairs of member states ensures that it is in no position to help restore state legitimacy by addressing these structural failures, bad faith and rights abuses. On the contrary, all that is achieved by the entry of Burma into ASEAN is that an illegal military government is propped up, the illegitimacy of the state persists, and ethnic violence continues. In a recent letter to the Thai newspaper *The Nation*, the secretary-general of the Shan Democratic Union urged ASEAN to recognise that Burma is becoming a failed state that will require the intervention of "the international community... to correct the balance of power between the SPDC[62] on one side and the NLD (National League for Democracy) and non-Burman ethnic nationalities on the other."[63]

We now turn our attention to Indonesia, which, like Burma, is a post-colonial state that did not exist as such prior to European colonization. As in the case of Burma, Indonesia's post-coloniality is seen as problematic by its own citizens. For example, Aditjondro asks:

> Before discussing the contemporary challenges, allow me first to crack the basic nut, by raising the basic question to expose the basic contradictions in what has been taken for granted during the last 50 years: is "Indonesia" indeed the rightful heir of the Dutch East Indies colony? Or, is Indonesia actually a "brand-new" nation-state, which has liberated itself completely from the Dutch—as well as the Japanese—colonial yoke?[64]

Also like Burma, Indonesia has a dominant ethnic majority—the Javanese who constituted 41.71 percent of the population in 2000.[65] According to the 2000 census, the Indonesian population of 201,092,238 is divided into 101 ethnic groups.[66]

However, despite the eruption of ethnic violence in several parts of Indonesia, the magnitude of its ethnic fragmentation is arguably less than in Burma, although such fragmentation does unquestionably exist. Moreover, in Indonesia, the prevalence of these conflicts increased perceptibly after the fall of Suharto in May 1998. Most notably, such violence has erupted, from west to east, in Aceh, Jakarta, West and Central Kalimantan, Maluku, Central Sulawesi, West Papua, and prior to its secession, former East Timor (now Timor-Leste). Unlike Burma with its 23 ethno-nationalist separatist groups going back to the 1940s, in Indonesia, there have been only three areas with long-standing ethno-nationalist movements—that is, Aceh, West Papua and former East Timor. Also unlike the situation in Burma, the majority of non-Javanese are not in armed conflict with the Javanese. The post-Suharto ethnic conflicts that occurred in Jakarta, West and Central Kalimantan, Maluku and Central Sulawesi are recent occurrences.

Two questions need to be answered:
1. Why is Indonesia less ethnically fragmented than Burma despite its larger territory, larger population and more numerous ethnic groups?
2. Why did ethnic conflicts in Indonesia increase in recent years after the fall of Suharto in May 1998?

Wee and Jacobsen[67] show that the conflicts that have emerged in Indonesia are not based solely on ethnic divisions. Rather, these conflicts derive from different political imaginings of the nation-state, the roots of which can be traced to the anti-colonial struggle in the Netherlands East Indies. The most relevant of these at the moment are:
- Secular nationalism in two versions: (a) centralized unitary state (b) decentralized federalism
- Political Islam seeking to make Indonesia more Islamic or indeed an Islamic state

While there are ideological struggles between these two views of what Indonesia should be, these are nonetheless non-ethnically based oppositions. The difference between ethnic conflicts and ideological struggles is significant. The former is based on an assertion of ascriptive identity (membership through birth), whereas the latter is based on professed belief (which can change).

Ascriptive identity requires "identity work"—that is, the work of constructing an identity that is simultaneously inclusive (to insiders) and exclusive (to outsiders). Such "identity work" focuses on linking oneself to local cultural markers, including:

- Genealogical accounts of kinship and descent relations
- Integration into local groups with co-villagers to vouch for one's identity
- Links to common places of origin—for example, ancestral graves, houses, fields
- Knowledge of ethno-historical narratives—for example, stories of collective ancestors, places, events
- Language use—for example, local languages and dialects
- Rituals
- Observable customs and habits—for example, dressing, etiquette

In contrast, achieved belief requires "cognition work"—that is, the work of constructing rationality that is simultaneously coherent (to insiders) and differentiated (to outsiders). Such "cognition work" focuses on linking oneself to a supra-local cultural domain that may be national or congregational, including:

- Access to and familiarity with a certain body of impersonal knowledge, such as the constitution or the Quran
- Integration into groups of varying sizes with co-believers who can vouch for one's belief, such as civic groups or religious groups
- Links to the sources of one's belief—for example, the national capital, government institutions, Mecca, religious schools
- Knowledge of historical narratives—for example, national history, Islamic history, stories of national heroes, religious stories
- Language use—for example, the national language or Arabic
- Rituals—for example, national day, prayers
- Observable customs and habits—for example, uniforms, etiquette.

We argue that while ethnic conflicts do occur in Indonesia, they are not the only and perhaps not the most significant types of political conflict to have emerged, precisely because competing ideologies play such a key role in the country. Since achieved beliefs have the potential of transcending ascriptive ethnic identities, Indonesia is less ethnically fragmented than Burma despite its larger territory, larger population and more numerous ethnic groups. This does not mean that political conflicts are not prevalent in Indonesia. They certainly do occur but include more types of conflicts than in Burma—namely, ethnic conflicts and ideological conflicts. Ethnic conflict and ethnic violence are indeed basically political in nature.

Not only is there an ongoing ideological struggle between secular national-ism and political Islam—a struggle that has gone on even before independ-ence—there are also struggles between competing versions within secular na-tionalism and within political Islam. For example, we can identify at least three Islamising trends in Indonesia that are in ideological conflict with each other: (1) compartmentalised Islam (2) the quest for an Islamic Republic of Indonesia (3) the quest for a trans-national caliphate. Compartmentalised Islam accords with the modernist divide between church and state. This trend was memorably ar-ticulated by Nurcholish Madjid who said in the 1960s, "Islam yes, Islamic party no."[68]

Contesting this acceptance of secular politics is Darul Islam (House of Is-lam), which declared itself the government of the Islamic State of Indonesia in August 1949. In 1950–1959, it launched armed revolts in South Kalimantan (1950–1959), South Sulawesi (1952–1965) and Aceh (1953–1962). The secular nationalists, led by Sukarno, successfully quashed this attempt at Islamic state-building in 1965.[69] Attempts to make Indonesia an Islamic state still persist and are currently most visible in advocates who have repeatedly proposed, both in-side and outside Parliament, that the *shariah* should become the law of the land.[70]

Radically different from the two mentioned above is Jemaah Islamiyah, which seeks to build a caliphate modelled on what supposedly had existed in the Prophet's time. It is this last group that was evidently involved in the Bali bomb-ing of 12 October 2002 and with al-Qaeda. Their ultimate goal is to have a world-wide caliphate in which modern nation-states, including Indonesia, would no longer exist. So this is not a secessionist movement in terms of a part of the state wanting to secede. Rather, it is an imperialist movement that wishes to sub-sume the secular nation-state within a larger empire.

Because of these long-standing struggles, a compromise was reached be-tween the contending groups during the inception of the nation-state, such that the current Republic of Indonesia is a hybrid state that combines a certain degree of secularism with a certain degree of political religiosity.[71] This hybridity is fragile and continues to be pushed and pulled in different directions, especially in recent post-Suharto years. But these struggles to shape and reshape the Indo-nesian nation-state are nevertheless qualitatively different from ethnic conflicts that may culminate in secessionist movements to take certain territories out of Indonesia.

As noted above, there have been three long-standing secessionist move-ments in Indonesia—Aceh, West Papua and former East Timor (now Timor-Leste). On 20 October 1999, through the intervention of the United Nations, the Indonesian parliament renounced all claim to East Timor and on 20 May 2002, Timor-Leste became formally independent.[72] However, separatist struggles are continuing in Aceh and West Papua. Why are these places the three sites of long-standing secessionist movements?

As in the case of Burma, the answer lies in colonial and post-colonial processes of conquest. East Timor was never part of the Netherlands East Indies. Instead, it had been colonized by the Portuguese since 1520. On 28 November 1975, following the withdrawal of the Portuguese colonial authorities, the left-wing party Fretilin declared the independence of a "Democratic Republic of East Timor." Ten days later, on 7 December 1975, with the tacit support of the US government, Indonesian troops invaded East Timor.[73] From that time on until East Timor seceded and became independent, there was armed conflict between East Timorese ethno-nationalists and the Indonesian armed forces.

West Papua remained under Dutch colonial rule until 1961 when the territory was granted self-rule. In 1962, following the New York Agreement facilitated by the US, Indonesia annexed West Papua, re-naming it Irian Jaya. Mass uprisings by the West Papuan population were forcibly suppressed by Indonesian troops. In 1965, the Free Papua Movement (*Organisesi Papua Merdeka* (OPM)) was formed, which is still engaged in armed conflict with the Indonesian military. In 1969, a West Papuan government-in-exile was set up in the Netherlands.[74]

Aceh was the very last area of the archipelago to be colonized by the Dutch. The Acehnese fought a bitter war of resistance, holding off the Dutch from 1873 to 1914. Even after that, there were constant rebellions in the 27 years of Dutch colonization until 1942 when the Japanese conquered Aceh together with the rest of the Netherlands East Indies.[75] In the prelude to Indonesian independence, Acehnese leaders (especially Teungku Daud Beureu'eh) sided with the Islamists that wanted Indonesia to be an Islamic state. Aceh became one of the three strongholds of Darul Islam that arose in armed revolt against a secular-nationalist Indonesia. As noted above, this revolt was put down in 1965 by Sukarno's government.

In 1971, the world's largest gas field, with a radius of more than 200 kilometres, was discovered in Arun in northern Aceh. In the following six years, Mobil (now ExxonMobil) built the world's largest gas refinery in Arun, closely guarded by Indonesian troops. This gas field has enabled Indonesia to become the world's largest supplier of liquefied natural gas. By the early 1990s, this field produced nearly a quarter of Mobil's global revenue.[76] Under the production-sharing contract system devised by the Indonesian government, all revenue generated through resource extraction by multinational corporations goes directly to the central government in Jakarta with nothing for the local population.[77] On 4 December 1976, under the leadership of Tengku Hasan di Tiro, a descendant of the last sultan of Aceh, the Free Aceh Movement (*Gerakan Aceh Merdeka* (GAM)) proclaimed Aceh as an independent sovereign state. Since then GAM has been in armed conflict with the Indonesian armed forces. In 1980, the leaders of the Free Aceh Movement formed a government-in-exile in Sweden.

It is clear from this discussion why the Indonesian state has come to be regarded as illegitimate by the indigenous populations of former East Timor, West

Papua and Aceh. It is also evident that from their perspectives, their conflicts with the Indonesian state are not "ethnic" conflicts but ethno-nationalist struggles against Indonesian imperialism. Their resentment has been further aggravated by the Indonesian government's transmigration programme. Between 1969 and 1995, more than eight million people from Java were relocated to less populated islands including Sumatra, Kalimantan, Sulawesi and West Papua.[78] The ethnic violence that has occurred in former East Timor, West Papua and Aceh has led to massive human rights violations, mostly committed by Indonesian troops utilizing their superior firepower with impunity. From the moment of Indonesia's invasion of former East Timor, the territory was sealed off completely from the outside world. "Two months after the invasion, an East Timorese leader inside the country told *The Age* that probably 50,000–60,000 people had already died. By the end of the year, priests in East Timor who were asked about the accuracy of that figure said that already 100,000 Timorese had died, out of a population of around 700,000."[79]

When the United Nations announced on 4 September 1999 that nearly 80% of the East Timorese population had opted for independence, the Indonesian military and its militias forced about 400,000 people from their homes.[80] What is particularly striking in this instance is the way the Javanese-dominated military were able to recruit about 7500 East Timorese men, from 11 out of 13 provinces, into militias to fight and kill other, pro-independence East Timorese.[81] This was done to show that there were East Timorese in favor of "integration" with Indonesia and to use these locals to penetrate the pro-independence opposition. These militias subsequently moved to West Timor (within Indonesia) where they controlled about 100,000 East Timorese refugees.[82]

Similar atrocities have occurred in West Papua and Aceh. Indeed, as in the case of former East Timor, documentation and analysis indicate that "many of these acts clearly constitute crimes against humanity under international law."[83] Large numbers of people have also died in West Papua and Aceh. For example, in 1977–1978, in West Papua, the military operation called *Tumpas* [Annihilation] reportedly killed 3000 people.[84] "The Baliem River was so full of corpses that for a month and a half...people could not bring themselves to eat fish."[85] In 1981, the military launched Operation Clean Sweep to intimidate supporters of OPM and to clear the territory bordering Papua New Guinea of local populations to make way for Javanese and other migrants. The latter objective was implied by the army's slogan: "Let the rats run into the jungle so that the chicken can breed in the coop."[86] There was thus a direct connection between the military operations and the government's transmigration programme. Similar kinds of military operations have been carried out in Aceh, also killing and displacing many.[87]

The ethnic violence happening in former East Timor, West Papua and Aceh, as well as that occurring in Burma, may be categorized as asymmetrical in that the antagonists are a majority-dominated state versus a minority-based nation-of-intent that is still a non-state. However, post-Suharto ethnic conflicts that have erupted in West and Central Kalimantan, Maluku and Central Sulawesi may be considered as symmetrical violence between ethnic peers. Most of these conflicts have not (yet) developed into ethno-nationalist struggles for independence, although such a tendency is also evident in Maluku—for example, with the establishment of the Front for the Sovereignty of Maluku.[88] As elsewhere, these conflicts may be understood in the context of the massive population of Javanese people.

From 1996 to 2001, the indigenous Dayaks in West and Central Kalimantan revived a long-abandoned tradition of beheading their enemies—namely, the Madurese migrants who have settled in these provinces.[89] Virtually no Madurese remain in Central Kalimantan. While the fighting appears to have stopped for now, violence is likely to break out again if the displaced Madurese settlers were to return.[90]

Maluku too has received many migrants—97,422 official transmigrants from 1969 to 1999 and many other "spontaneous" ones. What is particularly significant is that the 1995 census shows that Muslims now constitute the majority (59.02%) in this once predominantly Christian province.[91] The Field Coordinator for *Médecins Sans Frontières* in Ambon opines that the cause for the Christian-Muslim conflict stems, to a large extent, from the policy of transmigration.[92]

Furthermore, Muslim-Christian conflict has apparently been provoked by the military sponsorship of jihadist Muslim "warriors" from the Laskar Jihad group. Thousands of them were sent from Java to Maluku to wage "holy war" against Christians Indonesians.[93] There is evidence that in January 2000, the head of Laskar Jihad was approached by military retirees who told him that they approved of his plans to escalate the armed campaign against Christians in Maluku. The explicitly stated purpose was to undermine the reformist government of Abdurrahman Wahid, who was then President.[94] "Western intelligence has confirmed that at least $9.3 million has been transferred from the Army's main fighting section to the militant group."[95] In this case, therefore, what was overtly a symmetrical battle between ethnic peers was covertly an asymmetrical fight between the state and an ethnic minority.

Overtly, transmigration is a development programme aimed at population redistribution, which is why it has received the World Bank's sponsorship for as much as US$560 million. But human rights organisations argue that it has an underlying political agenda that acts against the interests of indigenous host populations.[96] For example, Clause 17 of Indonesia's Basic Forestry Act of 1967 says: "The rights of traditional-law communities may not be allowed to stand in the way of the establishment of transmigration settlements."[97] Investigations by the United Nations and the World Bank also show how Indonesian forestry and land laws have been systematically used to dispossess indigenous peoples of their lands.[98]

As recently as September 1998 (that is, after the fall of Suharto in May 1998), a new transmigration programme was launched in Aceh and Papua, with the aim of moving non-indigenous groups into these areas to bring about a mixing of religions and ethnicities, supposedly to strengthen a sense of Indonesian unity. This plan included the establishment of armed militias among transmigrants under the supervision of the Armed Forces.[99]

More recently, there is evidence of some new awareness of the political conflicts caused by transmigration. The government admitted that the existing policy failed to assess the social, cultural and environmental background of the target regions and people living there. In December 2001, it announced a reformed transmigration programme that will check the legal status of land before giving it to new migrants and that will ensure a 50:50 ratio between local people and transmigrants. But "critics say that the emphasis on the legal status of land will not improve matters for indigenous communities affected by transmigration unless the legal definition of land ownership is expanded to include *adat* (customary) land held by indigenous communities."[100]

Furthermore, the reformed policy is silent on the official intent of achieving "national integration" through transmigration.[101] *Act of the Republic of Indonesia No. 15 on Transmigration Matters (1997)* still states that the purposes of the implementation of transmigration are to improve the welfare of the transmigrants and neighbouring communities, increase and spread equally the development in the region and also strengthen *national unity* [my emphasis].[102] An extreme interpretation of "national unity" was articulated in 1995 by the then Minister of Transmigration, who stated that the goal of transmigration is "to integrate all the ethnic groups into one nation; ... the different ethnic groups will in the long run disappear because of integration... and there will be only one kind of man."[103] As stated in a relatively recent UN report, transmigration is a major cause of inter-ethnic conflict, because it "sought to spread Javanese culture throughout the archipelago," affected the demographic balance between different ethnic groups, and caused economic and political competition over scarce resources.[104]

The discussion above indicates that the Indonesian state is not a neutral party that qualifies to be an objective arbitrator of conflicting ethnics fighting among themselves. Rather, the state is complicit in the production of ethnic violence and is actively involved as an interested party with its own political agenda, either directly through its armed forces or indirectly through proxy militias, such as jihadists sponsored to fight Christians. The increase in ethnic conflicts after the fall of Suharto in May 1998 has to do with several factors: (a) the disappearance of a dictatorial regime that ruthlessly quashed all dissent (b) the emergence of competitors for state power among both civilians and military personnel (c) the sudden eruption of decades of mass discontent with corruption, nepotism and human rights violations (d) massive economic failure on the part of the state, particularly in maintaining the value of the currency.

This was the context which led to one particular incident of massive violence perpetrated against Indonesians of Chinese descent in Jakarta, which occurred on 13–15 May 1998. Observers noted the similarity of this attack to previous incidents in Indonesian history, going back to the Dutch colonial period: economic hardship brings insecurity and the often visibly prosperous Chinese are blamed and become scapegoats.[105] Thus, even these anti-Chinese attacks are related to the failure of economic development to bring benefits to the people.

Despite the prevalence of ethnic and non-ethnic violence in Indonesia, arguably, it is less of a failed state than Burma is. Even though there is widespread corruption and social fragmentation,[106] there are more functioning institutions in Indonesia than in Burma. Presidents and parliamentarians who are elected do take office in Indonesia, unlike in Burma. There is a Parliament and a multi-party political system. Even though the military continues to have a political role, they do not constitute the government. Civil society thrives in Indonesia, unlike in Burma. There are thus institutional avenues for disenchanted sectors of the population, ethnic and non-ethnic, to voice their demands and to negotiate for better deals. This comparison of Indonesia with Burma shows that even very imperfect political institutions play an important role in defusing the impetus to ethnic violence. Our analysis would indicate that if the legitimacy of Indonesia's political institutions could be enhanced, ethnic and non-ethnic violence would probably decrease. Therefore, apart from economic development, political development in the form of democratisation and institution-building is probably the key to ending political violence, both ethnic and non-ethnic.

Conclusion

The classic Hobbesian mission of the state is to enforce peace and security. This requires a monopoly on the use of coercion and violence, which in turn requires (unless the state is able and willing to use overwhelming force) popular acceptance of the use of such means exclusively by the state. Following Weber, we call this acceptance "legitimacy." The classic sign of a successful state is that there are no substantial communal rivals in the use of violence, and that state violence is minimal as a result of functioning institutions to mediate and resolve disputes.

But the "state" is a recent innovation in many parts of the world. In Southeast Asia, all of the contemporary states originated—in terms of their current territorial boundaries and identity—in the colonial era, and were elaborated mainly to facilitate exploitation of resources within a particular territory. In the post-colonial era, the state as a method of extracting surplus from a well-defined territory has been adapted by post-colonial majorities and post-colonial elites for their own purposes. This entity was superimposed on much older social groupings which survive, with various old or reworked symbolic overlays, within or across these new states. None of these Southeast Asian states is fully coterminous with older socio-cultural groupings.

In the absence of Weberian traditional authority, post-colonial regimes in Southeast Asia have sought to justify their rule through the developmentalist project, but lacking the political will to maintain trans-ethnic integration and joint enterprise, some of these states have been turned against minorities for the benefit of majorities or of centralized elite rule. Where there are few local institutions which allow these minorities to pursue collective advantage within the state-system, some of them have turned against failed developmentalist states with a vengeance, where there is either minimal development, as in the case of Burma, or where the development visibly benefits only the elite and the ethnic majority, as in the case of Indonesia.

In both Burma and Indonesia, pre-colonial local communities formerly maintained relative political autonomy, even if they were nominally part of kingdoms. In the colonial and post-colonial eras they have been incorporated into developmentalist states, subjected to rule by centralising elites, and have experienced aggressive intrusions into their territories for resource extraction. In both states, some of these groups have responded by engaging in armed struggle for many decades.

In the pre-colonial region which was eventually constituted as "Burma," the current territory of the state did not coincide with any polity, and a number of political entities of various sizes and potencies co-existed, albeit with some jostling among them. The colonial and early post-colonial regimes tried to incorporate these regions into a modern state-system. However, an early post-colonial attempt to establish a federalist system was aborted by centralizing military rule, precipitating revolts and the assertion of localised ethnic identities and the pursuit of political independence. The peripheral positions of these minorities, the lack of cross-cutting institutional systems, the overall failure of the Burmese state to provide beneficial development for these peripheral minorities, and oppressive rule from the centre have led to chronic ethnic violence. These conflicts continue to the present (2005), and have led to the decimation of some of these populations, and the ravaging of natural resources in their territories for the benefit of the elite.

In Indonesia, by contrast, a much larger and more diverse collection of ethnic minorities has produced only a few major "ethnic" rebellions against centralized rule. The reasons are instructive. First, the political struggles within Indonesia have involved both Islamic and secular-nationalist visions of the state which penetrated many different ethnic subgroups, providing competing but cross-cutting ties and moderating identities which had been rooted in pre-colonial political entities. The military struggle against the Dutch colonial regime helped to create pan-ethnic solidarity and a pan-ethnic vision of the future. The anticolonial resistance movements, however, used as their template for the state the political system and political boundaries which had been created by the Dutch.

Second, the developmentalist project led to certain benefits for many of the major ethnic populations in the Indonesian archipelago. The state earned at least a minimal legitimacy from this project, which succeeded in buying off major dissent until the Asian financial crisis in the late 1990s fatally undermined the Suharto regime through the huge contraction of the economy. Third, Indonesia's limited federalism and numerous civil society institutions have helped to moderate ethnic conflict and provide ways for most minorities to pursue collective advantage to a certain degree within the system.

The exceptions were populations in peripheral regions which were resource-rich—thus inviting intensive exploitation by central elites—but which were unable to gain a substantial share of the benefits from local resources in the face of aggressive extraction. Thus, in Aceh, West Papua, and former East Timor, local populations generated armed resistance movements which included the goal of reviving the previous political self-rule which they believe they had developed in the past, and which they hope to recover in the future. However, their aspiration for this alternative political future meets with bloody reprisals by the state, which further de-legitimate it in the eyes of these already marginalised peoples. The result is schismogenesis[107] where state delegitimation begets ethnic nations-of-intent, which then beget state violence, which then begets more non-state resistance, which then begets even more state violence. As of 2005, we have not yet seen the end of this process in either Burma or Indonesia.

Notes

1. In 1989, the military government tried to change the name of the country from 'Burma' to 'Myanmar,' but because this proposed name change was not approved by any sitting legislature in the country, it has not been accepted by a number of other states, including the United States and European Union. A compromise is sometimes made by writing 'Burma (Myanmar).'

2. Rogers Brubaker and David D. Laitin, "Ethnic and Nationalist Violence," *Annual Review of Sociology* 24 (1998): 423.

3. Pierre Van der Berghe, *The Ethnic Phenomenon* (New York; Oxford: Elsevier, 1981), 24.

4. Fredrik Barth, "Ethnicity and the Concept of Culture" (paper presented at the Conference of Rethinking Culture in Harvard University, 23 February 1995), 1.

5. Ashutosh Varshney, "Ethnic Conflict and Civil Society: India and Beyond," *World Politics* 53, no. 3 (April 2001).

6. Vivienne Wee, "Political Faultlines in Southeast Asia: Movements for Ethnic Autonomy as Nations of Intent," Southeast Asia Research Centre Working Paper Series, no. 16 (Hong Kong: City University of Hong Kong, November 2001), 19. Also see Donald Horowitz, *Ethnic Groups in Conflict* (Berkeley and Los Angeles: University of Berkeley, 1985), 15.

7. Vivienne Wee, "Political Faultlines," 10–11. Also see Vivienne Wee, "Ethnonationalism in Process: Ethnicity, Atavism and Indigenism in Riau," Asia Research Centre Working Paper Series, no. 22 (Hong Kong: City University of Hong Kong, March 2002), 19.

8. Vivienne Wee and Kanishka Jayasuriya, "New Geographies and Temporalities of Power: Exploring the New Fault Lines of Southeast Asia," *The Pacific Review* 15, no. 4 (2002): 489.

9. Horowitz, *Ethnic Groups in Conflict*, 41–54.

10. "License to Rape: The Burmese Military Regime's Use of Sexual Violence in

the Ongoing War in Shan State," The Shan Human Rights Foundation (SHRF) & The Shan Women's Action Network (SWAN) May 2002, <http://www.shanland.org /HR/Publication/LtoR/license_to_rape.htm>; "Rape by the Burmese Military in Ethnic Regions," Fact Sheet, Washington, D. C.: Bureau of Democracy 2002, <http://www.state.gov/g/drl/rls/16087.htm>; Suraiya Kamaruzzaman, Mass Rape in a Situation of Armed Conflict (1989–1998) in Nanggro Aceh Darussalam Province, Indonesia (thesis of LLM Degree in Human Rights of Faculty of Law at City University of Hong Kong, 29 September 2003); Elizabeth Brundige, Winter King, Priyneha Vahali, Stephen Vladeck and XiangYung, *Indonesian Human Rights Abuses in West Papua: Application of the Law of Genocide to the History of Indonesian Control* (New Haven: Lowenstein International Human Rights Clinic, Yale Law School, April 2004), 23–24, <http://www.law.yale.edu/outside/html/Public_Affairs/426/westpapuahrights.pdf>; George Aditjondro, *Violence by the State Against Women in the East Timor: A Report to the UN Special Rapporteur on Violence Against Women, Including its Causes and Consequences* (Melbourne: East Timor Human Rights Centre (ETHRC), 7 November 1997).

11. Varshney, "Ethnic Conflict," 365–366.

12. Berverly Crawford and Ronnie D. Lipschutz, eds., *The Myth of "Ethnic": Politics, Economics, and Cultural Violence* (Berkeley: University of California, International Area Studies, 1999).

13. Max Weber, *From Max Weber: Essays in Sociology* (translated, ed.) and with an introduction by H. H. Gerth and C. Wright Mills (London: Routledge & Kegan Paul, 1946), 78.

14. Brubaker "Ethnic and Nationalists," 424.

15. Muthiah Alagappa, ed., *Political Legitimacy in Southeast Asia: The Quest for Moral Authority* (Stanford, Calif.: Stanford University Press, 1995), 4–6.

16. Geoffrey Benjamin, "The Unseen Presence: A Theory of a Nation-state and its Mystifications," Department of Sociology Working Paper Series, no. 91 (Singapore: Nanyang Technology University, 1988), 2.

17. Max Weber, *Economy and Society: An Outline of Interpretive Sociology* (New York, Bedminster Press, 1968), 215.

18. Wee, "New Geographies," 7.

19. Wee, "New Geographies," 6.

20. The term 'nation-of-intent' was first used by Robert Rotberg, "African Nationalism: Concept or Confusion?" *Journal of Modern African Studies* 4, no. 1 (1967): 33–46.

21. Rotberg, "African Nationalism," 38.

22. Benedict R. O'G. Anderson, *Imagined Communities: Reflections on the Origin and Spread of Nationalism* (London: Verso. Second revised edition, 1991) and Stein Tønnesson and Hans Antlöv, *Asian Forms of the Nation* (Richmond, Surrey: Curzon, 1998), 37.

23. Tønnesson, Asian Forms, 37.

24. Vrshney, "Ethnic Conflict," 365–366.

25. Deepa Narayan, Raj Patel, Kai Schafft, Anne Rademacher and Sarah Koche-Schulte, *Voices of the Poor: Can Anyone Hear Us?* (Oxford: World Bank/Oxford University Press, 2000), 219–220.

26. Antonio Gramsci, *The Modern Prince, and Other Writings*, transl. by Louis Marks (New York: International Publishers, 1967).

27. Guibernau i Berdún and M. Montserrat (Maria Montserrat), *Nations Without States: Political Communities in a Global Age / Montserrat Guibernau* (Cambridge, UK;

Malden, MA: Polity Press, 1999).

28. Edmund R. Leach, "The Frontiers of Burma," *Comparative Studies in Society and History* 3, no. 1 (October 1960): 49–68.

29. Chao-Tzang Yawnghwe, "Putting Burma Back Together Again," *Legal Issues on Burma*, November 2002, <http://www.ibiblio.org/obl/docs/LIOB11-Chao-Tzang.htm> (7 May 2005), 3.

30. Geroge Aditjondro, "Liberating Our Colonial Mindset" (outline of a lecture presented in the Winter Lecture Series 1995, the AIA-CSEAS Monash Asia Institute in Melbourne, Australia, 16 August 1995), <http://www.hartford-hwp.com/archives/54b/34.html>.

31. M. N. Djuli, "Aceh for Beginners or the Process of Ethnic Dilution in Aceh," (New York: Graduate Faculty of Political and Social Science, New School University, n.d.) 2. <http://www.newschool.edu/gf/news/01-02/aceh_for_beginners.pdf>.

32. David Chanbonpin Kim, "Historical Background," *Holding the United States Accountable for Environmental Damages Caused by the U.S. Military in the Philippines: A Plan for the Future* (Manoa: University of Hawaii, 2003), 329.

33. See, for example, Heine-Geldern Wolters, *History, Culture, and Region in Southeast Asian Perspective* (Ithaca, N.Y.: Southeast Asia Program Publications, Southeast Asia Program, Cornell University, 1999)

34. Wolters, *History, Culture and Region*, 27–33.

35. Elsbeth Locher-Scholten, *Sumatran Sultanate and Colonial State: Jambi and the Rise of Dutch Imperialism, 1830–1907*, transl. by Beverley Jackson (Ithaca, NY: Southeast Asia Program, Cornell University Press, 2004), 59.

36. Sukhumbhand Paribatra and Chai-Anan Samudavanija, "Factors Behind Armed Separatism: A Framework for Analysis," in *Armed Separatism in Southeast Asia*, ed.,Joo-Jock Lim Joo-Jock and S. Vani (Singapore: Regional Strategic Studies Programme, Institute of Southeast Asian Studies, 1984), 41.

37. Yawnghwe, "Putting Burma Back," 3.

38. Yawnghwe, "Putting Burma Back," 3.

39. Yawnghwe, "Putting Burma Back," 3.

40. Yawnghwe, "Putting Burma Back," 3.

41. Anand Rajah, "A 'Nation of Intent' in Burma: Karen Ethno-Nationalism, Nationalism and Narrations of Nation," *The Pacific Review* 15, no. 4 (2002): 517–537.

42. Yawnghwe, "Putting Burma Back."

43. Richard A. O'Connor, "Agricultural Change and Ethnic Succession in Southeast Asian States: A Case for Regional Anthropology," *Journal of Asian Studies* 54, no. 4 (November 1995): 968–996. Also see Michael A. Aung-Thwin, Myth of the 'Three Shan Brothers' and the Ava Period in Burmese History," *The Journal of Asian Studies* 55, no. 1 (1996).

44. Edmund Leach, *Political Systems of Highland Burma. A Study of Kachin Social Structure* (Boston: Beacon, 1964).

45. Fredrik Barth, "Ethnicity."

46. Yawnghwe, "Putting Burma Back," 4 and Martin Smith, *Burma: Insurgency and the Politics of Ethnic Identity* (London: Zed Books Ltd., 1999).

47. "The Constitution of the Union of Burma,"Rangoon: Govt. Printing and Stationery, Burma, 1948, <http://www.shanland.org/History/Publications/consittution_of_the_union_of_bur.htm>.

48. Yawnghwe, "Putting Burma Back," 4.

49. See, for example, Josef Silverstein, *Burma: Military Rule and the Politics of Stagnation* (New York: Cornell University Press, 1977) and Josef Silverstein, *Burmese Politics: The Dilemma of National Unity* (New Brunswick: Rutgers University Press, 1980).

50. See, for example, Stephen Collignon, *The Burmese Economy and the Withdrawal of European Trade Preferences* (Brussels: European Institute for Asian Studies, March 1997); Economist Intelligence Unit, *Country Report: Myanmar (Burma)* (London: Economist Intelligence Unit, February 2001); Mya Maung, *The Burma Road to Poverty* (New York: Praeger, 1991); Mya Than and Myeit Than, eds., *Financial Resources For Development In Myanmar: Lessons from Asia* (Singapore: Institute of Southeast Asian Studies, 2000).

51. Smith, Burma and "Aung San Suu Kyi-biography," in *Nobel Lectures,. Peace 1991–1995*, ed., Irwin Abrams (Singapore: WorldScientific Publishing, 1999), <http://nobelprize.org/peace/laureates/1991/kyi-bio.html>.

52. United Nations, "Situation of Human Rights in Myanmar: Note by the Secretary-General 20," *General Assembly: Fifty-sixth Session Item 131 of the provisional agenda*, A/56/312 August 2001, <http://www.unhchr.ch/Huridocda/Huridoca.nsf/0/53f25867f d928877c1256ad9004b8e15?Opendocument>, 13.

53. Ananda Rajah, "Burma: Protracted Conflict, Governance and Non-Traditional Security Issues," Non-Traditional Security Issues in Southeast Asia Working Paper Series, no. 14 (Singapore: Institution of Defence and Strategic Studies, May 2001), 6.

54. Maureen Aung-Thwin, "Developments in Southeast Asia," *Capitol Hill Hearing Testimony* (Washington, D.C.: Asian and the Pacific Subcommittee, House International Relations Committee, 10 June 2003), 4.

55. Aung-Thwin, "Developments in Southeast Asia," 2003, 4.

56. "Burma 'using chemical weapons'," *Financial Times Information*, Global News Wire, and Guardian Unlimited, 21 April 2005.

57. Rajah, "A Nation of Intent."

58. Rajah, "Nation of Intent"; Smith, *Burma*, ix

59. Rajah, "Burma," 1.

60. "Ethnic Groups," The Burma Project n. d., <http://www.burmaproject.org/ethnic _groups.html>.

61. K. Heppner, "'My Gun was as Tall as Me': Child Soldiers in Burma," *Human Rights Watch 2002*, http://www.eldis.org/static/DOC11178.htm; Martin Smith, Burma, 30. Smith states that the numbers published by the SPDC "appear deliberately to play down ethnic minority numbers."

62. SPDC stands for State Peace and Development Council—the current name of Burma's military junta.

63. "Shan Leader Urges ASEAN to See Burma as Failed State," *Letters to the Editor, The Nation*, Thailand, 25 March 2005.

64. Geroge Aditjondro, "Liberating Our Colonial Mindset," 1.

65. L. Suryadinata, Evi N. Arifin and Aris Ananta, *Indonesia's Population: Ethnicity and Religion in a Changing Political Landscape Singapore* (Singapore: Institute of Southeast Asian Studies, 2003), 32. There has been a decline in the proportion of Javanese in the Indonesian population—from 47.02 percent in 1930 to 41.71 percent in 2000.

66. Suryadinata, *Indonesia's Population*, 7–9.

67. Vivienne Wee and Michael Jacobsen, "Assessing Project Indonesia: Endogenous

Aspirations and Exogenous Forces," in *Political Fragmentation in Southeast Asia: Alternative Nations in the Making*, ed., Vivienne Wee (London: Routledge, 2005 forthcoming).

68. Elizabeth Fuller Collins, "Islam is the Solution: Dakwah and Democracy in Indonesia" (Athens: Ohio University, 20 June 2004), 5. <http://www.classics.ohiou.edu/faculty/collins/islamsolution.pdf>.

69. Wee, "Ethno-nationalism," 9.

70. Those inside Parliament include a coalition of Islamic parties and politicians, including the current Vice President Jusuf Kalla, while those outside Parliament include groups like Hizb ut Tahrir, an Islamic mass organization, which launched a nation-wide campaign on 7 July 2002 called 'Save Indonesia Through Shariah Islam.' Interestingly, however, this advocacy for an Islamic state has been repeatedly rejected, not only by the secular parties, but also by the two largest Islamic organizations in Indonesia—Nahdlatul Ulama and Muhammadiyah.

71. This hybridity is articulated through the official state catechism known as Pancasila (Five Principles), which was included in the Preamble of the 1945 Constitution. The five Principles are: (1) belief in a supreme God (2) just and civilised humanitarianism (3) unity of Indonesia (4) populism that is led by the prudent wisdom in a context of consultation/ representation (5) social justice for all the people of Indonesia.

72. United Nations, "East Timor," United Nations Transitional Administration in East Timor (UNTAET) (Geneva: United Nations, 2001), <http://www.un.org/peace/etimor/etimor.htm>.

73. Kathy Kadane, "U.S. Officials' Lists Aided Indonesian Bloodbath in '60s'," *Washington Post*, 21 May 1990; Marian Wilkinson, "Indonesia: Hidden Holocaust of 1965," *Sydney Morning Herald*, 10 July 1999.

74. Anthony Reid, *An Indonesian Frontier: Acehnese and Other Histories of Sumatra* (Singapore: National University of Singapore, Asia Research Institute, 2005).

75. Reid, *An Indonesian Frontier*.

76. Jay Solomon, "Mobil Sees Its Gas Plant Become Rallying Point for Indonesian Rebels," *Wall Street Journal*, 7 September 2000.

77. Kurt S. Abraham, "Indonesia Poised to Lead Asian Rebound—Indonesian Petroleum Industry Will Play a Key Role," *World Oil* February 2000, <http://www.findarticles.com/p/articles/mi_m3159/is_2_221/ai_60499090> (26 Oct. 2004).

78. "Transmigration," *Building Human Security in Indonesia* (Programme on Humanitarian Policy and Conflict Research, Harvard College, April 2002). <http://www.preventconflict.org/portal/main/background_transmigration.php>.

79. Carmel Budiardjo, "A Global Failure on Human Rights: East Timor in Transition, Sovereignty. Self-Determination and Human Rights" (paper presented in a Conference at Nottingham University, May 1999).

80. Geoffrey Robinson, "The Fruitless Search for a Smoking Gun: Tracing the Origins of Violence in East Timor," in *Roots of Violence in Indonesia*, ed., Freek Colombijn and J. Thomas Lindblad (Leiden: KITLV Press, 2002), 243.

81. "East Timor Militias: Overview and Assessment," *Virtual Information Center* 16 October 2000, 1, <http://www.vic-info.org/RegionsTop.nsf/0/468941b4e411f39a8a256981007a4011?OpenDocument>.

82. Judy Aita, "US Calls on Indonesian Military to End Support for Timor Militias," *The Washington File* (Office of International Information Programs, US Department of

State). Associated Press 21 March 2000, <http://www.etan.org/et2000a/march/19-25/21usoffi.htm>.

83. Brundige, 27.

84. Brundige, 27.

85. Kompas, 28 November 1977 (cited from Carmel Budiardjo and Liem Soei Liong, *West Papua: The Obliteration of a People* (3rd ed., London: TAPOL, 1988)).

86. Robin Osborne, *Indonesia's Secret War: The Guerilla Struggle in Irian Jaya* (Sydney: Allen and Unwin, 1985).

87. "New Military Operations, Old Patterns of Human Rights Abuses in Aceh (Nanggroe Aceh Darussalam, NAD)," *Indonesia* (Amnesty International, Library Online Documentation Archive, 2004), <http://web.amnesty.org/library/Index/ENGASA 210332004>.

88. K. Turner, "Perception of Ethnic Conflict in Ambon, Indonesia" (paper presented at the Symposium on Political fault-lines in Southeast Asia: Movement for Ethnic Autonomy in Nation-state Structures by the Southeast Asia Research Centre, City University of Hong Kong, 15–16 October 2001).

89. Madura is an island off the north coast of Java; the Madurese constitute 7.5 percent of the population in Indonesia.

90. See "Kalimantan," *Building Human Security in Indonesia* (Programme on Humanitarian Policy and Conflict Research, Harvard College, April 2002). <http://www.preventconflict.org/portal/main/maps_kalimantan_resources.php>.

91. Richard Rowat, "Population and Religious Breakdown of Maluku," Ambon Information Website 2002, <http://www.websitesrcg.com/ambon/index.html#Data and Statistics>.

92. See Richard Rowat, "Ambon / Maluku?" *Ambon Information Website* November 1999, <http://www.websitesrcg.com/ambon/documents/Advocat1.htm>.

93. "Who are the Laskar Jihad?" BBC News, 20 June 2000, <http://news.bbc.co.uk/1/hi/world/asia-pacific/770263.stm>.

94. Robert W. Hefner, "Indonesian Islam in a World Context" (paper presented at the joint conference of the United States-Indonesia Society and the Asia Foundation, Washington, D. C., 7 February 2002), 6.

95. Reyko Huang, "In the Spotlight: Laskar Jihad," *Terrorism Project* (Washington D. C.: Center for Defence Information, 8 March 2002), <http://www.cdi.org/terrorism/laskar-pr.cfm>.

96. See, for example, Sidney Jones, "East Timor Alert: Stop Transmigration!" *Human Rights Watch* (New York: Human Rights Watch, 20 September 1999), <http://www.hrw.org/press/1999/sep/trans0920.htm>.

97. Bernard Nietschmann, Economic Development by Invasion of Indigenous Nations (Berkeley: University of Berkeley, 1999), <http://www.cwis.org /fwdp/Eurasia/indbang2.txt>.

98. See "Transmigration," Building Human Security in Indonesia.

99. See "Armed Civilian Militia Plan Comes Under Fire," *The Jakarta Post*, 12 December 1998; "Irja dan DI Aceh Pilot Proyek," Suara Pembaruan, 23 September 1998; "Lt-Gen (ret) Abdullah Mahmud Hendropriyono [Hendro Priyono]," *In Master of Terror: Indonesia's Military and Violence in East Timor in 1999*, ed. Hamish McDonald, Desmond Ball, James Dunn, Gerry van Klinken, David Bourchier, Douglas Kammen and Richard Tanter (Canberra: Strategic and Defence Studies Centre, Australian National University, 2002), <http://yayasanhak.minihub.org/mot/Hendropriyono.htm>.

100. See "Transmigration," *Building Human Security in Indonesia*.

101. See Robert Cribb, *Historical Atlas of Indonesia* (Honolulu: University of Hawaii Press, 2000), 57.

102. "Transmigration," *Government of Indonesia 2000*, <http://www.indonesia-ottawa.org/IHb2000/transmig.htm>.

103. Cited from "Transmigration," *West Papua Information Kit* (Austin: The University of Texas, Computer Science Department, 11 February 1997), <http://www.cs.utexas.edu/users/cline/papua/core.htm>.

104. United Nations Economic and Social Council (ECOSOC), *Specific Groups and Individuals: Mass Exoduses and Displaced Persons: Report of the Representative of the Secretary-General on Internally Displaced Persons Submitted in Accordance With Commission Resolution 2001/54, Addendum, Profiles in Displacement: Indonesia* (Geneva: United Nations Economic and Social Council, 5 February 2002), 5. <http://www.brook.edu/dybdocroot/fp/projects/idp/articles/SudanReportCHR2002.pdf>.

105. Scott McKenzie, "Jakarta: Riding the Bumpy Road to Democracy," CNN Interactive, June 1999. <http://edition.cnn.com/SPECIALS/1999/indonesian.elections/jakarta.profile/>.

106. Vivienne Wee, "Social Fragmentation in Indonesia: A Crisis from Suharto's New Order," *Southeast Asia Research Centre Working Paper Series*, no. 31 (Hong Kong: City University of Hong Kong, September 2002).

107. "Schismogenesis" is a concept developed by Gregory Bateson, *Steps to an Ecology of Mind: Collected Essays in Anthropology, Psychiatry, Evolution, and Epistemology* (New York: Balantine, 1972) for understanding antagonistic interactions that mutually exacerbate towards breakdown.

Chapter 3

Not Ethnicity, but Race: Unity and Conflict in Rwanda Since the Genocide

Helen M. Hintjens and David E. Kiwuwa

Unlike the term 'ethnic identity,' which can have some positive connotations, the term 'race' is now almost wholly discredited in mainstream academic literature. Yet in Rwanda, and more widely in the Great Lakes region of Africa, a politics of conflict along race lines is alive and well. In Rwanda, where the terms Tutsi, Hutu and Twa are now officially proscribed from public discourse, race politics operates in a covert fashion, and in spite of an appearance of overall peace and security within the country. In the chapter, we review debates about who died in the genocide, and who was responsible. There have been major institutional in-novations in Rwanda since 1994, and these were to overcome race conflict, and promote shared Rwandan citizenship values. If this were so, we ask, why is it that mixed Rwandans appear unable to find a safe place in the new, supposedly non-racial Rwanda? The whole question of democracy is debated, including the 'race' politics around the first set of elections after the genocide. Official unity cannot disguise the politics of race, which involves reading people's political identities and social status off their position in relation to that defining event of Rwandan history, the genocide of 1994. Rwandans returned from Uganda now control all the main levers of state power, and the army and Intelligence services almost as racially exclusive as before. Rural producers are neglected and sink into greater poverty and insecurity, with landlessness emerging as a major problem, making violent solutions along race lines potentially more attractive once again. Where a few are enriched and the vast majority neglected and stigmatised, there remains the potential for race conflict. International support for the Kigali regime is a key factor in explaining how the regime can—for the most part— retain an image of unity externally, whilst ruling over a society that is increasingly polarised and fragmented, and where conflict expressed in racial terms conflict remains a permanent danger, even when it changes its appearance.

> When populism is a response to a national, economic or political crisis [and]... is inspired by the need to defend a natural entity that can be represented only by a charismatic leader... in such cases, populism paves the way for totalitarianism.[1]

> Embittered and desperate young men, with no land, jobs or schooling—and without land or job, no prospect of marriage and family— made up the majority of militia and army recruits.[2]

Introduction

In Rwanda, the politics of 'race' has involved a great deal of killing of innocent civilians, culminating in the death of up to a million Tutsi in 1994 and of up to half that number of Hutu, including political moderates, leaders and mixed people. Since then Rwanda has been heavily involved in civil war in the Democratic Republic of Congo, in which an estimated three million people have died. A central role in these continuing conflicts in Rwanda and the wider region is the theory of distinct human racial types, and the political belief that violence will tend to polarise along lines of racial difference, rather than—for instance—along class or gender, or other lines. The two authors of this chapter suggest that this race ideology continues to be a central element in the framing and the perpetuation of cycles of violence in the Great Lakes. Taking Rwanda as an example, the authors show just how difficult it is for any government, whatever its ideological position towards race theories, to escape the legacy of an idea and a form of political action that has long outlived its usefulness as a means of social control during the colonial era.

We consider the policies of the Rwandan government in the transitional period ten year period following the genocide, and under the newly elected democratic regime in place since the first elections in 2003. In spite of appearances of unity, Rwandans have been unable to move beyond the divisive and conflict-laden politics of race inherited from the past. How has the post-genocide regime tried to get Rwandans to leave behind the legacy of race theory and its pernicious effects? The transitional government set out straight after 1994 to remove identity cards, race labels from official documents and laws, and from public debate. They saw race politics as a colonial hangover, and genocide as the result of an ideology of separate races inculcated through the administrative and political systems put in place under Belgian colonial control.

In this chapter, we suggest that the Rwandan government may need to relinquish its self-appointed task of preventing another genocide if it is to avoid falling into race politics of a different order. The officially constructed history of the genocide, taken to be the defining event for everything Rwandan, does not always serve to emphasise what Rwandans have in common in terms of their present political and social identities. It divides them in new ways which can overlap uncomfortably with race categories, now used so pervasively throughout the Great Lakes region of Africa. For too many Rwandans, being defined in terms of the events of 1994 casts them as criminals within their own society; for others their status as perpetual victims is almost as unwelcome and stigmatising. Throughout this chapter, the focus is on how the post-genocide governments have sought to divert conflict away from the racial politics of old. Of course the term 'race' is highly problematic, and we use it in this chapter quite conscious that it has been demolished as a theory. Following the experience of Nazism, as the apotheosis of 'scientific' approaches to race and race hierarchy, race however continued to be used in Rwanda until at least 1994 *as if* it were unproblematic and had not been challenged elsewhere. The Hamitic myth continued to live a life of its own long after race theories were debunked in mainstream scholarly and political circle.[3] The RPF/RPA have: "... an overwhelming sense of moral responsibility for the very survival of all remaining Tutsi, globally."[4]

There have been quite vociferous debates in Rwanda surrounding the legacy of the genocide, and its meaning for the present. The official story gradually constructed since 1994 about the genocide and its causes, legacies and lessons is taught both inside Rwanda and externally, through the institutions of media, schools and official statements. New institutions have been established, and new laws introduced, all of which are intended to forge a stronger sense of national or Rwandan identity. But have these innovations contributed to replacing race politics with something new? Have 'race politics' evolved into national politics by the time the transitional regime of 1994-2002 came to an end with the first round of democratic elections? Are the divisive forms of political mobilisation based on racial identities being altered in favour of more meaningful and unifying political identities based on a shared Rwandan citizenship and other common values?

The legacy of genocide has been dealt with in much more detail by Paul Magnarella elsewhere in this volume, and need not be dwelt on in this chapter. The centrality of pristine race theories to the construction of the Rwandan state needs to be emphasised, however. The situation in Rwanda till at least 1994 was thus in marked contrast to that in the West, where nineteenth century ideas about human races were largely discredited by the experiences of Nazism. In Rwanda past notions of physical race continued to have a powerful hold on the popular imaginations and on political discourse. Today, throughout the Great Lakes region and beyond, Africans themselves use the labels of 'Bantu,' 'Hamites' and 'Nilotic' as if the existence of such races were fact. Such ideologies spread further and became more accepted in the public imagination through the conflicts and killings in the DRC.

In this wider context, it is not surprising that race ideology remains deeply entrenched in the minds of Rwandans and their political leaders, even if it is only in terms of antipathy to such theories; that there are such theories is not in doubt. Race ideas seem to be able to survive banning through new laws, removal from identity cards, and being excised from school text books. It seems much harder to rub them out of people's awareness and judgements. Racial terms have been removed from the letter of Rwandan law, and from formal citizenship categories. From being enshrined into the very structures of state power and authority in the pre-genocide era, the terms 'Hutu,' 'Tutsi' and 'Twa,' and wider terms like 'Hamitic' and 'Bantu' are now politically taboo, unmentionable in public, indeed illegal. Banning race terms is one way of trying to undermine the destructive race politics of the past. The question remains: can it work? Can race be extirpated as a consideration in Rwanda's public affairs, and a new sense of a single Rwandan identity be created to override the old divisions and persecutory mentality of violence? This chapter addresses the question Antione Lema poses in a recent study, namely: "How could a political system be developed that guarantees democratic and political participation by the two communities?"[5]

To determine the modes of Rwandan politics today is no simple matter. Those in power seek to control how conflict is expressed in Rwandan society. At the same time, they continue to demand total obedience from the population, and are unwilling to tolerate open political opposition. Opponents have been crushed and forced into exile quite remorselessly. Rwanda's leaders self-appointed task is to do all they can, using all the military, intelligence and legal means at their disposal, including *gacaca*, the school system, solidarity camps and any other means to prevent what they see as the constant threat of a dangerous slide towards genocidal politics in Rwanda. To reiterate, the rest of this chapter is about the various legal and ideological innovations introduced by the transitional post-genocide government and by the post-transition government of the past few years. We ask whether these changes have brought Rwandans any closer to thinking about themselves as Rwandans first instead of Hutu, Tutsi or Twa first and Rwandan only thereafter. In other words, are Rwandans today divided and united by something other than race?

Understanding Rwanda?

A great deal has already been written about the causes of the genocide in Rwanda in 1994, and there are still many different ways of understanding what happened and why. What is quite clear is that a highly centralised, authoritarian state, where the leaders perceives themselves to be under siege, and are faced with a conformist society, is capable of producing and implementing quite frighteningly efficient plans for the systematic eradication of a perceived internal 'enemy'.[6] Rwanda is not the first, nor will it be the last example of this. In Rwanda the enemy was defined in racial terms, and political allegiance was read off a person's racial ascription. The opening quotations to this chapter link the lethal manipulation of those in power with the challenge of human insecurity, which remains a major cause of what are often terms ethnic conflicts and civil wars. In the decade since the genocide, Rwanda has changed significantly. However it must not be "written out of the rest of humanity,"[7] simply because of the genocide legacy; the genocide has this tendency to transfix us. Life continues in Rwanda, people make their livings in various ways, and the government in power has its own goals, plans and ways of operating that cannot be reduced to being against genocide or for it. The government is the main focus of this chapter for the simple reason that it is the specific institution with overall responsibility for human rights, development and 'ethnic' relations in the country.

'Primal violence' is not the problem in Rwanda today. It was not the problem during the genocide either. The problem is 'race politics,' which involves the manipulation of history by those in power in order to polarise people along pseudo-scientific lines. This has various purposes, and has the advantage of allowing for divide-and-rule. It can also result in deaths or even genocide, once race politics is transformed into war. Some accounts still insist on attributing the killings and deaths of 1994 to 'inter-tribal' conflict or 'ethnic violence,' including the editor of this volume. Rwandans too will often explain such killings as the outcome of senseless rivalry between 'Hutu' and 'Tutsi' people, a rivalry which is sometimes blamed on the Belgian colonisers, and sometimes thought to date back centuries. The regime currently in power in Rwanda blames race hatred among Rwandans on the divisive colonial policies of the Belgians, and on imperialist designs of Western countries. The government of Rwanda has even proposed that "The government of Belgium through its divisive colonial policies, must be held morally and legally accountable, under international law" for the genocide. The Belgian government might yet find itself asked to pay "compensation to the victims of the genocide."[8] Nigel Eltringham has helped us understand complex debates around the meaning of Rwandan history in his careful study of differing accounts of the genocide.[9] He also shows that academic accounts both overlap with and diverge from the explanations of Rwandans themselves, including official accounts.

What are we to make, then, of a recent study on ethnic cleansing and genocide, which concludes that: "Regardless of their complex origins, these events demonstrate the capacity of ethnicity and race to arouse the emotions, sometimes to the point of homicidal fury."[10] The Rwandan army, militias and later the RPA itself did indeed commit crimes of hatred, of revenge, of fury. It has been suggested that genocide in Rwanda was assisted by the tendency of most ordinary Rwandans to do what they were told.[11] Widespread popular compliance was achieved through a variety of means and ensured that killing Tutsi became a civic duty of all Hutu, rather than an exceptional or spontaneous act of cruelty. Threats and coercion were involved, but brute force was only one element of the ability to gain the consent of a large part of the population. Social and political control and the capacity to secure obedience "largely consists in the ability to make others inhabit your story of their reality."[12]

The 'Hutu Power' story was based on the idea that all Tutsi were potential or actual traitors, and all Hutu should feel threatened by them, even by Tutsi babies in the womb. Genocide was implemented in a very efficient manner in Rwanda, and social conformism played a large part in this. Official genocide policy from the start of the 1990s to 1994 was in fact a constant struggle against externally imposed, and domestically desired peace, and a means of denying other differences (regional, left-right, rich-poor, gender) among Rwandans. To get genocide started at all: "required a dogged uphill effort for Habyarimana's extremist entourage to prevent Rwanda slipping toward moderation."[13] Orders to kill were not given in a calm way once genocide started. Revenge became more common as the genocide achieved its aim of killing as many Rwandan Tutsi as possible, and more and more 'children' of Rwanda were swept up as victims.

The RPA entered Rwanda as the genocide came to an end, and for them the aim was to restore central control over the country, arrest those guilty of genocide crimes, and secure military peace. Some RPA soldiers however took revenge on Hutus in general, and also raped Tutsi married to Hutu, or imprisoned their Hutu husbands. These attacks were all more or less based on hatred; both sides used rape and killings of witnesses and civilians as weapons in their conflict with the other. Seizing property was sometimes the motivation for such revenge killings and also for rapes and forced marriages.[14]

The point here is that whilst fury and hatred are bound to be significant factors in war and violence, equally important, and indispensable to genocide, are obedience and the dread of punishment in case of disobedience. "I was only doing my job" is a far more likely explanation of how horrors are committed than "They deserve it, I hate them all." Our concern here is less to find out how hatred is cultivated and manipulated, and more to explain how people obey orders to do terrible things, including to those they love. In a recent conference on "Why Neighbours Kill" , the overall view of participants was that neighbours kill one another because they are ordered to do so, rather than because they actually hate their neighbours to start with.[15] Selection of a particular human target is always a gradual process, and it is only through various institutions that such organised hatred can find expression through mass persecution, killings or genocide.

To create specific hatreds convenient to those in power necessarily involves diverting other forms of resentment and anger into a specific channel. Spontaneous forms of hatred for the government itself, for instance, are not tolerated. For example, people may start to hate the leaders who have failed to provide economic security, employment and prospect for their children. But such hatred can be redirected towards a mythical or racial enemy, who can be blamed for the economic and social problems being experienced by millions of people. Government and the economic elite get off the hook, and blame is passed on. Very powerful groups and very weak groups may be equally vulnerable in the process, each in different ways. Yet since all groups contain both the powerful and the poor, inevitably any attack on a social group will include both powerful and less powerful people, labelling all as the enemy. Hatred thus becomes politically sanctioned, and socially conformist, when it is directed towards the selected scapegoat as target, as identified by the state. Logic or evidence has nothing to do with it, since: "The most compelling anthropological proofs that the Jews are not a race will... alter the fact that the totalitarians know full well whom they do and whom they do not intend to murder.[16]

So ethnic and race identities can be deliberately manipulated from above until it appears *as if* they act as primordial ties, in Rwanda's case as ties of 'race'. Social scientists are often as easy to take in concerned the 'reality' of ethnic or race differences as anyone else.

In Rwanda the idea that distinct 'races' do not exist among Rwandans is relatively new. It was expressed by Alexis Kagame and other early scholars of Rwandan society.[17] But in the post-independence era, it is a rediscovery of the post-genocide years. This may surprise students of race relations in Western Europe or North America, where the idea of race was discredited by the experience of the Holocaust. Elsewhere in the world, scholars and other 'right thinking' people still talk about races, and even cranial shapes, length of noses and so forth (Indian anthropology is an interesting case in point). Entire groups of people are still classified as if race theory had never been debunked. There common humanity is replaced with physical distinctions between entire groups of people, often based on measurement and 'types.' The human capacity to extend and limit compassion according to one's definition of 'us' lends race theories their fatal power and attraction, making them into a deadly weapon in the hands of determined and ruthless politicians. Race theories can disembowel entire countries and set people who previously loved one another into a frenzy of hatred. The post-genocide regime in Rwanda is trying to 'deracialise' not only the minds of Rwandans, but also the society itself.

How can we understand the process by which previously fluctuating social identities hardened into lethal barriers that prevented any compassion for those redefined as 'alien'; the Tutsi of Rwanda? It is likely, overall, that the sense of social solidarity among Rwandans was greater prior to the arrival of Europeans than afterwards, when race labels started to be employed for the purposes of colonial administration. That is not to say that all was well in the pre-colonial garden; but violent hatreds along 'race' lines are not primordial in Rwanda; they are a distinctly modern phenomenon, brought in with European languages, religious beliefs and science.[18] The role of colonial ideologies and administrative practices, the economic and political crisis of the early 1990s, and the use of national foundation myths based on race and gender by an increasingly totalitarian state are all factors. External manipulation by major Western powers under conditions of severe socio-economic and political stress also contributed to the ideology of genocide.

Notions of racial inferiority and superiority were adopted by Rwandans themselves (i.e. internalised) and made it very difficult to construct a shared anti-colonial form of nationalist identity.[19] As Sol Yurick suggests: colonization can be thought of not only as the control of somearea 'external' to the 'homeland' but as the process of *internalizing* the alienating code of the overarching nation-state.[20]

During the Belgian colonial era, "... with every schoolchild reared in the doctrine of racial superiority and inferiority, the idea of a collective national entity was steadily laid to waste."[21] Has the RPF government managed to rewrite Rwandans' social identities through a renewed sense of anti-colonial nationalism? This question is explored in the next section.

Reinventing Rwanda Identity?

The increasingly totalitarian nature of Rwandan politics was apparent from the early 1990s, when economic crisis started to take a hold on the country, and at the same time there were popular movements perhaps for the first time contesting the regime in power on the basis of mass mobilisation, at least in urban Kigali. Underlying pressures of economic reform and debt problems were squeezing Rwandans, who already lived at close to bare subsistence levels. Reform was imposed from outside, and money supplied by the World Bank and other international donor organisations fuelled the militarisation of Rwanda society and politics, given the context of a war with the RPA.[22] More generally, it can be noted that:

> ... the deepening of Africa's economic crisis tends to encourage sort of cultural fundamentalism, comparable to other religious fundamentalisms, as an escape for rural populations, constituting an obstacle to genuine democratisation.[23]

In Rwanda it was not so much the rural populations as the urban unemployed youth, led by the Northern-dominated political and military elite that became ardently fundamentalist in outlook. This class of unemployed young men still poses a real challenge for the regime, which finds it almost impossible to provide a secure livelihood for the increasing numbers of youth alienated from both the rural and urban economies. Continuing economic recession and war have "transformed politics into a drama based on shared emotions" on a more or less permanent basis. It seems that the emotion of ethnic hatred has been replaced by hatred of those who dare to use ethnic labels.

According to some writers, the appeal of exclusionist and chauvinist political ideologies can be traced back to repressed sexual impulses, and to what Fromm calls the 'fear of freedom.'[24] From Rwanda to the Balkans and from Armenia to Cambodia, self-styled representatives of the dominant 'people' claim that "the victim minority at home is linked with powerful foreign influences, whether another state or some kind of 'international conspiracy'."[25] In the case of Rwanda, once the Tutsi had been labelled as aliens, they lost their right to be protected as citizens. The creation of such lethal and divisive ethnic (in this case 'racial') political identities is not an unavoidable outcome of historical inevitability.[26]

> In the case of Rwanda, as in Germany in the 1930s and Bosnia of the 1990s, those who sought to consolidate their power did so by attributing the hardships of the people to an identifiable (and accessible) scapegoat: a group to serve as target. With that in mind, it becomes possible to mobilize people on such a scale that the group redefines its own morality, for genocide, if "everyone" from one group is involved, then killing others becomes not only acceptable but necessary.[27]

Particular conditions account for the emergence of totalitarian commands, such as genocide, and a predisposition to believe in the fantastical, or what Reich calls "a mystical upbringing" can become "the foundation of fascism when a social catastrophe sets the masses in motion."[28] Famine, war and disease all had this effect in Rwanda, at once fragmenting the Rwandan population by undermining their sense of social solidarity, and creating out of them a 'mass mentality' that could be manipulated by the regime in power, using carrots and sticks at once. Under totalitarian conditions, such as those which pertained in Rwanda in the run-up to genocide "the individual—always an annoyance to totality—ceases to exist."[29] A lot of this analysis applies as much to post-genocide Rwanda as to the pre-1994 era. Things have improved in many respects, and Rwandans are dying in far smaller numbers. Yet things have not improved in terms of people's economic and social security. If anything more are now likely to die from hunger and neglect than before 1994.

In Rwanda, it is traditionally said certain powerful truths should not be openly shared with strangers.[30] Knowledge which is not meant for outsiders is known as *amalenga*.[31] As in other conflict situations, so too in Rwanda: "to those who have no right to know one could adapt one's speech by using language that they would misunderstand through ignorance."[32] Presenting false information for outsiders (including naïve academics, journalists and diplomats) could be justified as necessary in a situation where the state wants to get away with mass murder.

Both during the genocide, and under the present regime, techniques are used familiar to any student of authoritarian propaganda the world over. For example, one strategy is to: "(v)erbally attack the victims, deny—even in the face of the clearest evidence—that any physical violence is taking place, or has taken place."[33] The state's propaganda machinery in Rwanda remains highly sophisticated today, in spite of continuing poverty across the country. Western stereotypes of 'tribal conflict' are no longer played up to, instead they are heartily condemned, and all ethnicist expressions of opinion attributed to malign Western and alien influences. The RPF version of 'Hutu Power' is a mythical Rwanda inherited from the forefathers where there was no conflict except against common enemies, including the Europeans.

All states and regimes need myths of origin to legitimise their dominance over society. The post-genocide regime in Rwanda is no exception. Sarah Benton notes that "(a) story of the origin of a nation is always of its moment... it always reveals the character of the nation, explains a conflict, proposes its destiny, justifies a current action."[34] Since 1994, myths of origin based on the 'ascribed' identity marker of race have been replaced by the genocide itself as the defining moment of the antithesis of everything that the Rwanda nation stands for. The Rwandan nation is united, it is peaceful, it is secure, it is not divided, not fearful, not a place of terror, but one of safety and calm. The feeling of belonging in today's Rwanda is to be based on common language, common history, common opposition to divisive race theories and politics, and an emerging sense of nationalism. The myth of origin is self-consciously reliant on images of Rwanda as a pre-colonial society with a high level of social cohesiveness, destroyed by the Europeans' divisive strategies of administration and governance.

> Whether considering traditions (cultural beliefs, rituals, ceremonies, ways of doing things) or collective memories of shared pasts, as nations, tribes, peoples or clans, a degree of scepticism is appropriate. Many such claims turn out to be recent, modern inventions or reinventions; the products of conflicts of material interests or struggles.[35]

Whereas some scholars claim ethnic identities in the Great Lakes region, and in Rwanda in particular, preceded European colonial rule, the present ideology is that all divisions were created through external manipulation. Along with some scholars, the present regime maintains that "those who hold the view that ethnicity already existed in pre-colonial Rwanda, always adhere to a version of Rwandan history... according to which, at some time in the past, Hutu (of Bantu origin) were conquered by Tutsi (of Nilotic stock)."[36] Interpretations of pre-colonial Rwandan society are highly polarised because of attempts to use pre-colonial history to justify present positions. The 'essentialist' view of Rwandan history is opposed by the 'socially constructed' view of race differences.[37]

The Rwandan reconstruction of national identity through a selective use of history contests the notion of race, and of purity. Hybridity should be the key to a new Rwandan identity. Has this in fact been the case? It is disturbing to note that evidence in this respect is not that promising. It seems that the position of mixed people, of partly Hutu and Tutsi ancestry, is that they are particularly vulnerable to persecution, both from the government, but also from ordinary Rwandans of both 'sides' who do not trust them. Racial purity is declared officially nonsense, yet real people of mixed background suffer daily abuses at the hand of neighbours and officials. Recent involvement of one of the authors in asylum advocacy in the UK has highlighted that most Rwandans seeking asylum are themselves mixed. At least in the UK context, their mixed identity is not seen as any defence in asylum cases, however. Two profiles of Rwandan exiles may help to illustrate this problem, which poses some serious questions about the extent to which the post-genocide regime has been able to deconstruct race identities inherited from the past. Identity in post-genocide Rwanda is being reconstructed in ways that do not seem to accommodate Rwandans of mixed heritage, who do not fall easily into any of the old or new definitions of political identity in Rwanda.[38] The two profiles presented suggest that below the smooth surface of shared Rwandan citizenship there still lurk the polarised 'race' identities of the past.

Case 1: Noelle Angelicas (Female—not real name)
    Noelle's father was a prominent official under the Habyarimana regime until he joined the first major opposition party in 1986. This automatically makes him a suspected *genocidaire* in post-genocide Rwanda. Noelle is the only known survivor of a family of ten, product of a mixed Hutu-Tutsi marriage. Both her parents were killed, each in very different ways. Her mother was Tutsi and was killed by militia in the first few days of the genocide. Noelle has inherited her mother's looks and is still generally taken for a Tutsi. Her father and seven siblings are all presumed dead, and either fled or was killed following attacks by RPA soldiers on their camp in former Zaire in 1996. Noelle survived for many years hidden in the house of priest in Kivu. There she was raped by an RPA soldier in 2001, and now has a young child as a result of that rape. In early 2002, by then heavily pregnant, Noelle moved to Rwanda to live with a relative also involved in the opposition party her father had joined in 1986. This party was then banned for its 'divisive' and 'ethnicist' outlook. Noelle's closest male relative with whom she was staying was arrested by RPA soldiers and disappeared.

Shortly afterwards, Noelle was warned that soldiers were looking for her too. She was in fear of her life, and shortly afterwards managed to flee to a third country. She has been refused asylum on the grounds that the security situation in Rwanda is fine. She is trapped between her father's reputation as a prominent political man, and her status as a victim of rape by an RPF soldier, an additional danger because of the possible risk of her being silenced as a witness.

This woman survived all her siblings, and her mother and father, all of whom have perished as a direct or indirect result of the genocide. Although her mother was a Tutsi victim of the genocide, and although she 'looks Tutsi' herself, she is not regarded as a survivor. Her siblings and father were killed by the RPA, and she was raped, marking her out as a potential threat to the government, and specifically the army. Her Tutsi appearance and the Tutsi identity of her mother have not protected this person; her family fled to the camps of former Zaire, and so she is a new caseload refugee—a Hutu. After her closest surviving relative was arrested for his political involvement in an opposition party, this person chose exile, paid for by a soldier who took pity on her.

Case 2: Julius Gasana (Male—not real name)

Julius Gasana is the son of a mixed marriage. Like Case 2, Noelle, his father was a Hutu and his mother Tutsi. His mother was killed at the very start of the genocide, on April 9th 1994. Julius' own father was killed for defending his Tutsi wife. Julius is a genocide survivor, by any definition of the term, and remained inside Rwanda until the RPF took over. However, Julius is unfortunately related on his father's side to an uncle who has been classified as a Category 1 genocide suspect, and whose name is on the list for Gitarama (not real location). As the oldest surviving male relative of this uncle, when he returned from studying in Kigali, Julius became vulnerable to severe persecution by Tutsi survivors in his home village. He was spat on every day and twice attacked and badly injured. When Julius complained to police and the local authorities, they did nothing to help. Despite losing both parents in the genocide, Julius is held accountable for killings by his missing paternal uncle. Moreover, because Julius's father was Hutu, even though he lost his mother and stayed inside Rwanda throughout the genocide, not leaving for the camps in Zaire, Julius is not able to identify himself as a genocide survivor. He looks Tutsi and considers himself loyal to the RPF, who saved him when they took over the country. He is a survivor in every sense of the term except the official one, but cannot escape being labelled a suspected *genocidaire* because of his uncle's crimes. He is an apparently innocent person being labelled suspected *genocidaire* for the simple reason that his (disappeared) uncle killed people during the genocide in 1994.

Julius's story shows how 'Hutu' and 'Tutsi' identity continue to be taken as metaphors for guilt and innocence with sometimes devastating effects. Mixed people, especially those with a Hutu father or male relatives suspected of genocide, seem rarely, if ever, to be accorded 'survivor' status. The political identities of these two individuals were profoundly altered by official accounts of the genocide, which removed from their lives the possibility of complexity and ambiguity. Instead of more hybrid identities being formed in post-genocide Rwanda, it seems that those caught in the middle, the 'in-betweenies,' find themselves squeezed between polarised political identities related to the genocide. In 1994 using the terms Hutu and Tutsi was compulsory, now such terms are proscribed. But the people in the middle still suffer from the distrust of both 'sides.'

In other ways, political identities in post-genocide Rwanda have become more complex, and potentially more Rwandan, since the genocide. There has been an influx of new kinds of Rwandans and the appearance of new schisms inside Rwandan society—particularly along language lines. However, official genocide history, the new regime's myth of origin, has 'frozen' political identity formation in time, in a polarised version of 1994. Most ordinary Rwandans refuse the over-simple and officially remembered categories of the genocide. They prefer to invent new terms, like 'Ugandans' to describe those in power. Some popular terms like 'Hutsi,' which used to be a way to express ideas about Rwandans' hybridity, have fallen into disuse since 1994.

Those with Tutsi mothers but Hutu fathers, even if they 'look Tutsi,' may be particularly vulnerable to being blamed for the sins of their paternal families. Even those who refused to flee to the camps, and remained inside Rwanda to await the RPA are not safe (Profile 2 above). They are not given 'survivor' status in their local communities. Claudine Vidal in an article in *Le Monde* at the occasion of the tenth anniversary commemorations notes that the first genocide commemorations of 1995 were a genuine exercise in mourning for all Rwandans. She claims that since then the commemorations increasingly screen the regime's own dictatorial policies. The government tends to use *genocidaires* as a by-word for Hutus, and survivor and old caseload returnees as euphemisms for Tutsi. Vidal regrets that by 2004: "Hutu are forbidden any collective mourning."[39] Neither Noelle nor Julius feels included among the 'survivor' of genocide today, yet from their accounts, neither can be described in any other way, objectively speaking. Both are suspected *genocidaires* because of Hutu family connections, or because their relatives oppose the present regime.

Permissible forms of political identification are almost as tightly restricted in today's Rwanda as they were in the past, but the actual terms used are now somewhat less racial, and somewhat more complex. The officially sanctioned classification system fits in with the official account of what happened during the genocide. This account more or less mirrors the image of the Hutu power account of Rwandan history and the genocide; both completely ignore the real complexity of Rwandan people's daily lives both in 1994 and since then. This means that Rwandans with a mixed Hutu-Tutsi background, or those who have suffered at the hands of the RPF, cannot form independent political identities outside the confines of official categories.[40] In terms of political identities, the legacy of genocide has been to polarise rather than cut across 'race' divisions.

There is anecdotal evidence emerging from Rwanda to suggest that inter-'race' marriages have become less—rather than more—common since 1994.[41] The race markers of the First and Second Republics lurk behind the terms '*genocidaires*,' 'new caseload refugees,' or 'old caseload refugee,' 'Ugandans' and 'survivors'. There is even a danger that race divisions will take on new life due to being officially banned. The complete repression of debates about the relative positions of Hutu, Tutsi and Twa in Rwandan political life is a potentially dangerous strategy according to one seasoned observer of 'ethnic politics' elsewhere in the African continent.[42]

Like other studies, this section has tried to "ease a number of complex voices back into the debate... the voices of people that have nuanced stories to tell."[43] Post-genocide strivings for 'Never again' have produced a rather simple tale of good and evil, which cannot reflect the growing complexity of political identity formation in Rwanda today. The logic, according to which everyone is either a victim or a perpetrator, has been bypassed by circumstances.

Institutions of Renewal? Solidarity Camps and *Gacaca*

A number of bold institutional innovations took place in Rwanda after 1994, for both security and ideological reasons. As we noted right at the start of this chapter, the regime's main aim was to ensure genocide never happened again. After 1994, a fund for survivors, and a National Unity and Reconciliation Commission were created. Prosecutions of suspected *genocidaires* proceeded at snail's pace, and by the end of the 1990s survivors and suspected *genocidaires* and their families all complained that justice was not being done.[44]

Solidarity camps (or *ingando*) are a form of re-education camp introduced by the post-genocide government, and have received surprisingly little attention in the literature. Such camps preach a secular form of nationalism, teaching practical skills at the same time. The participants are expected to obey rules and agree on who should cook, wash, clean and so on. More than one researchers accounts of such workshops run in early 2003 noted the emphasis on self-discipline, on sharing responsibilities and solving practical problems through cooperation, but also the superficiality of the exercise, which amounted to denial of continuing tensions at local level.[45] Another goal is to transmit a 'correct' version of Rwandan history to the participants. Belgian colonial rule is blamed for infecting Rwandans' minds with the virus of race theory; political commissars from the Unity and Reconciliation Commission run the solidarity camps, and see it as their job to instil a sense of shared citizenship among Rwandans. Participants are housed in simple tents, classrooms and community halls, supposed to facilitate a sense of interchange, equal status and shared public space.[46]

There are solidarity camps for the youth, for military and for ex-prisoners. All former FAR are taken through solidarity camps in preparation for reintegration into the mainstream Rwandan army. Former prisoners suspected of genocide crimes (usually lesser crimes) remain in the camps for up to three months, in preparation for reintegration into their home communities. In these cases, the camps also seek to ensure 'deparmehutization.'[47] Ironically, however, the senior posts in the army and Intelligence services are almost entirely 'tutsi-ised.'[48]

Civic sensitisation and shared citizenship are core values in the camps, in contrast with real life outside, where harmony seems harder to achieve. In February 2003, 40,000 low-priority prisoners, including the elderly, those arrested as children and those with no case files, were released from prison and held in solidarity camps. Here they were "taught how to be good citizens and how to re-establish themselves in society."[49] While in principle this is highly commendable, "(t)he dilemma is that to be a Hutu in contemporary Rwanda is to be presumed a *perpetrator*," and therefore in need of rehabilitation.[50] The camps are promoting an official national identity that is quite partial, and which may not remove obstacles to shared citizenship and public space. As was argued earlier in this chapter, there is a need to get beyond images of good guys and bad guys (and gals).

Bringing genocide suspects to trial in the courts has been a very slow process.[51] By 1998 it was estimated that it would take another two hundred years before all those accused could be brought to trial. By 2000 there was, as one survivor notes: "a general consensus that genocide took place, without any effective prosecutions, amounts to denying genocide in practice."[52] Most legal clerks, judges, lawyers and prosecutors were killed or exiled in 1994. From 1995 the Rwandan government asked the international community for resources to reconstruct the courts and legal system.[53] But after the genocide "international support was shamefully disappointing," and the French government in particular blocked EU aid to Rwanda.[54]

In 2000, the UK Minister for International Development, Clare Short pronounced herself more "hopeful about further progress on reconciliation in Rwanda,"[55] and there were promises of increased overseas aid for the judicial sector. By 2003, international confidence in the Rwandan criminal justice system had increased, and the UNHCR started to send Rwandan refugees back from neighbouring countries.[56] This was in no small part because of the introduction from 2001 onwards of the g*acaca* courts. These neo-traditional institutions were set up to try less serious crimes of genocide. Before they passed sentence on a single case, *gacaca* courts have been opposed by survivors associations, including Ibuka and Avega, who see them as 'cheap' justice'. One local NGO concluded that *gacaca* "looks set to further damage the relationship between the government and survivors."[57] Amnesty International criticised the lack of any right of appeal or legal representation for the accused.[58] One detainee feels sorry for the government:

> ... (the government)... has very good aims, but is hard pressed by
> both the survivors and the detainees. The international community is
> also pressurising the state because of the overcrowding of prisons.
> The government wants to correct the mistakes made at the beginning,
> especially the huge number of arbitrary arrests.[59]

Quoted in the same report, a journalist observes: "*Gacaca* means the privatisation of the judicial system" for Category 2, 3, and 4 genocide suspects.[60] 260,000 appointed men and women judges are starting to try around 150,000 genocide suspects, and possibly many more.[61] The huge numbers of cases being tried, and variations in local conditions and events during the genocide, mean the central state authorities are hard pressed to prevent discrepancies in judgements at local level. Killings of witnesses and suspected *genocidaires* in rural Rwanda have not reassured anyone, least of all survivors, who mainly view *gacaca* courts as rough justice for themselves.[62]

A more optimistic appraisal of *gacaca* is that it "... brings together the people of Rwanda in a spirit of equality and openness... (p)roperly implemented it may well prove an antidote to the social poison of the genocide."[63] Early signs are that *gacaca* seems to be working, but often in ways that polarise communities. In one set of communities observed, whereas at the first trials Hutu and Tutsi Rwandans sat in the audience together, after some weeks it was noted they sat separately, each on their own side of the open air court.[64] On the other hand, the films of Ann Aghion on *gacaca* proceedings show that breakthroughs and reconciliation are also possible outcomes. In the next section, developmental institutional changes are identified, including resettlement initiatives, and the impact on Rwandans' material security and well being is assessed.

Land, Poverty and Social Insecurity

Economic collapse in the mid-1980s set the stage for the disaster of genocide, and endemic mass poverty continues to haunt Rwanda, which is faced with rising inflation, declining agricultural production and the prospect of long-term food insecurity, rising morbidity and growing unemployment. These issues must be tackled if political and social order is to be maintained in Rwandan society. Belying the serious structural problems observed by many Rwandans themselves, official statistics indicate that the economy "has grown rapidly since the genocide."[65] At the macroeconomic level, the period since 1994 has seen economic growth after almost ten years of sharp and continuous economic decline since 1986.[66] The country reportedly now "has one of Africa's fastest growing economies thanks to foreign donors led by Britain, which is contributing £37 million" in 2004.[67] Those recently returned to Kigali are impressed by the "shiny new office blocks and hotels... popping up" all over the city.[68] Real estate development tends to disguise the huge problem of underemployment faced by the urban poor and the decline in production among Rwandan peasants.

After 1999, material considerations played a large part in Rwanda's continuing intervention in former Zaire. In a good example of how "... conflicts do not only bring destruction, they also shape new opportunities,"[69] the Democratic Republic of Congo has been subjected to a war of predation by its neighbours. Since 1998, the parallel economy has blossomed in Rwanda. Nzongola-Ntalaja sees this as typical of "the logic of plunder in the new era of globalisation... (and) the growing tendency of states... to enrich themselves from crises."[70] The consequences for ordinary Rwandans are not positive.

Rwandans remain among the poorest people in the world, with 40 per cent of all Rwandans (and 46 per cent of rural Rwandans) living below the extreme poverty line "at which one's entire budget must be allocated to food."[71] New illnesses including malaria and HIV/AIDS have increased, and water shortages and food insecurity have continued since the mid-1980s. It can be forcefully argued that mass poverty, and high levels of inequality, rather than race ideology *per se*, or political domination, is the single greatest obstacle to peace and reconciliation in Rwanda today.[72] After all, "(p)overty is itself a violation of human rights."[73] The impact of the genocide was devastating in terms of human development indicators; life expectancy at birth dropped from 45 years in 1970-75 to 39 years in 2000-05.[74]

Rwanda's status as a development 'basket case' reflects the economy's heavy reliance on coffee exports, and a growing agricultural population living at or below subsistence levels on land of diminishing quality and quantity with few prospects of alternative off-farm income or urban employment.[75] It is essential to consider Rwandans' economic situation; economics must come into questions of governance and how political identities are fashioned in the new Rwanda. Studies of post-genocide efforts to create a new Rwanda often proceed as if politics can be detached from how people live on a daily basis. As Uvin has shown, only through tangible improvements in Rwandans' material living conditions can the 'structural violence' of economic and social life be undone.

Combating social inequalities and absolute poverty can reduce the number of desperate people who might be attracted to extremist politics of whatever stripe. The socio-economic roots of intolerance and race persecution are by now well-established and hardly need be reiterated in detail.[76] When General Dallaire revisited Rwanda in 2004, on the occasion of the tenth anniversary of the genocide, he commented to journalists that he wanted to go into the Rwandan hills and do some manual labour in exchange for food.[77] Perhaps he had heard that things were not too easy for Rwandan farmers today.

A recent study places Rwanda alongside such countries as Somalia, Afghanistan and Haiti as 'UCEs,' ungovernable chaotic entities,[78] with high levels of absolute and relative poverty. Both before and after the genocide, Rwanda had the appearance of constantly teetering on the edge of demographic and political disaster.[79] A somewhat Malthusian view is that Rwandans 'have no more land.'[80] Seeing this as the cause of genocide ignores completely that what matters is land distribution, which is highly skewed. Land remains a sensitive and critical development issue ten years after the genocide, one governed by relations of class, gender and political identities (e.g relations between new and old caseload returnees). Problems of coexistence between new and old caseload refugees are acknowledged by the RPF, but it is less often acknowledged that some genocide accusations have been motivated by land grabbing.[81] The difficult coexistence of old and new caseload returnees has been the subject of some detailed academic attention,[82] as have gender relations and access to land.[83]

In an effort to deal with land issues and security—military rather than economic and social—the Rwandan government decided in 1995-96 on a policy of villagisation. This was to "... change the mode of habitat in Rwanda, moving away from dispersed units which use too much space."[84] New caseload refugees on their return from Zaire, Tanzania or Burundi, found their homes occupied by old caseload refugees who had arrived shortly after the RPF victory.[85] Old caseload refugees were supposed to vacate the property, but not all did so.[86] Severe housing shortages and the rapid return of civilian populations meant that many NGOs and donor agencies supported official imidugudu (villagisation) programmes as a form of reconstruction. Few serious reservations were expressed about forcing people to relocate; donors seem to have believed the government's argument that imidugudu could not be compared with other, generally unsuccessful villagisation schemes in Eastern Africa. The uniqueness argument did not convince everyone however.[87] Suspicions remain that the imidugudu policies of village resettlement "... aims to compensate genocide survivors and 'old caseload' refugees for not being allowed to repossess property under the Arusha Accord."[88]

Villagisation in Rwanda was supposed to achieve several things: (1) concentrate land use; (2) release vacant fertile land in an equitable manner; (3) mix communities residentially and promoting reconciliation; (4) make it easier to provide services and overcome the handicaps of dispersed dwellings.[89] Actual results vary in different parts of the country. In the North-West, for instance, security considerations took precedence over other aspects of resettlement.[90] Between December 1997 and March 1998, 478,000 people were resettled in 172 sites in Gisenyi and Ruhengeri provinces, as insurgency and RPF reprisals took hold of the region.[91] By contrast in Southwest Rwanda villagisation was almost entirely voluntary, with some popular involvement in construction.[92]

Houses are sometimes abandoned because they are poorly constructed and there is no land or services; some new villages did not even have a clean water supply when constructed. Rwandans also complain at the lack of privacy, with new houses being uncomfortably close by local rural standards.[93] Allocating adjacent plots of land has been used as a material incentive to get people to move into some villages.[94] In addition, the transitional government has claimed that "one of the criteria in these villages is multi-ethnicity."[95] Yet certain groups—notably women survivors and their children—have found themselves regrouped together in isolation, sometimes making them feel more vulnerable to attack rather than more secure.[96] In recent years, some released genocide suspects have been involved in building houses and service infrastructure including schools and clinics as a form of 'community service'. This tendency is likely to be expanded with community service being an option for part of sentences handed out by *gacaca* courts.

Rwanda's whole rural productive system, based on assistance from one's neighbours with major jobs, and a "system of community obligation" was "turned on its head" during the genocide and discredited.[97] With *imidugudu* collective systems of self-help have been given a death-blow. Rural social dynamics have been completely altered, since "Rwanda has no history of villages."[98] The *imidugudu* programme therefore represents a very radical break with the past indeed, and does not seem to have achieved its ambitious aims. It may further have demotivated agricultural producers, who now have to travel further to the fields. Whatever the verdict on villagisation, land issues remain extremely fraught in Rwanda. Excluded and marginalized rural producers, landless and unemployed can be exploited for lethal ends, and this is an unpredictable state of affairs. Most Rwandans farm and households averaging nine people before the genocide, have less than one hectare (2.5 acres) each for all their food needs and to grow cash crops of diminishing value.[99] Conflicts over land are frequent and widespread, and the land allocation systems of inheritance have been undermined by the sale of land. Privatisation and commercialisation of land use started in the late colonial period and accelerated markedly from the 1980s with a growing class of impoverished and landless peasant families. Larger land-holdings have been consolidated through crisis and rural inequalities are higher than ever. Such pressures are unlikely to diminish as *gacaca* start to operate and prisoners are released, following the first mass release of 40,000 in early 2003. Up to 80,000 more people are expected to return in 2004-5 from the DRC, demobilised ex-combatants who need to be reintegrated into Rwandan society under the terms of international agreements.[100] DfID assess the level of risk relating to "a possible breakdown in internal stability" as high and increasing.[101]

There are some important gender politics involved in access to land. During genocide itself, militia members sometimes obtained land through 'marriages' with women known to have access to lineage land.[102] After the genocide Hutu widows of Tutsi husbands, and Tutsi women survivors married to Hutu men, became victims of inter-community conflicts. The Tutsi woman married to a Hutu might find her husband imprisoned as a result of accusations of crimes of genocide (whether genuine or not). The woman would have her property seized.[103] The introduction of a new law in 1999, which allowed women to inherit property for the first time, signalled that the government wanted to tackle the issue of rural women's landlessness (law 22/99 of 12.11/1999). It is however

notoriously difficult to implement such laws in favour of widows whose husband's land is generally taken back by his family.[104] Already in 1995, of the de-
tainees in Rwanda's prisons it was said that: "many among... (them) were innocent victims of disputes over property or of attempts to acquire property."[105]
With high mortality levels among Rwandan prisoners, women-headed families
could be permanently deprived of land.[106]

The results of land conflicts can be messy politically; as Stiefel observes;
"... peasants will attempt to avoid 'problems' and conflicts and seek to accommodate rather than confront," but when pushed beyond passive dissent, peasant-
based protests can rapidly become lethal.[107] The view that Rwanda is ungovernable is not a minority opinion. DfID insists on providing support for those who
seek peaceful change within the Rwandan state because the stakes of not doing
so are seen as high. Whilst the rural economy suffers from rising inequality, the
urban economy is booming by all accounts.

Pervasive poverty and widespread popular economic insecurity do not seem
to have undermined the solidity of public institutional and political structures,
which retain a powerful hold over Rwandans. The population can still be mobi-
lised in its virtual entirety, as for example during the recent spate of elections.
Virtually all rural voters obediently voted for Kagame and the RPF. It was only
in Kigali, with its more prosperous and growing middle class, that some resistance to mobilisation by the RPF was expressed. Presidential election results
contained an interesting paradox; there were record votes for the RPF (almost 99
per cent) in former Prime Minister Faustin Twagiramungu's relatively impoverished rural home area, and the highest vote for opposition candidate was Twagiramungu (15 per cent), in the prosperous, Tutsi-dominated suburbs of Kigali.
Whatever this implies, there is no reason to imply, as do some observers, that
Rwanda now constitutes an example of an 'ungovernable entity' along the lines
of Somalia or Afghanistan.[108] Despite the massive deprivations and sufferings of
rural Rwandans, and the insecurity of those in petty urban employment, Rwanda
remains as much as ever a country of 'effective' if not 'good' governance.

Conclusions of Others

Prognoses for the future by prominent scholars concerning Rwanda's future
vary greatly from understandably gloomy predictions of further rounds of civil
war and even genocide to images of a future where democracy can flourish and
militarisation can come to an end. Here are choice selections of conclusions
drawn by recent scholarly studies either specifically about Rwanda's future or
more generally about the wider Great Lakes region of which Rwanda forms an
integral—and increasingly closely inter-connected—part. The quotations start
with the gloomiest and end with the most positive.

1. "For someone like the present author, who warned against massive violence during the years leading up to 1994, it is frustrating to wonder whether, in two, five or ten years from now, the international community, again after the facts, will have to explain why Rwanda has descended into hell once more."[109]

2. "The war (in Congo)... crystallised two volatile regional diasporas—one Hutu, the other Tutsi—each determined to set the region on fire if the demands it considered legitimate were not met."[110]

3. "Arguably ethnic identity is more important today than it was during preparations for the genocide."[111]

4. "Without a vision of the past which acknowledges that different interpretations of history will exist, Rwanda... and the Great Lakes Region generally, will remain entrapped in an official discourse which legitimates the use of violence and makes some, leaders and led, *genocidaires.*"[112]

5. "... a critique of colonialism and its effects on people's categories of perception was never allowed to develop and mature in Rwanda. Although this critique is not the only measure needed in order to bring about reconciliation in Rwanda, Rwandans must start here. They must acknowledge, then question, then criticize the enduring effects that colonialism has had on their own minds."[113]

6. "For the Congo, as for Rwanda, Burundi and Uganda [a political solution]... implies the resolution of the crises of democratic transition by putting an end to governments established by the force of arms, and embarking on a path of genuine national reconciliation, justice and inclusiveness...."[114]

This brief sample shows an increasing readiness to be critical of the RPF and in general of all purely military solutions to the problems of security and coexistence in post-genocide Rwanda and the wider Great Lakes region, which has been so profoundly affected by events in Rwanda in 1994. Immediately after 1994, Pottier argues that many scholars fawned before Rwanda's post-genocide leaders. Today there may be an opposite danger of disbelieving everything the Rwandan government says. This is just as faulty as believing their every word. Academic researchers and other observers need to view events in the country in their wider and historical context. Unfortunately as the human rights climate in Rwanda worsens prominent critics of the post-genocide government, even those who were formerly supporters, are finding it almost impossible to return, either to do research or to live in Rwanda.[115] Those who suffer exclusion and exile include some previously close to the RPF, including Faustin Twagiramungu and researchers like Prunier.

Varied conflicts between old and new caseload refugees, a growing urban middle class, uprooted from rural life, and a growing class of landless rural poor, with no secure claims to land and few livelihood choices, have all made it much harder to realise a basic level of economic and social rights for ordinary Rwandans after the genocide. Some things are more complex than before: there are now four national languages in Rwanda (English, Kinyarwanda, French and Kiswahili).[116] French is less widely spoken in official circles than before 1994.

In part the new regime's legal suppression of race identity labels has worked; references to Hutu, Tutsi and Twa are already less acceptable even in unmonitored internet and media outlets.

Not every conflict can be reduced everything to a supposedly age-old conflict between two 'races,' Hutu and Tutsi, this has allowed other, more complex, perspectives on political identity to emerge. The realities that underpinned the polarised politics of the past may remain, but the terms 'Hutu' and 'Tutsi' seem to have been defused of their ticking time bombs, surely a change for the better. Within Rwanda, and in the wider Rwandan diaspora, social divisions that can not be reduced to the Hutu-Tutsi divide, have been able to come to the fore, including divisions of class, region, politics and religion. The official categories of identity, survivors and *genocidaires*, new and old caseload refugees, rural and urban Rwandans, anglophone and francophone, have also taken on new meanings. Researchers, journalists and academics have at the very least been challenged by the RPF regime in Rwanda to rethink the categories through which they explained Rwandan history and contemporary politics, and this is a positive development. "Only time will tell whether Rwandan politics can be de-ethnicised to a degree that makes democracy meaningful and secure."[117] Letting go of the clichés that informed most popular academic and media understandings of Rwanda prior to 1994 is a welcome development, and one that is surely to be welcomed.

Conclusions

The post-genocide transitional regime's search for national unity has involved it increasingly adopting a form of 'victim' ideology through its diasporic nationalism. The ideal for the regime is a romantic one, implying as it does national unity and fixity in time. The practical difficulties involved in managing an increasingly complex society with a more deeply class divided society than ever, are hard to overcome. If our profiles of mixed Rwandans are in any way indicative (and the suggestion is that they are), then the signs for genuinely national post-colonial political identities emerging from Rwanda are not promising. If more complex form of Rwandan nationalism could only find expression, then it might be possible for Rwandans collectively to:

> ... move beyond fixed identities... (and) advocate a more generous and pluralistic vision of the world, where the possibilities for oppressive identity claims are minimised.[118]

In the absence of such changes, the future for Rwandans and other people in the Great Lakes region, still carrying the poisonous legacy of out-dated notions of race-based identities even whilst denying and opposing them, is to restore law and order, let go of old hatreds and confront their difficulties in integrating into the increasingly competitive global economy. To the fatal consequences of race theories in Rwanda can be added the fatal consequences of international complicity, commercial interests and politicking.[119] To underpin the post-colonial reimagining of political identities and state-society relations in Rwanda, the full range of individual human rights (economic and social as well as civil and political) needs to be much more central to the Rwandan state and the donors' priorities in future. The Rwandan government needs to recognise that if it expects a high level of loyalty and trust from Rwandan people, and wants all Rwandans to feel equally 'at home' in Rwanda, then it must be prepared reciprocally to make every effort to ensure that all Rwandans achieve a decent minimum level of well-being, based on securing their socio-economic rights as citizens.[120] Social inequalities should also be reduced as far as possible, especially in land holdings and access to markets. If these goals are not achieved, then Rwanda's people will continue to be sacrificed on the altar of a version of the nation that only has room for two mutually antagonistic stories; that of the victors and that of the vanquished, with each side deprived of both social justice and the respect of their own individual human rights.

Notes

1. Alain Touraine, *Can We Live Together? Equality and Difference* (Cambridge: Polity, 2000), 221. David Kiwuwa is a US doctoral student, studying and teaching in the Politics Department of Nottingham University. David recently made an extended visited to Rwanda, conducting interviews and carrying out extensive fieldwork for his doctoral thesis on democracy and ethnicity in Rwanda. This will be presented soon, probably early in 2005. Helen is a long-serving academic, who has been writing about the genocide and its legacy since 1996. She is preparing to return to Rwanda for the first time since the mid-1980s. She has been involved in writing 'expert' reports for asylum seekers from the Great Lakes region, occasionally enabling Rwandan refugees to be allowed to remain in the UK. Rwanda is a large part of both our lives, and it is a common concern to understand what is going on there that brought us together, as well as our mixed bags of experience and expertise. By putting our heads together in this chapter, we hope to have provided some new insights into the current situation in Rwanda, and to have clarified the problem of ending race conflict. Some authors have written on Rwanda without ever having been there: "I have never set foot on Rwandan soil" says Michael Barnett. He then says "the Rwanda that now dwells inside me is not a geographical territory. Rather it is a metaphysical space" (Michael Barnett, *Eyewitness to a Genocide: The United Nations and Rwanda* (Ithaca: Cornell University Press, 2002), xiii). Some other academics who have worked on Rwanda for decades are now no longer allowed in because the regime considers them hostile and ethnicist (Filip Reyntjens is the main case in point). This chapter has been written specifically with the idea that Rwanda is a real and not a meta-

physical entity. We have tried to keep the real concerns of Rwandans we know in mind when writing it, even if the language is at times regrettably too dense for the lay person. This chapter has drawn on David Kiwuwa's forthcoming thesis, and on a number of published and unpublished studies by Helen Hintjens. We would like to thank the two reviewers of this chapter for their helpful comments.

2. Meredeth Turshen, "The Political Economy of Rape: An Analysis of Systematic Rape and Sexual Abuse of Women During Armed Conflict in Africa," 55–68 in *Victims, Perpetrators or Actors? Gender, Armed Conflict and Political Violence*, ed. Caroline O.N. Moser and Fiona C. Clark (London: Zed Books, 2001), 62.

3. The term 'race' is used here in spite of its being very contentious, because it was used in Rwanda in this way prior to the genocide, as if it were 'natural.' One of the most influential and convincingly argued studies debunking the theory of race is Ashley Montagu, *Man's Most Dangerous Myth: the Fallacy of Race* (New York: Harper & Brothers, 3rd. ed., 1953). The 'race' theory most relevant in Rwanda is the Hamitic hypothesis which is discussed in detail in Mahmood Mamdani, *When Victims Become Killers: Colonialism, Nativism and the Genocide in Rwanda* (Princeton: Princeton University Press, 2001), Chapters 2 and 3.

4. Mamdani, *When Victims Become Killers*, 261.

5. Antoine Lema, "Causes of Civil War in Rwanda: The Weight of History and Socio-cultural Structures," 68–86 in *Ethnicity Kills? The Politics of War, Peace and Ethnicity in Sub Saharan Africa*, Einer Braathen, Morten Boas and Gjermund Saether, eds. (New York: St Martin's Press 2000), 85.

6. Helen Hintjens, "Explaining the 1994 genocide in Rwanda," *Journal of Modern African Studies* 37, no. 2 (June 1999): 241–86.

7. David Newbury, "Understanding Genocide," *African Studies Review* 41, no. 1 (January 1998): 73–97, 88.

8. Republic of Rwanda, *Recommendations of the Conference on 'Genocide, Impunity and Accountability: Dialogue for a National and International Response'* (Kigali: Office of the President, 1995), 32.

9. Nigel Eltringham, *Accounting for Horror. Post-genocide debates in Rwanda* (London: Pluto Press, 2004).

10. Stephen Cornell and Douglas Hartmann, *Ethnicity and Race: Making Identities in a Changing World* (Thousand Oaks, CA.: Pine Forge Press, 1998), 32.

11. Newbury, "Understanding Genocide."

12. Philip Gourevitch, *We Wish to Inform You That Tomorrow We Will be Killed with Our Families. Stories from Rwanda* (London: Picador, 1999), 181.

13. Gourevitch, *We Write to Inform You*, 95.

14. Turshen, "The Political Economy of Rape," 63 for both points in this paragraph.

15. "Why Neighbours Kill: Explaining the Breakdown of Ethnic Relations" (paper presented at Nationalism & Ethnic Conflict Research Group Conference, Social Sciences, University of Western Ontario, 4–5 June 2004).

16. Theodor Adorno, *Minima Moralia. Reflections from a Damaged Life* (London: New Left Books, 1974), 102.

17. Johan Pottier, *Re-Imagining Rwanda. Conflict, Survival and Disinformation in the late Twentieth Century* (Cambridge: Cambridge University Press, 2002).

18. George L. Mosse, *Toward the Final Solution. A History of European Racism* (London: J.M.Dent & Sons, 1978), 191.

19. Hintjens, "Explaining the 1994 genocide;" Jean-Paul Harroy, *Rwanda* (Brussels: Hayez, 1984), 28–9.

20. Sol Yurick, "The emerging Metastate versus the politics of ethno-nationalist identity," 204–24 in *The Decolonisation of Imagination: Culture, Knowledge and Power*, ed., Jan Nederveen Pieterse and Bikhu Parekh (London: Zed Books, 1995), 214.

21. Gourevitch, *We Wish to Inform You*, 57–8.

22. Andy Storey, "Ethnic Scapegoating: Elite Manipulation and Social Forces in Rwanda" (paper presented at Conference on Ethnicity, Uganda Martyrs' University, 3–6 September 2001.

23. Solofo Randrianja, "Nationalism, Ethnicity and Democracy," 20–41 in *Africa Now: People, Policies and Institutions. Stephen Ellis*, ed. (London: Heinemann/James Currey, 1996), 39.

24. Wilhelm Reich, *The Mass Psychology of Fascism* (London, Souvenir Press, 1970); Erich Fromm, *The Fear of Freedom* (London: Routledge, 1960).

25. Michael Mann, "The Dark Side of Democracy: the Modern Tradition of Ethnic and Political Cleansing," *New Left Review* 235 (May–June 1999): 18–45, 41.

26. Marion O'Callaghan "Continuities in imagination," XX–XX in *The Decolonisation of Imagination: Culture, Knowledge and Power*, Jan Nederveen Pieterse and Bikhu Parekh, eds. (London: Zed Books, 1995), 40.

27. Newbury, "Understanding Genocide," 77.

28. Reich, *The Mass Psychology of Fascism*, 131; Adorno, *Minima Moralia*, 238–41.

29. Gourevitch, *We Write to Inform You*, 95.

30. Gourevitch, *We Write to Inform You*, 95.

31. Filip Reyntjens, *Rwanda: Trois Yours Qui Ont Fait Basculer l'Histoire* (Paris: L'Harmattan/Institut Africain Cahiers Africains/Afrika Studies, No 16, 1995), 7.

32. Perez Zagorin, *Ways of Lying: Dissimulation, Persecution and Conformity in Early Modern Europe* (Cambridge, MA.: Harvard University Press, 1990), 251.

33. Gerard Prunier, *The Rwanda Crisis 1959–94. History of a Genocide* (London: Hurst & Co, 1995), 241.

34. Sarah Benton, "Founding Fathers and Earth Mothers: Women's Place at the Birth of Nations," 27–45 in *Gender, Ethnicity and Political Ideologies*, Nickie Charles and Helen Hintjens, eds. (London: Routledge, 1998), 27.

35. Sheila Allen, "Identity: feminist perspectives on 'race', ethnicity and nationalism," 46–64 in *Gender, Ethnicity and Political Ideologies*, Charles, 49.

36. Didier Goyvaerts, *Conflict and Ethnicity in Central Africa* (Tokyo: Tokyo University of Foreign Studies, 2000), 6.

37. In the wider Great Lakes region, the Hamite-Bantu distinction has become pervasive, expressing the view that a single, supposedly 'racial' conflict, can be spread out over most of East, Central and Southern Africa. In Nairobi, Kinshasa, Kampala and Harare the pastoral/agricultural divide is viewed increasingly in dangerous, racially laden terms.

38. Mamdani, *When Victims Become Killers*, 45.

39. *Le Monde*, 7 April 2004.

40. Rwandans are not all equally 'at home' in the new Rwanda; some are forced into exile, and many others feel unwanted. The relatives of suspected genocidaires may be particularly vulnerable. See for instance Filip Reyntjens, "Rwanda: Ten Years on: from Genocide to Dictatorship," *African Affairs* 103, no. 411 (May 2004): 177–210.

41. David Kiwuwa, "Slouching Towards a Democracy: Rwanda and the Ethnic Hurdle," Ph.D. thesis in progress, Department of Politics, University of Nottingham.

42. Conversation with Tunde Zack-Williams at the Review of African Political Economy Conference, University of Birmingham, 8–10 September 2003.

43. Pottier, *Re-Imagining Rwanda*, 202.

44. Paul Magnarella, *Justice in Africa: Rwanda's Genocide, its Courts and the UN Criminal Tribunal* (Aldershot: Ashgate, 2000); Nigel Eltringham, *Accounting for Horror: post-Genocide Debates in Rwanda* (London: Pluto Press, 2004), 49; African Rights, *Confession to Genocide* (London: African Rights, 2001).

45. Phil Clark, "Gacaca Courts in Rwanda" (presentation at On Justice in Rwanda, Oxford University, 15 May 2004).

46. Kiwuwa, "Slouching Towards Democracy;" Chi Mgbako, "*Ingando* Solidarity Camps: Reconciliation and Political Indoctrination in Post-Genocide Rwanda," *Harvard Human Rights Journal* 18, Spring 2005: 201–28.

47. Republic of Rwanda, "Reconciliation and Democratization Policies: Experiences and Lessons learned in Reconciliation and Democratization from Germany, South Africa, Namibia and Rwanda (Kigali: National Unity and Reconciliation Commission, October 2003), 58.

48. See table in Reyntjens, "Rwanda Ten Years On," 187.

49. Hirondelle press release, Government of Rwanda, <http://www.rwanda1.com/government>, 5 May 2003.

50. Quotations from Mamdani, *When Victims become Killers*, 267; Eltringham, *Accounting for Horror*, 69–77.

51. Magnarella, *Justice in Africa*.

52. African Rights, *Confession to Genocide*, 96, 139.

53. Republic of Rwanda, *Recommendations of the Conference on 'Genocide, Impunity and Accountability*, 54.

54. Pottier, *Re-imagining Rwanda*, 141.

55. Government of Rwanda website, 10 May 2000.

56. UN Office for the Coordination of Humanitarian Affairs, IRIN update 2.5.2003, <http://www.irinnews.org/report.asp>.

57. African Rights, *Confession to Genocide*, 8.

58. Amnesty website "Gacaca: a question of justice," AI Index, AFR 47/007/2002 at <http://www.amnestyusa.org/countries/rwanda/document.doc>.

59. African Rights, *Confession to Genocide*, Confession of Dr Eustache Muntanhirwa, 36.

60. African Rights, *Confession to Genocide*, Confession of Dr Eustache Muntanhirwa, 128.

61. Martin Ngoga, *Post-genocide Justice Systems in Rwanda* (Presentation at Oxford University, 15 May 2004).

62. Lionel Cliffe "African Renaissance?," 40–59 in *Africa in Crisis: New Challenges and Possibilities*, Tunde Zack-Williams, Diane Frost and Alex Thomson, eds. (London: Pluto Press, 2004), 55.

63. African Rights press release, January 23, 2003.

64. Kiwuwa, "Slouching Towards Democracy."

65. *Independent*, 4 July 2004.

66. Michel Chossudovsky, *The Globalisation of Poverty: Impacts of IMF and World Bank Reforms* (London: Zed Books, 1997).

67. *Independent*, 4 July 2004.

68. *Independent*, 4 July 2004.

69. Rudi Doom "Changing Identities, Violent Conflict and the World System," 15–91 in *Politics of Identity and Economics of Conflict in the Great Lakes Region*, Ruddy Doom and Jan Gorus, eds. (Brussels, VUB University Press, 2000), 41.

70. Georges Nzongola Ntalaja, *The Congo: From Leopold to Kabila, A People's History* (London, Zed Press, 2003), 227.

71. Department for International Development (DFID), *Rwanda Country Assistance Plan* (London, DFID, May 2003) 6.

72. Alison des Forges, talk on post-genocide justice and the history of the genocide, at Oxford University Conference, 15 May 2004; Andy Storey, "Ethnic Scapegoating"; Department for International Development, *Rwanda Country Assistance Plan.*

73. Juliet Hausermann, *A Human Rights Approach to Development* (London, Rights and Humanity, 1998), 24.

74. UNDP "Human Development indicators 2003: Rwanda" in *Human Development Report* <http://undp.org/hdr2003/indicator/cty_f_RWA.html>.

75. Oswaldo de Rivero, *The Myth of Development: Non-viable Economies of the Twenty First Century* (London-Dhaka-Bangkok-Cape Town, Zed Books/University Press/Fernwood/White Lotus/David Philip/Books for Change, 2001), 144–5, 168.

76. Peter Uvin, *Aiding Violence: the Development Enterprise in Rwanda* (West Hartford, CT, Kumarian, 1998); Montagu, Man's Most Dangerous Myth, 77; Guardian, 7.4.2004.

77. *Guardian*, 4 July 2004.

78. De Rivero, *The Myth of Development*, 147.

79. David Waller, *Rwanda: Which Way Now?* (Oxford, Oxfam Country Profile, Oxfam Publications, 1993); Reyntjens, "Rwanda: Ten Years On."

80. Catherine Andre & Jean-Philippe Platteau "Land Relations under unbearable Sstress: Rwanda Caught in the Malthusian Trap," *Journal of Economic Behaviour & Organisation* 34, no. 2 (Spring 1998): 1–47.

81. Johan Pottier, "Reporting on the 'New' Rwanda: the Rise and Cost of Political Correctness, with reference to Kibeho," in *Politics of Identity and Economics of Conflict in the Great Lakes Region*, ed. Ruddy Doom and Jan Gorus (Brussels: VUB, 2000), 122.

82. Pottier, *Re-imagining Rwanda*, 179–201; Mathijs Van Leeuwen, "Rwanda's Imidugu programme and earlier experiences with villagisation," *Journal of Modern African Studies* 39, no. 4: 623–44.

83. Turshen, "The Political Economy of Rape."

84. Emmanuel Gasana, Jean-Bosco Butera, Deo Byanafashe and Alice Kariekezi "Rwanda," 141–73 in *Comprehending and Mastering African Conflicts: the Search for Sustainable Peace and Good Governance*, ed. Adebayo Adedeji (London: Zed Books, 1999), 167.

85. Van Leeuwen, "Rwanda's Imidugu Programme."

86. Pottier, *Re-Imagining Rwanda*, 87.

87. Van Leeuwen "Rwanda's Imidugu Programme."

88. Pottier, *Re-Imagining Rwanda*, 88; Van Leeuwen "Rwanda's Imudugu Programme."

89. Gasana, "Rwanda," 168.

90 African Rights, *Rwanda The Insurgency in the Northwest* (London, African Rights, 1998); Nigel Eltringham and Saskia Van Hoyweghen "Power and Identity in Post-Genocide Rwanda," in *Politics of Identity and Economics of Conflict*, Doom, 237.

91. Michael Dorsey, "Violence and power-building in post-genocide Rwanda," 311–48 in *Politics of Identity and Economics of Conflict*, 322.

92. Shigetsugu Komine, "Towards National Reconciliation in Rwanda: the Challenge to a Japanese NGO," in *Conflict and Ethnicity in Central Africa*, ed. Didier Goyvaerts (Tokyo, Tokyo University of Foreign Studies, 2000), 263–86.

93. Van Hoyweghen "The Rwandan Villagisation Programme," 213–4.

94. Komine, "Towards National Reconciliation in Rwanda," 265; Van Leeuwen, "Rwanda's Imidugu Programme," 639.

95. Gasana, "Rwanda", 168.

96. Gourevitch, *We Write to Inform You*, 34.

97. Eltringham and Van Hoyweghen, "Power and Identity in Post-Genocide Rwanda."

98. Eltringham and Van Hoyweghen, "Power and Identity in Post-Genocide Rwanda," 236.

99. Van Hoyweghen "The Rwandan Villagisation Programme."

100. DFID, *Rwanda Country Assistance Plan*, 13.

101. DFID, *Rwanda Country Assistance Plan*, 14.

102. Turshen, "The Political Economy of Rape," 62.

103. Turshen, "The Political Economy of Rape," 60.

104. Turshen, "The Political Economy of Rape," 66; Pottier, *Re-Imagining Rwanda*, 190–2.

105. Pottier, "Reporting on the new Rwanda," 133.

106. Turshen, "The Political Economy of Rape," 63.

107. Marshall Wolfe, *Elusive Development* (London: Zed Books, 1996), 45.

108. de Rivero, *The Myth of Development*, 145.

109. Reyntjens, "Rwanda Ten Years On," 210.

110. Mamdani, *When Victims Become Killers*, 263. The importance of a rights-based approach is formally recognised by most of the major international donors, including even the World Bank, most recently. The importance of economic and social rights alongside civil and political rights is now fully acknowledged by DFID, for instance, and officially by the Rwandan government as well.

111. Suzanne Buckley-Zistel, "Between Past and Future: An Assessment of the Transition from Conflict to Peace in Post-Genocide Rwanda" (paper presented at Oxford University Conference on Rwanda, 15 May 2004).

112. Pottier, *Re-Imagining Rwanda*, 207.

113. Christopher Taylor, *Sacrifice as Terror: The Rwandan Genocide of 1994* (Oxford: Berg, 1999), 177.

114. Nzongola-Ntalaja, *The Congo: From Leopold to Kabila*, 264.

115. Doom, "Changing Identities, Violent Conflict," 83.

116. Government of Rwanda, <http://www.rwanda1.com/government>.

117. Fergal Keane, *Season of Blood: a Rwandan Journey* (Harmondsworth: Penguin, 1996), 118–9.

118. Rita Abrahamsen, "African Studies and the Postcolonial Challenge," *African Affairs* 102, no. 407 (April 2003): 189–210, 207.

119. Hintjens, "When Identity Becomes a Knife"; Mamdani, *When Victims Become Killers*, 20, 261; Linda Melvern, *Conspiracy to Murder: the Rwandan Genocide* (London: Verso, 2004); Linda Melvern, *A People Betrayed: the role of the West in Rwanda's Genocide* (London: Zed Press, 2000), 261.

120. Giles Mohan and Jeremy Holland, "Human Rights and Development in Africa: Moral Intrusion or Empowering Opportunity?" *Review of African Political Economy* 28, no. 88 (June 2001): 100, 177–96.

Chapter 4

The Hutu-Tutsi Conflict in Rwanda

Paul J. Magnarella

Editor's Introduction

The author begins this article with a discussion of significant events and socio-political relationships in Rwandan history leading up to the 1994 mass murder and genocide. He offers an explanation of these crimes based on an analysis of certain ecological, economic, cultural, and political factors peculiar to Rwanda, but shared to an important extent by much of East Africa. He divides the causes into ultimate and proximate, and argues that ultimate causes of the mass murder of Hutu and genocide of Tutsi had less to do with ethnicity than with the increasing imbalance in land, food, and people that led to malnutrition, hunger, periodic famine, fierce competition for land to farm, and periodic massacres and wars. The proximate causes included the policies of the ruling elite. Rwanda's leaders refused to employ the kinds of demographic and economic policies that would have addressed these problems in a peaceful and more effective way. Instead, they responded to these conditions by employing the weapons of indoctrination and coercion to convince the Hutu masses that eliminating the Tutsi portion of the population was the right strategy.

Introduction

In 1994 Rwanda erupted into one of the most appalling cases of mass murder the world had witnessed since World War II. The killings fell into three
categories: (1) combatants killing combatants; (2) Hutu citizens, military and
paramilitary killing Hutu citizens because the victims were either moderates
willing to live and work with Tutsi or persons whose land and wealth the murderers wanted to appropriate; and (3) Hutu killing Tutsi because they were Tutsi.
Of these, the second was mass murder; the third amounted to genocide.[1] Since
these are the most aberrant of human behaviors, they cry out for explanation. In
this chapter I offer an analysis and explanation that involves the consideration of
those ecological, historic, economic, cultural and political factors that I believe
contributed significantly to the mass murder of Hutu and the genocide of Tutsi.

Rwanda: The Place

Rwanda, the landlocked "land of a thousand hills," consists of only 26,340
square kilometers, making it one of Africa's smallest countries. Rwanda's terrain is dominated by mountain ranges (in the west), hills, and highland plateaus.
Throughout the twentieth century, Rwanda's people have placed tremendous
pressure on the land. As early as 1983, when Rwanda's population reached 5.5
million, expert observers writing for the Economist Intelligence Unit noted that,
"with the population increasing at an average annual rate of 3.7 per cent, in a
country with the highest population density in Africa, the authorities are worried
that it will be impossible to increase food sufficiently."[2] At the time, an estimated 95 per cent of the gainfully employed populations were engaged in agriculture.[3] By 1993, one year before the genocide, the population had climbed to
7.7 million without any substantial improvement in agricultural output. To the
contrary, food production had been seriously hampered by periodic drought,
overgrazing, soil exhaustion and soil erosion.

Rwanda's Pre-Colonial Era

The history of Rwanda prior to German penetration in the late nineteenth
century is not well known. One of the first Europeans to explore Rwanda was
Count G.A. von Gotzen, a member of an 1894 German scientific-military expedition.[4] Historians believe the area's first known inhabitants were a pygmoid
people, the hunting-gathering ancestors of the present-day Twa. Around 1,000
AD, Bantu-speaking Hutu horticulturists arrived, probably from the east, and
began clearing and settling the hills. Physically, they resembled other Bantu-
speakers of central Africa. Their language—Kinyarwanda, a branch of the Ni-

ger-Congo subfamily—eventually became the idiom of Rwanda. Hutu became the dominant population, far outnumbering the Twa with whom they bartered agricultural goods for forest products.

Between the eleventh and fifteenth centuries the Tutsi, a pastoral people with long-horned cattle, moved into the region, probably from southern Ethiopia where other pastoralists such as the Oromo resided. Typical of cattle pastoralists, Tutsi men were armed and accustomed to fighting to protect their herds against raiders and to raid for cattle and village goods themselves. Being more aggressive and better organized for military purposes than were the Hutu farmers, the Tutsi eventually conquered central Rwanda and established their rule there. According to Maquet, "Tutsi came into Ruanda as conquerors.... They wanted to settle in the country and they built a permanent system of economic and political relations with the Hutu whereby they established themselves definitely as masters and exploiters.... [A] caste society evolved from their will to stabilize the conquest."[5]

During the reign of Tutsi warrior King (mwami) Kigeri Rwabugiri (1860–1895), the Tutsi conquered and firmly established central control over much, but not all, of Rwanda, despite the fact that they represented only about 10 per cent to 14 per cent of a population that was over 80 per cent Hutu. Importantly, a number of Hutu principalities in the north, northwest and southwest remained independent until the late nineteenth and early twentieth centuries.[6] The Tutsi dominated the Hutu and Twa militarily, politically, and economically. According to their common religion, the Tutsi king was a divine and absolute monarch.[7]

Theoretically, the king owned all the land and livestock; subjects held usufruct rights.[8] Succession to property rights was mainly patrilineal, but the king could and did dispossess subjects of all their property if they displeased or opposed him. King Rwabugiri's rule was harsh and his taxes were heavy. Royal tribute was collected by a group of land chiefs, cattle chiefs, and hill chiefs, who served the king. All cattle chiefs and most land chiefs were Tutsi; Hutu and Twa could serve as hill chiefs.[9] "The dominance of cattle as a form of disposable wealth meant that cattle chiefs—all of them by definition Tutsi—were able to dominate most of Rwanda. To mobilize an army required capital, which came only in the form of livestock, and the Tutsi controlled the cattle."[10]

In some cases Tutsi royalty ennobled or elevated politically and economically successful Hutu and Twa to the rank of Tutsi. Mbanda writes that "a Hutu who gained status through wealth or by becoming a chief could become a Tutsi through a ritual of Kwihutura—literally, a cleansing of one's Hutuness.... [I]f a Tutsi lost his cattle and turned to farming for a living and married into a Hutu family, that person could become a Hutu."[11] No scholar, however, has been able to offer reliable statistics of these kinds of social transformations. Maquet maintains that "the number of Hutu and Twa assimilated to Tutsi because of the holding of political offices or because of wealth has always been tiny.... There was no egalitarian ideology.... Cases of intercaste mobility were extremely rare in

Rwanda."[12]

Some modern historians stress that during the pre-colonial period there were no Tutsi-Hutu conflicts as such.[13] Tutsi and Hutu lived intermingled on the same hills and formed alliances against other groups of allied Hutu and Tutsi. It is important to remember, however, that during the strict reign of Tutsi King Rwabugiri, most of the king's agents were Tutsi and the vast majority of those who suffered were Hutu. Consequently, it is highly probable that many Rwandans believed an effective political cleavage between Tutsi and Hutu did exist.

The Tutsi aristocracy ruled by force, and the army was its main instrument of power. Only Tutsi males were specially trained to be warriors.[14] Hutu and Twa fought also or acted as auxiliaries who carried supplies, but they did not receive the special Tutsi warrior education. As part of their training, young Tutsi warriors were indoctrinated with an ideology of Tutsi superiority. Their status, military training, and ideology set them apart from non-Tutsi.

Wealthy Tutsi owned large herds of cattle and extensive tracts of land that they had expropriated from the Hutu. By the late nineteenth century many Hutu were experiencing a crippling land crisis and abject poverty.[15] As their population grew, increasing numbers of Hutu had insufficient land or none at all. In order to survive they entered into feudal patron-client relations with Tutsi. *Uburetwa* (corvée labor service and offerings of beer in return for access to land) became a principal means of Hutu subjugation. All poor Hutu were bound by *uburetwa*, but Tutsi were exempt.[16] For the Hutu, *uburetwa* became the most hated of the feudal contracts.[17]

Another feudal contract, the *ubuhake*, could be initiated by a poor man who approached a rich Tutsi and ritually asked for milk or acceptance as the Tutsi's child. If the Tutsi agreed, he granted the poor man, usually a Hutu, protection and usufruct rights over one or more head of cattle. In return, the client or vassal Hutu provided a variety of services to his patron or lord, including cultivating his fields, repairing his huts, and possibly providing him with wives or daughters as concubines.[18] In 1950–51, elderly Tutsi informants told Maquet that by giving one or two cows to a Hutu, "he becomes our client (*mugaragu*) and then has to do, to a large extent, what we ask of him."[19]

Given the prevalence of protein-poor diets among the Hutu and the frequent occurrence of drought and famine, they desperately needed access to Tutsi land, milk and the meat from bulls and barren cows. The penalty for stealing cattle was a brutally painful death by impalement. Hence, safe access to cattle was through service contacts with rich and powerful Tutsi, who needed Hutu servants to work their land since they regarded farm labor as degrading.

During the nineteenth century, Tutsi, Hutu, and Twa corresponded roughly to occupational categories. The socioeconomic and political division appeared so rigid to some Western scholars that they referred to it as a caste system. For example, the American anthropologist Helen Codere writes:

Occupational specialization, cultural differences and endogamy justify the use of the term 'caste' for each of these three groups. The Hutu agriculturists also did all manner of menial services for the Tutsi; the Tutsi monopolized all administrative positions and were warriors as well as being pastoralists. The Twa were hunters or potters but in addition they performed a number of special services for the Tutsi: royal dancers and choreographers, musicians, torturers and executioners, pimps, commando raiders, messengers and jesters. Marriages between members of each caste were extremely rare.[20]

A number of modern scholars and early explorers have commented on the physical differences between these three peoples. For example, anthropologist Codere writes that "although there has been sufficient intermixture to blur racial lines, the majority of each caste is racially [sic.] distinct. In stature, for example, the differences are striking: the average stature of the Tutsi is 1 m. 75; the Hutu 1 m. 66; and the Twa 1 m. 55."[21] Unfortunately, Codere does not reveal the source, time, or sample size of her data. Of the Tutsi, Lemarchand writes that "physical features suggest obvious ethnic affinities with the Galla tribes of southern Ethiopia."[22] Duke Frederick of Mecklenburg, who traveled through Central Africa in 1907–08, writes:

> The Watussi [i.e., Tutsi] are a tall, well-made people with an almost ideal physique. Heights of 1.80, 2.00, and even 2.20 meters (from 5 ft. 11 1/2 in. to 7 ft. 2 1/2 in.) are of quite common occurrence.... their bronze-brown skin reminds one of the inhabitants of the more hilly parts of northern Africa.... Unmistakable evidences of a foreign strain are betrayed in their high foreheads, the curve of their nostrils, and the fine oval shape of their faces.[23]

His measurements most probably apply only to full grown Tutsi men. By contrast, he described the Twa as a pygmy tribe and the Hutu as a people of medium size "whose ungainly figures betoken hard toil."[24]

Despite the caste or rigid class structure, there was some genetic mixing among these people as a result of intermarriage and concubineage. Maquet maintains that Tutsi fathers gave their unmarried sons the wives and daughters of Hutu clients as concubines. He also writes that Tutsi wives did not accompany their husbands on trips. Instead their husbands took concubines, probably the women of Hutu clients.[25]

National statistics on intermarriage rates are unavailable. In July 1995 when Mamdani visited Ntarama, a *secteur* in Rwanda near the Burundi border, a local resident told him that prior to the genocide about one-third of Tutsi women had been married to Hutu, whereas only about one per cent of Hutu women had been married to Tutsi. The local explained that because of the discrimination against Tutsi, Hutu (in this community of about 3,500 Hutu and 1,500 Tutsi) were very reluctant to give their daughters to Tutsi in marriage, while many Tutsi parents believed their daughters would have better opportunities if they married Hutu. However, he said that once the genocide began, the administration, "forced Hutu men to kill their Tutsi wives...."[26]

Tutsi notions of superior worth were reflected in the laws they imposed on the parts of Rwanda they controlled. For example, although cattle theft was generally prohibited, a Tutsi could steal cattle from a Hutu with impunity so long as the Hutu had no Tutsi lord or patron to protect him.[27] Murder was also generally prohibited, but the penalty for it varied with the classes of the parties. If an ordinary Tutsi murdered a Hutu, the king might authorize the retaliatory killing of one of the murderer's kinsman; if a Hutu murdered a Tutsi, the king would order the killing of two of the murderer's kinsmen.[28]

Rwanda was not a land of social harmony and equality prior to European colonization. Based on his review of the historical evidence, Pottier writes that "ethnic divisions (and 'obvious hatred' toward the Tutsi overlords, according to Grogan and Sharp) were well entrenched by 1898, the time the Germans began to colonise Rwanda."[29]

Pre-Colonial Rwandan Culture

The Hutu, Tutsi and Twa each possessed their own unique cultural segments of a larger multi-cultural system. Their shared religion both socially integrated and culturally differentiated them. For example, one common version of the Rwandan origin myth goes as follows: Imana, the maker, created Kazikamuntu—the common ancestor of all humans. Three of Kazikamuntu's children—Gatutsi, Gahutu and Gatwa—became the ancestors of the Tutsi, Hutu, and Twa. Kazikamuntu cursed Gatwa because he had killed one of his brothers. Kazikamuntu originally had chosen Gahutu to be his successor, but because Gahutu fell asleep at an inappropriate time and failed to perform an assigned task, Kazikamuntu turned to Gatutsi, who accomplished the task with sobriety and cleverness. Consequently, Kazikamuntu chose Gatutsi to be the chief of his brothers.[30]

Another myth explains the origins of the Tutsi and Twa differently. It has the Tutsi coming to Rwanda from heaven with a Twa servant. In Rwanda the servant mates with a forest ape, and their offspring become the ancestors of modern Twa—a people many Tutsi regarded as sub-human.[31] Lemarchand writes that from the Rwandan legends of the time "the Tutsi emerged as Imana's elect, endowed with superior military skill, extraordinary courage, great wealth and commensurate intelligence."[32]

The customary and preferred diets, or food cultures, of the three peoples also differed. Tutsi preferred dairy products over all else. They also consumed beef and agricultural products, but "milk [was] the beverage of the high caste. It was considered a complete food, and true Batutsi were said to live on milk alone."[33] Hutu generally had poorer diets. While most consumed mainly agricultural products, those with a *ubuhake* contract had access to limited amounts of milk and meat. Twa ate game meat and traded for agricultural and dairy products. Even leisure-time culture also varied among the three. As a result of their exclusive military training and ideological indoctrination, Tutsi men belonged to a fraternity closed to others. Maquet explains: "[Tutsi] boys at an early age begin their military training which gives them a complete education in the skills, knowledge, and virtues pertaining to their noble condition. This training is given to them as *intore* (chosen ones) at the royal court or at the court of an important chief."[34]

A set of 'caste stereotypes' reinforced the social, economic, and political stratification of Rwandan society. Maquet writes that many Rwandan folktales contained the following characterizations: "Batutsi are intelligent (in the sense of political intrigues), apt to command, refined, courageous, and cruel. Bahutu are hard-working, not very clever, extrovert, irascible, unmannerly, obedient, physically strong. Batwa are gluttonous, loyal to their Batutsi masters, lazy, courageous when hunting, lacking in restraint."[35] Maquet claims that the Banyarwanda considered the above qualities to be "innate, not acquired. A Mututsi is born clever and a Muhutu impulsive.... Inferiority and superiority are due not to personal qualities but to membership of certain groups."[36]

German and Belgian Rule

From 1894 until the end of World War I, Rwanda, along with Burundi (similar in population size and "ethnic" composition to Rwanda) and present-day Tanzania was part of German East Africa. Belgium claimed it thereafter, and in 1924 Belgium became the administering authority under the League of Nations mandate system. Belgium ruled Rwanda and Burundi (then called the Territory of Ruanda-Urundi) as a single administrative trusteeship until 1962. By then, the two countries had evolved different political systems. Hutu political leaders declared Rwanda a republic in January 1961 and forced the Tutsi monarch, Kigeri, into exile. Burundi, by contrast, remained a constitutional monarchy until 1966.

During their colonial tenure, the Germans chose to rule Rwanda indirectly through the existing Tutsi monarch (*mwami*) and his chiefs. This had the effect of continuing the "pre-colonial transformation towards more centralisation, annexation of the Hutu principalities and increase in Tutsi chiefly power."[37] "Mutually advantageous relations were the result: the Germans used [Tutsi king] Musinga to establish their authority in the northwest of the colony; Musinga used the Germans to strengthen his own position in Ruanda."[38] The principal means by which the Germans maintained authority was the often brutal punitive expedition.

The early Europeans were generally impressed with the ruling Tutsi. Reasoning from the premises of Social Darwinism, an evolutionary theory prevalent in Europe at the time, many Europeans believed that Tutsi political and economic success evinced their superior fitness in the struggle for survival. Because the Tutsi ruled over the Hutu and Twa, Europeans concluded that they were indeed, like the colonialists themselves, a people superior to common Africans. In fact, some Europeans concluded, the Tutsi were not really sub-Saharan Africans at all, but rather a Hamitic people, probably descendants of the ancient Egyptians. Hence, the colonialists developed the "Hamitic myth" or "hypothesis" which held that the Tutsi and everything humanly superior in Central Africa came from ancient Egypt or Abyssinia. The Europeans made it known to the people of Ruanda-Urundi that they regarded Hutu and Twa as inferior to Tutsi. Prunier writes that sixty years of such prejudicial fabrications "ended by inflating the Tutsi cultural ego inordinately and crushing Hutu feelings until they coalesced into an aggressively resentful inferiority complex."[39] The hypothesis had the consequence, according to Mamdani, of racializing Tutsi identity, establishing Tutsi as foreign settlers and Hutu as natives.[40] The Hutu revolution of 1959 built on and reinforced these identities.

The Belgians initially favored the Tutsi over the Hutu even more than the Germans had. Belgian administrators replaced Hutu chiefs with Tutsi. The replacement policy was so extensive that by 1959, 43 out of 45 chiefs and 549 of 559 sub-chiefs were Tutsi.[41] In addition, "83 per cent of posts in such areas as the judiciary, agriculture and veterinary services" were held by Tutsi.[42]

Initially Christian missionaries spread their religion to the more receptive Hutu, since the Tutsi king and aristocracy rejected it. Christian theology had the effect of discrediting the indigenous belief in the Tutsi king's divine nature; it also prohibited polygyny, a practice common among rich Tutsi and Hutu. By contrast, poor and marginal Hutu regarded the European churches as their new, protective patrons. By 1930, however, some of the Tutsi realized that to remain part of the elite in a Rwanda dominated by Christian Belgians, they, too, had to convert. The process of Tutsi conversion accelerated after 1931 when the Belgians deposed King Yuhi Musinga and replaced him with his son who converted to Christianity.[43] Henceforth, the Christian schools, both Catholic and Protestant, had much larger Tutsi than Hutu enrollments.

In order to profit from their colonial investment, the Belgians instituted a number of agricultural and infrastructural projects (e.g. coffee cultivation, terracing, road building and maintenance, construction of railway lines, etc.) that required a huge amount of cheap or free native labor. Hence, they redesigned the traditional corvée system so that every man had to contribute time and energy to government-designated projects. Those who failed to meet government expectations were often brutally beaten by enforcers appointed by local Tutsi chiefs.[44]

The people grew to hate the forced labor requirement, the brutal punishments and the government functionaries (usually Tutsi) who applied them. "Nothing so vividly defined the divide [between Tutsi and Hutu] as the Belgian regime of forced labor, which required armies of Hutus to toil en masse as plantation chattel, on road construction, and in forestry crews, and placed Tutsis over them as taskmasters."[45] The Tutsi compradors directed the corvée laborers with whips. If the Tutsi supervisors did not get the job done, their white colonial masters whipped and replaced them. Corvée work demands were so great that they could consume 50 per cent to 60 per cent of a native's time.[46] This huge amount of labor, having been forcibly diverted from the production of food, most probably contributed to the famine of 1940–1945. Due to the brutal Belgian regime, land shortages, and famine, "hundreds of thousands of Hutus and impoverished rural Tutsis fled north to Uganda and west to the Congo to seek their fortunes as itinerant agricultural laborers."[47]

During 1933–34 the Belgians conducted a census and introduced an identity card system that indicated the Tutsi, Hutu, or Twa "ethnicity" (*ubwoko* in Kinyarwanda and *ethnie* in French) of each person. Most writers on the subject, trace the recent Hutu-Tutsi distinction to the Belgians' use of the 10-cow rule for the 1933–34 census and identity cards. Supposedly, any male who owned 10 cows was classified as a Tutsi; those with fewer than 10 cows were classified as Hutu. No explanation for Twa is usually given. Relying on a doctoral dissertation by Tharcisse Gatwa, Mamdani writes that the Belgians actually used three major sources of information for their census classification: "oral information provided by the church, physical measurements, and ownership of large herds of cows."[48] "The fact is," writes Mamdani, "that the Belgian power did not arbitrarily cook up the Hutu/Tutsi distinction. What it did do was to take an existing sociopolitical distinction and racialize it."[49] "The origin of the violence," Mamdani maintains, "is connected to how Hutu and Tutsi were constructed as political identities by the colonial state, Hutu as indigenous and Tutsi as alien."[50] The census determined 85 per cent of the population was Hutu, 14 per cent Tutsi, and one per cent Twa.

The identity card "ethnicity" of future generations was determined patrilineally; all persons were designated as having the "ethnicity" of their fathers, regardless of the "ethnicity" of their mothers. This practice, which was carried on until its abolition by the 1994 post-genocide government, had the unfortunate consequence of firmly attaching a sub-national identity to all Rwandans and thereby rigidly dividing them into categories, which, for many people, carried a negative history of dominance-subordination, superiority-inferiority, and exploitation-suffering. In their Hutu Manifesto of 1957 (discussed below), Hutu leaders referred to the identity card categories as "races," thereby evincing how inflexible these labels had become in their minds.

Move to Independence

Belgium altered its policy of discrimination in the late 1950s to favor the Hutu. Foreseeing the inevitable dominance of the Hutu majority, Belgian colonial administrators sided with them, claiming to promote a democratic revolution. In 1957, a group of nine Hutu intellectuals had published the so-called

"Hutu Manifesto," which complained of the political, economic, and educational monopoly of the Tutsi "race" and characterized the Tutsi as foreign invaders. The Manifesto called for promoting Hutu in all fields and argued for the maintenance of "ethnic" identity cards so as to monitor the race monopoly.[51] Tutsi royalty rejected the Manifesto and blamed colonial administrators for any interethnic problems. The monarchists also advocated "the eviction of the trust authorities at the earliest possible date, so as to reassert their control over the destinies of the country."[52]

Political activists formed a series of pro-Tutsi, pro-Hutu, and integrationist parties. "But the political struggle in Rwanda was never really a quest for equality; the issue was only who would dominate the ethnically bipolar state."[53] In November 1959, the pro-Hutu PARMEHUTU party led a revolt that resulted in bloody ethnic clashes and the toppling of King Kigri V. Beginning in 1960, the colonial administrators began replacing Tutsi chiefs with Hutu, who immediately led persecution campaigns against the Tutsi living on those hills the Hutu controlled. By 1963, these and other Hutu attacks had resulted in thousands of Tutsi deaths and the flight of about 130,000 Tutsi to neighboring countries, with 50,000 going to Burundi.[54] The land and cattle that the fleeing Tutsi left behind were quickly claimed by land-hungry Hutu.

Belgian authorities organized communal elections in mid-1960. The PARMEHUTU and other pro-Hutu parties won the vast majority of posts. Of 229 mayoral (*bourgmestre*) positions, only 19 were Tutsi, and 160 were PARMEHUTU.[55] As a result of the national election held under UN supervision in 1961, Gregoire Kayibanda (an author of the 'Hutu Manifesto') became Rwanda's president-designate. Kayibanda, the son of Hutu farmers, had studied for the priesthood at a Catholic seminary and had been employed as a secretary by a Belgian bishop. By 1960, he had become a leader of the PARMEHUTU. For him and many other Hutu, neither Christian ethics nor marital ties with Tutsi were deterrents to presiding over or engaging in vicious attacks on Tutsi.[56]

As a result of a referendum, Rwanda was declared independent on 1 July 1962. President Kayibanda soon established a style of rule that resembled that of the traditional Tutsi kings. He became remote, secretive, and authoritarian. His demand for "unquestioning obedience was to play a tragic and absolutely central role in the unfolding of the 1994 genocide."[57]

Supported by the Tutsi-dominated government in Burundi, Rwandan Tutsi refugees there began launching unsuccessful attacks into Rwanda. These invasions were usually followed by brutal Hutu reprisals against local Tutsi. The Hutu government used a failed 1963 invasion as the pretext "to launch a massive wave of repression in which an estimated 10,000 Tutsi were slaughtered between December 1963 and January 1964. All surviving Tutsi politicians still living in Rwanda were executed."[58] Lemarchand writes the following about this period:

The recent history of Rwanda is punctuated with countless examples of bloodshed and violence; but there are no precedents for the appalling brutality employed after independence by some Hutu officials. In late 1963 and early 1964 thousands of innocent Tutsi were wantonly murdered in what has been described as genocide.... [T]he scale and methods by which it was perpetrated suggest that it can only be regarded as an extreme example of pathological behavior, as the blind reaction of a people traumatized by a deep and lasting sense of inferiority.[59]

The Rwandan situation was exacerbated by events in neighboring Burundi. In the spring of 1972 some Burundian Hutu rebelled against the Tutsi military regime. The regime put down the rebellion and then embarked on a campaign to eliminate educated Burundian Hutu. A genocidal frenzy ensued; about 100,000 Hutu were killed and another 200,000 fled for their lives, many into Rwanda. President Kayibanda capitalized on the situation by eliminating several hundred Rwandan Tutsi in the name of public safety and sending another 100,000 fleeing out of the country as refugees. Consequently, more Tutsi land and cattle were taken over by rural Hutu.

Kayibanda's government had earlier installed an ethnic quota system whereby the proportion of Tutsi in schools, civil service, and other employment sectors was officially limited to nine per cent, their under-estimated proportion of the general population. On occasion, but especially in 1972–73, Hutu "vigilante committees... scrutinised the schools, the University, the civil service and even private businesses to make sure that the ethnic quota policy was being respected. Those eager to carry out this 'purification'...were educated people who could expect to benefit from kicking the Tutsi out of their jobs."[60]

The Second Republic

In July 1973, Major Juvénal Habyarimana, a northern Hutu, overthrew Kayibanda, a southerner, and declared himself president of the Second Republic. Over the next few years, his security forces would eliminate former president Kayibanda and many of his high ranking supporters as part of a plan to eradicate serious Hutu opposition. Habyarimana's kin and regional supporters filled high level positions in the government and security forces. Close relatives of the president and his wife dominated the army, gendarmerie and, especially, the Presidential Guard.

Habyarimana's Rwanda became a single-party dictatorship. His party, the *Mouvement Révolutionnaire National pour le Développement* (MRND), was enshrined in the constitution. He relegated the Tutsi to the private sector. "Throughout the Habyarimana years there would not be a single Tutsi *bourgmestre* or *préfet*, there was only one Tutsi officer in the whole army, there were two Tutsi members of parliament out of seventy and there was only one Tutsi minister out of a cabinet of between twenty-five and thirty members."[61] Regulations prohibited army members from marrying Tutsi. Habyarimana also maintained the 'ethnic' identity card and "ethnic" quota systems of the previous regime.

Up until 1990, when the Tutsi-dominated Rwandan Patriotic Army (RPA) invaded from Uganda, Rwanda's main internal political issue was the north/south divide. "Habyarimana had consistently favored his home region in the north-west. The north received a disproportionate share of resources, and northerners enjoyed better educational opportunities and were over-represented in government and state companies. The leading advocates of change within Rwanda were Hutu from the south, who felt they were entitled to a greater share of the country's resources."[62]

The principal foreign issue confronting Rwanda concerned refugees. By the mid-1980s, the number of Rwandan refugees in neighboring countries has surpassed one-half million. Thousands more were living in Europe and North America. Habyarimana adamantly refused to allow their return, insisting that Rwanda was already too crowded and had too little land, jobs, and food for them.[63] However, the surrounding countries were also poor and had insufficient resources to accommodate both their own citizens and large refugee populations.[64]

Many Rwandan Tutsi refugees in Uganda joined forces with the Ugandan revolutionary Yoweri Museveni, helping him to overthrow the government of Milton Obote in 1986. In the process they received military training, and a few became high-ranking officers in the Ugandan military. Together with some Rwandese Hutu refugees, they formed the Rwandan Patriotic Front (RPF) and committed themselves to return to Rwanda. In 1990–92 RPF troops conducted a number of assaults into Rwanda from Uganda in unsuccessful attempts to seize power. The fighting caused the displacement of hundreds of thousands of people. Habyarimana retaliated by heightening internal repression against Tutsi. His security forces indiscriminately interned and persecuted Tutsi solely because of their ethnic identity, claiming they were actual or potential accomplices of the RPF.[65] From 1990 to 1992 Hutu ultra-nationalists killed an estimated 2,000 Tutsi; they also targeted human rights advocates, regardless of their ethnicities.[66]

The slaughter of Tutsi was not solely the result of RPF threats from the north. Radical indoctrination also played a role. In April 1990, six months before the RPF's October invasion, President Habyarimana attended a Franco-African summit in France. French President François Mitterrand, one of Habyarimana's supporters, advised the Rwandan president to permit multi-party politics. Habyarimana quickly did so, thereby allowing a platform for political groups, such as the Coalition pour la Défense de la République (CDR), that were even more radically pro-Hutu and 'racist' than his own MRND. Hasan Ngeze, a CDR member and Hutu supremacist, became a major preacher of anti-Tutsi hatred. In the sixth issue (December 1990) of his newspaper, Kangura, he vilified the Tutsi in his infamous "Ten Commandments of the Hutu." The most inflammatory and discriminatory of these were the following:

> 1) Every Hutu must know that a Tutsi woman, wherever she may be, is working in the pay of her Tutsi ethnicity. Therefore, a traitor is any Hutu who marries a Tutsi woman, makes a Tutsi his concubine, or makes a Tutsi his secretary or protégé.
> 4) Every Hutu must know that every Tutsi is dishonest in business. He aims only at the supremacy of his ethnicity. Therefore, a traitor is any Hutu: Who makes an alliance with the Tutsi in his business.
> 5) Strategic posts such as political, administrative, economic, military, and security posts must be given to the Hutu only.
> 7) The Armed Forces of Rwanda must be exclusively Hutu. No member of the military should marry a Tutsi.
> 8) The Hutu must stop feeling pity for the Tutsi.
> 9) The Hutu must be firm and vigilant in their enmity against their common Tutsi enemy.[67]

The Ten Commandments circulated widely and became a major anti-Tutsi indoctrination text. "Community leaders across Rwanda regarded them as tantamount to law, and read them aloud at public meetings."[68] The eighth commandment—"The Hutu must stop feeling pity for the Tutsi"—would be invoked mercilessly during the 1994 genocide.

The Arusha Accords

Rwanda's 1990–92 war with the RPF occurred while the country was experiencing a financial and economic crisis. At the urging of the Organization of African Unity and some West European governments, Habyarimana agreed to a series of meetings with RPF representatives in Arusha, Tanzania to negotiate peace and a new governmental plan for Rwanda. Despite strong opposition from the growing right-wing and ultra-racist Hutu Power movement in Rwanda, Habyarimana's government signed a series of agreements with the RPF. These included accords for a cease-fire, a power-sharing government, return of refugees to Rwanda, and integration of the armed forces. In addition to allowing hundreds of thousands of Tutsi to return to Rwanda, the RPF was to constitute 40 per cent of the integrated military forces and 50 per cent of its officer corps. It would also be allotted five ministries (including the important Interior Ministry) in a broad-based government.[69] Habyarimana's own MRND would be allocated only five ministries and eleven MPs in the new 70-member National Assembly. The extremist CDR was to be excluded completely. The presidency would become largely ceremonial. The final accord was signed on 3 August 1993.

Gourevitch correctly notes that for Habyarimana the Arusha Accords amounted to a suicide note. After enjoying exclusive power for twenty years,

Hutu Power leaders could never accept these changes. "They cried treason, and charged that the President himself had become an 'accomplice.'"[70] If the Accords were implemented, many Hutu elitists in government and in the military would lose their privileged positions. Within days of the signing, *Radio Milles Collines*, a new, private station devoted to genocidal propaganda, began broadcasting anti-Accord and anti-Tutsi diatribes from Kigali.

Events in Burundi

Events to the south, in neighboring Burundi, contributed to the call in Rwanda for Hutu power and Tutsi elimination. After nearly thirty years of Tutsi dictatorship in Burundi, the people participated in the country's first free election in July 1993 and chose Hutu Melchior Ndadaye as their president. Ndadaye headed FRODEBU (*Front pour la democracy au Burundi*), a political organization whose roots go back to the 1972 Burundian refugees in Rwanda.[71] "Motivated by a deep hatred for the Tutsi-dominated army [in Burundi] and the 1972 massacre [of Burundian Hutu], the Hutu overwhelmingly voted for FRODEBU" in the 1993 election.[72]

Leaders of FRODEBU immediately urged Hutu citizens to kill any Tutsi they could get their hands on. Four ministers in Ndadaye's cabinet used Radio-Kigali in Rwanda for their genocide message.[73] "Hutu hoodlums took revenge on innocent Tutsi throughout the countryside. Armed with machetes, spears, knives, and clubs, they roamed from village to village and house to house, hacking every Tutsi in sight. Churches and schools were transformed into killing fields."[74] The Tutsi-dominated Burundi army responded by killing Hutu. Altogether, about 50,000 people were murdered, and approximately 375,000 Burundians, mostly Hutu, fled into Rwanda for safety.

Members of Rwanda's Hutu Power movement and President Habyarimana, who had been close to Burundian President Ndadaye, became alarmed by these events. Consequently, they refused to implement the Arusha Accords and integrate refugee Tutsi back into the country. The MNRD and CDR had begun training and indoctrinating anti-Tutsi youth militias, known respectively as the *Interahamwe* ('Those who attack together') and *Impuza-mugambi* ('Those with a single purpose'). They would soon become vicious death squads. Hutu extremists drew up death lists containing the names of prominent Tutsi and Hutu political opponents. Attacks on Tutsi and Hutu who supported the Arusha Accords became commonplace.

Assassination and Genocide

Fearing that the reigning instability in Rwanda would threaten the region, the heads of the surrounding states pressured Habyarimana to honor the Arusha

Accords. During a regional meeting of heads of state in Dar-es-Salaam, Tanzania, President Yoweri Museveni of Uganda and President Ali Hassan Mwinyi of Tanzania appeared to have won a commitment from Habyarimana that he would indeed begin implementing the accords. On 6 April 1994, however, as Habyarimana's presidential plane neared the Kigali Airport on his return from Dar-es-Salam, it was struck by a missile and plunged to earth, killing the president and all aboard.

Although the identity of his assassins is still not generally known, many foreign observers believe Habyarimana was killed by Hutu extremists in his own military, the *Forces Armées Rwandaises* (FAR), a Hutu institution that may have had the most to lose from the Arusha agreements.[75] Only a month before, the Hutu Power publication, *Kangura*, had run the banner headline "Habyarimana will die in March." The same issue carried a "cartoon depicting the President as a Tutsi-loving RPF accomplice."[76]

"Within the hour following the crash, and prior to its official announcement over the radio, Interahamwe militiamen had begun to set up road-blocks in Kigali. During April 6 and 7, the young men checked the identity cards of passers-by, searching for Tutsi, members of opposition parties, and human rights activists. Anyone belonging to these groups was set upon with machetes and iron bars. Their bleeding bodies lined the roads of the city."[77] The Presidential Guard began killing Tutsi civilians in Ramera, a section of Kigali near the airport. *Radio Milles Collines* blamed the RPF and a contingent of UN soldiers for Habyarimana's death and urged revenge against the Tutsi. Extremists in the president's entourage had made up lists of Hutu political opponents, mostly democrats, for the first wave of murders.

> The assassins' first priority was to eliminate Hutu opposition leaders.... After that, the wholesale extermination of Tutsis got underway.... With the encouragement of [radio] messages and leaders at every level of society, the slaughter of Tutsis and the assassination of Hutu oppositionists spread from region to region. Following the militias' example, Hutus young and old rose to the task. Neighbors hacked neighbors to death in their homes, and colleagues hacked colleagues to death in their workplaces. Doctors killed their patients, and schoolteachers killed their pupils. Within days, the Tutsi populations of many villages were all but eliminated.... Radio announcers reminded listeners not to take pity on women and children.[78]

The approximately 1,500-man Presidential Guard (GP) was responsible for the assassination of hundreds of political opponents. The GP itself played a key role in organizing, training and arming the Interahamwe militias.[79] In turn, the Interahamwe recruited and trained Hutu refugees from Burundi, who earned reputations for their extreme brutality.[80] One of the most depressing accounts of the slaughter is the African Rights publication sub-titled *When Women Become Killers*. It describes the general participation in the genocide:

The killings would never have claimed so many lives if the killers had not adopted a strategy to involve as much of the population as possible—men, women and even children as young as eight. The hundred days' genocide was no spontaneous outburst. It followed instructions from the highest levels of the political, military and administrative hierarchies. At an intermediate level, huge numbers of [people from all occupations] were involved, both directly and indirectly.

Some women, including young girls in their teens, were participants in the carnage, hacking other women and children, and sometimes even men, to death. Some of these women joined willingly. Others were forced in the same manner that men were forced.... They participated in massacres and in the murder of their neighbors as well as strangers. They joined the crowds that surrounded churches, hospitals and other places of refuge, wielding machetes, nail-studded clubs and spears.... Above all, women and girls stripped the dead—and the barely living—stealing their jewelry, money and clothes.[81]

The organizers of the massacres wanted to create a new Rwanda, a community of murderers, who shared a collective sense of accomplishment or guilt. The new Rwandans would undergo an initiation rite by killing their former neighbors. In the process, they would take on a new identity and shared responsibility for the killings. What would have been crimes under ordinary circumstances became expected and common behavior.

The extremists exhorted the Interahamwe and ordinary Hutu to kill Tutsi and "eat their cows." The later phrase had both symbolic and practical significance. Symbolic, because historically Tutsi supremacy had been built on cattle ownership. "Eating their cows" meant devouring the basis of Tutsi past dominance. Practical, because it also meant looting Tutsi homes, farms, offices, business, churches, and so on. "Theft was one of the principal weapons used to bribe people into betraying and killing their neighbors."[82] Some Hutu leaders urged their followers "to send the Tutsi back to their country of origin, Ethiopia, by the quickest route, via the Akanyaru River."[83] Consequently some northerly flowing rivers were filled with the dead. People in Uganda recovered about 40,000 bodies from Lake Victoria and buried them.[84]

The murderers were not content with simply killing Tutsi and Hutu rivals, they expended a great deal of time and effort torturing and mutilating their victims. The murderers enjoyed watching the suffering and agony. They hacked off Tutsi penises as if to disempower their historic rulers. Some victims were burnt alive. Rape was used extensively, even against wounded women. The psychological need to eliminate the Tutsi was so great, that Hutu extremists hunted down and killed the pregnant Hutu wives of Tutsi men, so that their "Tutsi fetuses" would not survive.[85]

RPF troops from the north began fighting their way south in early April in an attempt to stop the slaughter. "But the RPF's advance simply could not match the pace at which the militiamen and soldiers were massacring civilians."[86] The

RPF took Kigali on July 4th and Butare, the second-largest city, on July 5th. By July 18, the RPF had reached the Zairian border, having captured the town of Gisenyi the previous day. Having defeated the Hutu FAR and militias that opposed them, the RPF unilaterally declared a cease-fire.

Within a period of only three months approximately 800,000 Tutsi and between 10,000 to 30,000 Hutu or 11 per cent of the total population had been killed.[87] This Rwandan tragedy may have set an historic record for the largest number of people killed in such a short time. About two million people were uprooted within Rwanda, while the same number of Hutu fled from Rwanda into Tanzania, Burundi, and Zaire. Many were driven out by remnants of FAR and Hutu militias that planned to rearm and organize the refugees into a fighting force that they hoped would reenter Rwanda and finish the job.

The RPF and moderate Hutu political parties formed a new government on 18 July 1994, but the country was in chaos. The government pledged to implement the Arusha peace agreement on power sharing previously reached by Habyarimana's regime and the RPF on 3 August 1993. On 10 August 1995, the UN Security Council called upon the new Rwandan government to ensure that there would be no reprisals against Hutu wishing to return to their homes and resume their work, reminded the government of its responsibility for a national reconciliation, and emphasized that the Arusha Peace Accords constituted an appropriate framework for reconciliation.[88]

The new Rwandan government was a coalition of twenty-two ministers drawn from the RPF (with nine ministers) and four other political parties. Both Tutsi and Hutu were among the top government officials. Pasteur Bizimungu, a Hutu, was named president, while Paul Kagame, a Tutsi, was appointed vicepresident and minister of defense. Faustin Twagiramungu, a Hutu, was prime minister until late August 1995, when he was replaced by Pierre Claver Rwigema, also a Hutu. The government publicly committed itself to building a multiparty democracy and to discontinuing the ethnic classification system utilized by the previous regime.[89]

Causes of Genocide

When analyzing major events in complex political societies, such as states, one fruitful research strategy recommends an initial focus on the material, demographic, and leadership sub-components of infrastructure as potential causal variables.[90] In the case of Rwanda, I argue, the interaction of these infrastructural components led to the genocide.

Rwanda was faced with a critical food-people-land imbalance. In the years leading up to the genocide there had been a marked decline of kilocalories per person per day and overall farm production.[91] Famines occurred in the late 1980s and early 1990s in several parts of the country.[92] Emergency sources of food in neighboring countries also were limited. Seavoy, writing generally about famine in East Africa, notes that "hunger is endemic among all peasant societies in East Africa.... Malnutrition often affects one-third of a village's population."[93]

"In some areas population densities exceeded 400 people per square kilometer—over 1000 per square mile. In many parts of the country, the average family had scarcely half a hectare of land, while increasing amounts of land were being taken over by the wealthy. Youths faced a situation where many (perhaps most) had no land, no jobs, little education, and no hope for a future."[94] Without a house and a source of livelihood, they could not marry.

The previous historical sections of this chapter discuss the political foundations of Hutu-Tutsi distinctions and antagonisms. Important Hutu-Tutsi sociopolitical and cultural distinctions existed prior to the arrival of Europeans. The foreign colonialists attempted to explain these distinctions in terms of the Hamitic hypothesis, which recast the Tutsi as Northerners who were genetically and culturally superior to both the Hutu and Twa. Later, during the Republican periods, the Hutu Power movement further racialized the distinction and charged that the Tutsi were foreign exploiters who should be expelled from Rwanda.

Importantly, while these people may have lived together relatively peacefully prior to the mid-nineteenth century, that was a time when their total population was comparatively low (probably less than two million, versus over seven million in 1993) and land supply for both farming and cattle grazing was ample. With rapid population growth in the twentieth century, the situation changed.[95]

Because of their historically different modes of ecological adaptation—Hutu horticulture and Tutsi cattle pastoralism—within the context of a society over 90 per cent agrarian, a rapidly growing rural population, no significant employment alternatives, and diminishing food production and consumption per capita, the Hutu and Tutsi became natural competitors. Those Tutsi still engaged in cattle pastoralism wanted open ranges to graze their herds. In direct opposition, landless Hutu wanted those very lands, marginal as they may have been for agriculture, to build homesteads on and to farm.

By flight or death of more than half of Rwanda's Tutsi population from the early 1960s to 1973, vast tracts of land in the eastern region were freed up for Hutu settlement and cultivation.[96] The political elites exploited these developments, which appeared to prove that Hutu farmers could have sufficient land if the Tutsi were eliminated. By the mid-1980s population increases had again outstripped the amount of arable land. Farmers' attempts to increase food production by double- and triple-cropping their dwindling plots resulted in soil exhaustion. While foreign experts looked for means of increasing the country's food production potential, they usually had to admit that they are impressed by the relative sophistication of the traditional intensive methods of farming.[97] "Research efforts to-date has not succeeded in developing more than a few varieties of traditional food crops that are more productive and resistant than local varieties."[98] Foreign technical experts could do little to help farmers; the problem was the increasing imbalance of the land: people ratio.

There were few employment alternatives to farming. The country's major employer was the government. In the late 1980s, the central government was employing 7,000 people and the local governments 43,000.[99] By law, only nine per cent of these employees could be Tutsi. Eliminating the Tutsi would open up 4,500 more government jobs for Hutu. Because the country had no social security program, the thousands of unemployed young people who entered the job market each year lived on the very margins of survival.[100] Many became easy subjects for recruitment and manipulation. "In Kigali the *Interahamwe* and the *Impuzamugambi* tended to recruit mostly among the poor. As soon as they went into action, they drew around them a cloud of even poorer people, a *lumpenproletariat* of street boys, rag-pickers, car-washers and homeless unemployed. For these people the genocide was the best thing that could ever happen to them.... They could steal, they could kill with minimum justification, they could rape and they could get drunk for free."[101]

"Before the [1994] war a statistically significant relationship was found between regional variations in the incidence of juvenile delinquency on the one hand and regional variations in per capita availability of calories on the other As a matter of fact, together with population density, the latter variable explained as much as 58 per cent of the regional variations in offences committed by persons between 21 and 15 years old."[102]

"It is not frivolous to conclude that economic desperation, blighting individuals' presents and their perceived futures, was a major contributor to the willingness of many thousands of poor farmers and urban dwellers (a) to fear the possibility of a Tutsi land- and jobs-grab under a victorious RPF regime, (b) to be tempted by more specific hopes for land and jobs, or, more crudely still, to participate in order to grab a share of the victims' property."[103]

As stated above, Habyarimana had adamantly refused to allow Tutsi refugees back into the country, insisting that Rwanda was too small and too crowded to accommodate them. What did ordinary people think about the country's demographics? According to André and Platteau, "It is not rare, even today, to hear Rwandans argue that a war is necessary to wipe out an excess of population and to bring numbers into line with the available land resources."[104] The economists André and Platteau conclude that the "strained situation engendered by economic scarcities goes a long way towards explaining why violence spread so quickly and so devastatingly throughout the countryside."[105]

The human materialist research strategy also recommends taking into account the strategies of Hutu leaders to determine to what extent they contributed to the genocide. In this poor country, regional Hutu elites vied with each other to acquire the economic resources, especially tax revenue and foreign aid that the reins of political power controlled. Their common plan involved marginalizing the educated Tutsi to eliminate any domestic competition from them and demonizing all Tutsi so as to dupe poor Hutu, the vast majority of the population, into believing that the elites protected them and represented their interests. With the Tutsi sidelined, Hutu regional elites competed with each other.

Rwanda's poor economy rests on peasant subsistence agriculture. The governing elite could extract only limited surplus value directly from the peasant masses. In addition to taxes, the governing elite had two other potential sources of enrichment: skimming export revenues and foreign aid. During the late 1980s and early 1990s the three sources of export earnings—coffee, tea, and tin—all declined. According to a UN source, the tin mining company set up by Rwanda's government in 1990 was losing about $5 million a year.[106] The mine itself had been closed in the mid-1980s owing to the collapse of world tin prices.[107] Coffee export receipts declined from $144 million in 1985 to $30 million in 1993.[108] Hence, export revenues declined, government budgets were cut, and the only remaining source of enrichment was foreign aid. Those who could benefit from it had to be in positions of political power. Consequently, elite Hutu engaged in a fierce competition for control of the rapidly shrinking economy.

The 1990–92 war with the RPF contributed further to the devastation of Rwanda's economy. It displaced thousands of farmers in the north, thereby causing reductions in food and coffee production. It closed Rwanda's main land route to Mombasa and the outside world. It destroyed Rwanda's small tourism industry, which had become the third major foreign exchange earner.[109] But, rather than negotiate in earnest with the RPF, Habyarimana chose to increase the size of his armed forces (from 5,000 in 1990 to 30,000 in 1992), thereby diverting scarce resources from needed food imports, health care, and education.

The rule of dominant persons does not depend on political or economic power alone, but on persuading the ruled to accept an ideology that justifies the rulers' privileged positions and convinces the ruled that their best interests are being protected. "Ideas and myths can kill, and their manipulation by elite leaders for their own material benefit does not change the fact that in order to operate they first have to be implanted in the souls of men."[110]

From the 1960s to 1994, the ideology promoted by the Hutu ruling elite was as follows: Tutsi were foreign invaders, who "could not really be considered as citizens.... The Hutu had been the 'native peasants,' enslaved by the aristocratic invaders: they were now the only legitimate inhabitants of the country.... A Hutu-controlled government was now not only automatically legitimate but also ontologically democratic."[111] This political ideology validated both the persecution of Tutsi and the autocratic rule by some elite Hutu.

As for its economic ideology, the government promoted the idea that the Hutu "holy way of life" was farming. It strictly limited rural migration to the city. People could not change their residences without government permission, and that was rarely given.[112] "The myth reigned supreme that Rwanda had its own way to go and this way was largely inspired by agrarian and paternalistic values based on the continuation of tradition, food self-sufficiency and the simplicity of rural life (immune from the corruption of modern cities)."[113]

Consequently, the government made no attempt to significantly diversify the economy so as to create a viable non-agricultural sector or to limit population growth (except by killing and expelling Tutsi). Religious ideology also contributed to the country's deepening demographic problems. The majority of Rwanda's population was Catholic. Despite Rwanda's evident overpopulation, those in the church and government hierarchy not only refused to promote birth control programs, they actively opposed them. Evaluating Rwanda's pro-natal policy and almost exclusive agro-economic strategy, the economists André and Platteau write: "The fact that so few people understood that the path followed by Rwanda was a blind alley still remains something of a mystery."[114]

Conclusion

In short, the *sine qua non* and ultimate cause of the Rwandan genocide was the increasing imbalance in land, food, and people that led to malnutrition, hunger, periodic famine, and fierce competition for land to farm. Too many people were relying on rapidly diminishing amounts of arable land per capita for their subsistence level existences. This situation extended beyond Rwanda's borders to Burundi, Uganda, and Eastern Zaire (Congo). Hunger and malnutrition were endemic among all peasant societies in East Africa. Because of rapid population growth throughout the region, emigration or flight of people from one country to another, the traditional means of alleviating internecine violence over land, only moved the problem from one place to another. Many of those Hutu who periodically fled into Rwanda to avoid death at the hands of Tutsi in Burundi enthusiastically participated in the slaughter of Rwandan Tutsi when the opportunity came. And those Rwandan Tutsi refugees who fled north sometimes clashed violently with Ugandans over land for pasturage, farms and settlements.[115]

Among the proximate causes of the mass murders in Rwanda were:

(1) the Hutu Power ideology in Rwanda, which fanned the flames of hatred of Tutsi by recalling and rewriting the history of Tutsi domination and Hutu subservience;

(2) the characterization of Tutsi as foreign exploiters belonging to a different race;

(3) the practices of a small, corrupt Hutu elite who consolidated the limited wealth available and blamed the Tutsi for the deprivations of the masses;

(4) the Museveni government's perceived need, for political and economic reasons, to evacuate Rwandan refugees from Uganda, and,

(5) the failure or refusal of the Rwandan government to employ the kinds of demographic and economic policies that would have addressed the ultimate causes in a peaceful and more effective way. These policies could have included birth control, economic diversification into non-agrarian sectors, requests for significant foreign food aid, sincere negotiation with the RPF, and attempts at a regional solution to the refugee problem. Rwanda's leaders chose instead to respond to these conditions by eliminating the Tutsi portion of the population. They employed the weapons of indoctrination to convince the Hutu masses that

this strategy was right. These ultimate and proximate causes combined to result in the tragedy of 1994.

Notes

1. According to international law, the mass murder of members of a civilian population for political, racial or religious reasons constitutes "crimes against humanity," while committing acts with the intent to destroy in whole or in part a national, ethnic, racial or religious group constitutes "genocide." See Roy Gutman and David Rieff, eds., *Crimes of War* (New York: W.W. Norton, 1999), 107–108, 153–157. For an explanation of how the International Criminal Tribunal for Rwanda dealt with these concepts, especially with the legal concept of genocide, see Paul J. Magnarella, *Justice in Africa: Rwanda's Genocide, Its Courts, and the UN Criminal Tribunal* (Aldershot, England: Ashgate, 2000), 95–110.

2. Economist Intelligence Unit, *Rwanda Country Report* (1983) No. 4, 18.

3. Economist Intelligence Unit, *Rwanda Country Report* (1983) Annual Supplement, 28.

4. Jacques J. Maquet, "The Kingdom of Ruanda," in *African Worlds*, ed. D. Forde, (London: Oxford University Press, 1954), 185.

5. Jacques J. Maquet, *The Premise of Inequality in Ruanda* (London: Oxford University Press, 1961), 170.

6. Gerard Prunier, *The Rwanda Crisis* (London: Hurst and Co., 1997), 19. See generally Catharine Newbury, *The Cohesion of Oppression* (New York: Columbia University Press, 1988).

7. Maquet, *Premise*, 124.

8. Maquet, *Premise*, 89–91.

9. Maquet, *Premise*, 103–105.

10. African Rights, *Rwanda: Death, Despair, and Defiance* (London: African Rights 1995), 4.

11. Laurent Mbanda, *Committed to Conflict* (London: SPCK, 1997), 4.

12. Maquet, *Premise*, 150.

13. Prunier, *Rwanda Crisis*, 39.

14. Maquet, *Premise*, 118.

15. Johan Pottier, "Representations of Ethnicity in Post-Genocide Writings on Rwanda," in *Ethnic Hatred: Genocide in Rwanda*, ed. O. Igwara (London: ASEN, 1995), 45.

16. Pottier, "Representations of Ethnicity," 43.

17. Pottier, "Representations of Ethnicity," 42.

18. Maquet, *Premise*, 77, 138.

19. Maquet, "The Kingdom of Ruanda," 177. For a more complete discussion of this contract and its variations, see Prunier, *Rwanda Crisis*, 13–14.

20. Helen Codere, "Power in Rwanda," *Anthropologica* 4 (1962) 48.

21. Codere, "Power in Rwanda," 48.

22. Rene Lemarchand, *Rwanda and Burundi* (London, Pall Mall, 1970), 18. Duke Frederick of Mecklenburg, *In the Heart of Africa* (London: Cassel, 1910), 47–48, who traveled through Central Africa in 1907–08 (offering physical descriptions and measurements of Tutsi and stating that 'their bronze-brown skin reminds one of the inhabitants of the more hilly parts of northern Africa ....').

23. Duke Frederick of Mecklenburg, *In the Heart of Africa* (London: Cassel, 1910), 47–48.

24. Mecklenburg, *Heart of Africa*, 47.

25. Maquet, *Premise*, 77–78.

26. Mahmood Mamdani, *When Victims Become Killers* (Princeton: Princeton University Press, 2001), 4.

27. Maquet, "The Kingdom of Ruanda," 185.

28. Maquet, "The Kingdom of Ruanda," 187.

29. Pottier, "Representations of Ethnicity," 39. E. Grogan and A. Sharp, *From The Cape to Cairo: the First Traverse of Africa South to North* (London: Hurst and Blackett, 1900), 19.

30. Maquet, "The Kingdom of Ruanda," 173–74.

31. Maquet, "The Kingdom of Ruanda," 185–86. For another, but similar myth, see Christopher C. Taylor, *Sacrifice as Terror: The Rwandan Genocide of 1994* (Oxford, New York: Berg, 1999), 75.

32. Lemarchand, *Rwanda and Burundi*, 34.

33. Maquet, "The Kingdom of Ruanda," 178.

34. Maquet, "The Kingdom of Ruanda," 177.

35. Maquet, "The Kingdom of Ruanda," 185.

36. Maquet, "The Kingdom of Ruanda," 185.

37. Prunier, *Rwanda Crisis*, 25.

38. W.R. Louis, *Ruanda-Urundi, 1884–1919* (Oxford: Oxford Clarendon Press, 1963), 122.

39. Prunier, *Rwanda Crisis*, 9.

40. Mamdani, *When Victims Become Killers*, 16.

41. Alain Destexhe, *Rwanda and Genocide in the Twentieth Century* (New York: New York University Press, 1995), 40.

42. Dixon Kamukama, *Rwanda Conflict: Its Roots and Regional Implications* (Kampala, Uganda: Fountain Press, 1997), 21.

43. Prunier, *Rwanda Crisis*, 31.

44. Lemarchand, *Rwanda and Burundi*, 123–124.

45. Philip Gourevitch, *We Wish to Inform You That Tomorrow We Will Be Killed with Our Families* (New York, Farrar Straus and Giroux, 1998), 57.

46. Prunier, *Rwanda Crisis*, 35.

47. Gourevitch, *We Wish to Inform You*, 57.

48. Mamdani, *When Victims*, 99.

49. Mamdani, *When Victims*, 99.

50. Mamdani, *When Victims*, 34.

51. Lemarchand, *Rwanda and Burundi*, 149.

52. Lemarchand, *Rwanda and Burundi*, 153.

53. Gourevitch, *We Wish to Inform You*, 58.

54. Prunier, *Rwanda Crisis*, 51, 55.

55. Prunier, *Rwanda Crisis*, 52.

56. Edward L. Nyankanzi, *Genocide: Rwanda and Burundi* (Rochester, VT, Schenkman, 1998), 134.

57. Prunier, *Rwanda Crisis*, 57.

58. Prunier, *Rwanda Crisis*, 56.

59. Lemarchand, *Rwanda and Burundi*, 44.

60. Prunier, *Rwanda Crisis*, 60.
61. Prunier, *Rwanda Crisis*, 75.
62. Guy Vassall-Adams, *Rwanda* (Oxford: Oxfam, 1994), 23.
63. Vassall-Adams, *Rwanda*, 10.
64. Mbanda, *Committed to Conflict*, 74.
65. Villia Jefremovas, "Acts of Human Kindness: Tutsi, Hutu, and the Genocide," *Issue* 23, no. 2 (1995): 29–30; Catharine Newbury, "Background to Genocide in Rwanda," *Issue* 23 no. 2 (1995): 12–14.
66. Newbury, "Background to Genocide," 15.
67. Jean-Pierre Chrétien, *Rwanda: Les Médias du Génocide* (Paris: Karthala, 1995), 39–40.
68. Gourevitch, *We Wish to Inform You*, 88.
69. Prunier, *Rwanda Crisis*, 192–193.
70. Gourevitch, *We Wish to Inform You*, 99.
71. Rene Lemarchand, *Burundi: Ethnic Conflict and Genocide* (Cambridge, Cambridge University Press, 1996), 143.
72. Nyankanzi, *Genocide: Rwanda and Burundi*, 43.
73. Lemarchand, *Burundi*, xv.
74. Nyankanzi, *Genocide: Rwanda and Burundi*, 46.
75. For an excellent discussion of various assassination theories, see Prunier, *Rwanda Crisis*, 213–229. Two of the best books covering the events of 1994 in detail are Alison Des Forges, *Leave None to Tell the Story: Genocide in Rwanda* (London: Human Rights Watch, 1999) and African Rights, Rwanda (1995).
76. Gourevitch, *We Wish to Inform You*, 108.
77. Vassall-Adams, *Rwanda*, 32.
78. Gourevitch, *We Wish to Inform You*, 114–115.
79. African Rights, *Rwanda*, 49.
80. African Rights, *Rwanda*, 63–64.
81. African Rights, *Rwanda: Not So Innocent: When Women Become Killers* (London, 1995), 1–2.
82. African Rights, *Rwanda*, 1002–1003.
83. Rene Lemarchand, "Rwanda: The Rationality of Genocide," *Issue* 23, no. 2 (1995): 62.
84. Prunier, *Rwanda Crisis*, 255.
85. Judgment, Akayesu (ICTR-96-4-T), Trial Chamber I, 2 September 1998, para. 428.
86 Vassall-Adams, *Rwanda*, 37.
87. Prunier, *Rwanda Crisis*, 265.
88. UN Doc. S/PRST/1994/42.
89. Raymond Bonner, "Rwanda's Leaders Vow to Build a Multiparty State for both Hutu and Tutsi," *New York Times* (7 Sept. 1994): A10.
90. The particular research strategy or paradigm employed here is human materialism. Readers interested in a full description of this paradigm are invited to read Paul J. Magnarella, *Human Materialism: A Model of Sociocultural Systems and a Strategy for Analysis* (Gainesville, FL.: University Press of Florida, 1993).
91. Catherine André and Jean-Phillipe Platteau, "Land Relations under Unbearable Stress: Rwanda Caught in the Malthusian Trap," *Journal of Economic Behavior and Organization* 34 (1998): 3.

92. André and Platteau, "Land Relations," 3.

93. Ronald E. Seavoy, *Famine in East Africa: Food Production and Food Policies* (New York: Greenwood, 1989), 85–86.

94. Newbury, "Background to Genocide," 14–15.

95. Here, I do not argue that Rwanda's relatively large and dense population was the only cause of the genocide. I do believe that the relationship among land-population-food availability was the sine qua non and the ultimate cause of the genocide. But for the conditions of that relationship, there would have been no genocide. It would have been impossible for the government, military and Hutu Power movement to motivate so many people in such a short time to kill as many as they did.

96. André and Platteau, "Land Relations," 4.

97. Economist Intelligence Unit, *Rwanda Country Report* 4 (1983): 18.

98. André and Platteau, "Land Relations," 4.

99. Vassall-Adams, *Rwanda*, 12.

100. Vassall-Adams, *Rwanda*, 12.

101. Prunier, *Rwanda Crisis*, 232.

102. André and Platteau, "Land Relations," 37, citing J. Maton, *Développement économique et social au Rwanda entre 1980 et 1993. Le dixiéme décile en face de l'apocalypse*, (University of Gent, Belgium: Department of Economics, 1994): 27–28.

103. André and Platteau, "Land Relations," 38–39, quoting G. Austin, "The Effects of Government Policy on the Ethnic Distribution of Income and Wealth in Rwanda: A Review of Published Sources," *Consultancy Report for the World Bank* (Washington, DC, 1996): 10.

104. André and Platteau, "Land Relations," 40.

105. André and Platteau, "Land Relations," 38.

106. Economist Intelligence Unit, *Rwanda Country Report* 1 (1993): 25.

107. Prunier, *Rwanda Crisis*, 84.

108. André and Platteau, "Land Relations," 3.

109. Vassall-Adams, *Rwanda*, 13, 23.

110. Prunier, *Rwanda Crisis*, 40.

111. Prunier, *Rwanda Crisis*, 80.

112. Prunier, *Rwanda Crisis*, 77.

113. André and Platteau, "Land Relations," 5.

114. André and Platteau, "Land Relations," 5.

115. The literature on regional genocide and mass murder includes: Lemarchand, Burundi: Ethnic Conflict and Genocide; Jean-Pierre Chretien, "Burundi: The Obsession with Genocide," *Current History* (1996): 206–210; H. Adelman and A. Suhrke, eds., *The Path of a Genocide: The Rwanda Crisis from Uganda to Zaire* (New Brunswick, NJ: Transaction Publishers, 1999); G. Nzongola-Ntalaja, "The Congo Holocaust and the Rwanda Genocide," *CODESRIA Bulletin* 2 (1999): 66–70; C.P. Scherrer, *Genocide and Crisis in Central Africa: Conflict Roots, Mass Violence, and Regional War* (Westport, CT: Praeger, 2002).

Introducing the Issue

Religion as a component of ethnic identity is important in dividing as well as integrating groups in conflict-torn societies. Given the intense cross-boundary ethnic linkages, and deep class and ethnic cleavages in the contemporary Indian society, each conflict is interlocked with another in a variety of ways. It is argued here that the Indian state does not behave as an agent of the majority nor is the hegemonic *Hindutva* movement is largely responsible for ethnic riots. Rejecting the arguments of conflict prone thesis of the Indian Marxists and leftists, I claim that conflict is not the inevitable outcome of Hindu-Muslim religious ethnicity. Consciousness of one's ethnic origin and background is not a psycho-sociological reality and certainly is not universal in nature. We need to seek mechanism by which socio-psychological construction happens. All of our ideas are learned but we forget that they are learned, partly because they conform to social arrangements that so dominate our organization of experience that appear to be inevitable. Internalization of ideas involves, not simple imitation, but complex processes of interpretation and deduction. Ideas in conflict situations need to be put to critical appraisals.[1]

Large-scale ethnic violence is an important topic both because of the enormous suffering it causes and because it could be an important piece of evidence in the larger puzzle of how Indian politics are now evolving.

In India, lethal ethnic riots, mostly between the majority Hindus (81%) and the minority Muslims (12%) have in recent years occurred in 4 of India's 28 states, and primarily in urban, not rural settings. Eight cities in India account for a hugely disproportionate share of deaths (46%) resulting from communal riots.[2] In areas where ethnic/religious violence is a recurring problem, governments—central and state—tend to act in political strategies, not legally correct ways. Generally, Hindu-Muslim riots, which are being characterized as intense and sudden, not necessarily wholly unplanned, are deadly attacks on the civilians of one religious group by members of a different religious background, with the victims chosen because of their group membership.[3] It has been argued that an identity seeking effort necessarily leads to violence because the embattled groups become involved in a mutually futile attempt to modify each other's perception, and meanwhile violence continues as the identity issue recedes to the background.[4] My argument is that a genuine hatred that is not reinforced by something from the hated, such as regularly occurring hostile action, can hardly last for long. By labeling this negative sentiment as "primordial," we seem to have explained something, when in fact we have only labeled it. It is a "know-nothing" (US Know-Nothing Party) stance that labels what we do not understand.[5]

Behavioral social psychology has not adequately explained the reasons for communal violence, and other explanatory paradigms in social sciences also appear to be partial. A multidimensional approach may be better suited for an analysis of ethnic conflicts. Jonathan Spencer argues that the nature of ethnic

What is responsible for partiality?
— more inclined to use only one form of analysis

Chapter 5

Politico-Psychological Dimensions of the Ethnic and Political Conflicts in India: Conflicting Paradigms at Work

Academic studies of communal conflicts in India have traditionally argued that religious violence between Hindus and Muslims are intrinsic to the conflict region. This simplified interpretation overlooks the complexities of relations. We need not find causes of violence only in individual psyches or group interests because contentious conversation follows its own causal logic. Of course, the role of cultural identity in making riots may not be minimized. My present study represents a heady interdisciplinary mix. A related thesis has so far been that social discrimination by the majority Hindus has caused grounds for violence. In contrast, my argument is that Indian Muslims have kept an "oppression psychosis" that arises out of the suspicion with which under-privileged minorities view dominant majority groups. In India, due to the particularistic quality of most social interaction situations, the oppression psychosis of the minority has been further reinforced but causes of physical violence are complex.

violence can be explained, but there appears to be deficiency in the explanatory power necessary to furnish answers to the more basic question of why it occurs.[6] Even intense and deeply held identities that appear to be "almost primordial" to an observer, can quite easily be "recently constructed."[7] Although there is some merit in the psychological, Marxist, new religious politics paradigm (NRP) as well as other models explaining Hindu-Muslim conflict in India, these theories have basic weaknesses.

In this connection, I would claim that that much-maligned contemporary Hindu reformist revivalism, which is quite different from Jehadist Islamic fundamentalism expressed in parts of the disturbed world, has developed a bicultural identity that has combined a legitimate Hindu identity with an identity linked to an all-Indian national culture that is espoused by Westernized Indian secularists as well. Revivalist communalism, by postulating a fundamental identity along religious lines, has greatly contributed to conflict, but has not contested the validity of Indian composite nationalism, as alleged by secularists. Hindu fundamentalism is not "simply nonsense," or a paradox.[8] It is possible to argue that that the Bharatiya Janata Party (BJP), the Rashtriya Swayam Sevak Sangh (RSS), the Vishwa Hindu Parishad (VHP) and their associates "have used the destruction of the Babri mosque to build another vote bank, this time a Hindu vote bank,"[9] but these revivalists need not be blamed for sustained Hindu-Muslim riots, although they are often contributors to political generation of tension.

see computer notes (2/13/13)

Understanding Ethnicity in Conflict: Misplaced Emphasis

Several cultural markers—language, race, religion, etc.—serve as identity axes for ethnic groups and their political mobilization. In recent Hindu revivalism, more than one of these cultural markers is pertinent for identification. Ethnic[10] conflict, or "communal conflict" in the terminology used in India involving Hindus and Muslims, refers to the historical processes of how confrontational identities of religious communities are formed and expressed with physical violence. Whereas the concerned public considers communalism a result of the politicization of religious communities and a threat to the cohesion of social fabric in India, scholars move from ethnicity to ethnic violence. Discourse about ethnic riots in India has been dominated by the wrangling between the Left Secularists and the Revivalist nationalists and their intellectuals. There is a need to develop a viable alternative that goes beyond a concept of secularism "devoid of any psychological meaning and the rigid *Hindutva* ideology." Leftist scholars, including Amrita Basu, would go so far as to suggest that even revivalist women activists are "determined crusaders" looking for a cause for violence.[11] For me, the secularist minority's stigmatization of the majority as superstitious and irrational is both moral arrogance and political folly.[12] Obviously, ethnicity has been misinterpreted by many authorities.

PARTIALLY (see prev. pg.)

First, secular scholars have blamed ethnic religious resurgence as a significant fomenting cause of riots in India. To Paul Brass, revivalist resurgence is a "process of nationality formation rather than state-building," implicitly arguing that renewed Hindu-ness itself is a national ethnic and political problem.[13] But it is legitimate to argue that the ethnos of a nation is its cultural foundation in language, religion, and a shared sense of history. Either as a functional prerequisite or as a reference point for identification, revivalism, not fundamentalism, has been a moral basis. Religion plays a leading secular constructive political role in Ireland, Poland, and Israel as well. At the same time, it is admitted that the nation is more than an ethnos because territorial nationalism is a broader and stronger force while religious ethnicity is an intense narrow force. Thus, equating Indian identity with Hindu identity—a logical but not a valid equation for a nation with large Muslims (12%), Sikh, and Christian components—the revivalist parties, including the Bharatiya Janata Party (BJP), urge the promotion of ancient values in all aspects of national life, causing some socio-political tension between communities. Ashutosh Varshney sees in this revivalist attitude a starting point for the use of violence to alter the minority's hostile behavior.[14] It is a kind of an ideological war against the Muslims, as Vijay Prasad finds in his field research, in which high caste Hindus took the "Dalits" (suppressed lower class) into confidence to fight the Muslims, projecting the image that culturally Hindu lower and upper classes are very much different from the Muslims. Thus, an anti-Muslim confrontation was made possible.[15] In adding a missing link between demonstration of glory and violence, Donald Horowitz adds that "political entrepreneurs" who float ethnic parties in ethnically divided societies can get a "ready-made clientele" waiting to be led.[16]

Critics of revivalism fail to observe the progression in the development of violence. In her in depth study of riots in riot-prone Meerat city, Usha Menon sees the surface current of Hindu stereotyping of Muslims as "coarse, cruel, bloodthirsty, and eater pet goats," but she forcefully affirms that "prejudice does not get translated immediately and inevitably into violence." Besides, there were restrictive conditions from other quarters. After the demolition of the Ayodhya mosque, she adds, there appeared reflective writings, both in English and Urdu, stressing peaceful coexistence. As Tajfel insightfully explains, even the most trivial of category, religious or racial, distinction may lead to the extreme forms of discrimination but inter-group physical conflict cannot be attributed exclusively or even mainly to the content of pre-existing stereotypes or the meaning of pre-existing social identities.[17]

Indeed, a systematic analysis of the revivalist literature, including election slogans and political speeches, testifies that the revivalists have not tried to invent new villains or solutions at will. They have succeeded when they have broadly articulated the existing sentiments on which they could build. They have built on what Habermas calls "pre-cultural understandings" (mythologies, etc.) in society, but it is too simplistic to argue, as a Muslim scholar does, that in India's ethnic spectrum, there is a subordinate/dominant pattern between two major religious groups.[18] This paradigm has a fault line. As Gurr argues, there are four processes, conquest, state building, migrations, and economic development that create inequalities dividing the dominant groups from the subordinate groups. To generate violence, the dominant group must be sharply distinct from the subordinate group. According to Gurr and his associates, a group must be "at risk" which essentially means that a group is either mobilized, subject to discrimination, or at a major economic disadvantage.[19] In India, there has been no planned discrimination against the Muslims, nor has Hindu revivalism been directed against any minority. On the other hand, the federal arrangements for Muslim reservations have exacerbated ethnic tensions.

To refer to the secularists' thesis, no doubt culturally valorized civility, tinged with ethnic Hindu traditions, provides a limit on what the consensus may encourage or require of all members in the revivalist concentric circle. Brass notes that "anti-Muslim pogroms" are the culminating events of religious resurgence, police inaction and politicians' collaboration as was evidence in the Aligarh's riots.[20] Paul Brass (1993) and Christophe Jaffrelot (1996) trace the transformation from ethnocentrism to actual violence arguing that the revivalist rituals and mass religious processions are more of hostile posture than religious celebrations. Daniel Gold adds to this argument by arguing that the "ratha jatras," i.e., the countrywide religious mass processions in modern Toyota cars amidst worldwide broadcasting via satellite and the vivid display of "Trisuls" (heavy divine weapons), were symbols of revivalist civilizational glory and moral superiority, apparently to make a point. He depicts how revivalists draw upon various metaphorical images and rhetorical strategies to define certain phenomena as social problems and to build consensus suggesting that suitable actions need to be taken to constrain the behavior of others who appear to be culturally threatening.[21] In this mode of culture-specific presentation, the "righteous representatives" of the majority act like an "embattled minority" who must stand firm as the majority on the defensive and consequently develop effective confrontational tools. Revivalist news organs thus editorialized by claiming that "holy men" were above the judicial court's orders.[22]

Admittedly, revivalist consensus building process encounters some problems. Lord Bhikhu Parekh correctly maintains that civility requires that cultural minorities not only be tolerated within limits, but free to challenge the consensus.[23] What makes civil society liberal, as Galston argues, is not the officially promoted or required notions of the Good, but that the strategy of coercion is held "to a minimum" for the common good.[24] Interestingly, what constitutes the minimum is itself a matter of cultural interpretation.[25] What is true in secularists' argument is that in the mode of the revivalist social engineering, some people's cultures are more fully reflected in public policy than others (Hindu values and practices rather than Muslim norms).

Second, the existing literature unduly finds fault with ethnicity itself. It is not enough to ask: in whose interest are ethnic identities constituted? Rather, we need to inquire the processes through which ethnicity, in our case religious ethnicity, becomes a significant site of identification, which may or may not entail construction of the interests of a particular group. Following a constructivist approach, one should examine why and how revivalist religious identification is interlinked to the "production of violence." In India, conflict between the groups remains in the realm of politics, and not in that of nature. To spark a conflict there is a need of a detonator, an ethnic lie. Even when one group consider the next door neighbors as threatening alien, the first step is to describing them as such, exasperating the elements that make them different, or inventing them if they do not exist.[26] Propaganda workers on rival sides create "positive myths" and "negative myths" regarding the rival. But is there any need to ignore myths? The anthropologist Ashis Nandy worries that we try to overcome our cultural differences at our peril; that we somehow need the mystery of these differences.[27] Ethnic identity is normal and perhaps harmless, but violence is the creation of the politicized communal mind. Ethnicity may be a "backlash," a violent reaction, partially justified, to what a significant number of Hindus perceive as excessive privileges retained by Muslims. "Reservations" of seats for the Muslims in government offices and university admissions created an adverse political condition affecting the material life of the majority. The politically mobilizing backlash, whether objectively valid or not, was exacerbated by "ethnic number games," a fear that Muslims had been growing at a faster rate than the majority.[28] Kashmir ethnic conflicts did not stem from incompatible identities, but rather from tensions between political elites in this northern state and successive central governments insisting on the maintenance of the unity of a territorial state at all costs.[29] A basic question is, however, how would one identify the rightful holders of the self-determination? Exactly what is the extent of the territory under question?

In sum, ethnicity itself is not a cause of violence. A recent work by Posner argues that high levels of ethnic fractionalization per se are in fact not a concern; rather, it is the presence of two or three large competing ethnic groups coupled with weak public institutions that spells danger of violence.[30] Rajni Kothari also argues, India's socio-political problem is a problem of governability. Civilians who actually participate in riots seem to do so in the belief that they are acting morally, imposing a justice, which the official organs of the state cannot or will not impose. In doing so, they seem to be able to invert the most obvious interpretation of their actions.[31] Quite apart from its ethnocentric baggage (R. Howard, 1995), the ancient hatreds based on religious grouping are not the cause of violence. Historians ignore the prosaic politic-economic roots of Hindu-Muslim riots. While identity politics of the revivalists may well depend on ethnic collective memory, it is not a reinvention of myths, as alleged by Romila Thapar and others.

The Hindu Group Psychology and Communal Riots

Psychoanalytical theory attempts to explain inter-group conflicts by applying theories of personality development to group dynamics, and by assuming that groups need enemy, groups which serve as targets to project their negative images, and as reservoirs of their negative feelings.[32] In analyzing the causes of Hindu-Muslim riots, Sudhir Kakar of New Delhi, who is widely known as the father of Indian psychoanalysis and a former trusted associate of Erik Erikson of Harvard, argues that a primordial instinct in ethnicity takes an upper hand in an adversarial situation simply because anger is the natural outcome of "ancient hatred." He deliberately sets his primordialist account of Hindu-Muslim conflict against the instrumentalist or constructivist accounts that have been predominant in current social-scientific explanations. He observes that the Hindu revivalists perceived even such governmental administrative action as raising the official status of Urdu language in the Hindu majority Bihar state as "Muslim separatism," signifying the existence of an ancient and inherent perception.[33] This "religious intimacy," fueled by idealization and ritual symbols, he goes on, makes riots much more violent and difficult to control.[34] In fact, Kakar concludes, the religious "ultimacy," based on *Hindutva* (Indian-ness) forces, was expressed during the Ayodhya riot over temple-mosque controversy in 1992, demonstrating the peril in Hindu-Muslim cultural differences."[35] Here he submits that ethnic identities are given and flow directly from cultural identities. In contrast, we would claim that an ethnic identification is an instinctive notion only; if we have it, we have learned it in our lifetime.[36]

First, Kakar begins with the idea that a Hindu child develops some habits in Muslim hating either out of fear or community's inherent belief. He blames the Hindu child raising process that grounds the childhood in his religious community identity. Hindu joint family is based, he argues, on the "naturant dependency" of the son to the mother and then to the absolute authority of the father. As the child transfers his allegiance from mother to father at the age of about five, he is "twice-born," a rebel, infused with confusion and anger. Additionally, a Hindu child's preoccupation of sexual guilt and constant feelings of inadequacy leads to his inner frustration. This child, unhappy but angry, then externalizes his positive and negative images into certain people or objects in the outside world. For Kakar, this Hindu ego is an underdeveloped ego created by the rigid social norms and practices.[37] According to this thesis, the imaging is necessary to maintain the socially integrated self-images. This analysis bears striking similarities with the "Suitable Targets of Externalization" (STEs) theory that argues that the people who are negative STEs (reservoirs of unintegrated bad representations) are regarded as enemies. This theory explains how individuals adopt group identity, how it can prevail over individual identity, and how it can contribute to the emergence and perpetuation of inter-group conflict.[38]

Second, in this transformation from community to violent religious communalism, the community aspect of religious identity becomes "hyperconscious." During the riots in Hyderabad city, both Hindu and Muslim wrestlers stopped killing only when they found that they had already killed more people than the wrestler of the other community. The atmosphere was so charged with religious hatred that no body dared to testify against the killers or the wrestlers due to fear. The arrest of a wrestler in the city erupted into wide spread riots, because of the common theme of communalists who cherished "a primordial antagonism" between the Hindus and Muslims. The distinction between crime and valor thus disappeared and honor religious killing was committed in the name of community. For Kakar, this was an expression of ancient hatred and thus he writes, the Muslim butcher in his "blood-flecked undervest and lungi, wielding a huge carving knife" was a figure of awe and dread for "the Hindu child and fear-tinged repulsion for the (Hindu) adult."[39] This is the work, Kakar notes, of super-ego that drives the personality system into a social interaction on moral grounds. The process in fear arises from inherent and pathological apprehension, concludes Kakar.

In Ritambhara's (a religious activist supporting the politically charged *Hinduva* values), construction of a post-Babri mosque "Hindu identity," there is a "splitting that enhances (Hindu) group cohesion." Fire eating Ritambhara invokes the Hindu gods and heroes as symbols of "ego ideals" to reach the "overreaching Hindu community." The Hindu gods and mythical ancient religious heroes are then linked through the ardent action by other *karsevaks* (volunteers) religious activists, prepared to die to build the temple at the birth spot of Lord Ram. In this process of divine invocation, the Hindu religious ethnic unity is sought while at the same time the Muslim others are hated. The scapegoating of the Muslims inevitably generates the desired "the bad, the dirty, and the impure Muslim other."[40]

Kakar explains the progressive stages in hate producing emotion. He complains that the *Hindutva* agenda to restore classical glories is bound to psychologically spur Muslim suspicion when it is presented an adverse situation. The *Hindutva* agenda is likely to create an outgroup, the Muslims that rationalizes arson and killing. Although Kakar occasionally admits that the revivalist anti-Muslim stance is also "socially constructed,"[41] his main thrust is that when the Hindu-Muslim primordial instinct is submerged in the political psychology of rival mass movements, large-scale communal violence is inevitable, and that revivalists were largely responsible for riots.

In Kakar's psychoanalysis, the revivalist ethnicity is more than an "unconscious" emotion. He projects this emotion as illness, or something like a disease, a sign of physical decay. To him, the anti-modernist revivalist is a pathological character obsessed with the motives of the Muslim *mullah*.[42] Asha Mukherjee (2002), in her psycho-analysis, adds to Kakar's hypothesis by arguing that revivalism is not only a spiritual urge but also a psychological therapy for the removal of "distress."[43] Methodologically, this psychoanalysis of Kakar is itself a sub-culture of broad Western civilization.

Kakar's psychoanalysis is a branch in psychology that studies human behavior as determined by the "unconscious," the Freudian typography. For Freud, interior identity and psychic structure are emotional rather than conscious and rational in inspiration. It can be analyzed, but not explained rationally. The "unconscious" is that part of a subject that silently communicates with others in inter-subjectivity that is reverberating empathy.[44] Empathy here is an imaginative projection of a subjective state into an object so that the object appears to be infused with it. It is vicariously experiencing the feelings and thoughts of another without having the feelings and thoughts fully communicated in an objectively explicit manner.

Uncertain Steps in Psychoanalysis

First, Kakar ignores the immensely complex question of the interplay between individual minds and social groups such as the political parties, religious organizations, and institutions. Donald Horowitz, who has done massive studies in conflict, is perhaps nearer the truth when he disagrees with the pure primordialists. The so-called "primordial" link becomes "a resource" that is mobilized to serve "instrumental" needs in contact and competition with other groups.[45] To Horowitz, this link is not inherent but "situationally" invented as self-defense mechanism.[46] However, this argument turns collective ethnic conflict into a rational response removing it from any mysticism.[47] We may concur with Clifford Geertz who argues that psychological ties, stemming from a common linguistic, racial, tribal, or religious background, are totally separable, though often reinforcing, fundamental identities.[48]

Unlike Kakar, Horowitz argues that that sociality and group affiliation constitute universal human condition, antedating globalization, the modern state, and the power of the printing press. In this social psychology, the leading elites face certain constraints, which, he adds, stem from the "cognitive" basis of ethnic affinities and disparities. In the Indian context, the manipulative individual political leaders, in order to redress specific grievances, purposely create a cynically organized plot.[49] In this case, individual initiatives, mostly political in nature, merge into collective religious mobilization.

On balance, Horowitz stands with the "primordialists" ("essentialists") who argue that primordialists emphasize each individual's and group's deeply held ethnic heritage. His argument is that inherent cleavages drive culture, more than culture drives cleavages,[50] and thus he writes, "The roots of mass antagonism may reside in the domain of psychology, rather than in the realm of material interest." [51] Unlike Kakar, Horowitz more accurately maintains that the social realities of language, ethnicity, religion, and traditions evoke "existential feelings or emotions called primordial sentiments" during the individual's encultur-ation.[52]

However, both Sudhir Kakar and Donald Horowitz contend that the indi-viduals invest their own existence within the group because the group is more likely to bring expected results. The greater is the threat to individual existence, the higher the individual's identity is with the group.[53] A revivalist individual, it is alleged, tends to identify with the larger ethnic group for the group victory that satisfies individual's immediate goal, though in a minor way. For Hindus and Muslims, violence becomes morally acceptable when communally and re-ligiously sanctioned.[54] It is the change from community to communalism that makes "the community aspect of religious identity hyperconscious," Kakar con-cludes.[55]

Kakar's is culture-specific psychology, different from the psychology model of classical psychoanalysis: Freud, and Melanie Klein. Stanley Tambiah agrees with Kakar when he writes that religious "processions can be precursors of violence" in India, and the crowd becomes the sum total of individuals be-cause of inherent bias.[56] But Tambiah differs from Kakar in suggesting that in-dividuals take "extreme actions in response to rather moderate dangers"[57] be-cause of communal identity. Kakar's culture-specific psychoanalysis misses the role of self-motivated rioters. Kakar seems to suggest that given the inherent survival value of emotional reaction such as fear and rage that prepare an organ-ism to flee or fight, negative emotions tend to be more powerful as conditioning stimuli.[58] Stated differently, fear-inducing stimuli proceed directly to the amyg-dala and unleash a variety of somatic and emotional reactions that focus our attention and put the agitated ones on high alert before the rational brain has a chance to act.[59]

In contrast, Stanley Kurtz sees a positive Hindu path to psychological healthy development and maturity. Confronting Kakar's thesis and backed by a large body of secondary material, he cogently argues that Hindu mother's physi-cal indulgence, coupled with her personal distance, is a healthy combination which reassures the infant of the world's basic benevolence (you will be fed, never be left out). This assumption rejects Kakar's thesis of angry and alienated Hindu child, who likes to take sides with any group with a constructive bond.[60]

Indeed, the processions such as annual Muslim Muharram processions in Aligarh city and Calcutta, or Hindu processions traversing neighborhoods of rival Muslim groups in Hyderabad city and elsewhere become a psycho-cultural contest that divides the rivals but may not cause conflict. Because ethnic con-flicts are subject to psychological interpretation, the element of perception and misperception is present during processions.[61] Thus, psycho-analysts would do justice by acknowledging the role of sociopolitical and economic circumstances of man's making in aggression. Also, there is a need to make a distinction be-tween defensive and offensive aggression.

Second, Kakar's analysis neglects the "cultural conditioning" and thus re-stricts the ego to a purely cognitive reading of its external environment. The work of collective identification is left to the super-ego upholding moral values. As some authorities argue, what drives the personality system is not the instincts but a social interaction that is already operative.[62] Kakar ignores Erik H. Erikson's two sided personality development. Erikson argues that associated with each stage of proper psychological development there is a positive virtuous resolution of an identity conflict and a negative pathological failure to resolve a conflict and often pathological aspect takes on a violent development depending on individual intensity.

Third, the moot point is: Why anger begets actual violence? Horowitz argues that ethnic parties create congenial atmosphere in which followers are created for political reasons.[63] A balanced explanation is found in sociobiologists including Reynolds and others (1987), who, after reviewing the biological explanations for ethnocentrism, reject the idea that negatives such as ethnicity, selfishness, and racism are "genetic imperatives" of human nature, although they point to instinctive behavior like kin selection among animals.[64] Indeed, we know very little about the psychology of the prejudiced group. Collective psychology is at best a psychology of the "crowd." In this case "collective interest" is a potentially confused notion. Milosevic may successfully mobilize sections of Serbs behind his Serbian nationalist program, but it is unlikely that the same people will concur on other major policy matters that will eventually arise.[65] Allan Barton puts this in a provocative fashion by writing that a sample of individuals merely guarantees "no one in the investigation interacts with anyone else."[66] What is certain is that without feelings of antipathy, there can be no ethnic conflict, and there is plenty of antipathy between Hindu revivalists and Muslim radicals for multiple reasons.

Unlike Kakar, Horowitz more appropriately finds that institutional arrangements rather than human habits are responsible for ethnic conflict in India. Horowitz argues that the failures to deal with ethnic conflict do not derive from a lack of knowledge as to what to do, or from "an unalterable human nature," but from deficiencies in political will and often radicalized will becomes a driving force.[67] This "Rational Choice" approach, a rational "cost-benefit analysis," presupposes that ethnocentric behavior is responsive to constitutional political manipulation.[68] The implicit idea is the revivalist organized parties have both religious ethnocentrism and political will to cause harm to the non-Hindus. But we would contend that it is easy to blame ethnicity (in our case, Hindu religious ethnicity), a pleasingly simple thesis that seems to fit the facts and gives the government an excuse for indifference and inaction.

Moreover, there is a related un-answered question: why an individual or a group would take a risk in physical violence? Benedict Anderson wonders why there are "such colossal sacrifices" to build an "imagined community."[69] Hindu revivalists, who are believed to be primordialists by some, are instead the "imagined communities" that Benedict Anderson introduced in the 1990s. Here the nation is given as the typical example of the imagined community. To the degree that revivalists hold overlapping memberships in several associations such as

Farmers Associations their sense of identification and trust may be transferred to
several contexts and society as a whole. Russell Hardin, a political scientist,
correctly assumes that self-interest can successfully match with group interests,
and when it happens that way, the result is "often appalling." The result of
strong identification with an ethnic group is "willingness to run grotesque risks
of personal harm for a meager group benefit."[70] What is clear is that violence
results from group identification when both the group and the other group are
faced with increasing incentives for preemptive action. People who do not take
risks at early stages, but do take greater risks at later stages, when they are more
subject to group commitments and when they are fewer opportunities for doing
anything other than joining in the group violence.[71]

Fourth, while giving due credit to Kakar' analysis that that a driving force
in violence is often a psychological and emotional attachment to collective identity,[72] we need to admit that the economic and political factors also do stir up
ethnic passions. In defense of revivalism, it is legitimate to remind ourselves of
the aggressive force of radical Islam. Some authorities have established that
when Islamic groups are involved in a conflict, religion is generally more relevant. When one group is Islamic, on average the relevance of religion nearly
triples.[73]

Fifth, Kakar argues that only when normative social actualities are distorted
or contrasted with other social actualities does the arbitrary nature of emotions
become apparent. The straight dogmatic reductionism is not a good methodology to explain complex Hindu-Muslim riots. It is not enough to explain recurring civil conflict by postulating an aggressive instinct, and then to claim that
occurrence of conflict itself is proof enough for the existence of an aggressive
instinct. At the same time, within the confines of the experimental situation,
argue Tajfel and Billiing (1976), the hypothesis that anxiety and /or uncertainty
would lead to in-group affiliation was disconfirmed.[74] As Watson (1973, 1974)
posits with reference to Black rage in the United States, ethnic movements contain strong political ideologies, and these are ideologies that need to be understood in relation to the inter-group context of black and white racism.[75]

Last, we tend to claim that primordial sentiments and bonds are not in
themselves good or bad, but they are the sources of constructive (patriotic) and
destructive (nativistic, xenophobic) behaviors with regard to others within and
across cultures. Their specific development depends on social history.[76] Psychological explanations fail to see the role of the interlocutors in causing violence.
Debating about whether ethnicity is primordial or instrumental, Francis Robinson and others explain the factors that drive the Muslim mobilization around the
issue of the status of Urdu.[77] While Robinson asserts that the Muslim view of
Urdu as a symbol of religious and cultural identity predated the Hindi-Urdu
competition, Paul Brass counters that Urdu, and many other symbols of Islamic
culture, became important in the elite competition for economic and political
advantage.[78] This explanation fits into the model of the unethical political use of
ethnicity and testifies to the inadequacies in psychoanalysis.

Interlocutors

Behavioral psychologists does not explain why the violent incident takes place where it does and when it does. Why is it that only some cities, not others, with a comparable mix of Hindu and Muslim populations, both economically and sociologically, are prone to occurrence of violence? Additionally, is there any state connivance in aiding the causation of violence?[79]

Psycho-analysis ignores the intermediate process in interaction leading to violence. There is a need to recognize the conversational dynamics of Hindu-Muslim disputes. Their conversation engages multiple interlocutors in varied settings and as such takes place in many explosive modes. For instance, Majid Khan's interchanges with his counterparts, who mobilize their own wrestlers-thugs-activists on behalf of Hindu causes, differ greatly from the initial angry conversation between Golam Fakir (Muslim) and Kumar Tarkhania (Hindu) in the Panipur in Bangladesh of 1954. Interchanges, which differ in form from the exchanges between high-caste Panipur resident Mr. Ghosh and the Muslim officials, who came to Panipur when the local conflict started drawing in outsiders. More importantly, Muslim Fakir and Hindu Tarkhania did not initially respond to each other as representatives of competing categories. Only as their conflict escalated did they fall into ranks of self- identified Muslims on one side, self identified Hindus on the other. Every contentious conversation proceeds through incessant improvisation. In short, the crucial processes of contentious politics did not stem from a competition of elites for political power and economic resources. Without organization and command, many thousands of Hindus and Muslims rushed each other, but did not attack. Instead, they sat in tidy lines as if they were a canal separating them. The Panipur riot was not a true communal confrontation; it was a "pre-industrial" event.[80]

They are not primordial or, Kakar's ancient inherent instinct, in the sense of expressing deeply grounded individual hatred. They were conversational in the sense that they proceeded through historically situated, culturally constrained, negotiated, and consequential interchanges among multiple parties.[81] The conceptual language of psychology is not equipped to address primary issues in riots because psychological languages is generally in a-historical and a-social terms such as instinct and drive. Social psychology needs more culture and historic-specific concepts for explaining group conflicts like riots. Just before the actual riot in Panipur, Muslim Altaf-uddin, supporting the Muslims, was in agreement with Freud when he declared, "People...are animals." This simple but powerful assertion does not say why and how people came together in the particular groupings as they did. Why did Altaf elect to indulge his feelings when and as he did, not earlier, not later, not in the market place or at the polls?[82] This aspect in the development stages has been largely ignored mainly because many of the riot studies have been undertaken by peace and civil rights activists, specifically with a view to pressurizing the government to intervene in an ongoing episode of violence, or to attend to the process of rehabilitation in the aftermath.

New Religious Politics Paradigm (NRP)

Atul Kohli observes that the ethnic self-aggrandizement movements are social movements that can be interpreted as a variant of power politics in which election politics is forceful. In India, political parties assume a role of critical outsider vis-vis-vis the state and as a result democracy is weakened.[83] This points out to the "new religious politics paradigm," which has gained considerable currency in locating causes of riots in recent years in India because politics and religion, as many analysts argue, have been mixed to produce ethnic conflict. Several Western and many Indian social scientists and historians subscribe to this model which, they believe, may explain the frequency of Hindu-Muslim riots. Paul Brass exposes the mechanisms by which endemic communal violence is deliberately provoked and sustained. He implicates the police, criminal elements, members of Aligarh's (in Uttar Pradesh state) business community, and many of its leading political actors in the continuous effort to "produce" communal violence. Riots, he concludes, become key historical markets in the struggle for economic and political dominance of one religious community over another but local politics act the catalyst.[84] Ranajit Guha, of the sub-altern historiography, postulates that at the local level, where the action is, agents of hate speech in all homes prepare the "politically correct" atmosphere in the midst of religious antagonism and then are supplemented by a range of "learned professions," such as teaching, vernacular journalism, and books that are not free from prejudice. Eventually, the official political power holders permit the commission of violence that is augmented by regional circumstances. To political leaders, this manipulative act appears to be a "moral task," attempting to "manufacture" causes of "social and political violence" in India.[85] However, Guha makes an interesting difference between Indian conditions and those of other countries. He recognizes that India falls in between the two ethnic conflict systems - "centralized" (Rwanda, ethnic groups are very large and strong) and "dispersed" (India, weak and dispersed), and local politics often tend to vitiate communal harmony in India.[86] Sub-alternists, however, ignore individual consciousness and community dialogue although they use articulate tools of cultural analysis in friction and conflict.

Secular purists also agree with the new religious politics paradigm when they argue that religious processions become powerful vehicles of violence when "local politics is at stake." In the 1980s and 1990s, Hindu religious leaders used processions to mobilize supporters more and more frequently during the elections, both local and central. Even B.G. Tilak's re-interpretation of processions in honor of God *Ganesh* in the 1890s had represented an anti-Muslim political mobilization, it has been argued by some.[87] Here the secular scholars

Hindu Revivalism direct result of fundamentalist Islamic movements

rightly blame the manipulation of Hindu religious symbols during elections. The "politics of ethnicity" has obviously caused enormous harm to modern Indian developmental state, and *Hindutva* forces are to share some responsibility.[88]

Of course, means and motives to "manufacture" religion based violence differ. Revivalists, it has been argued by scholars, want to gain political power in the name of their redefined, but in theory the age-old view of Hinduism. Several volumes edited by Martin E. Marty and R. Scott Appleby exclude some of the more purely religious trends found in many discussions of fundamentalism, but encompasses new religious politics in South Asia and Israel. Nikki Keddie, a leading proponent of the "New Religious Politics" paradigm, argues that revivalists in India gain election success by presenting the Muslims as having conquered and corrupted Hindu society, and with the creation of Pakistan, broken off part of "Hindu patrimony."[89] He correctly sees the rise of Hindu revivalism as a necessary reaction to the "fundamentalist movements in nearly all Muslim countries."[90] In an article (1998), he uses the model with the adjective "religio-political," rather than "fundamentalist," because he regards crude politics as instrumental. He elaborates two types in religious politics: one type is directed at replacing or radically changing one's government, believed to be hostile to dominant religion, and the other type includes religious nationalism, targeted primarily against another religious or national group (Revivalist movements against Muslims). Keddie calls the second type "communal," leading to riots. Indian religio-nationalist movements led by parties and groups such as the BJP, VHP, and RSS, etc., he adds, do not only stress particular religious practices, but also want to increase religion in government.[91] At times, even the Hindi-Urdu competition in northern India intensified the Hindu and Muslim conflict when local economic and political conditions were manipulated by the elite who wanted political advantage.[92] In short, the NRP explains that political parties exist not only to distribute goods, but to distribute rage, anger, and hatred, using religious sentiments. In this psychodynamics, private ambitions, miseries, and pleasures are politicized and transformed into public concerns.

The new religious paradigm is based on the assumption that the individual enters the political culture with a dual identity—civic identity based on the national question and a cultural identity based on primordial sentiments. But historically, these two identities have been more or less concordant. The primordial sentiment dominates when intermingled with religious issues. The new religious politics paradigm vehemently upholds that religious attachment and emotion is transformed into primal violence through political action that is manipulative.[93]

NRP Paradigm in Gujarat Riots: All Politics are Local

Advocates of the new religious politics paradigm have found a fertile ground in the Gujarat riots of 2001 when at least 900 Muslims were killed. The main contention of their analysis is that the Hindu-Muslim riots have been the results of the revivalist cultural aggression, forcefully led by the BJP Chief Minister Narendra Modi, who, it is alleged, has manipulated politics for BJP's election gains. David Singh of Oxford Centre for Mission Studies, writing on Gujarat riots in 2001, argues that Hinduism failed to "unequivocally eschew interreligious violence" in its new version of Hindu-ness, admitting, however, that the phenomenon of violence associated with religions has more that one center.[94] Paul R. Brass maintains that the "retributive genocidal massacres" in Gujarat from February to June in 2001 by the Hindu militants was a transformation, through the "institutionalized riot systems," of a local incident into the statewide riots by the "fire tenders" (Hindu militants) to derive gains in elections. The election of December 12, 2002, resulted in an overwhelming victory for the BJP, which won 126 seats in the revivalist dominated state assembly of 182 members.[95] This analysis has gone so far as to claim that riots in Gujarat were efforts to "erase Islam from the perceivable present."[96] Professor Mahmood Mamdani of Columbia University perceptively contends that political identities are not reducible to cultural ones. He emphasizes the necessity of distinguishing between cultural/religious and political identity because we need to situate violence in its political context. In short, political violence, as in Gujarat, is not a product of pre-modern cultures, nor of fundamentalist forms of religion, but are deeply associated with particular types of modernist politics, both secular and religious.[97]

It is worth noticing that the issues involved in Gujarat conflicts were invariably mixed with questions of sharing economic resources and decision-making power. Atul Kohli, who in reference to the Gujarati riots of 1985 in which minority Muslims heavily suffered, says that as democracy evolved, representatives of poorly organized but numerically significant underprivileged Hindu groups gained control of government in Gujarat, and the socio-economically privileged groups reacted violently. He writes, "The major target of the insurrections is the state itself." Once Solanki government retracted the reservation policies, antireservation caste-oriented agitation was sustained on the basis of other issues. Muslims were easy targets for such hostility.[98] As the Sakaria Commission (1988) indicated, some ethnically based political parties built their strengths by exploiting the linguistic frustrations of their constituencies.[99] Moreover, during the 2001 riots in Gujarat, there was no visible movement for peace from the Islamic community; even today no Muslim radicals in the state hardly make an attempt at reconciliation with the majority.

Many analysts argue that the Gujarat riot was an example of brutal and effective form of campaign expenditure, directed toward winning over swing voters in the most competitive seats. Seats were Hindu-Muslim violence occurred in the state of Gujarat in the spring of 2002 had both higher turnouts and greater swings toward the BJP than other seats in the subsequent elections. The BJP derived benefit from a subsequent riot-induced swing toward the party.[100]

All said, the new religious paradigm has some validity here. Revivalist governing elites and party supporters played their role for political success. An exercise of silent political "rights" to kill people, rights aggravated by governmental bystanderism, provides a congenial "social environment for killing."[101] As some rightfully argued, the Modi government in Gujarat used "a right to collective vengeance and retaliation," an "anticipatory right to self-defense," believed to be a massive message for future deterrence. These were "purificatory practices of politics of mass cruelty" to serve the cause of future revivalist politics in which "popular" consciousness ignored the constitutional secularism.[102] In Gujarat, the political deterrence seems to be weak due to constant election fear. Therefore, the "lonely crowds" are now fearful of the future militancy by constitutional and religious majorities.[103]

NRP and Its Deficiencies

Now, a question arises: why do the common people take part in political manipulation? Masses follow, it has been argued, the elite's manipulation only when there is a payoff. Horowitz rightly argues that "ethnicity ...entails not the collective will to exist but the existing will to collect."[104] The material benefits take precedence over psychological fear and frustration. Violence is merely potential until the incentive structure is right (or wrong). The incentive structure might change quickly if leaders opt to mobilize violence, or if economic opportunities change in the face of limits to growth, economic malaise, or attempted transition from one economic system to another.[105] Thus, Amiya Kumar Bagchi, an economic historian with strong Marxist leanings, argues that the major ideological influence on the consciousness of the poor in the country stems from religion, but such influences are not immutable. A militantly secular ideology has to be diffused into the people's consciousness. He confirms that, despite occasional communal disturbances, the leftist West Bengal government (CPM) long maintained social harmony by active secularizing consciousness. He correctly warns that unless "material conditions of living" are improved, riots are "likely" to recur.[106] Here the "new religious politics" paradigm falls short of an adequate explanation for riots. Indeed, some studies offer more pertinent response in arguing that secular ideologies such as liberalism and socialism, which are the basis of many state governments in India, are suffering from a crisis of legitimacy primarily due to their failure to meet the political and economic expectations of their people in several areas. As a result, religion has become alternative basis of legitimacy.[107] Others argue that religion becomes so important that it is beyond protest and "only violent responses are considered appropriate."[108] In this analysis, radical religion is a significant cause.

There are other dimensions in the new religious politics model. The pure political manipulation becomes effective when rumors are acted upon. Rumors have become occasional and proximate instruments for political mobilization in India. Rumors that undue justice has been given to Hindus, or Hindus have killed Muslim boys, etc., have at times caused the transformation of usual politi-

cal machine to active violence, without verifying the events. Those who participate in riots are aroused by the organizational and mobilizing activities of prac-
tioners, who are skilled in the production of rumors and riots. There is a difference between ordinary rumors that abound in daily life, which may provide
source material for psychologists, psychoanalysts, and rumors, that have specific
functions that may or may not arouse demonizing fantasies. The latter are the
material for political and sociological analysis of riot production. When two
types of explanations become complimentary, as they have been in contemporary India, they act together to perpetuate riotous conditions.[109] Specifically,
when rumors are spread in India just before the heightened election tension, the
crowds are given instruments such as voters' lists to feed on unconscious images.[110] In this psychological case involving rumor, a number of secular and
non-ethnic factors such as the pattern of economic development, quality of political elites, and existence of prior local grievances play a critical role.[111] Rumors reach a special intensity in special circumstances. The rumors which circulated in Delhi in 1984 after India Gandhi's assassination drew upon pre-existing
stereotypes about Sikhs and provided a plausible interpretation of what must
otherwise had been threateningly disorientating time.[112]

It is equally important to observe that, as Mushirul Hasan reminds us, during the Ayodhya crisis, the Hindu Muslim political life was not molded by religious consideration alone. In the 1989 elections, most people in a predominantly
"Hindu" constituency voted for secular candidates of the Communist party of
India (CPI), who stood for Hindu-Muslim amity and opposed the communaliza-
tion of polity and society by outside forces.[113] Many Muslims in Calcutta think
of the Communist Party of India (CPM), the larger of the two communist parties, as more secular than Congress and less likely to utilize anti-Muslim communal themes for electoral mobilization. The Indian Muslims have moved toward the CPM, hoping to relieve their sense of communal vulnerability.[114] Thus,
political use of religion has been successful in some cases, but the NRP model
may not be uniformly applicable in explaining frequent bloody riots. A summary
assessment should clarify our arguments.

First, the new religious politics paradigm does not provide enough clues to
remedial measures. Does the political manipulation leave the masses in constant
despair? Second, the new religious politics paradigm is not universally applicable to Indian many riots. Historians and analysts have to debate about whether
riots in Gujarat have been socially/culturally constructed, or simply dictated by
material incentives. Perhaps a combination of new religious model and materialistic interpretation will reveal a fuller explanation. It is wise to argue that the
strength of associational life and the local organization matters most because
communities of the same religion act together for shared interests or identities.
This strong identity sense heightens tension among the rival groups[115] Keddie
has failed to observe that religious politics has several expressions: cultural revivalism (strong defense of traditions), prevention of perceived threat from religious groups, politics of self-organization among minority groups, and of

course, the cruel means of attaining political power. The precise form it takes depends on local historical traditions and objectives of ethnic organizations and parties. The environment of a peaceful city makes a difference between politically motivated violence and peace. Violence that erupts in a city is not the cause and consequence of "civic engagement," but rather a robust criticism of civil society that is plagued by corrupt political practices.[116] Third, people are intoxicated with politics as in Gujarat because the premium on political power is very high and as such leaders take extreme measures to win power. Implicit in the argument is the idea that the religion-based communal discord is a lesser issue than the access to power,[117] and the NRP paradigm has certainly some validity in explaining several cases of riots.

Social Identity Theory and Communal Violence in India

Social Identity Theory (Henri Tajfel, 1978) is particularly good in explaining how minority and majority groups define themselves. The theory assumes that group members have a basic need for a positive social identity and that inter-group conflicts arise because each group inevitably compares itself to the other. According to this theory, every individual divides his social world into distinct classes or social categories. Then, within this system of social categorization, individuals locate themselves and the others. Tajfel, a psychologist using tools in laboratories, predicts that an individual automatically identifies with some categories (occupation, religious affiliation, etc) and rejects others. This creates a difference between "in-groups," with which one identifies, and "out-groups," with which one does not identify. The goal of the comparisons is to establish the superiority of one's own group, or the group's uniqueness on some level such as cultural heritage and spirituality.[118] This analysis in identity formation has led some scholars to argue that the revivalist cultural affirmation has increased revivalist ethnocentrism causing social friction and even violence. According to the judgment of these analysts, revivalists tend to view Indian society, or at least, Hindu society, as unitary and relatively undifferentiated. In this mode, the revivalists see themselves less as individuals, defined by their personal differences from others, and more as interchangeable representatives of their social group, defined by their intergroup similarities. Social identities in this sense are "public selves" projected in social interaction or "internalizations of such public selves."[119]

In explaining the transformation from revivalist religious ethnocentrism to actual riots, Paul Brass (1993), Christophe Jaffrelot (1996), and many others argue that the revivalist rituals and mass religious processions demonstrate Hindu superiority to provoke an outbreak of riots.[120] M.G. Smith suggests that if one group infringes on the precious norms of another, value dissensus may lead to conflict.[121] Daniel Gold observes that using tools such as the "ratha jatras," country-wide religio-politico processions in Toyota cars, amidst worldwide broadcasting via satellite, and some other vivid symbols like "Trisuls,"[122] revivalists have placed the Hindus in a superior civilizational moral height, compared to Muslims. He depicts how revivalists draw upon various metaphorical images and rhetorical strategies to define certain phenomena as social problems and to build consensus that action needs to be taken to constrain the behavior of others who appear to be culturally inferior.[123] Some policy statements by revivalists conform to the above argument. Revivalist parties- the BJP, Bajrang Dal, the Vishwa Hindu Parishad (VHP)- editorialized by arguing that holy men were above the court's orders, thereby highlighting the spiritual superiority of Hindu values.[124]

Many analysts support the conventional hypothesis that there is an intrinsic confrontational political power hidden in the comparison highlighting ethnic differences.[125] This model in explaining violence falls under a false pretext of the social identity theory. In this thought process, many argue, revivalists unjustifiably believe that Muslims, compared to pacifist Hindus, are essentially aggressive by nature, and a demonstration of superior Hindu physical strength is believed to be the only way to alter the minority's hostile behavior.[126] A social prejudice is being frequently created by the revivalists by way of comparison. Interestingly in this stance, caste Hindus sided with lower castes. Vijoy Prasad finds in his field research that revivalist Hindus used the Dalits (suppressed lower castes) in an ideological war against Muslims, and Hindus in this case identified the Muslims as culturally and psychologically different from the majority Hindus,[127] and as such an anti-Muslim action is generated.

In claiming a unified superior identity, revivalists made direct references to the Muslims. Usha Menon, in her thorough field research on ethnic violence, observes that revivalism's cultural identity stressing "Hindu tolerance, compassion, depth of insight, and width of social cohesion," and the constantly stereotyping of the Muslims, especially in Meerut city in northern India, as "coarse, cruel, bloodthirsty, and eater of pet goats," a combating communal atmosphere was generated. At the same time, she affirms with some justification that "prejudice does not get translated, immediately or inevitably, into violence." Physical violence must have "prejudices plus other factors." Elaborating her point, she correctly argues that riots did not begin in many northern cities even after the demolition of the Ayodhya mosque, because, among others, there appeared reflective writings, both in Urdu and in English, about the need of peaceful coexistence.[128] Tajfel's insight is that even the most trivial of category (religion, race, etc.) distinctions can be the cue for the most extreme forms of discrimination, but inter-group conflict cannot be attributed exclusively or even mainly to the content of pre-existing stereotypes or the "meaning" of pre-existing social identities.[129] Some authorities have made more specific references to social identity formation and its results on community relations.

In sum, the cultural "other" in India refers to relationships of plurality, addition, diversity, and exclusion. Both self and other could thus be viewed from endless standpoints, with differing messages and meanings. Therefore, a comparative assertion by the revivalists does not qualify us to claim that the "other," even if inferior, has to be confronted.

Identity in Confrontation with the Muslims

C. Ram-Prasad, a social scientist, who is critical of revivalist cultural essentialism and ethnocentrism, argues that the radical "para-religious conservatism" performs a hegemonic function by insisting on a national culture that is confrontationally ethno-centric.[130] Dennis Austin and Peter Lyon (1992) interpret the revivalist comparative civilizational argument as demonizing the religious minorities as evil aliens. A virile punishment has to be given to Muslims, who through polygamy increase their number, which is politically damaging for Hindus. The critical "ethno-centrist idea," as Ralph R. Premdas notes, underscores the need for identity to be asserted by favorable comparisons in quest not only of parity but superiority.[131] If the group fails to satisfy this requirement, the individual may seek a new way of comparison that would favor his group and hence reinforce his social identity. This comparison phase often turns out to be an ethnocentric orientation to cultural differences. In short, revivalists as a group are denounced for their civilizational confrontation, a kind of one dimensional clash of civilization.

Robert Bates, Albert Breton, and others are nearer the truth in maintaining that besides civilizational superiority complex, other factors such as material benefits, jobs, land, and markets, are also motivational factors in group identification.[132] The implication is that value dissentions may equally impede conflict by focusing the ambitions of various groups on alternative sources of gratification, thereby preventing them from impinging on each other. Thus, dissensus may foster or retard conflict, and consensus (political behavior) may be integrative or disintegrative. The comparative model has generally tended to denigrate the importance of political variables.[133] The revivalist complex appears to be a Durkheimian perspective on religious fundamentals that appeared as totems of the group, authentic symbols of collective identity, and there is as such no inherent violent conviction.

Indeed, the effect in the group comparison is open to debate. Tajfel contends that a positive social identity is the outcome of a "favorable social comparison" made between the in-group and other social groups. He admits that inter-group comparison, per se, can either be positive or negative in its effects upon inter-group relations.[134] In fact, both Tajfel and Turner (1985) observe that groups discriminated against often are not ethnocentric but just the opposite.[135] In that sense, the revivalist identification urge and comparative stance are non-confrontational. The revivalist's primacy in individual character building, especially by the RSS, is based on the assumption that most non-revivalist parties, including the Islamic parties, are more organized. The revivalist parties have a kind of defensive mentality (not offensive) and in their comparative vision there is no urge for violence. In a comparative scenario, a confrontation is not inevitable. As the philosopher Charles Taylor (1989) argues, in any inter-group comparison, the "misrecognition" can inflict harm as well as imprison someone "in a false ... mode of being,"[136] but the outcome may not be physical violence. Charles Taylor correctly takes a middle course in alluding to the shift in modern identity from attributes that are essentially determined at birth (one's religion, occupation, and economic status in life) to identities that are much less deterministic and more subject to choice in the modern era.[137] Taylor postulates that people's identity is "partly shaped by the recognition or its absences, often by misrecognition of others.[138] Thus, it becomes a politics of conviction. Comparison in religion, education, occupation, and domestic roles can now be fashioned at will largely than was possible in the past.[139] In Festinger's (1954) words, a notion of social comparison, being part of normal psychological functioning, is only a "social creativity," an artificial creation without the force of ferocity. In other words, most identity theories unnecessarily perceive the society as a place of conflict rather than cohesion. In short, the revivalist identity is not inherently all that aggressive as alleged by identity theorists such as Brass and Jaffrelot and others.

Further Arguments in the Causation of Violence Relating to Identity

Donald Horowitz offers two basic reasons for ethnic conflict. His reasons for violent activity such as communal riots are: (a) the relative absence of over-reaching identities with the state, which compete with those felt for the ethnic group, and (b) the absence of strong alternative identities "within" the ethnic group, e.g., class and language, which might form the basis of political action in non-ethnic parties. In this case, ethnic politics is the social norm that includes class and language, the attributes of socioeconomic position. These factors together produce a high density of ethnic conflict.[140] In short, a conflictual relationship between ethnic collectivities may exist only when one group tries to dominate the other.[141] Thus, revivalist historians, who reject the comparison as inconsequential, claim that since the rebellion of 1857, the Indian Muslims fell into a state of depression and increasing backwardness due to the refusal of British education, and nostalgia for the medieval imperial glory. During the 1920s, the politically frustrated separatist Muslim minority "took to the unscrupulous use of muscle power in a big way, creating street riots, tacitly encouraged by the colonial administration. In the first months of 1990, the entire Hindu population of the Kashmir Valley was driven out. The Hindu psyche failed to react because what an author calls "negationism" policy of the secular Hindus.[142] Ashis Nandy and Rajni Kothari, who are by no means supportive of revivalism, correctly argue that the issue of comparative perception and analysis is irrelevant because there is nothing like "Hindu civilization;" the Indian polity has always been "a confederation of cultures," and as such the issue of comparison in conflict is irrelevant.[143]

It is relevant to observe other factors in conflict situation. Radical Muslim groups calculate that assimilation and improvement of their status will not be possible in India. This highly placed non-assimilated minority Islamists, conscious of the existence of political Islam in neighboring Bangladesh or more importantly in Kashmir, begin to raise the "consciousness" of their group to claim that the stratification should change, not just at the level of individuals, but at the group level as well. In this instance, the Franz Fanon's "self-hate" by the minority is replaced with magnified pride and Muslim ethnocentrism. The minority elite now attribute the responsibility for its low status to discrimination on the part of the dominant group. The minority begins to struggle, often violently, against what it now perceives as social injustice.[144] It is an aggressive communalism, both Hindu and Muslim that poses people of different religions against each other; comparative stance may not have caused actual violence.

In sum, comparative identity analysts ignore that ethnicity is a flexible feature. As Cohen (1978) notes, ethnic boundaries are not enduring and stable.[145] Indeed, they ignore also a real world that is affected by history and culture.[146] Religion-based social groupings are not universal and in most cases harmless in India. For example, the Muslims of Kerala are part of the Malayam cultural stream and in that sense are closer to the Kerala Hindus and Christians than to the Urdu-speaking Muslims of north India. The Muslims of Tamil Nadu are much closer to Tamil Hindus and Christians.[147] An anthropological investigation in Karnatak state reports that good community relations are cemented during ceremonies of fakirs, across hybrid cults or within the individual community, in daily life as well as on the occasions of festivals.[148] Incidentally, the revivalist concern about the designs of hostile ideologies, globalization, and Westernization is not as paranoid as the defenders of social identity theorists as well as secular intellectuals in Calcutta, Aligarh, and New Delhi have alleged. As Elias Canetti investigates and Neera Chandhoke perceptively elaborates, riots have a short-span, and when the psychic high of emotion is spent, people return to normal ways of living with each other, and boundaries are restored to their "rightful place" in society.[149] This reinforces my underlying thesis that revivalism, in its attempts to glorify ancient past, has not caused any permanent friction in Indian society. As Ashutosh Varshney eloquently argues, communal identity by itself does not lead to conflict. For instance, in the state of Kerala, religious identities are principal basis of regional politics and yet communal violence is rare.[150]

Materialistic Interpretations of Riots

Rioters demonstrate a mixture of clear calculation and irrational passion in their action, carefully targeting their victims but finding emotional release in their killing. To a Marxist historian, it is a deeper hidden factor rather than an emotion that causes (as alleged by psychoanalysts such as Sudhir Kakar) violence. The Marxist analysis is comparable to the Freudian analysis in that both refuse to accept outward meanings at their face value and seek instead their underlying, and often hidden determinants. In the Marxist argument the structure of society must be analyzed to reveal the objective significance of the subjectively held ideologies. The analysis that basic social and class disparities cause riots has been testified by analyses of many case studies in different regions in the world.[151]

It appears that the materialistic interpretation has a broad range of varieties. Some have strong Marxist convictions, a few are liberal leftists, and many are simply advocates of "economism" (economic rationalism, a phrase used in Australia). Several Indian Marxist historians examine the entire gamut of Hindu Muslim relations from the colonial era up to today, arguing that in terms of education, trade, and industry, the Indian Muslims were "backward" from the early twentieth century. In the absence of a strong middle class attitude, the reactionary backward looking Muslim leaders, in their own self-interest, turned to inflammatory religious appeals.[152] Reporting on the Hindu side, Prem Shankar Jha, a political analyst and a senior columnist for *Outlook* magazine, offers a materialist interpretation when he writes that in Gujarat, the largest proportion of petit bourgeoisie, the shopkeepers and small businessmen (mostly Hindus) take the leadership role because owner-managed small businesses always feel the least control over their future. That breeds certain general insecurity and becomes a factor in causing riots, as communal relations get tense.[153] Highlighting an adverse effect of globalization, Neo-Marxists, including Immanuel Wallerstein, link the recurring ethnic conflicts directly to the economic distortions fostered by the global capitalist order, thus making ethnic struggles far more relevant than class conflicts. He adds that in India, the conflicts caused by an economic development strategy based on a substantially indirect trickle-down effect tend to aggravate the existing socio-economic disparities and to polarize further communal rivalries.[154]

This argument is advanced by Asghar Ali Engineer, a scholar-activist, who has written profusely on Hindu-Muslim riots, entertains a proto-Marxist belief, arguing that the roots of communal violence lie in uneven capitalist development and competitive politics. The poor and working classes so easily succumb to an elite conspiracy that is not in the poor men's material interests. He claims that social changes brought by economic development and technological progress decide the pattern of behavior and political perceptions.[155] For Engineer, the Muslims whose "economic situation was far from enviable" showed aggressive behavior as part of their social movement for justice.[156]

Differing from the mainstream Marxist analysis, and arguing for the poor Muslims, Engineer explores the Muslim elite's role in the political use of religion, claiming that a section of Muslim leadership in India has acquired "a vested interest" in an aggressive assertion of Islam and Islamic identity. Lower "caste"

Muslims such as Ansaris and Qureshis have acquired a measure of economic affluence in middle-sized cities and towns and they need their Islamic identity and religious symbols for social legitimating vis-à-vis Muslims of traditionally high status.[157] The Muslim artisan class is generally more formally religious than other classes, Engineer believes. Their oppressive and exploitative conditions and increasing anonymity in big towns make them even more religiously oriented. The political leadership exploits this religiosity of "lower middle class Muslims" and riots are expressions of these economic disparities.[158] But this is a partial explanation. As some historians of ethnic conflicts find, if political institutions historically provided preferential material benefits to ethnic groups whose political relevance had been previously established, then politicized ethnicity would continue, but it would not necessarily lead to violence. Nirvikar Singh, a culture historian, finds in reference to conflict in Kashmir and the Punjab that economic inequalities can exacerbate conflict but they are not always an essential ingredient for cultural conflict between Hindus and Muslims.[159]

Gail Omvedt, who teaches sociology at the Shivaji University in south India, sees conflict over religious ideologies as basic to the struggle for a more "egalitarian" economic order. Here ethnic violence is explained in terms of class conflict. Engineer relies on structural or societal assumptions.[160] Whereas for Marx, civil violence is integral to the transition process from one mode of production to the other, for Engineer, conflict is a direct expression of economic frustration. When the Muslims, with their rallying cry, "Islam is in danger," get support from the low castes and argue for a new call, "Harijan-Muslim bhai bhai" (lower caste solidarity with Muslims), they signal the importance of communal appeals against high cultured and rich Hindu classes. This is an example of interest-based, rather than religion based, competition for resources, and the results are communal violence in varied forms.[161]

Now the question is: Which is more important in causing violence, inequality or discrimination? Research by Clayton D. Peoples (2004) suggests, in a sociological survey, that political discrimination against a minority will most likely increase the likelihood of interethnic violence, followed by economic discrimination, and finally cultural discrimination, in accordance with their respective "pervasiveness."[162] Messner (1989) finds that discrimination has a stronger effect than inequality on the likelihood of violence.[163] Therefore, Engineer's conclusion that economically depressed Muslims reacted, almost in a typical linear Marxist mode, appears to be less than truth.

Like the Marxists the hegemonic left-liberal conceptualize and treat ethnicity as non-existent beyond administrative interventions. They stressed class as the crucial category to explain riots in which ethnic concerns, such as the revivalist reconstruction of epic age values, are reduced to a mere epiphenomena (superfluous baggage) of the past. Thus, for Gyandenra Pandey, Sumit Sarkar, and Amiya Bagchi and many others, revivalist religious ethnicity is a false consciousness, or a purely surface reflection of more basic class variables. Implicitly and with obvious misinterpretation, these Marxist intellectuals blame the forceful and purposeful construction of Indian identity for an immanent Indian proto-nation, present from antiquity onward. Their basic assumption is that this identity seeking effort by itself amounts to not only subversion of secularism but also an invitation for communal tension.

Several observations are due at this stage. First, most Marxists deduce that since there is poverty amongst the Muslims, they are likely to fight more than the Hindus, who are economically better off. Implicitly the burden of causing riots is laid on the discriminatory social system and supposedly richer Hindus. We may counter argue that if Hindu-Muslim conflicts are about resources, then bargains are possible, and in fact, have been made in history. In addition, poverty and low income are often symptoms of corrupt and incompetent government, and these symptoms can also provoke communal riots between communities. Second, as subaltern studies, which emerged in India in the 1980s, gaining some respectability among the university and college circles, demonstrate, the Marxists are correct in utilizing the analytical tools necessary to study material conditions, but they would do justice by analyzing more direct interactive relations between capital and violence, instead of attacking "modernity and classes."[164] Indeed, there is a difference between the existence of the class system and the assumption of being-consciousness. Thus, a combination of various disciplines may explain more fully the ethnic component of violence. While the economic factor is necessary to explain the communal attitude, it per se does not constitute an expression of communal violence because economic growth is only one instrument of human action.[165] The economic sphere does not mechanically translate into class identities. That communalism is an important problem among the nation's many other problems cannot be denied. It is true that economic stress has fuelled diverse ethnic insurgencies in India. Yet, riots cannot be prevented by mere "institutional engineering," i.e., Marxist redistribution of resources.[166]

It is fair to argue that most ethnoreligious conflicts involve at least some religious issues. Yet, religion is not a factor in many cases, as a broad empirical study indicates. Of the 105 ethnoreligious cases, only in 12 (11.4%) is religion a primary issue, but in another 65 (61.9 percent) it is only a secondary issue. In short, religion is not an issue at all in many cases.[167]

In sum, there is a gap in the leftist scholars' analysis. Because of their economic backwardness the Muslims have run into an insurmountable barrier to social modernization. Unrealistic demands are made upon the minority to become socially modernized even though the facilitating economic conditions for such modernization are absent.

Lack of Social Capital

Ashutosh Varshney (2001) demonstrates that where there are cross-cutting ties to connect different groups, such as associations that bring together Hindus and Muslims, conflict is addressed constructively and rarely descends into street violence; where these ties are lacking, there are no established channels for dealing with violence.[168] Varshney's studies involving 28 Indian cities involving Hindu-Muslim conflict have this conclusion: (a) if inter-group ties are weak, there are regular incidents of violence; (b) extensive bridging ties between Hindus and Muslims reduce incidence of conflict; and (c) membership in formal associations such as business clubs and recreation clubs are important in keeping the peace. The general argument of Varshney is that civic engagement between Hindus and Muslims can prevent violence.[169] A robust discussion on the linkage between civil society and maintenance of civil order has been introduced by several sociologists. Sanjeev Prakash and Per Selle (2004) doubt whether social capital in the form of associational contacts, formal or informal, can bridge differences between groups and communities. There are several analytical problems in the social capital faith. First, as Paul Brass demonstrates with concrete examples, it is likely that the creation of institutionalized riots systems override and displaces whatever forms of civic engagement and interethnic cooperation exist at some specific sites.[170] Second, one has to assess the normative contents or purposes of the group within which bonding ties are developed, and not on the form of institutional structures alone. There is often a trade-off between the "demands of strong groups or bonding ties and development of crosscutting and bridging linkages." Perhaps, social capital theory may distract us from more valuable tools in conflict analysis.[171] R.D. Putnam (1993) excluded Catholic associations from those relevant for the formation of social capital. Likewise, the *Rashtriya Sevak Sangh,* a member of the Hindu family of organizations, which is structured on Leninist-style of principles of leadership, may not qualify for social capital formation, and as such might not have contributed to communal harmony.

Fortunately, the notion of "associational life" in India does not include associations defined on particularistic and primordial identities such as kinship and religion.

Conclusion

India does not have the typical situation of frontier settings, as are the cases in Congo, Somalia, and Liberia.[172] Whether Hindu-Muslim ethnic violence is on the rise is debatable, but we are simply more aware of it now, as Yahya Sadowski (1999) observes. The literature on ethnic identification and communal violence is patently distorting (use of Nazi "pogrom" in narratives against the revivalists) and its distortion pervades much of the explanations about riots in recent years, both in the press and in more substantial works. Some concluding comments are due.

First, psychoanalysts, such as Sudhir Kakar, often think that they can ignore philosophy or ideas. In fact, their empirical analytical psychology rests on extensive systems of hidden metaphysics.[173] Indian psychologies clearly lack the West's sophisticated understanding and detailed analysis of areas such as psychodynamics, psychopathology, the unconscious and divided consciousness, and appear to have very little to offer in explaining conflict prone religious attitudes. The result is a current distortion in explanations.

Social science has shown decisively that any significant system of human behavior must have a substantial aspect of cultural determination. Psychoanalysis cannot escape from this fact. Rather, we should identify the cultural elements of what we do, so that we can think about them competently and appropriately. We may begin to understand psychoanalysis as culture by reflecting on our norms, our world-view, and our ethos.[174] Nevertheless, we must admit that the psychoanalysis of Hindu-Muslim violence provides a much-needed corrective to a complacent analysis fostered by the increasing categorization and description of contemporary lives by focusing on the social and political events. Primordialists well emphasize the "thick, compelling character of group membership," but they need to be more sensitive of ethnic conflict in varying circumstances. Conflict analysts tend to overemphasize the theories from the disciplines they are most familiar with, and do not pay enough attention from disciplines that are foreign to them.

Third, the Marxist interpretation that class and ideology is a more genuine basis of political alignment or that ethnicity is, for all purposes, poisonous to political health, is debatable. Ethnic affiliations and revivalist civilizational attitude provide a sense of security in a divided society, as well as a source of trust, certainty, reciprocal help, and protection against hostile neglect of one's interests by strangers.[175]

Fourth, a sustained faith in "muscular Hinduism" has not provided a "solid" cause for riots. Revivalists demand a cultural revival to strengthen Hindu community attachment. What is partly true is that religion, for the revivalists, is the vehicle by which they seek to achieve political power. Here is the relevance of the new religious politics paradigm. It is worth observing that secularism in India does not erect a "wall of separation" between church and state, but rather seeks to recognize and foster all religious communities. The form and degree of state accommodation of religious practice have been matters of controversy. Sociologist T.N. Madan insightfully argues that religion is not a subsystem of society; "holism and pluralism are not necessarily in conflict."[176]

In India, the sense of an ethnic group as a community and its competition with others to constitute the whole community creates a strong impetus toward party organization along revivalist ethnic and religious lines, but that situation does not provide an adequate explanation for communal riots. Hindu revivalist organizations today use advanced computers and other technologically developed gadgets to organize and monitor their agitational political activities. To justify their political agitation, they have tried to use religious prejudices combined with fear.

Fifth, commenting on ethnicity, it is wise to note that Max Weber justifiably argues that ethnic honor is a specific honor of the masses and ethnic member-ship does not constitute a group; it only facilitates group formation of any kind, particularly in the political sphere.[177] Implicit in his statement is the existence of actors who can find with ease among second-order identities some consolation, but the diverse social identities as citizens are never disturbed. Ashis Nandy espouses a view of Indian sense of "self" or identity that differs markedly from our everyday Western perceptions. In India, there is a continuum of civilization consciousness. "It is our ignorance of the psyche if these appearances appear mystic," claims Carl Jung.[178] Jung concludes that the personal unconscious or shadow includes those things about ourselves that we would like to forget. The collective unconscious refers to events that we all share, by virtue of having a common heritage, humanity. An anthropologist may readily discern an ethnic group, but until the members are themselves aware of the group's uniqueness, it is merely an ethnic group. While an ethnic group, including revivalists, may be other-defined, the nation is self-defined.[179] Thus, employing ethnicity in rela-tionship to several other types of identities beclouds the relationship between ethnic group and the nation. Exclusion and cultural superiority (ethnocentrism) is not Hindu revivalism's sole ingredient. To consider revivalist religious ethnic-ity only as a divisive obstacle to nation building remains one-sided.

Sixth, while new religious politics paradigm has largely and in many cases (including recent Gujarat riots) successfully explained the political misuse of religion, but its one-sided explanation is open to questions. Likewise, social identity model is thin in blaming revivalism and its comparative attitude. From the occasional anti-revivalists writings of sociologist Veena Das on riots to the philosophical arguments of Ashis Nandy on revivalist religious militancy and the psychoanalytical explanations of Sudhir Kakar, or Asghar Ali Engineer's Marxist interpretations about Hindu-Muslims frequent riots, we observe that one-dimensional analysis is inadequate. Many have not examined the role of the party dominated state. Is state connivance a crucial reason in the outbreak of violence or is it only a subsidiary cause?[180] An inter-disciplinary mix in explana-tion is desirable.

Seventh, the old "primordialist"/ "instrumentalist" debate is largely over but there is no scholarly unanimity on the issue of what ethnic identity entails. There are two propositions: (A) "Ethnicity-as-affect," where ethnic identities are cho-sen and valued because of the emotions they inspired. (B) "Ethnicity-as-strategy" which stresses the economic benefits. Where the first operate at the subconscious level, the second is a result of rational calculation. Both are "in-strumental" in the sense that both involve a choice of the ethnic groups.[181] For our analysis of Hindu-Muslim riots, perhaps it is wise to accept the perspective of ethnicity-as-strategy because rioters, not the masses, of both communities carefully calculate about how best to secure political and economic resources. In this sense, psychological rewards, associated with community affinity, are not enough for violence.

Last, as Ashutosh Varshney (2002) recommends, "strong association forms of civic engagement" such as integrated business organizations, trade unions, political parties, and professional associations, are able to control outbreaks of ethnic violence. The integrated "associational life" can serve as an agent of peace restraining those, including powerful politicians, who would polarize Hindus and Muslims along communal lines. Extensive inter-communal engagement in civic life, as was demonstrated by the engagement of Hindu-Muslim cooperation during the Gandhian popular political mobilization in the 1920s and 1930s, created a kind of "institutionalized peace system," and it is this, rather than administrative action, that determines whether or not bloody riots take place due to political use of religion. A dialogue and dialectic between revivalist movements and secularism would create an atmosphere of peace and stability; mere blame game, as is done by secularists, is not only un-moral but also historically un-authentic.

Notes

1. Beth Roy, *Some Trouble with Cows: Making a Sense of Social Conflict* (Berkeley: University of California Press, 1994), 146–47. The basic thesis in my argument is that common sense can be questioned, disputed, and affirmed. See Antonio Gramsci, *Selections from the Prison Notebooks*, edited by Quintin Hoare and Geoffrey Nowell Smith, New York: International Publishers, 1980. Two conceptualizations of ethnic identity seem to prevail in the main stream of the existing literature. There is a narrow definition stressing cultural attributes like language, customs, and origins, and which places emphasis on objective criteria and authenticity, and broader definition which lays emphasis on political behavior. From the standpoint of the second definition, ethnic groups reveal themselves the best only in interaction with other groups. There is a need to depart from the "false consciousness" paradigm by which we construe ethnic conflict as simply being the result of imperialism, class domination, or colonial stereotypes.

2. United States Institute of Peace, "Special Report 101: Lethal Ethnic Riots, Lessons from India and Beyond," February 2003 <http://www.usip.org/pubs/specialreports/sr101.html>.

3. Donald L. Horowitz, *Ethnic Groups in Conflict* (Berkeley: University of California Press, 1985); Horowitz, *The Deadly Ethnic Riot* (Berkeley: University of California Press, 2001).

4. Ravinder Kaur, *Religion, Violence and Political Mobilization in South Asia* (Thousand Oaks, Calif.: Sage Publications, 2005).

5. Russell Hardin, *One for All: The Logic of Group Conflict* (Princeton: Princeton University Press, 1995), 149.

6. Jonathan Spencer, "Problems in the Analysis of Communal Violence," *Contributions to Indian Sociology* 26, no. 2 (1992): 262–279.

7. Hardin, *One for All*, 150.

8. Iain Chambers and Lidia Curti, eds., *The Post-Colonial Question: Common Skies, Divided Horizons* (London: Routledge, 1996), 110. These two authors argue that Hindu revivalists have transformed the nature of traditional Hinduism, from tolerance to aggression.

9. *India Today,* cited in John McGuire, Peter Reeves and Howard Brasted, eds., *Politics of Violence From Ayodhya to Behrampada* (New Delhi: Sage Publications, 1996), 139.

10. Ethnic group refers to the nominal members of an ascriptive category such as race, language, caste, tribe, or religion. An ethnic party has set of categories to the exclusion of others, and that makes such a representation central to its strategy of mobilizing voters.

11. Usha Menon, "Do Women Participate in Riots? Exploring the Notion of 'Militancy' Among Hindu Women," *Nationalism & Ethnic Politics* 9, issue 1 (Spring 2003): 42–44.

12. T.N. Madan, "Secularsim in Its Place," *The Journal of Asian Studies* 46, 4 (1987): 747–59.

13. Paul R. Brass, *Language, Religion and Politics in Northern India* (London: Cambridge University Press, 1974), 14.

14. Ashutosh Varshney, "The Local Roots of India's Riots," *The Milli Gazette* 3, no. 7 (March 1, 2004): 1.

15. Vijoy Prasad, *Untouchable Freedom: A Social History of a Dalit Community* (Oxford: Oxford University Press, 2000).

16. Horowitz, *Ethnic Groups in Conflict,* 308.

17. J. Richard Eiser, "Acctuation Revisted," in *Social Groups and Identities: Developing the Legacy of Henri Tajfel,* ed. Peter Robinson (Oxford: Butterworth-Heinmann, 1996), 139.

18. Samina Ahmed, "The Politics of Ethnicity in India," *Regional Studies* (Islamabad) IX, no. 4 (Autumn 1991): 22–50.

19. Ted G. Gurr, *Minorities at Risk: A Global View of Ethnopolitical Conflicts* (Washington, D.C.: United States Institute of Peace Press, 1993), 3–5.

20. Paul R. Brass, *The Production of Hindu-Muslim Violence in Contemporary India* (Seattle: University of Washington Press, 2003).

21. Daniel Gold, "Organized Hinduisms: From Vedic Truth to Hindu Nation, " in *Fundamentalism Observed* 1, ed. Martin Marty and Scott Appleby (Chicago: University of Chicago Press, 1991); 576–77.

22. *Navabharata Times* (in Hindi, Bombay) (December 26, 1992), 6.

23. Bhikhu Parekh, *Rethinking Multiculturalism: Cultural Diversity and Political Theory* (London: Macmillan, 2000).

24. William Glaston, *Liberal Purposes: Goods, Virtues, and Diversity in the Liberal State* (Cambridge: Cambridge University Press, 191).

25. Lawrence E. Cahoone, *Civil Society: The Conservative Meaning of Liberal Politics* (London: Blackwell, 2002), 262.

26. Eric Hobsbawm and Terence Ranger, *The Invention of Tradition* (Cambridge: Cambridge University Press, 1983); Benedict Anderson, *Imagined Communities* (London: Verso, 1983).

27. Vinay Lal, ed., *Dissenting Knowledges, Open Futures : The Multiple Selves and Strange Destinations of Ashis Nandy* (Oxford: Oxford University Press, 2000), 274.

28. Theodore P. Wright, Jr., "The Muslim Minority Before and After Ayodhya," in *Hinduism and Secularism After Ayodhya,* ed. Arvind Sharma (New York: Palgrave, 2001), 3.

29. Sten Widmalm, "The Rise and Fall of Democracy in Jammu and Kashmir, 1975–1989," in *Community Conflicts and the State in India*, eds., Amrita Basu and Atul Kohli (Delhi: Oxford University Press, 1998), 149–182.

30. Daniel Posner, "Ethnic Fractionalisation: How (not) to measure It? What Does (and Does it Explain?" (paper presented at the Annual Meeting of the American Political Science Association, Atlanta, 1993).

31. Spencer, "Problems in the Analysis of Communal Violence," 266.

32. Dimostenis Yagcioglu, "Psychological Explanations of Conflicts between Ethnocultural Minorities and Majorities: A Overview" <http://www.geocities.com /Athens/8945/sycho.html>.

33. Sudhi Kakar, *The Colors of Violence: Cultural Identities, Religion, and Conflict (Chicago: Chicago University Press, 1996)*, 12–13, 52.

34. Kakar, *Colors of Violence*, 40.

35. Review by C.J.S. Walliam in *India Star Review of Books* (February 24, 2004), 9. <http://www.indiastar.com/wiilia5.html>.

36. Walker Connor, *Ethnonationalism: The Quest for Understanding* (Princeton: Princeton University Press, 1994), 220–21.

37. Sudhir Kakar, *The Essential Writings of Sudhir Kakar, with an Introduction by T.G. Vaidyanathan* (Oxford: Oxford University Press, 2001), xxvii–xxix.

38. Vamik D. Volkan, *Cyprus: War and Adaptation*, 78.

39. Sudhir Kakar, *The Inner World: A Psychoanalytic Study of Childhood and Society in India* (Delhi: Oxford University Press, 1981), 135.

40. Gananath Obeyeskere, *The Work of Culture: The Symbolic Transformation in Psychoanalysis and Anthropology* (Chocago: University of Chicago Press, 1990), 83.

41. C.J. Wallia, *Review of the Colors of Violence* <www.indolink.com/Book /book27.html> (2/24/2004); T.G. Vaidyanathan and Jeffrey J. Kripal, eds., *Vishnu on Freud's Desk: A Reader in Psychoanalysis and Hinduism* (Delhi: Oxford University Press, 1999); Sudhir Kakar, *Culture and Psyche*: *Psychoanalysis and India* (New York: Psyche Press, 1997).

42. Sudhir Kakar, *The Essential Writings of Sudhir Kakar* (with an introduction by T.G. Vaidyanathan) (Oxford: Oxford University Press, 2001), xxvii–xxix.

43. Asha Mukherjee, "Hindu Psychology and Bhagavat Gita," in *Religious Theories of Personality and Psychotherapy: East Meets West*, ed. R. Paul Olson (New York: The Haworth Press, 2002), 19–70.

44. Mario Rendon, "The Psychoanalysis of Ethnicity and the Ethnicity of Psychoanalyis," *The American Journal of Eethnicity and the Ethnicity of Psychoanalysis*, Vol. 53, no. 2 (1993), 111.

45. Horowitz, *Ethnic Groups*, 131.

46. Ralph Premdas, "The Political Economy of Ethnic Strife," *Ethnic Studies Report* (Fall 1989).

47. Ralph R. Premdas, "Public Policy and Ethnic Conflict,"in Mamangement of Social Transformations: Discussion Paper Series No. 12. <http://www.unesco.org/most /premdas.htl> (2/23/2004).

48. Clifford Geertz, "The Integrative Revolution: Primordial Sentiments and Civil Politics in the New States," in *Old Societies and New States*, ed. Clifford Geertz (New York: 1963), 109.

49. Horowitz, *The Deadly Ethnic Rio, 102*.

50. Mahesh Daga, "The Making of a Riot Narrative," <http://www.india-seminar.com/2002/519/519%20mahesh%20daga.htm> (3/5/2004).

51. Horowitz, *Ethnic Groups in Conflict*, 131.

52. E.A. Shils, "Primordial, Personal, Sacred, and Civil ties," *The British Journal of Sociology* 8 (1957): 130–45.

53. S. A. Giannakos, ed., *Ethnic Conflict: Religion, Identity, and Politics* (Athens: Oxford University Press, 2002), "Introduction," 10–11.

54. Kakar, *Colors of Violence*, 56.

55. T.G. Vaidyanathan, *The Essential Writings of Sudhir Kakar* (Oxford: Oxford University Press, 2001), xxx.

56. Stanley Jeyraja Tambiah, *Leveling Crowds: Ethnonationalist Conflicts and Collective Violence in South Asia* (Berkeley: University of California Press, 1996), 241.

57. Horowitz, *Ethnic Groups in Conflict*, 383.

58. Douglas S. Massey, "A Brief History of Human Society: The Origin and Role of Emotion in Social Life," *ASA: American Sociological Review* 67, no. 1 (2002): 22.

59. T. Ono et al., *Perception, Memory, and Emotion: Frontiers in Neuroscience* (Oxford: Pergamon, 1996), 90.

60. Stanley N. Kurtz, *All Mothers are One: Hindu India and the Cultural Reshaping of Psychoanalysis* (New York: Columbia University Press, 1992), 12 and 275.

61. Earl Conteh-Morgan, Collective *Political Violence: An Introduction to the Theories and Cases of Violent Conflicts* (New York: Routledge, 2004), 82.

62. Talcott Parsons and Robert Bales, *Family, Socialization and Interaction Process* (New York: The Free Press, 1955), 98.

63. Horowitz, *Ethnic Groups in Conflict*, 308.

64. V. Reynolds, V.S. Falger, and I. Vine, eds., *The Sociobiology of Ethnocentrism: Evolutionary Dimensions of Xenophobia, Discrimination, Racism and Nationalism* (London: Croom Helm, 1987), xv.

65. Hardin, *One for All*, 223.

66. Barton in E. Rogers, *The Diffusion of Innovations* (New York: Free Press, 1995), 4th ed, 120.

67. Horowitz, *Ethnic Groups in Conflict*, 1985, 684.

68. E.A. Tiryakian and R. Rogowski, eds., *New Nationalalisms of the Developed West* (London: Allen & Unwin, 1985).

69. Benedict Anderson, *Imagined Communities*, 7.

70. Russell Hardin, *One for All*, 23.

71. Russell Hardin, *One for All*, 24.

72. Walker Connor, *Ethnonationalism: The Quest for Understanding* (Princeton: Princeton University Press, 1994), 73–74, 153, 174.

73. Jonathan Fox, "Is Islam More Conflict Prone than Other Religion? A Cross Sectional Study of Ethnoreligious Conflict," *Nationalism and Ethnic Politics* 6, no. 2 (2000): 1–23.

74. Michael Billing, *Social Psychology and Intergroup Relations* (London: Academic Press, 1976), 279.

75. W. James, *The Principles pf Psychology* (New York: Dover, 1950), 97–98.

76. Eugene Weiner, ed., *The Handbook of Interethnic Coexistence* (New York: Continuum, 1998), 135–36.

77. David Taylor and Malcolm Yapp, *Political Identity in South Asia* (London: Curzon Press, 1979).

78. Brass, *Ethnicity and Nationalism*, 84.

79. Daga, *The Making of a Narrative*, 4.

80. Beth Roy, *Some Trouble with Cows: Making Sense of Social Conflict* (Berkeley: University of California Press, 1994), 82.

81. Charles Tilly, "Contentious Conversation." <http://www.geocities.com/ usman-far82/contentious.html> (18 March 2004).

82. Roy, Some *Troubles with Cows*, 138.

83. Atul Kohli, *Democracy and Discontent: India's Growing Crisis of Governability* (Cambridge: Cambridge University Press, 1990).

84. Paul R. Brass, *The Production of Hindu-Muslim Violence in Contemporary India* (Seattle: University of Washington Press, 2003), 89.

85. Veena Das, ed., *Mirrors of Violence, Communities, Riots and Survivors in South Asia* (Delhi: Oxford University Press, 1990.

86. Horowitz, *Ethnic Groups in Conflict*, 56.

87. Christophe Jaffrelot, "The Politics of Processions and Hindu-Muslim Riots," in *Community Conflicts*, ed. Amrita Basu and Atul Kohli 60–61.

88. Jaffrelot, "The Politics of Processions."

89. Nikki Keddie, "The New Religious Politics and Women World-wide: A Comparative Study," *Journal of Women's History* 10, no. 4 (2004): 2–5.

90. Keddie, "Secularism and the State: Towards Clarity and Global Comparison," *New Left Review* (November/December 1997): 34–35.

91. Keddie, "The New Religious Politics and Women Worldwide: A Comparative Study," *Journal of Women's History* 10, no 4.

92. Paul Brass, *Ethnicity and Nationalism: Theory and Comparison* (New Delhi: Sage Publictaions, 1991), 84.

93. Primal Eugene Weiner, ed., *The Handbook of Interethnic Coexistence* (New York: Continuum, 1998), 138.

94. David Singh, "The Conflict Between Hindus and Muslims in India," <http://staff-www.uni-mar.de/-vonredo/remaposingh.html> (25 April 2005).

95. Paul R. Brass, "The Gujarat Pogrom of 2002," *Contemporary Politics* (SSRC HOME) <http://conconflicts.ssrc.org/Gujarat/brass/> (29 March 2004).

96. Anna Bigelow, "Hulladiya Hanuman: the Return or the End of History?" <http://conconflicts. Ssrc.org/Gujarat/biglow/> (29 March 2004).

97. Cited in Veera Vaishnava, "Faith, Diplomacy and India," <http://www.india-forium.com?columbus/Veera_Vaishnava?Faith,_Diplomacy_and India/26> (25 April 2005).

98. Kohli, *Democracy and Discontent*, 266.

99. S.D. Muni, "Ethnic Conflict, Federalism, and Democracy in India," 9.

100. Steven Wilkinson, "Ethnic Violence as Campaign Expenditure: Riots, Competitions and Turnout in Gujarat 2002," internet.

101. Horowitz, *Deadly Ethnic Rio*, 326–73.

102. Upendra Baxi, "The Second Gujarat Catastrophe," <http://conconflicts.ssrc.org/ gujarat/baxi/> (29 March 2004).

103. Tambiah, *Leveling Crowds*, 285.

104. Horowitz, *Ethnic Groups in Conflict*, 104.

105. Hardin, *One for All*, 9.

106. Amiya Kumar Bagchi, "Predatory Commercialization and Communalism in India," in *Anatomy of a Confrontation: The Babri Masjid-Ramjanmabhumi Issue,* ed. Sarvepalli Gopal (Delhi: Penguin Books, 1991), 213.

107. Mark Juergensmeyer, *The New Cold War?* (Berkeley: University of California Press, 1993).

108. Jonathan Fox, "Counting the Causes and Dynamics of Ethnoreligious Violence," *Totalitarian Movements & Political Religions* 4, no. 3 (Winter 2003): 128.

109. Brass, *The Production,* 35.

110. Veena Das, "Introduction: Communities, Riots, Survivors—The South Asian Experience," in *Mirrors of Violence: Communities,* ed. Veena Das, 28.

111. Cited in S.D. Muni, "Ethnic Conflict, in 2–25–04. S.D. Muni, "Ethnic Conflict, Federalism, and Democracy in India," <http://www.unu.edu/unupress/unupbooks /uu12ee/uu12eeOj.htm> (25 February 2004).

112. Spencer, "Problems in the Analysis of Communal Violence," 271.

113. Mushirul Hasan, "Competing Symbols and Shared Codes: Inter-Community Relations in Modern India," in *Anatomy of a Confrontation,* ed. Sarvepalli Gopal, 113–14.

114. Atul Kohli, *Democracy and Discontent: India's Growing Crisis of Governability* (Cambridge: Cambridge University Press, 1990), 152–53.

115. John Harriss, Review of Ashutosh Varshney, Ethnic *Conflict and Civic Life: Hindus and Muslims in India; Frontine* 19, issue 11 (May 25–June 7, 2002), 6.

116. Robert Putnam, *Making Democracy Work* (Princeton: Princeton university Press, 1993).

117. Kohli, *Democracy and Discontent,* 402.

118. Nancy A. Piotrowski and Tracy Iron-Georges, eds., *Psychology* 4 (Pasadena, CA.: 2003): 1483–84.

119. Alan E. Kazdin, ed., *Encyclopedia of Psychiology* (New York: Oxford University press, 2000), 342.

120. Paul Brass, "The Rise of the BJP and the Future of Party Politics in Uttar Pradesh," in H. Gould and S. Ganguly, eds., *India Votes* (Boulder, Co: Westview Press, 1993), 274; Christophe Jaffrelot, *The Hindu Nationalist Movement* (New York: Columbia University Press, 1996), 392.

121. M. G. Smith, *The Plural Society in the British West Indies* (Berkeley: University of California Press, 1966), 90–91.

122. Daniel Gold, "Organized Hinduisms: From Vedic Truth to Hindu Nation," in Martin E. Marty and R. Scott Appleby, eds., *Fundamentalisms Observed* 1 (Chicago: University of Chicago Press, 1991), 576–77.

123. Joel Best, *Threatened Children* (Chicago: Chicago University Press, 1990), 89; Gary Alan Fine, "Scandal, Social Conditions, and the Creation of Public Attention: Fatty Arbuckle and the Problem of Hollyhood," *Social Problems* 44 (1998),:297–323.

124. *Navbbharat Times* (in Hindi) (Bombay, December 26, 1992), 6.

125. Varshney, *Ethnic Conflict and Civic Life,* 27.

126. Ashutosh Varshney, "The Local Roots of India's Riots," *The Milli Gazette* 3, no. 7 (March 1, 2004):1.

127. Vijoy Prasad, *Untouchable Freedom: A Social History of a Dalit Community* (Oxford; Oxford University Press, 2000).

128. Usha Menon, ""Do Women Participate in Riots? Exploring the Notion of 'Militancy' among Hindu Women," *Nationalism & Ethnic Politics* 9, issue 1 (Spring 2003): 42–44.

129. J. Richard Eiser, "Accentuation Revisted," in *Social Groups & Identities: Developing the Legacy of Henri Tajfel* (Oxford: Butterworth-Heinemann, 1996), ed. W. Peter Ropbinson, 139.

130. Emile Durkheim, *The Elementary Forms of Religious Life*, trns. Joseph Ward Swain (New York: Free Press, 1965); C. Ram-prasad, "Hindutva Ideology: Extracting the Fundamentals," *Contemporary South Asia* 2, no. 3 (1993): 304.

131. Ralph R. Premdas, "Public Policy and Ethnic Conflict," *Management of Social Transformation—MOST*, 19 <http://www.unesco.org/most/premdas.html> (23 February 2004)

132. Robert Bates, "Ethnic Competition and Modernization in Contemporary Africa," *Comparative Political Studies* 6, no. 4 (1974): 457–83; Albert Breton, "The Economic of Nationalism," *Journal of Political Economy* 72, No. 4 (1964),:376–86.

133. Horowitz, *Ethnic Groups*, 138.

134. Weiner, *Handbook of Interethnic*, 207.

135. H. Tajfel and J.C. Turner, " The Social Identity Theory of Intergroup Behavior," in S. Worchel and W. G. Austin, eds., *Psychology of Inter-group Relations* (Chicago: Nelson-Hall, 1985), 90–92.

136. Charles Taylor, *Multiculturalism and the Politics of Recognition* (Princeton: Princeton University Press, 1992), 25.

137. Charles Taylor, *Sources of the Self* (Cambridge, MA: Harvard University Press, 1989).

138. Taylor, "The Politics of Recognition," in *Multiculturalism Examining the Politics of Recognition*, ed. Amy Gutmann (Princeton, New Jersey: Princeton University Press, 1994), 25.

139. A. Giddens, *Modernity and Self Identity: Self and Society in the Late Modern Age* (Cambridge: Polity, 1991).

140. Giddens, *Modernity and Self Identity*, 18.

141. Giddens, *Modernity and Self Identity*, 5.

142. "Negotionism in India" <http://www.bharatvani.org/books/negaind/ch2.htm> (31 March, 2004).

143. Ashis Nandy and Rajni Kothari, "Culture, State and the Recovery of Indian Politics," *Economic and Political Weekly* (December 8, 1984). 23.

144. Dimostenis Yagcioglu, "Psychological Explanations of Conflicts between Ethnocultural Minorities and Majorities," <http://www.geocities.com?athens/8945/sycho.html> (30 March, 2004).

145. Ronald Cohen, *Ethnicity: Problem and Focus in Anthropology. Annual Review of Anthropolgy* 7 (1978): 379–87.

146. Leonie Huddy, "From Social to Political Identity: A Critical Examination of Social Identity Theory," *Political Psychology* 22, no. 1 (2001): 127.

147. Asghar Ali Engineer, "Muslims and the Mainstream," *South Asian Voice: Views from South Asia* (May 1998 Edition).

148. Jackie Assayag, *At The Confluence of Two Rivers: Muslims and Hindus in south India* (New Delhi: Manohar, 2004).

149. Elias Canetti, Crowds and Power (New York: Farrar, Strauss, 1984), 9; Neera Chandhoke, *Beyond Secularism: The Rights of Religious Minorities* (New Delhi: Oxford University Press, 1999), 211.

150. Ashutosh Varshney, "Postmodernism, Civic Engagement, and Ethnic Conflict: A Passage to India," *Comparative Politics* 30, issue 1 (October 1997): 2.

151. Valery A. Tishkov, "Ethnic Conflicts in the Context of Social Science Theories" <http://www.unu.edu/unupress/unupress/unupbooks/uu12ee08.htm (February 26, 2004).

152. Bipan Chandra, *Indian National Movement, the Long Term Dynamics* (New Delhi: Vikas Publishing House, 1988), 203, 205–06, 212, 258–59.

153. Scott Baldauf, "India Watches Quietly as Communal Riots Intensify," *The Christian Science Monitor* (April 25, 2002).

154. Immanuel Wallerstein, *The Capitalist World Economy* (Cambridge: Cambridge University Press, 1979).

155. Asghar Ali Engineer, ""Hindu-Mus*lim* Relations before and After 1947," in *The Babri- Masjid-Ramjanmabhumi Issue*, ed. Sarvepalli Gopal, 191.

156. Ashgar Ali Engineer, "Indian Muslims in Contemporary MultiReligious Society," in Religi*on and Political Conflict in South Asia: India: Pakistan, and Sri Lanka*, Douglas Allen (Delhi: Oxford university Press, 1993), 60–61.

157. Ashgar Ali Engineer, *Indian Muslims—A Study of Minority Problems in India* (Delhi: Ajanta Publications, 1986), 45.

158. Asghar Ali Engineer, "Indian Muslims in a Contemporary Multi-Religious Society" in *Religion and Political Conflict in South Asia*, Allen, 62.

159. Nirvikar Singh, "Cultural Conflict in India: Punjab and Kashmir," in Beverely Crawford and Ronnie D. Lipschutz, eds., *The Myth of 'Economic Conflict': Politics, Economics, and 'Cultural Violence'* (Berkeley: University of California Press, 1998), 346.

160. Gail Omvedt, "Dalit Literature in Maharashtra," *South Asia Billetin* 7, nos. 1 and 2 (Fall 1987): 78–85.

161. Ghanshyam Shah, cited by Amedeo Maiello, "Ethnic Conflict in Post-Colonial India," in *The Post-Colonial Question*, ed. Iai Chambers and Lidia Curti, 108.

162. Clayton D. Peoples, "How Discriminatory Policies Affect Inteethnic Violence: A Cross-National, Group-Level Analysis," *International Journal of Sociology* 34, no. 1 (2004): 85, 97.

163. Steven S. Messner, "Economic Discrimination and Societal Homicide Rates: Further Evidence on the Cost of Inequality," *American Sociological Review* 54 (1989): 507–611.

164. Frederick Cooper, "Conflcit and Connection: Rethinking Colonial African History," in David Luddened., *Reading in Subaltern Studies: Critical History, Contested Meaning and the Globalization of South Asia* (London: Anthem Press, 2002), 259.

165. S.C. Dube, *Modernization and Development: The Search for Alternative Paradigms* (London: Zed Books, 1988), 62.

166. Amedeo Maiello, "Ethnic Conflcit in Post-Colonial India," in *The Post-Colonial Question: Common Skie: Divided Horizons*, ed. Iain Chambers and Lidia Curti (London: Routledge, 1996), 110.

167. Jonathan Fox, "Counting the Causes and Dynamics of Ethnoreligious Violence," *Totalitarian Movements & Political Religions* 4, issue 3 (Winter 2003): 119.

168. Ashutosh Varshney, *Ethnic Conflict and Civic Life: Hindus and Muslims in India* (New Haven: Yale University Press, 2001).

169. Ashutosh Varshney, "Ethnic Conflict and Civil Society: India and Beyond," *World Politics* 53, no. 3 (April 2001): 362–98.

170. Paul R. Brass, *The Production of Hindu-Muslim Violence in Contemporary India* (Seattle: University of Washington Press, 2003), 27.

171. Sanjeev Prakash and Per Selle, *Investigating Social Capital*, 31.

172. An American psychoanalyst has explained the nature of frontier conditions. See Ken Jowitt, "Ethnicity: Nice, Nasty, and Nihilistic," in *Ethnopolitical Warfare: Causes, Consequences, and Possible Solutions*, ed. Daniel Chirot and Martin E.P. Seligman (Washington, D.C.: American Psychological Association, 2001), 30–33.

173. Roger Wals, "Two Asian Psychologies and Their Implications for Western Psychotheraphists," *American Journal of Psychotherapy* XIII, no. 4 (1988): 546–48.

174. Robert T. Fancher, "Psychoanalysis as Culture," *Issues in Psychoanalytic Psychology* 15, no. 2 (1993): 81–93.

175. Donald L. Horowitz, "Democracy in Divided Societies," in *Nationalism, Ethnic Conflict, and Democracy*, eds. Larry Diamond and Marc F. Plattner (Baltimore: The Johns Hopkins University Press, 1994), 49.

176. T.N. Madan, "Epilogue: Religion in India: An Essay in Interpretation," in *India's Religions: Perspectives from Sociology and History*, ed. T.N. Madan (Delhi: Oxford University Press, 2004), 407.

177. D.P. MacAdams, *Power, Intimacy, and the Life Story: Personological Inquiries into Identity* (New York: Guilford Press, 1985), 90, 92–93.

178. C. Jung cited in G. Adler, ed., *Letters* (Princeton: Princeton University Press, 1972), 535.

179. Charles Winick, *Dictionary of Anthropology* (New York: Palgrave, 1956), 193.

180. For a summary interpretations, see Mahesh Daga, "The Making of a Narrative" <http://www.india-seminar.com/20002/519/519%mahesh20daga.htm>.

181. Daniel Nolan Posner, "The Institutional Origins of Ethnic Politics in Zambia" (Ph.D. thesis, Department of Government, Harvard University, 1998), 16.

Part II

Contemporary Regional Ethnic Conflict

Chapter 6

Multifaceted Ethnic Conflicts and Conflict Resolution in Nigeria

Abdul Karim Bangura

The oil rich Federal Republic of Nigeria, Africa's most populous nation with hundreds of different ethnic groups, has over the past decades had a surfeit of ethnic conflicts that have escalated as a result of several differences, and they continue to impede its economic growth and development. As a result, there has been an insurgence of third-party intervention all through the ages in an effort to douse tension and de-escalate fratricidal carryings-on. Under the guidelines of several theories explaining conflict and its resolution, this qualitative essay sets out to examine the nature of the escalation of the Nigerian ethnic conflict through religious, economic, and social differences. The role played by 'third parties' over the years as well as the role played by Nigerian women in the on-going conflict in the Niger Delta region of the country are also assessed.

Introduction

All around the world, human existence seems to be at risk not only because of such social aberrations like mutual mistrust, intolerance and hatred, insecurity, ethnocentrism, language differences, religious fanaticism, intra- and inter-state conflicts, but also because of the human's inability to predict, manage and control intending disorders. As a result, there has been an insurgence of internal violence especially in most developing countries, with Africa being the most severely hit. The African continent has witnessed a surge of ethnic conflicts, which is threatening to the development, stability and security of African states.

In the past few years, ethnic conflicts have presented the most daunting challenge to both national and international security. In order to attempt to contain this situation, an understanding of the root causes and escalatory mechanisms of these conflicts is utterly essential. In attempting to shed more light on conflicts in Africa using Nigeria as a case study, this essay focuses on the background of ethnic conflicts in Nigeria and their current manifestations.

During the 19th Century, social scientists sought to understand the forms of social life and the psychological character of social control. Although there is a large volume of literature written about the nature and theory of conflict, "social scientists are divided on the question whether social conflict should be regarded as something rational, constructive, and socially functional or something irrational, pathological, and socially dysfunctional."[1]

Given that the majority of conflicts in the developing world are characteristically protracted, theorists such as Edward Azar have directed attention to the fact that an all-inclusive approach identifying and analyzing their multiple causal factors is crucial. Azar used the term protracted social conflict "to suggest the type of on-going and seemingly unresolvable conflict."[2] This line of argument is also supported by Stephen Ryan who defines protracted conflicts as "usually conflicts between ethnic groups which have been going on for some time, and which may appear to be un-resolvable to the parties caught up in them."[3] These conflicts are fuelled by political and economic underdevelopment. As Azar states, "The roots of protracted social conflict are to be found at the interlocking nexus of underdevelopment, structural deprivation (political, economic, and psychological) and communal or identity cleavages."[4] In a country such as Nigeria where social, political, and economic inequalities are enormous, ethnic discrimination ensues. This leads to structural victimization, actual physical and psychological deprivation which Azar argues bursts into hostile and violent actions.[5]

There is the primordial perspective which presents the ubiquity of ethnocentrism. Primordialism originated in the anthropological writings of Shils and Geertz who hypothesized that all modern humans are subject to the strong and prevailing emotional influence of ancient primordial bonds of their ethnicities.[6] This perspective argues that ethnic conflicts are irrational blood feuds that cannot be eliminated.[7] The argument introduced here is that the hostility of the we-group or in-group toward the others-group or out-groups has its roots in primordial desire, an attempt to connect group identity, which is established through conflict. The socio-psychological dynamics of primordial attachments form a very powerful basis for the articulation of a sense of group consciousness. Ethnicity comes to resemble a double-edged sword in that it reassures the individual that he or she is not alone, "which is what all but a very few human beings most fear to be," yet it may be just as easily used as a vehicle for mobilizing "us" against "them."[8] According to David Carment, "Collective identities in underdeveloped societies are particularly conflict prone because identities are derived from *fundamental, incontrovertible,* and *non-negotiable* values such as language, history, and religion."[9]

Georg Simmel, in his study of group-binding functions of conflict, holds that conflict sets boundaries between groups within a social system by strengthening group consciousness and awareness of separateness, thereby establishing the identity of groups within the system. Simmel also states that reciprocal "repulsions" maintain a total social system by creating a balance between various groups.[10]

Opposing the primordial perspective, instrumentalists hypothesize that ethnic conflict is not a function of the natural division of groups into nation states, but rather a product of elite machination of nationalist sentiments for their political ambition.[11] Reinforcing this line of reasoning is Merton's citation of several instances of positive gestures of in-group toward out-group members in social interaction.[12] Singer has provided support for this perspective in a study of the cultural factors on prolonged rivalries. Elite manipulation of cultural differences, according to Singer, is the main cause of conflict, not culture.[13]

The majority of the literature on post-Cold War conflicts takes culture into consideration as the root cause of these conflicts. The current emphasis on ethnic groups or cultures as units of analysis in international security and the only way to ensure peace is a result of the acceptance of this culture-based paradigm.[14] While the dominant theories in ethno-nationalist studies approach the topic from varying perspectives, they cannot account for some of the conflicts that have occurred on the African continent.

The qualitative/simple case study method is employed in this essay. It is qualitative because the analysis of the various theoretical explanations is based on non-numerical data. For the reason that it examines the particular case of Nigeria using secondary data sources, it is a case study. Robert K. Yin explores the concept of a case study and defines it in three ways: (1) to look at a present day phenomenon in the context of real life, and when (2) the separation between the phenomenon and real life is blurred, and (3) when many sources are used.[15] In the following analysis, the escalation of conflicts in Nigeria is scrutinized. Due to the availability of information, time constraints, and the relative cost involved in using alternative techniques of data collection, the archival or document analysis technique was used to collect the data for this study of various references and the subsequent analysis of their content.

Nigerian Conflicts and Attempted Resolutions: A Kaleidoscope

Conflict can be linked to cultural differences, and a conflict is usually a direct challenge of a person's beliefs. According to David Newsom, negotiation is not the core of the problem; instead, it is the final stage in a process that involves profound understanding of other cultures.[16] Thus, negotiation requires creative approaches which, according to Louis Kriesberg, minimize violence and hostility between rivals and attain agreements mutually acceptable to the parties[17].

In Nigeria, conflict resolution is practiced by indigenous organizations that are set up to resolve interpersonal and group conflicts between members of communities. The ability of urban residents to join together to form associations creates a formidable platform for conflict management. Rothchild rightly asserts that the development of a bargaining culture has been crucial for moderating conflict within African states. A sense of shared fate prevents ethnic or religious differences from becoming completely devastating. With its emphasis on commonality and sharing, community asserts that conflict comes from perceptions of differences, and, therefore, solutions to conflict must work to create a common identity among people. Conflict can be linked to cultural differences, which definitely need to be taken into consideration when approaching conflict management. Conflict is all about context.[18]

Ever since independence in 1960, many Nigerians have found it difficult to live together as one nation. In fact, some have never forgiven the British colonialists for arbitrarily throwing together multifaceted ethnic groups and then leaving them to try and get along with one another. Sometimes, Nigerians have appeared to have nothing more in common with one another than a mutual suspicion of whoever was in power and love for soccer. Yet overwhelming majorities of Hausa and Yoruba have always lived peacefully side-by-side and are traditionally tolerant of each other's customs. Although it had one of the greatest potential among countries that achieved independence in the post-World War II era, Nigeria now exhibits a profound crisis in virtually every dimension of public life.[19]

Ethnic security dilemma, a concept borrowed from international relations, posits that groups' war when no sovereign authority can ensure a group's security. Although this concept is particularly important when explaining conflicts where governments are absent or weak, it has explanatory power for all cases where groups feel threatened. Ethnic conflict occurs as an outgrowth of group fears of being dominated, in both material and cultural ways, by other groups. This leads to a desire for hegemony. A hegemonic group seeks to have its way of life become dominant while subjugating rival groups. A subjugated rival group also seeks to have hegemony over weaker subjugated groups. The ambitions of ethnic elites, who play on ethnic fears, hatreds, and ambitions to gain or to maintain power, do nothing to ease the situation.

The quest to ensure security often continues to the point that it threatens other groups, which in turn mobilize and arm themselves. This leads to a dilemma as seeking to enhance one's own security causes reactions that, in the end, can make one less secure.[20] Elite members manipulate their groups into accepting and practicing the dehumanization of rival groups. However, as Stuart Kaufman argues, exaggerations about the dangers rival groups pose can lead to actual violence, which may expose the vulnerability of a rival group, or other structural problems, creating a self-sustaining conflict spiral.[21]

The history of "Nigeria" is as complex as the origin of the name. While some argue that the name suggests the agglomeration of pagan and Islamic states under British rule,[22] others suggest that the name arose from the artificial boundaries set by and at the convenience of the British and French during colonial rule in West Africa and the diverse cultures and vast distances that separate the people(s).[23] There are 10 principal national groups in Nigeria, which constitute about 80 percent of the entire population. They are as follows: Hausa-Fulani, Yoruba, Igbo, Efik/Ibibio, Kanuri, Tiv, Ijaw, Edo, Urhobo, and Nupe (Nigerian Constitution Section 15(3)). Among these groups, the religiously bicommunal Yoruba from the Southwest, the Muslim Hausa-Fulani from the North, and the predominantly Christian Igbo from the Southeast are the three major ethnic groups, which have historically dominated the political and economic spheres of the country since independence, even though the Yoruba and Igbo have generally maintained marginalization by the Hausa-Fulani hegemony. The rest of the population is believed to be made up of between 250 and 400 ethnic minority groups, ranging in size from several thousand to a few million, comprising adherents of Christianity, Islam, and traditional indigenous religions, with each group having its own distinct language.[24]

Ethnicity in Nigeria is "an exceedingly complex amalgam of multifaceted and interpenetrating identities" that are still very much in the process of evolution and are ever "shifting up or down" in scale and intensity depending on the political or economic context.[25] The principal reason for the collapse of the asymmetric three-region system bestowed by the British at independence was precisely that it gave inadequate recognition to the multiplicity, complexity, and latent fluidity of ethnic territorial interests in the federation. Instead, this system reified the country's major tripartite ethnic cleavage and transformed "a multiple ethnic balance of power," with no single ethnic group forming a majority, into a "federal imbalance" with the Northern Region alone comprising more than half the country's population and three-quarters of its territory.[26] The consequences of this faulty structure included the ethno-regional polarization of party competition in the ill-fated First Republic (1960-1966) and the eventual outbreak of a civil war in 1967.

In 1960, at the time Nigeria won its independence, the Nigerian and British governments jointly signed a defense agreement. Because of the difficulty felt by Nigeria to sustain such an agreement while trying to improve its own image as a regional power and also encouraging the francophone African countries to renounce their defense links with France, the agreement was eventually abrogated in January of 1962.

On May 30, 1967, the Biafran Republic started a two-and-a-half-year civil war when it declared independence and seceded from the Nigerian Federation. On July 6, 1967, the hostilities of the Nigerian civil war broke out when the Federal government of Nigeria under General Yakubu Gowon used military force to put an end to the secession of the Biafran province in eastern Nigeria. The Biafran leader, General Odumegwu Ojukwu, had declared Biafra's independence a few days earlier on May 30, 1967. The Igbos, the majority of whom were Catholics, were by far the dominant ethnic group in Biafra, which contains most of the country's oil resources, as well as a thriving agricultural sector. The war was one of the bloodiest in African history, with over one million lives lost, mainly Biafran civilians who starved to death.[27]

Outside support was essential for both factions, and it enabled them to continue the fighting. An initial arms embargo by a number of Western nations, including France and the United States, on all parties involved proved insufficient to end the conflict. Britain and the Soviet Union did not subscribe to the embargo. International support was split among the two factions and formed highly unusual alliances. While Britain, Egypt, the Soviet Union and Algeria strongly supported the federal authorities, France, Portugal, Israel, Spain, China, South Africa, and Rhodesia (now Zimbabwe) sided with the major ethnic group—the Igbos—in the secessionist Biafra.

Escalatory Mechanisms

Religious-ethnic Differences

"Paradoxically, ethnicity is an effective means of mobilizing around common material interests precisely because of its non-material, that is symbolic, content, which masks or 'mystifies' those interests for the group members themselves."[28] Nigeria is a multiethnic and multi-religious society. Each of the ethnic and religious groups has beliefs and values, which could ignite hostility, anger, and violent conflict with ethnic and religious basis. Religious affiliation in the country is equally as dynamic as ethnic identity. Before the arrival of Christianity and Islam, the people of Nigeria had and were already deeply rooted in their own religious institutions and beliefs. However, the Christian missionaries who established formal education in this region influenced southern Nigeria, leading to a concentration of Christianity in this region. Although the Northern region has remained dominated by Muslims, primarily as a result of an agreement between the colonial administration and Northern emirates that barred Christianity from the North, southern Christians that migrated to the North established churches there. Prior to the 1970s and the oil boom period, there were few incidents in which religion was manipulated for political purposes. Coinciding with a global rise in fundamentalist movements in the 1980s, however, the country experienced a rise in blood-shedding religious conflicts primarily between Christians and Muslims. As at 1999, the country was reported to have had more than 10 major ethnic/religious riots in about five major cities in its northern and southern regions.

The religious division was further strengthened in 1986 when, under the military rule of Ibrahim Babangida, a Northern Muslim, his administration recommended that Nigeria join the Organization of Islamic Conference (OIC). The proposal by the Abacha administration, in June of 1997, of Nigeria becoming a member of the Developing Eight, a group of Muslim countries that planned to ascend the ladder of industrialization in June of 1997, opened old sores and led to an escalation of religious tension across several Nigerian states. At the heart of this tension is the recent decision by some of the southern states to adopt the Islamic legal principles of *Shari-ah* law, a requirement to the practice of Islam, which represents the concrete embodiment of the divine will versus secular laws. Since Nigeria is not an Islamic state, promulgation the *Shari-ah* by Northern leaders appears to be inconsistent with the Nigerian constitution and clearly serves as a threat to the secular foundation of the nation. The *Shari-ah* is a way of life for Muslims, but some have argued that those oushing the *Shari-ah* in the North may have a different agenda ending attempts to lasting democracy and getting rid of the present government, which is headed by a southern Christian. In this regard, one must view the recent religious tension as detrimental to efforts of political integration in Nigeria. The problem with this argument is that the Vice President of the current government is a Muslim from the North.

Religious conflict broadened into regional conflict by the end of the 1980s. The succession to the Sultanate of Sokoto split the Muslim community into supporters of the late Sultan's son from the North and those, including Babangida, favoring Ibrahim Dasuki from the Middle Belt, setting off riots in Sokoto among those supporting the northern traditional hierarchy.[29] At the same time, as two leading southerners were dismissed from their cabinet posts, southerners charged that the ruling coalition had become heavily weighted in favor of northern Muslim interests.[30] Instigated by Christian military officers from the Middle Belt who claimed to represent "the patriotic and well-meaning people of the middle belt and the southern parts of Nigeria,"[31] these issues figured prominently in the April 1990 coup d'etat.

The role of religion and ethnicity in Nigeria is real and intractable in the country's politics and people's social experiences,[32] and both have been used by the leaders to unite their respective members for defensive and offensive purposes. The process of mobilization of one group's membership along lines of religion and ethnicity often involves the negative labeling of the other group. Each group's members view the other as an enemy and judges the other based on assigned stereotypical roles. Over time, these misconceptions become permanent and reinforced from one generation to another. As civil society becomes more differentiated and new interest groups coalesce to articulate claims on the state, existing governments encounter an increasingly complex mix of demands. Since these claims are not readily reduced to demands of moderate intensity, there is a resulting threat to political stability and sustained development.

Politics

The military intervention in 1966 was the ultimate move in the gradually escalating use of physical violence to settle political conflicts. Since their success in quelling the Tiv ethnic riots in 1960, the military forces intervened to seize political power in 1966. This intervention resulted in the death of the federal prime minister, Tafawa Balewa, as well as the premiers of northern and western regions and other prominent politicians. While the coup d'etat was not successful, most of the coup plotters were Igbo and all the victims, except one, were northern officers. This incensed the northerners who, although the coup was foiled by Major General Johnson Aguiyi Ironsi, an Igbo, inferred that it was a sectional coup intended to serve Igbo political interests. This resulted in a protest, which quickly turned into a riot, by Ahmadu Bello University students apparently acting with the consent of northern leaders. The situation worsened and was followed by the assassination of Major General Johnson Aguiyi Ironsi and several army officers, most of them being Igbo, by northern army officers. This action led to the *de facto* regionalization of the army and the massacre of thousands of Igbo's all over the northern region. New military administrations came and were toppled. During this period, the country was divided into twelve states—six in the North and six in the South. The Middle Belt people had two states, Benue-Plateau and Kwara, while the southeastern minorities also had two, Cross River and Rivers. The twelve-state structure dealt decisively with one of the vexations of the Nigerian federal system, its imbalanced structure.[33] More states that would all benefit from the allocation of federally collected revenue were later carved out. The impact of this change was to leave the oil-producing states of Cross River, Rivers, and Bendel—the Niger Delta Region—disappointed and disgruntled.

The Second Republic (1979-83) was a replay of the politics of the First Republic. Although there were new rules and new players, the same old ethnic banners were still in place. The only change was in the definition and scope of the concept of ethnic group. Indeed, as many have observed, the ethnic groups in Nigeria today and the boundaries they claim are actually the parcels of influence carved out by the powerful.

Oil, Politics and Development in Nigeria

The first discovery of commercial quantities of oil in Nigeria was in 1956 at Oloibiri, about 90 kilometers west of Port Harcourt in what is now Bayelsa

State. Other discoveries soon followed, and Nigeria began exporting oil in 1958. Significant quantities only began to flow in 1965, when the Bonny Island Terminal, on the Atlantic coast, and its pipeline network were completed. Production dropped during the Biafran war of 1967-1970. This war also served as the motivation for the government to establish the 1969 Land Use Act, which effectively gave the federal government control of all oil producing land in Nigeria. The act provided oil-producing states with only 3% of oil revenues received by Nigeria.

Estimates of Nigeria's oil reserves range from 24 to 31.5 billion barrels. Most of this oil is found in small fields in the coastal areas of the Niger Delta. According to the Ministry of Petroleum Resources, there are 159 oil fields, producing from 1,481 wells.[34] The main onshore exploration and production activities undertaken today by foreign oil companies in Nigeria are through joint ventures with the Nigerian National Petroleum Corporation (NNPC), the state oil company. NNPC controls at least 50 percent of each joint venture. The NNPC was created by Decree No. 33 of 1977, as a successor to the Nigerian National Oil Company, itself created in 1971 as the first major effort to "indigenize" the oil industry, in response to the OPEC call for member states to participate more actively in oil operations. NNPC is responsible for production, transportation, refining, and marketing of oil and petroleum products. In 1986, the Petroleum Inspectorate, responsible for regulation and policy formulation, was detached from NNPC and given instead to the Department of Petroleum Resources; while preferable to the previous situation, in which NNPC regulated itself, the inspectorate still lacks independence. NNPC became a "commercial and autonomous" entity in 1992, though it remains state owned.[35]

In 1980, oil export revenues peaked at $24.9 billion, external indebtedness reached $9 billion, oil accounted for 27 percent of Gross Domestic Product (GDP), about 80 percent of government revenues and expenditures, and 96 percent of total export receipts.[36] In recent times, Nigeria's economy remains heavily dependent on the oil sector and these figures still hold true.[37]

The current government of President Olusegun Obasanjo, inaugurated on 29 May 1999, faces a tough job of turning around an ailing economy crippled by decades of mismanagement, corruption and political instability.[38] Ranked for a time as a middle-income country, Nigeria rejoined the category of low-income countries in the mid-1980s. According to the World Bank, its per capita Gross National Product (GNP) was $290 in 2000, compared with an average of $688 for sub-Saharan Africa as a whole and $430 for low-income countries.[39]

In recent years, economic growth has barely kept pace with population growth, estimated at 2.5 percent per annum. Despite the country's immense human and natural resources, little social progress has been made. Two-thirds of a population of more than 100 million lives below the poverty line, and one-third survives on less than a dollar a day. Over 33 percent of the adult population is illiterate. Life expectancy is 45 years, a decade below the average for developing nations, and less than half the population has access to safe water and adequate sanitation.[40]

Economic Interests

Ethnic groups engage in conflict for reasons ranging from financial motives to cultural values that glorify feuding. Given the distribution of ethnic identities in Nigeria, it is important to note that these ethnic groups are not homogenous and have had a pre-colonial history of rivalries which is frequently resurrected by political and economic competitions.[41] Such was the case in 1997, in the economic capital of the Delta region, Warri. An inter-ethnic conflict erupted between the Itsekiris and the Ijaws over the relocation of local government headquarters from the Igbe-Ijoh and Ijaw enclave to Ogidigben and Itsekiri town in Warri North. In the ensuing conflict, hundreds of lives were lost on both sides, waterways were blocked, and more than 120 Shell Petroleum workers were held hostage.[42] Concomitantly, in Edo State on October 6, 1998, an inter-ethnic crisis at Ikpako-Ekewan, in Ovia North-East local government, led to the death of several people. This particular conflict was between the Ijaws on one side and the Urhobos with the Itsekiris on the other.[43]

Then on July 22, 1999, more than 300 lives were lost as a result of inter-ethnic conflicts between the Yoruba and Hausa in the northern city of Kano and also in Sagamu, a southeastern city. This particular conflict began in Sagamu, Ogun State, a Yoruba dominated state. The Yoruba indigenes of this town attacked Hausa settlers for defiling their sacred Oro festival with the alleged nocturnal outing of two Hausa prostitutes. This festival is usually celebrated in secrecy with a curfew for all residents.[44] The anxiety that has emerged in Nigeria as a result of these ethnic conflicts is also a reflection of the economic frustration endured over time by these groups. This is the case in the Delta region where the bulk of Nigeria's revenue is derived from crude oil extracted from this area. The Delta communities are provoked that the proceeds from oil were being used by the government to develop other areas of the country while the Delta region was left to bear the environmental hazards of oil exploration.[45] The disappointment and disgruntlement felt by the people of the oil-producing states under the First Republic due to the allocation of federally collected revenue was finally brought to light.

In Nigeria, the struggle between oil as a source of development and oil as symbol of oppression has been apparent for several decades. In the Niger Delta, the base of oil extraction for both Shell and Chevron/Texaco operations in Nigeria, the people of the region have been struggling against the two oil giants in dramatic and often violent ways. The people of the Niger Delta complain of environmental degradation and lost economic opportunities, while Nigeria is one of the largest oil producers in the world. Within these ongoing struggles, there was one demonstration in 2002, which caught the attention of the world. For the first time, senior representatives of the oil companies met with people of the Delta, and the women were able to glean substantive concessions from the oil companies.

Third-party Interventions

British Intervention

Under Prime Minister Harold Wilson, British authorities adopted a policy of open support to the Nigerian Federation and agreed to deliver arms, with the exception of aircraft and bombs. It was the Commonwealth Office that this show of support would demonstrate Britain's restraint in avoiding an escalation in the level of violence. The British was trying to avoid Soviet primacy in support of the Federation thereby protecting British primacy. As Wilson noted, "Nigeria would have been put in the pawn to the Russians had we refused [the supply of arms]. Whatever military supplies we felt it right to withhold, they in fact provided; they were tightening their grip on Nigeria's life."[46] The pro-Nigerian stance that the Organization of African Unity (OAU) took allowed for justification of the British government's policy of arms sales to the Federation. Wilson gathered support from all avenues. As John Stremlau notes,

> African unity had been a popular symbol among British socialists, and the prime minister hoped that African solidarity against Biafra would restrain the mounting antiwar sentiment among British liberals. Wilson did not expect his pro-federal policy to be challenged by a Conservative opposition that was committed to the need to offset the Soviet presence in Lagos, and was anxious about the future of British investments in Nigeria.[47]

However, the influence Britain could gain through its arms sales policy was marginal and "was not sufficient to end the war."[48]

Official British sources estimated arms supplied by the British to be 15 percent of the federal government's military needs while critics of the British arms deliveries estimated the supply to be 45 percent.[49] The Nigerian federal government did eventually turn to the Soviet Union after the British government refused to deliver modern bomber and fighter aircraft and heavy artillery. The Soviet Union provided 44 modern MIG fighters (piloted by Egyptian mercenaries), Ilyushin bombers, and 122-mm guns.[50] This gave the federal government total control over the air. The Soviet military and economic assistance was a substantial part of the federal government's eventual success.

French Intervention

The French interference was based on two aspects: first, the involvement with a country outside the traditional French zone of influence; second, French policy was geared toward the break-up of a country and a redefinition of colonial borders. It also put two allies, France and Britain, in opposing camps during the entire conflict, from 1967 to 1970.

French aid to Biafra paled in comparison to the British and was even worse compared to the Soviet Union. It was only in August of 1968 that de Gaulle reversed his decision to maintain the embargo on Biafra. De Gaulle was not exactly displeased by the prospect of weakening Nigeria due to the fact that the relations between France and Nigeria, the giant of Africa, had historically been antagonistic. The explosion of France's third nuclear bomb in the Algerian Sahara on December 27, 1960 had had an immensely negative effect on Franco-Nigerian diplomatic relations.

Initially, French involvement in the Biafran secession was limited and covert. It seemed that France was "meticulously careful not only to avoid being drawn into the conflict but to discourage the buildup of arms and armaments in any part of Nigeria."[51] French arms helped to keep Biafra in action for the last 15 months of the war, but were not enough to avoid the gradual worsening of the situation in Biafra.

French involvement in Nigeria has been viewed as not only insufficient to sustain the secessionist forces, it was also counterproductive. In an interview with John J. Stremlau concerning the French role, Biafra's chief of staff, Major General Philip Effiong, snapped: "[they] did more harm than good by raising false hopes and by providing the British with an excuse to reinforce Nigeria."[52] The whole war would no doubt have been much shorter without foreign interference, simply as a result of the exhaustion of military supplies. By January of 1970, the secession had failed, and so did the French attempt at weakening the Nigerian Federation.

The goals of conflict resolution are to assist severely alienated parties in conflict to analyze the causes of their conflict, to imagine methods of reconstructing or replacing the system that is generating the conflict, to investigate various conflict-resolving options, and to implement the options agreed upon. This was not the case in Nigeria during the civil war. The Nigerian civil war was a unique case of post-colonial Franco-British rivalry in Africa, each providing weapons to one of the antagonists. Both countries limited their assistance to the supply of weapons, refusing to be dragged into the conflict with troops.

The Niger Delta Region

In a 1986 lecture delivered at the University of Lagos, "Oil in World Politics," the late Chief M. O. Feyide, Nigeria's former Secretary to the Organization of Petroleum Exporting Countries (OPEC), underscored the importance of oil in defining the destiny of the world as follows:

> All over the world, the lives of people are affected and the destiny of nations is probably determined by the results of oil industry operations. Oil keeps the factories of industrialized countries working and provides the revenues which enable oil exporters to execute ambitious national and economic development plans. The march of progress would be retarded and life itself could become unbearable if the world was deprived of oil. That is why oil has become the concern of governments, a vital ingredient of their politics and crucial factor in political and diplomatic strategies. Oil has been given the image of a big business ruled by naked politics and dominated by ruthless men who are sensitive to nothing except their profit.[53]

In Nigeria, the struggle between oil as a source of development and oil as symbol of oppression has been apparent for several decades. In the Niger Delta, the major base for international oil companies where the black lifeblood of the Nigerian economy is pumped from nearby offshore platforms, the people of the region have been struggling against two oil giants in dramatic and often violent ways. Nigeria, one of the largest oil producers in the world and the fifth exporter of oil to the United States, heavily depends on the oil extracted from the Niger Delta Region. About 90% of the country's revenue comes from the export of crude oil. However, the lives of the indigenes whose livelihoods depend on the land have been of no interest to the government of the country and the oil multinationals based in the region. When oil is drilled, there is the possibility of oil spills, burst pipes, and other eventualities that should be taken into consideration. Oil spills resulting in extreme environmental degradation, loss of property, and contamination of aquatic life and crops are common occurrences in the Niger Delta Region. Over the years, the people of the Niger Delta have complained to the government and the multinationals but have gone unacknowledged. Intracommunal conflicts have occurred over limited existing resources. Within these ongoing struggles, there was one demonstration in July of 2002 that caught the attention of the world. In an act reminiscent of the role played by women in the struggle for independence, the women of the Niger Delta took a dramatic united stand; they overran, without weapons, many production facilities of Chevron Nigeria Limited (CNL), the Chevron-Texaco joint venture with the Nigerian government, in the region. Production was essentially halted for several weeks, as the women held the oil companies hostage. For the first time, senior representatives of CNL met with people of the Delta, and the women were able to glean substantive concessions from the oil companies.

Nigeria's Niger Delta Region, also known as the Riverine Area, is home to 40 ethnic groups speaking over 25 languages. Before the discovery of oil the Niger Delta, people enjoyed financial independence and were even considered wealthy. When oil was discovered in the 1950s, the Riverine people were unprepared for the consequences of oil drilling that was to come. From the effects of poisonous gases, spilled oil, and a lack of concern on the part of both the federal government and the oil-drilling multinationals, to the loss of their ancestral land for which they were offered no compensation, the Riverine people, dependent on the land and surrounding rivers for their survival, were faced with starvation, abject poverty, and a general demoralization of life itself. This has resulted in decades of inter-communal conflicts over existing resources, as well as a growing disapproval, distrust, and detestation of the multinationals.

After retired General Obasanjo was elected president, he acknowledged decades of neglect by previous governments. He then pledged to address the grievances of the ethnic minorities that inhabit the Niger Delta (Ogonis and Niger Delta Commission). The Escravos is a community devised of seven villages and approximately 50,000 people, most of whom maintain their rural lifestyle by fishing from the Niger Delta. The Niger Delta is fed through many different water sources, including but not limited to, the Atlantic Ocean and numerous rivers and creeks in Africa. However, Obasanjo also increased the military presence at key installations. On a number of occasions in the past several years, soldiers have opened fire on militant youths attempting to invade oil facilities, killing or wounding a significant number of them. This has acted as a deterrent, and the result has been a substantial decline in invasions recorded recently. Nonetheless, Obasanjo's inclination to concentrate oil revenue in the federal government, his reluctance to concede a bigger share to oil-region states, and the fact that his election promises have been slow to materialize appear to have fueled a renewed surge of restiveness in the oil areas. In April 2000, President Obasanjo signed into law a new revenue sharing formula with the nine oil producing states by which the latter receive 13% of oil revenues versus the previously allotted 3%. However, the Niger Delta communities are not satisfied with this agreement and want a larger share of the profits.[54]

From this backdrop rose one of the most famous acts taken by a group of unarmed women to peacefully fight for what they considered their rights.[55] Angry at the unemployment of their children and husbands and the neglect of infrastructure and economic empowerment by successive governments and multinational oil companies since production of oil began over four decades ago, plus the loss of the fattening room and other traditions, the women had had enough. The Niger Delta women made a conscious decision to organize against the oil industry operating on their land—a force they saw as being clearly responsible for their cultural degradation. With their traditions gradually fading away and survival becoming increasingly difficult, the Niger Delta women were left with no other choice but to take matters into their own hands.

The Niger Deltans have lost their wealth and prestigious status in the region. Today, while the region provides the country with 95% of its foreign income, the oil-rich Niger Delta region is one of the poorest in the country. For example, the state-owned power utility has not supplied power and there is only one major road.[56] Consequently, the Riverine people have now focused their anger at the multinationals and the federal government—the beneficiaries of the region's oil wealth. This has resulted in the region's volatility.

Farmed by the women, who traditionally are given a piece of land by their husbands as part of their dowry, the high yields of crops gave the people an abundance of produce and allowed for trade within and beyond the region. This provided for the Niger Delta women and the region as a whole a decent level of independence. Oil exploitation, with the resultant pollution from the industry, has left the women with very little means to feed or support their families. Where they once were able to get unpolluted water very near their homes, they now have to go further away from home to find unpolluted water for their domestic chores. The region's waters were once inundated with fish, but today the people have to import edible fish due to the level of pollution and toxicity attributed to oil and gas spills. About 50 Riverine people were employed in the oil industry a decade ago, but mainly as cleaners and unskilled labor. The young people of the region, due to unemployment regardless of their academic qualifications, continue to depend on their mothers. This has resulted in a rise of pressure on the women.

Before the discovery of oil, the Niger Delta people enjoyed financial independence and were even considered wealthy. When oil was discovered in the 1950s, the Riverine people were unprepared for the consequences of oil drilling that were to come. From the effects of poisonous gases, spilled oil, and a lack of concern on the part of both the Federal government and the oil-drilling multinationals, to the loss of their ancestral land for which they were offered no compensation, the Riverine people, dependent on the land and surrounding rivers for their survival, were faced with starvation, abject poverty, and a general demoralization of life itself. This has resulted in decades of inter-communal conflicts over existing resources, as well as a growing disapproval, distrust, and detestation of the multinationals. The Niger Deltans have lost their wealth and prestigious status in the region. And today, while the region provides the country with 95% of its foreign income the oil-rich Niger Delta region is one of the poorest in the country. Consequently, as noted earlier, the Riverine people have now focused their anger at the multinationals and the federal government—the beneficiaries of the region's oil wealth.

From sabotaging pipelines and taking expatriate workers hostage to publishing articles in all potential media, the Niger Deltans have not kept quiet about their displeasure in the way that the region is being run by the Nigerian government and the powerful multinationals that have over the years constantly showed their lack of interest in the affairs of the Niger Delta people by their continued neglect of the region. In 1995, The Nigerian government executed nine Niger Delta activists of the Ogoni ethnic group, including the prominent Ken Saro-Wiwa, who was very instrumental in bringing the damage caused by Shell to the international scene. His death brought international attention to the Niger Delta and condemnation of the oil companies. The people are constantly demanding amenities and access to more of the oil wealth. The demands of the people have always been the same. The negative responses have never changed. However, a group of Riverine women led by the Ogoni women, with the very same demands, were able to successfully and nonviolently negotiate these demands.

Role of the Niger Delta Women in Crisis De-escalation

On July 19, 2002, for the first time, the Niger Delta women joined the protest against oil companies operating in the oil-rich Niger Delta Region. They expressed their concern, in an act similar to the role the women of Aba played in the struggle for independence, by occupying oil-drilling facilities of Chevron Nigeria Limited. After occupying the territory for a while, the women finally placed four demands on ChevronTexaco and Shell. The next day, the women had collectively requested that all four demands be addressed. The demands were for the oil companies to provide the community with jobs, education for their children, electricity, water, a community center and economic support. Unfortunately, what started as a peaceful protest ended with the Nigerian police using Chevron helicopters resulted in the deaths of two people and dozens of others were severely injured.

While previous protests did not prove to be peaceful from all ends, the women continued to make efforts to ensure that their demands were heard and met by the oil companies. Only three days after the second protest, on July 23, 2002, the women worked in shifts of 200 and placed five more demands on Chevron. The demands were as follows:

(1) The oil companies should stop killing their sons for protesting peacefully for the right to work and have jobs.
(2) The pollution of farms and rivers should end and a clean up process begins immediately.
(3) The oil companies should begin to respect local customs and traditions by first of all negotiating with the traditional leaders and elders.
(4) Clean water, electricity, health care, free education should be provided.
(5) The right to live in peace in their homeland away from military and political violence must be ensured.

The women were able to force Chevron to the negotiating table because of the threat that their demonstrations posed. Nigeria is a patriarchal society, as are Western oil companies. As many observers have pointed out, when male youth demonstrated against Chevron, the company used a military strategy to quell the demonstrations. But the women prepared no one for nonviolent action. Military action against the women would have caused both the men of the region and the Nigerian government to lose face and create a greater conflict. The Itsekiri women drove the issue further by their threat to take off their clothes, a local taboo. Many Nigerians consider displays of nudity by wives, mothers and grandmothers as a damning protest and an act that shames and brings evil to all those at which it is aimed, an act to be avoided or prevented at all costs.

While Chevron is making money in the region and keeps its company property to Western living standards, the people of the region are impoverished. The people of the region, particularly the women, are highlighting Chevron's responsibility to improve the living conditions for the region as a whole while extracting the resources. The women employed a crisis negotiation strategy of nonviolence and decent consultation. Juxtapositional to this is their threat to strip naked publicly. All they craved was for a win-win solution. On the other hand, the government tried to use force as a tactical strategy and succeeded in killing some of the protesters. Fearing reprisals from the international community, Chevron asked the government to discontinue this line of action. The company's officials eventually realized that they were faced with crucial demands of needs and interests rather than positions and decided to negotiate. While officials of the oil company deemed it beneath them to sit with and address the locals, the women would only negotiate with a senior representative of Chevron rather than a community liaison officer, forcing the company to acknowledge the need for respect in its relationship with the community.

The women's protest forced the company to shut the pumping station, which normally accounts for production of 40,000 barrels of crude a day. All of the women's efforts proved to be worthwhile because on July 26, 2002, after four days of negotiations, the women lifted their occupation of four flow stations. Chevron seemed to agree to most of the demands of the women, the most important being the protection of the people and their commitment to trouble free environment. Although the accord was signed and peace was to be imminent, it did not occur that quickly; and once again, over 3,000 women found themselves back at the flow stations protesting for the protection of their homeland.

Finally, in August, Chevron reached a resolution with the women to end their occupation of the company's facilities by signing an agreement that would guarantee regular job offers and some amenities for the communities. The deal, regarded as a landmark in the relationship between Chevron and its host communities, had Chevron promising to raise the bursary for students in tertiary institutions from N50, 000 (Nigerian Naira) to N75, 000 effective from the 2002/2003 academic session, while that for secondary schools would be raised to N20, 000 from N10, 000.

Chevron was also supposed to put in place a N20-million credit scheme for 10 Ijaw communities, totaling N200 million, to aid business development. The scheme would be run by a yet-to-be-named non-governmental organization. The company also committed itself to providing two speedboats for each of the 10 communities and electricity and water projects in all the communities. The deal is up for review every three years. These brave women, armed only with lists of urgent community needs, who shut down Chevron Texaco ports and oil flow stations, have vowed to do it again if promises are not kept.

As discussed above, the nonviolent protests by the Itsekiri and Ijaw women in the summer of 2002 were largely resolved in a relatively peaceful manner because Chevron responded not just to the women's demands but also to the issues highlighted in that situation. A large aspect of the demonstration was the need for the women to be recognized and their voices to be given respect through direct meetings with representatives of ChevronTexaco. Also notable in the demonstrations was that, even though the women took hostages, they held them with respect and their statements were void of the language of hate. This situation was also remarkable because it marked the first time Chevron executives met with people of the Niger Delta, instead of sending the community liaison representative.

But it was simply only one protest in a long and ongoing struggle against the oil industry by the people of the Niger Delta. There are many parties who play a part in this broader conflict, not just the foreign oil companies and the Niger Delta communities. The players include the Nigerian government and its state-run organizations, the international community supporting the oil companies, and the international community supporting the Niger Delta communities.

There is a lack of attunement manifested in the very divergent worldviews of the parties to this situation. The people of the Niger Delta see their struggle with the oil companies in very simple terms: the oil industry is taking wealth from their communities while not putting the money back into their communities in the form of development, jobs and education. At the same time, their economy, health, and environment are threatened. On the other hand, the oil companies and the Nigerian government are not simply focused on the Niger Delta. The oil companies believe that they are doing all they can to assist development in the Niger Delta while also facing continued security threats and disruption to production. The Nigerian government is juggling economic, governmental and foreign relations decisions at all times. The point is that it is rare to see in statements from any of these groups, or from the international community, that they recognize the worldview and perspective of the other party. Resolution of this conflict will require more significant recognition of the perspective each party brings to the conflict.

In the preceding discussion, I have outlined the perspective of the Niger Delta people, but it is useful to this discussion to also provide more details of the perspective from which one international oil company, Chevron Texaco, might be viewing the conflict. A *New York Times* article in 1999 poignantly illustrated Chevron's perspective with the following:

> ...a rough and ready American Chevron employee named Leonard Hutto hovers in a helicopter above an oil facility occupied by angry Nigerians. The landing pad, a few hundred feet below, was thronged with hundreds of angry young Nigerians peering up at the midmorning sky, clearly shouting and shaking their fists. Seeing that they did not have guns, Hutto finally told the pilot to land. At the same moment, down on the flow station, standing atop a table inside a tiny of-

fice, surrounded by dozens of young men brandishing machetes, Hutto's Nigerian assistant, Tony Okoaye, was relieved to hear the helicopter's engine drone out the shouts of his captors...the young men, many drunk or high on marijuana, [had] made him stand on the table for hours, slapping his pudgy frame and jabbing forefingers into the soft belly above his Tommy Hilfiger jeans. "Ah, hah!" they taunted. "You're a big man!" This, to judge by Hutto's reaction, is a commonplace occurrence, the cost of doing business in a place where the breakdown of law and social order has "transformed the simple task of pumping crude into a strange exercise in diplomacy, civics, and bluff, less the oil business than an exercise in velvet-gloved imperialism."[57]

When looking at the operations in Nigeria, a ChevronTexaco executive is looking at a constant flow of security threats to the company's facilities and personnel through hostage taking and equipment sabotage, similar to the incident above. An extreme example of these threats occurred in March of 2003 when Chevron shut down production in the Niger Delta because of the violence between Ijaw and Itsekiri youths. Chevron evacuated its workforce at the Escravos terminal. Additional threats to Chevron's bottom line include the corruption in the Nigerian government, strikes throughout Nigeria, and illegal siphoning of production for the black market. Corruption starts at the local level, where Chevron pays local leaders to keep them from causing additional trouble.

At the same time, Chevron Texaco believes that its investment in Nigeria is good for Nigeria. In a speech in 2002, the Chairman and CEO of ChevronTexaco, David O'Reilly, praised his company's strategy of investment in Africa, contrasting the benefits to aid, with the following statement: "One ingredient of the fuel that will solve these challenges is investment. Investment brings jobs; it brings education; it brings a stronger healthcare infrastructure. Investment brings stability and growth. And, most important, investment attracts additional investment."[58] ChevronTexaco's fact sheet on Nigeria highlights the following points, which are in stark contrast to the perspective of the Niger Delta communities:

• More than 2,000 jobs, more than 90 percent held by Nigerians
• Nearly 75 percent of managers are Nigerian
• Community investments for schools, health, scholarships and environment total about $90 million since 1991
• CNL has invested $400 million to upgrade production facilities, including reducing discharges and the risk of oil spills.[59]

Also framing Chevron Texaco's response to the Nigerian situation is its reputation internationally. Rather then being castigated for its work in Nigeria, Chevron is being rewarded. In 2002, it received the Sullivan Leadership Award from the organization of Reverend Leon Sullivan for its positive approach to international investment. In October of 2003, Chevron received the United States Secretary of State's Award for Corporate Excellence for its outstanding

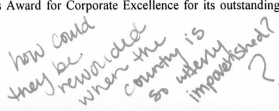

how could they be rewarded when the country is so utterly impoverished?

corporate citizenship in Nigeria. In presenting the award to ChevronTexaco, Secretary Colin Powell specifically highlighted three CNL initiatives, including the airlift of more than 2,000 villagers to safety in March during interethnic and political conflicts in the western Niger Delta, a River Boat Clinic that brings healthcare to thousands of people in the Niger Delta, and ongoing HIV/AIDS prevention efforts in the country.[60]

With such recognition from governments and peer groups, there is little incentive for ChevronTexaco to make significant changes in the way it does business in Nigeria. It is easy for executives to look at the security situation as something to be dealt with and not to view as legitimate the concerns of the Niger Delta communities.

To Chevron's arguments, the representatives of the Niger Delta may argue that Chevron Nigeria Limited (CNL) may employ Nigerians, but not Nigerians from our regions; the development projects funded only benefit certain people or are not of any use to them. And finally, they may argue that the security threats would go away if Chevron really addressed the substantive requests of the Niger Delta region.

These counter arguments illustrate not just the distance between the two positions, those of the Niger Delta communities and the oil companies, but the distance between perspectives, between worldviews. Currently, there is little effort being made to bridge these two perspectives and develop trust and respectful relationships. Little effort is also being made to address the overarching attunement issues in the conflict. A key to resolving the conflict in the Niger Delta will be to bring the parties into relationships and discussions from which trust can be built. Sustainable development of the area is an absolute must for conflict resolution.

Conclusion

State and society are intertwined in complex ways, as societal interests penetrate and sometimes achieve control of the state and as state institutions exercise a direct influence over societal activities. In a society, the interaction between local groups, state groups, national groups, and regional and global non-state actors involves governance. With the institution of a multi-state federal system in 1967, Nigeria has arguably functioned to decentralize and defuse ethnic conflict in several ways. The country has witnessed a history of the incorporation of the main ethno-regional groups in key federal institutions in a balanced manner. Beginning as early as 1958, the federal government initiated a quota system for the recruitment of enlisted personnel into the military services and extended this practice to the officer corps three years later.[61] And although the majority of Nigeria's presidents have favored their ethnic groups while choosing cabinet members, representatives from other ethnic groups have also been included in a number of cabinet appointments. The creation of additional states and the decentralization of significant powers to the states and local authorities have increased ethnic and sub-regional participation.

The success of governance rests on leadership abilities that include the proper management of demands. There is also the need for well-versed and widely accepted rules aimed at forming cooperative relationships. Critical to achieving these cooperative relationships is the emergence of accepted ties of reciprocity among elites and between these elites and their constituents. The existence of recognized rules of political exchange, based on formal rules and regulations, is also important for social stability. As a multi-ethnic and multi-religious country, Nigeria is constantly under the power of political leaders who, in order to divert the attention of the people away from the main issues of national development and in order to pursue and achieve their own selfish objectives, exploit the ethnic and religious sensitivities of the people. The multifaceted conflicts in Nigerian are reflected in the ongoing melee over the intergovernmental distribution of constitutional responsibilities and economic resources, the sharing of federal political power among ethnic blocs of the population, and the internal territorial configuration of the federation. The problem with Nigeria is not the absence of laws for preventing or managing ethnic, religious or political conflicts. The problem is with the implementation of the laws. Nigerian political leaders have not been known to have respect of the country's constitution. While third-party intervention as an approach to peace can be constructive, it can also be very destructive. What works in one situation may very likely not work in another situation. In Nigeria, as well as other parts of West Africa, demands are linked to the prevailing scarcity of resources, and the inequalities in the distribution of the existing goods prevail along ethnic, religious, and political lines.

The struggle to control resources has been cited to be a compelling cause of ethnic conflicts. Nigeria consists of hundreds of ethnic groups that were forcibly made to cohabit. The damage is done and is irreparable. There will always be a struggle over limited resources, and this will continue until all parties to the conflict have attained an acceptable level of economic development. According to James Gustave Speth, "Too often, short-term military, political and economic interests rather than the goals of poverty eradication have shaped development assistance."[62] New policies that address the development of underprivileged countries need to be formulated. New approaches to peace need to be developed. Sustainable development, political reconstruction, and nation building should be investigated by international actors as means for ending ethnic strife and as eventual approaches to world peace. If the underprivileged ethnic groups within Nigeria can achieve a level of political, social, and economic development comparable to that enjoyed by the more dominant groups, existing ethnic divisions may no longer result in conflict. Of course, the country is in dire need for internal reconstruction, which can only be achieved through the help of unbiased third parties. As Huntington aptly observes:

> A society with weak political institutions lacks the ability to curb the
> excesses of personal and parochial desires. Politics is a Hobbesian
> world of unrelenting competition among social forces—between man
> and man, family and family, clan and clan, region and region, class
> and class—a competition unmediated by more comprehensive politi-
> cal organizations.[63]

Politics is by nature conflict generating. The problem in Nigeria is not the
existence of conflict strictly among social forces, but the absence of a strong
central institution, which has the legitimacy and independent power base to
achieve authoritative and binding allocation of the scarce resources and, thereby,
delimit the conflict.

Acknowledgement

This essay benefited from the research assistance of one of my effulgent students, Mobolaji Art-Alade.

Notes

1. James E. Dougherty and Robert L. Pfalzgraff, *Contending Theories of International Relations* (New York: Harper & Row Publishers, 1981), 187.

2. E. Azar, "Protracted International Conflicts: Ten Propositions," in J. Burton and
F. Dukes, eds., *Conflict: Readings in Management and Resolution* (London: Macmillan
Press, 1990), 145.

3. Stephen Ryan, *Ethnic Conflict and International Relations* (Aldershot: Dart-
mouth, 1990), xxvii.

4. Azar, "Protracted International Conflicts," 90.

5. Azar, "The Theory of Protracted Social Conflicts and the Challenge of Transforming Conflict Situation," in D. Zinnes, ed., *Conflict Process and the Breakdown of
International System* (Denver, Colo.: University of Denver Press, 1983), 90.

6. Jack David Eller, *From Culture to Ethnicity to Conflcit* (Ann Arbor,MI: University of Michigan Press, 1999).

7. Donald L. Horowitz, *Ethnic Groups in Conflict* (Berkeley: University of California Press, 1985).

8. Harold A. Isaacs, *Idols of the Tribe: Group Identity and Political Change* (New
York:
Harper and Row, 1975), 43.

9. David Carment, "Modelling Ethnic Conflict: Problems and Pitfalls," *Politics and
the Life Sciences* 16 (September 1997), 2.

10. Georg Simmel, *Conflict,* trans. Kurt H. Wolf (Glencoe, Ill.: The Free Press,
1955).

11. V. Gagnon, "Ethnic Nationalism and International Conflict," in *Global Dangers:
Changing Dimension of International Security*, ed. S. Lynn and S. Miller (Cambridge,
Mass.: MIT Press, 1995).

12. Robert K. Merton and Alice S. Kitt, "Contributions to the Theory of Reference Group Behavior," in *Studies in the Scope and Method of "The American Soldier,"* ed. Merton and Lazarsfeld (Glencoe, Illinois: The Free Press, 1950).

13. J.D. Singer, "Accounting for International War: The State of Discipline," *Journal of Peace* 98, 1 (1981):37–48.

14. Chaim Kaufmann, "Possible and Impossible Solutions to Ethnic Civil Wars," *International Security* 20, 4 (1996); Barry Posen, "The Security Dilemma and Ethnic Conflict," *Survival* 35, 1 (Spring 1993): 27–47.

15. Janet B. Johnson, and Richard Joslyn, *Political Science Research Method, Congressional Quarterly Weekly Report* 49 (Washington, D.C.: Government Printing Office, 1991).

16. S. W. Thompson K. M. Jensen, eds., *Approaches to Peace* (Washington, D.C., United States Institute of Peace, 1991).

17. C.A. Croaker and F.O. Hampson, and P. Aall, eds., *Turbulent Peace: The Challenges of Managing International Conflict.* (Washington, D.C., United States Institute of Peace, 2001).

18. Francis Deng and I. William Zartman, *Governance as Conflict Management Politics and Violence in West Africa* (Washington, D.C.: The Brookings Institution Press, 1996).

19. Wole Soyinka, *The Open Sore of a Continent: A Personal Narrative of the Nigerian Crisis* (New York: New York University Press, 1996).

20. Barry Posen, "The Security Dilemma and Ethnic Conflict," *Survival* 35 (Spring 1993): 1, 27–47.

21. Stuart Kaufman, "An International Theory of Inter-Ethnic War," *Review of International Studies* (1996): 2, 22.

22. F. Schweartz in *The London Times* (June 8, 1897), 30.

23. Obafemi Awolowo, *Path to Nigerian Freedom.* (London: Faber, 1947).

24. Obafemi Awolowo, *Thoughts on Nigerian Constitution* (London: Faber, 1996).

25. Crawford Young, "Patterns of Social Conflict: State, Class and Ethnicity," *Daedalus* 3 (1982): 2:73; Larry Diamond, "Issues in the Constitutional Design of a Third Nigerian Republic," *African Affairs* 86 (1987): 343.

26. Arend Lijphart, *Democracy in Plural Societies: A Comparative Exploration* (New Haven, Conn.: Yale University Press, 1997).

27. Keith Somerville, *Foreign Military Intervention in Africa* (New York: St. Martin's Press, 1990).

28. David Turton, ed., *War and Ethnicity: Global Connections and Local Violence* (Rochester, New York: University of Rochester Press, 1997),1.

29. Reporter in *Africa Confidential* 31 (April 6,1990): 8.

30. W. Keeling and M. Holman, "Religious Tension behind Challenge to Babangida," *Financial Times* (London) (April 23, 1990).

31. Editorial, *West Africa* (April 1999): 9.

32. S. Gbadegesin, ed., *The Politicization of Society During Nigeria's Second Republic, 1979–1983* (Lewiston, New York: The Edwin Mellen Press, 1991).

33. Awolowo, *Thoughts on Nigerian Constitution*, 34.

34., *Environmental Resource Management* (Nigeria's Ministry of Petroleum Resources, 1997), 195.

35. Sarah Ahmed Khan, *Nigeria: The Political Economy of Oil* (Oxford: Oxford University Press, 1994), 28.

36. Khan, *Nigeria: The Political Economy of Oil* (Oxford: Oxford University Press), 133.

37. United States Energy Information Administration (USEIA), *Nigeria Country Analysis,* 2003: 2.

38. Olusegun Obasanjo, *Rationale of the People's Budget 2000: Fiscal Policy Measures 2000* (New York: Nigeria Consulate general, July 20, 2000).

39. World Bank, *World Economic Indicators* (Washington D.C.: World Bank Publications, 2003).

40. World Bank, *World Economic Indicators,* 2003.

41. Oladimeji Aborisadet and Robert J. Mundt, *Politics in Nigeria* (New York: Longman, 1999).

42. Akin Obasa, "Oily Wheels of Discontent," *The Week,* 1998.

43. Akin Obasa, "Oily Wheels of Discontent," *The Week,* 1998.

44. Wola Adeyemo, "The Day of Rage," *Tell Magazine,* 2 August 1999.

45. Obasa, "Oily Wheels of Discontent," 1998.

46. J.D.B. Miller, *Survey of Commonwealth Affairs: Problems of Expansion and Attrition, 1953–69* (London: Oxford University Press, 1974), 255.

47. John Stremlau, *The International Politics of the Nigerian Civil War, 1967–1970* (Princeton, N.J.: Princeton University Press, 1977): 11.

48. Keith Somerville, *Foreign Military Intervention in Africa* (New York: St. Martin's Press, 1990), 256.

49. Someville *Foreign Military,* 257.

50. Somervile *Foreign Military,* 258.

51. Uwechue cited in Stremlau, *International Politics,* 11, 225.

52. Stremlau *Interenational Politics of the Nigerian Civil War* (Princeton: Princeton University Press, 1977): 130.

53. M.O. Feyide, *Oil in World Politics* (Lagos: University of Lagos Press, 1987), 7.

54. USEIA (2003).

55. Ruth Rosen, "The Power of Peaceful Protest" *Women's World,* 22 July 2002.

56. Norimitsu Onishi, "As Oil Riches Flow, Poor Village Cries Out," *New York Times* (December 22, 2002).

57. Onishi, "As Oil Riches Flow," *New York Times* (22 December 2002).

58. <http://www.ChevronTexaco.com/news/speeches/2002/20jun2002_oreily.asp>.

59. *Chevron Niger Fact Sheet.*

60. <http://www. ChevronTexaco.com/news/spotlight/5oct2003_corpexcellence .asp>.

61. Rothchild cited in Deng and Zartman, *Governance as Conflict Management,* 204.

62. James Gustave Speth, "The Plight of the Poor: The United States Must Increase Aid," *Foreign Affairs* (May/June 1999): 13–18.

63. Samuel P. Huntington, *Political Order in Changing Societies* (New Haven, CT: Yale University Press, 1975), 24.

Chapter 7

Georgetown Shuffle: Ethnic Politics of Afro-Guyanese, Amerindians, and Indo-Guyanese in Postcolonial Guyana[1]

Sabita Manian

Since the 1950s, the inter-ethnic politics in Guyana has manifest itself in the form of violence—forms of collective social action resulting from rivalries among the Afro-Guyanese and the Indo-Guyanese population, even as the indigenous Amerindians (a minority in postcolonial Guyana) tussle for resources and participation in the political and economic landscape. The Afro- and the Indo-Guyanese, with ethnic identities that are rooted in Hindu, Muslim, Christian and secular values, reveal a ruthless power struggle for control of Georgetown's politics. While separatism in the form of irredentism is not a factor in Guyana, it is nevertheless expressed through violence and parliamentary politics. This article will specifically focus on the resurgence of Hindu nationalist revivalism by the Rise Organize and Rally (ROAR) since the 1990s, which provides another turbulent dimension in intra-Indo-Guyanese politics with serious ethnic implications for the other groups in the country.

Introduction

Since the pre-independent era of the 1950s, two main political parties have dictated Guyanese politics. Identified with and controlled by the two main ethno-racial groups, the Afro-Guyanese dominated People's National Congress (PNC) and the Indo-Guyanese dominated Progressive People's Party (PPP) have polarized politics to the near disenfranchisement of other minorities such as the Amerindians, the Chinese and the mixed ethnic population. The role of these two major political parties in ethnic violence that has rocked Guyana was highlighted thus by a 2003 UN Report "Ethnic Polarization Between Guyanese of African and Indian Descent," reflected in the composition of political parties, [has] greatly affected the structure of state mechanisms and perpetuated economic and social underdevelopment."[2] The Land of Six Peoples—constituted by East Indian, African, Amerindian, White, Chinese, and mixed population—with a population that is less than 800,000, in this third smallest country in South America (after Surinam and Uruguay), witnessed a disturbingly high number of racially motivated killings in 2002 which set a record of 162 and within the first six months of 2003 had already reached more than a hundred.[3]

These killings result from post-election violence as seen after elections in both 1996 and in 2001, leading to one recent report that warned: "Guyana has teetered for years on the brink of serious ethnic conflicts.... on the street, the noises are increasingly ominous."[4] Indeed this forecast was affirmed with reports of death squads and allegations of direct involvement of the home affairs minister that became headline news by mid-2004 with opposition parties and human-rights groups such as the Guyana Human Rights Association (GHRA) insisting on a commission of inquiry. Violence along the East Coast (of Guyana) raised the racism flag with the Indo-Guyanese (who largely vote for the PPP) victimized by "Afro-Guyanese criminals and neglected by the mainly Afro-Guyanese police."[5] The GHRA, in response to the racial polarization has tried to be even-handed in its comments by condemning "without reservation the renewed attempt to provoke racial confrontation by violence against the Indo-Guyanese" while advising the Indo-Guyanese government to "refrain from trying identifying the PNC with East Coast violence... [Since] such comments serve as a slur to tarnish the Afro-Guyanese community as a whole and strengthen racial polarization."[6] To offset the accusations of ineptitude in dealing with racially motivated crimes as well as for reserving employment opportunities, scholarships, government contracts, and landholding awards to benefit those of East Indian origin, the ruling PPP established the Ethnic Relations Commission. Having taken that step forward the PPP took two steps back and antagonized the Afro-Guyanese, other minority parties, and the GHRA, by reinstating the much vilified home affairs minister a step that also caused the EU, the US, and Canada to register their dissatisfaction with the decision.[7]

Meantime, this legacy of ethnic politics has left a bad taste in the mouths of the nation's young people who often see little relevance in becoming involved with a polarized political process and who may, like hundreds of thousands of fellow Guyanese, consider emigration a better alternative than engagement. Since they comprise about three-fifths of the country's population this is of no little concern. The land that at one time was known as El Dorado is now punished for its poison of ethnic violence that has discouraged economic growth so that it is ranked 104 (in descending order out of 177 countries) in the 2004 UN Human Development Report.[8]

So what then are the postcolonial politics and economics of ethnicity that direct such dire economic and societal instability? One hypothesis is that *ethnicist*, hyper-nationalist, and therefore exclusivist political discourse exacerbates violence among ethnic groups in Guyana, particularly during elections that strengthen and legitimize the pillar of democracy. This in turn undermines the consolidation of democracy and socio-economic development thereby rendering the state as unstable and failed. *Ethnicist* political discourse is crafted by the political elites to keep groups distracted with identity issues so that the latter may not identify political corruption and power-mongering with the governing elites. The empirical testing of these hypotheses will refer to questions central to this book's ethos: Is ethnic identity culture-bound? Is the devastating or recurring conflict ethno-political or primordial, something ancient and/or pre-social? How is ethnic conflict expressed in Guyana today different from previous times? When does the interface between ethnic issues and potential conflict situations result in violence and why? What is the linkage between ethnic violence and ethnic issues—above all, is violence a necessary or inevitable form of collective social action?

This chapter begins with an introduction of dominant Guyanese political parties to examine (a) the political discourse and rhetoric that foment ethnic hatred, and (b) the policies that act as a catalyst in increasing or decreasing ethnic tensions. During such scrutiny of the political party process, two relatively under-examined dimensions will be investigated—first, the emergence since the 1990s of the nationalist Hindu dominated ROAR (Rise Organize and Rally) party that has implications for molding the public discourse as it relates to ethnic differences; and second the role that the Amerindian population are developing in the fight for political and economic resources by the Indo- and the Afro-Guyanese. It is hoped that the implications of this study will lead to: (a) a better understanding of ethnic politics in Guyana that includes less explored themes - the politics of the Indo-Guyanese ROAR and the Amerindians; (b) alternative policy approaches through a critical examination of political discourse and rhetoric; and (c) discerning the extent to which regional stability is linked to a state's democratic political stability especially in an age of globalization where regional trade politics tie the local to the global.

Guyanese Political Parties and Political Discourse

> The struggle for control continues today. It is the African-Indian
> Guyanese subplot which has now moved centre stage. The ghost of
> colonialism continues to torment the land.[9]

Seecoomar's words express the continuity of Guyanese ethnicist history that since the pre-independence period has been a rather ruthless power struggle between Afro-Guyanese and Indo-Guyanese groups through their respective parties. In short, Amerindian interests have been marginal concerns, at best. The Land of Six Peoples is constituted racially by a majority that is East Indian (nearly 50 percent), followed in second place by those of African ethnicity (approximately 36 percent). In third position of numerical strength is the Amerindian (7 percent) population, with the remaining minority of Whites, Chinese, and "mixed" constituting 7 percent approximately.[10] The main political parties, the PNC and the PPP, persistently prevail over the parliamentary politics of Georgetown—dynamics that remain firmly entrenched today. Even socialist-oriented governments until the early 1990s routinely played the ethno-cultural card and of course such dynamics serve only to further the fission of society. Afro-Guyanese represent just over one-third of the population and almost exclusively vote for the PNC, while Indo-Guyanese comprising about one-half of the population vote almost exclusively for the PPP.[11] Leanings of Guyanese of mixed race vary widely, but they generally throw their support to the PNC or various smaller minority parties (see Table 1).[12]

The minority parties emphasize how years of abuse of power and the manipulation of elections by both the PNC and the PPP has bred mistrust that prevents their cooperation and progress on a national agenda in a multiparty unicameral parliamentary system. Such mistrust is a legacy of Guyanese pre-independence party politics, beginning in the 1940s and the 1950s.

The "first free and fair elections" held in 1992 brought the Indo-Guyanese Cheddi Jagan (PPP) to power as president and in an ethno-cultural twist, upon his demise, his North American wife Janet Jagan succeeded him in 1997 until her resignation in 1999.[13] Since then, the consolidation of Indo-Guyanese political power through the PPP/Civic party under the leadership of Bharrat Jagdeo, has launched a trend that dares to upstage the Afro-Guyanese (and other minorities') voice in power politics. Such political cleavages go hand-in-hand with prevailing racial prejudices and ethnic violence, while also effectively ignoring the voices of other minorities.

Table 1

POLITICAL PARTIES	ACRONYM/SEATS	LEADER
Guyana Action Party & Working People's Alliance coalition	GAP-WPA (2) – 9,451	Rupert Roopnaraine
Guyana Action Party	GAP	Paul Hardy
Working People's Alliance	WPA	Rupert Roopnaraine
People's Progressive Party/Civic	PPP/C (34)—210,013	Bharrat Jagdeo
People's National Congress	PNC (27)—165,866	R.H.O. Corbin
Rise Organize and Rebuild	ROAR (1)—3,695	Ravi Dev
The United Force	TUF (1)—2,904	Manzoor Nadir

Source: Statistics derived from BBC Monitoring Americas, 06 April 2001. The numbers in bold parentheses denote the number of seats in the unicameral National Assembly and the numbers in bold-italics denote the number of votes won by each of the parties in the March 19, 2001 elections.

The degree of ethnic polarization is aggravated by the *division of labor* along ethnic lines—Afro-Guyanese tending toward the civil services (including the military), and professions in urban areas, while most Indo-Guyanese live in rural areas along the coast and deal primarily in agriculture or merchandise trade. The decades long labor divisions and economic differences led to the opposition PNC party's claims that President Bharrat Jagdeo's government has been unfairly selecting Indo-Guyanese for government contracts and non-traditional employment opportunities. During a 2003 trip to India, President Jagdeo in turn, accused the PNC opposition leaders of encouraging youths to perpetrate the 18 months long racist crimes and violence.[14] The tit for tat accusations further led to a countercharge by the opposition that police squads have been used to kill rather than prosecute Afro-Guyanese suspects. This scenario has also produced mistrust among other minority parties who claim that neither the PPP nor PNC will hear or respond to them. One may ask: why doesn't the PNC reach out more to the Amerindians and court the other minorities since they are natural allies against the PPP? The answer to this question lies in the ethnic history of party politics in Guyana where political discourse developed along ethnic lines and contemporary politics appears to fail irrevocably in changing that tide. The next sub-section will trace this ethno-political discord before discussing contemporary racial politics through the involvement of ROAR and other minority parties.

Ethnic-history of Party Politics

Given the aforementioned conditions, the genesis and the development of Guyanese party politics may be traced to two prominent figures in the pre-independent period—the East Indian Cheddi Jagan and the African Linden Forbes Sampson Burnham—whose legacies are borne by the PPP and the PNC respectively. Cheddi Jagan along with his spouse (Janet Jagan), Jocelyn Hubbard and Ashton Chase launched the Political Action Committee (PAC) in 1946, the precursor to the PPP, with an objective of "political education" and a vision that "class, and not race, was the most important factor in the historical development."[15] The PAC thus began as a multiracial working class group which within a decade was torn by racial differences that played itself out in the power politics of the day.

Forbes Burnham was a charismatic Afro-Guyanese lawyer, steeped in Marxist rhetoric, which joined the PAC in the 1940s, but soon diverged from the Jagan faction on issues of ideology and race.[16] In 1950 when PAC formally declared itself a political party, the Progressive People's Party was born with Jagan as its leader and Forbes Burnham as its Chair. Dr. Jagan's "tactic" of identifying an African leader within the PPP to rally the Afro-Guyanese only ended up pitting the various African power contenders against one another, who together turned against Jagan himself.[17] In 1953 the "period of apprenticeship in self-rule" crafted by the British led to the socialist PPP winning 18 out of 24 legislative seats.[18] The Afro- and the Indo-Guyanese factions within the PPP, led by Jagan and Burnham respectively, fought over cabinet positions; proffering this clash of personalities as the perfect opportunity to the British—alarmed already by the radical Marxist overtones of Jagan's leadership and joined in this apprehension by the United States in the era of the Cold War—to dismiss the Jagan government. In the interim, the economic policies that were framed by the Jagan faction focused primarily on the agricultural sector that would have favored the Indo-Guyanese, adding fuel to the racial fire.

In the meantime, the governmental crisis of 1953 not only thrust the Jagan-Burnham contention to the forefront but it simultaneously precipitated domestic racial tensions and ultimately resulted in the PPP split. Burnham, in contrast to Jagan, presented himself as less of a socialist radical and not only courted the attention of the West but also gained the support of Indo-Guyanese business groups (as opposed to the farmers and workers)—thus belying the claim that class rather than race mattered to the groups. Consequently, in 1955 the People's National Congress led by Forbes Burnham was born from the division of the PPP—and "from this time forth, politics in Guyana became explicitly racialized."[19] No one ethnic group single-handedly was responsible for the divisiveness at this point, as a visiting Indian author to British Guiana, V.P. Vatuk, commented:

> Both groups (Africans and Indians) suffer from superiority. Indians feel that no culture is greater than that of India, while Africans feel that since they have copied more thoroughly the dress, manners, and religion of their masters, they are more civilized.[20]

The controversial Kean Gibson underscores this point more extremely by emphasizing the separatism of East Indian communities as based on ideological and fundamental Hinduism, and accuses Jagan's politics of being "a system of conquest that had always been Jagan's dream."[21] It was at this juncture that some "big powers," to suit their vested interests, propelled the candidate they backed to supercede the other. As a result, Burnham who now stood in contrast to the Marxist-leaning Jagan was a more favorable candidate to the British and the United States, especially when he called for Guyana not to be "used as a satellite of the Soviet Union." Arthur Schlessinger was led to declare: "an independent British Guiana under Burnham (if Burnham will commit himself to a multiracial policy) would cause us many fewer problems than a British Guiana under Jagan."[22] This did not mean that Burnham had given up the socialist rhetoric altogether; he astutely shaped a populist rhetoric for the PNC while devising a regional trade effort in the form of the Caribbean Free Trade Area, the precursor of the CARICOM (Caribbean Community). To be fair, Jagan also made chameleon like revisions to his "communism" while in office, according to Percy Hitnzen:

> He advocated the strengthening of economic ties with the US as a basis for securing the country's independence and actively sought out US support in a campaign for independence. He provided assurances against nationalization, and he complained about representations about himself in the US press as a communist.[23]

Subsequent elections in 1961 saw the Indo-Guyanese PPP defeat the PNC by 9 seats with a 90 percent electoral turnout which was clearly a response to racially mobilized campaigns.[24] The following year, Jagan, with his popular mandate, demanded full independence, which even the Labour Party in Britain ignored. A PPP minister, during the 1961 election had declared: "When I return to power I'll shoot Black man like birds falling from trees."[25] This rhetoric was evenly matched by Burnham's ominous warning soon after the birth of the independent Cooperative Republic of Guyana: "If it comes to a showdown, the East Indians must remember that we could do more killing than they could."[26] One wonders whether he was referring to the Afro-Guyanese throttlehold on the military and police that have often been accused of either perpetrating, or turning a blind eye to, violence against the Indo-Guyanese.

Needless to say, from this point onwards, the nationalist struggle for full independence was doomed not to unite the various sub-national groups but began to erode at any previous unity. Underscoring of ethnic differences led the public to identify Jagan "as the leader of the Indians while Burnham was as-

signed the mantle of African leadership."[27] Thus, 1961-64 saw widespread ethnic strife and carnage. In the first half of the 1960s the "virtual civil war" that
tore Guiana left hundreds dead, wounded and scores of women raped. Some
authors describe the situation as "an experience that left the country as one of
the most racially segmented polities" where "prospects of independence had
brought to fore a leadership that stoked the fires of racial hatred."[28]

The next round of elections in 1964 witnessed the substitution of the first-
past-the-post system with proportional representation, as proposed by the US,
leading Jagan's PPP to enjoy 46 percent of the vote (24 seats) while Burnham's
PNC, which had 40 percent (20 seats), teamed up with the UF which scored 12
percent (7 seats). Consequently, as leader of the PNC, Burnham was invited to
form the government as prime minister. The new electoral system of 1964 precipitated yet another violent outburst beginning with arson in the sugarcane
fields by August of that year. Along with hundreds killed and injured, thousands
of homes were destroyed by arson and looting, and 15,000 people were forced
by the violence to re-settle in their respective ethnic communities. Two years
later, on May 26, 1966 Guyana finally gained its independence, but as a deeply
racially-divided nation.

Most authors trace the ethnic divides in Guyana to the colonial era; [29] Perry
Mars in contrast observes that inter-ethnic rivalry was once rare, but it was "in
the wake of the contest for political power which emerged since 1953 in particular that ethnic consciousness as a rallying point for political competition became
manifest in overt racial violence."[30] In the political literature about Guyana, Joan
Mars' work[31] is unique in its methodical study of the structural context of colonial and post-independence police violence in Guyana.[32] However, the sophisticated examination of police violence and brutality does not lend itself to clarifi-
cations about the nature of ethnic differences nor does she examine such
violence through the prism of ethnicity per se. For such comprehensive analyses
one has to review Seecoomar's work that singularly stands out in providing a
robust examination of ethnic differences especially among the Afro-Guyanese
and the Indo-Guyanese.[33]

The latter years of British colonialism coincided with the Cold War era in
global politics so that the complicity of both the US and British governments in
fueling this racial-ethnic polarization is acknowledged by Jagan.[34] It is now
widely accepted that under a Cold War strategy to stem the spread of communism, the Kennedy administration decided to deny assistance to the Jagan government and at the 1963 Constitutional Conference in London, British demands
for a new proportional representation in exchange for independence was a calcu-
lated move to remove Jagan from power in favor of the "merely socialist" Burnham. Such divide-and-rule strategies were perfected by the British over centuries of colonial domination, and when the conservative United Force Party threw
its weight to the PNC in 1964, the regime change—and racially divided politics—was complete.[35]

The violence, carved out of racist discourse begun during the 1950s, ripples through Guyana today in rhetoric and action, as evidenced in the 1996 and 2001 elections and their immediate aftermath. The two dominant racial groups, the Afro- and the Indo-Guyanese tried to outdo one another with their racist rhetoric. Such has been the recent history of race-driven party politics on the eve of Guyana's independence those four decades hence, this multiracial country continues to be plagued by extreme ethnicism. More recently, the PPP and the PNC came to a showdown with the out-of-office PNC boycotting Guyana's parliament for nearly fourteen months until they returned, in May 2003, following the PPP/C government fulfilling some of their demands (including establishing a Commission of Enquiry into allegations of brutality and corruption in the Guyanese Police Force).[36] In a recent letter to the *Stabroek News*, a concerned citizen evoked the image of 1962 and applied it to 2004:

> The PNC has collaborated with ROAR, GAP/WPA and trade unions to stage a series of protests in Georgetown. Does this ring a bell? Of course it does! In February 1962 the PNC, UF [United Front] and TUC mounted protests against the PPP Government. In the process, rioters burned down businesses in Georgetown.[37]

Clearly, memories of 1962 and post-election riots loom large in today's context of ethnic politics while also shedding light on another political dimension: parties such as ROAR and the GAP/WPA have also made incursions into the party structure. ROAR is another Indo-Guyanese directed party; and it too appears to add to the divisiveness of Guyanese politics with its own ethno-nationalist rhetoric, thereby stealing the thunder from the PPP. The role of other ethnic minorities, such as the Amerindians, unfolds through the political machinery of the WPA and GAP. These dimensions of Guyanese politics will be examined in the subsequent two sections.

ROAR Guyana and Ethno-nationalism

Rise Organise and Rebuild (ROAR), is the brainchild of Ravi Dev, an expatriate Guyanese who returned to Georgetown in the 1990s after having trained in law in New York City.[38] Like his predecessors in the PPP and the WPA, he began challenging the dominant political elites and the power structure, through pre-party political structures such as the Jaguar Committee for Democracy established in 1988,[39] and a rights advocacy groups called GIFT—the Guyana Indian Foundation Trust. GIFT claimed that the rights and needs of the East Indian population were not being met by the largely Indo-Guyanese PPP, despite the fact that it was this very constituency that had helped the PPP win seats in the December 1997 elections. In mid-1998, GIFT first began to cause ripples in the bi-party race politics of Guyana by taking out full-page advertisements exhorting East Indian victims of election violence (from December 1997-January

1998) to make their statements public. GIFT alleged that the racial violence that spiraled into rioting and looting began with street protests led by the Afro-Guyanese Desmond Hoyte, then leader of the PNC.[40] GIFT urged the PPP government to set a commission of inquiry into the violence against East Indians rather than turning a blind eye to the perpetrators.

It is worth noting the *international* dimensions of an ethnicist discourse emerging from Ravi Dev's calls for the revitalization of Indian "culture" (as seen below). Dev's activities appear to have gained a momentum at about the same time in the 1990s when the Hindu BJP (Bharatiya Janata Party) government in India, and its international wing, the VHP (Global Hindu Forum), shaped the discourse of "otherness" vis a vis Muslims in India.[41] The Muslims were caricatured as betrayers of the nation while calling for a revival of Hindu culture and icons that according to the BJP was eroded under secularism. Concurrently, another international group, the Global Organization of People of Indian Origin (GOPIO), like the VHP, active in mobilizing the Indian Diaspora in Asia, Africa, the Caribbean and Pacific Islands, hosted a meeting in New York (April 2004), where the former prime ministers of Indian origin, Basdeo Panday (Trinidad), Mahendra Chaudhry (Fiji) were guest speakers—Ravi Dev was one among them as a member of the Guyanese Parliament representing ROAR.[42] The main theme of the GOPIO meeting was the abuse of human rights of people of Indian origin resulting in a resolution calling on the Indian government to "monitor such violations targeting the diaspora in various countries and 'take all necessary measures... to put an end to those abuses." In other words, Ravi Dev's populist campaign appears to have benefited from the pan-Indian activities that sharpen identity issues of "Indianness." Clearly, Ravi Dev and ROAR's influence in ethnic politics has now gone beyond advocacy groups, and is getting increasingly strident through party politics as he takes on the might PPP and competes with them for the same constituency of voters.

The confrontation with the PPP began to gain ground during Ravi Dev's US tour in 1999, when he accused the PPP of a policy of appeasement (to the Afro-Guyanese) by surrendering to "demands of black militants" to "shorten its tenure of office by two years," after being elected in a "fair election".[43] The PNC's Hoyte, echoing his predecessor Burnham's rhetorical ethos after the 1962 elections, had sworn to "make the country ungovernable" unless the election results were turned around.[44] What Dev failed to note, in his denunciation of the PPP, was that the 1997 election was considered controversial by Britain, Canada, and the United States as well; and it was not until a few months following the December elections that the Janet Jagan-led PPP government was finally recognized as legitimate.[45] Further, Ravi Dev was able to capitalize on the fact that attacks against Indians had continued to be on the rise from June 1998 to March 1999. Meanwhile, during the same 1999 US tour Dev declared at a press conference:

> We want our fair share of rights as citizens of a multicultural, multi-ethnic Guyana... while the PPP wishes to impose a *unitary* Guyanese nationalism.... We want our fair share of positions in the Guyanese Army which is now 80 percent black.... In the National School of Dance the syllabus is restricted to African dancing. Of all the instruments only the steel pan [which is of African origin] is taught. Why not the tabla [East Indian drum]? Why not Bharat Natyam [a South Indian classical dance form]?[46] [Emphasis added].

A closer scrutiny of the above commentary divulge the following features of ethno-nationalism: First, Dev's comments reveal the reassertion of *Indian* culture in the name of multiculturalism but against the backdrop of the "otherness" of African cultural manifestations—what Paul Gilroy would label as "ethnic insiderism."[47] In the eyes of non-East Indians, such talk becomes tantamount to ultranationalist rhetoric, though as with all cultural nationalists, he would disagree with such a label. The assertion of multiculturalism in the form of a revival of Indianism on Ravi Dev's part is no different from the general historical path of ethnicist discourse plaguing Guyanese politics and fragmenting society. What is different, however, is the person delivering it, the *Indian* ethnicity of the accuser (that is similar to the accused PPP government).

Second, Dev drew attention to a select segment of the *labor* sector (divided along ethnic lines as discussed in the previous section) by calling for a "fair share of positions in the Guyanese Army which is now 80 percent black."[48] While the Afro-Guyanese, the mixed race population, and the Amerindians have complained about lack of equal access to government contracts, land holdings, jobs, and scholarships, Dev in turn, drew notice to the one sector where the Indo-Guyanese are in a minority—the police and the military forces which is largely Afro-Guyanese. In nationalist discourse, defense of one's motherland is a primary function of the true patriot-citizen and it appears that Ravi Dev's call to guns reveals such a sentiment. Guyana is not a praetorian state with a heavy influence of the military in civilian rule, but as Ivelaw Griffith has pointed out, even though no external threat warrants such high military spending as Guyana's, the defense forces have been used, by both the PPP and the PNC, for security of specific regimes rather than the security of the nation-state.[49] One may speculate that increase in numbers of the Indo-Guyanese leading to a change in the currently existing ethnic composition of the Guyana Defense Forces will strengthen the perception of nationalist defense undertaken by East Indians. Additionally, it serves as a solution to allegations from the Indo-Guyanese that the largely Afro-Caribbean police have been negligent of crimes committed against the former.

Third, by charging the ruling PNC with the imposition of a "unitary nationalism" Ravi Dev has articulated an alternative solution to the ethno-pluralism of Guyana—a federal state drawn along ethnic lines so that majority ethnic groups can have their own administrative units. Dev has elaborated elsewhere about his concept of "Integrative Federalism" —a notion, he claims, does not imply the

Balkanization of Guyana along ethno-racial lines. Integrative federalism has been constructed although, within the context of an "ethnic *security* dilemma" as a structural reform proposed by ROAR—the term "security" underscores the aforementioned point about nationalist rhetoric.[50]

What is clear is that despite Dev's various calls from his parliamentary seat to eliminate governmental corruption, or to make the government accountable, which is needed in every democracy, issues of ethnocultural identity are closest to his heart. He pointedly articulates the divisive political discourse of cultural identity along with the promise of the trains running on time. In a commentary following a TV appearance with a fellow speaker, Ravi Dev exclaimed with consternation:

WHY PROBS PERSIST?

Re-alert

> I observed him mystifying the term "Guyanese" - which refers to one's citizenship, with "African" and "Indian", which refers to *the cultural roots or ethnicity of the citizen.* I figured if a bright politician could be confused on *the issue of identity,* which impacts so much on politics, then what can we expect from the average Joe? We're all citizens of Guyana... At the same time, we are "Amerindians," "Africans" or "Indians" because of some *cultural particularities.*[51] (Emphasis added)

These "cultural particularities" that are at the core of identity issues has been expressed differently by Ravi Dev at various times as either "race" or "ethnicity" though more recently (since mid 2004) all his writings and comments have focused on the latter term. Thus, whether the issue of identity is one that is race- or ethnicity-related is often obfuscated. In an editorial in January 2005, Dev asserted: "We like to say ethnicity because it is not just race, it is how you identify yourself within an area."[52] Previous writings, however, contradict this point—"The *racially and criminally* motivated depredations against entire villages on the East Coast were also violations" (referring to the criminal violence targeting the Indo-Guyanese on the East Coast that began in 2002-03).[53] Keeping the 2006 elections in mind and in crafting a strategic rhetoric, Dev more recently has emphasized the word "ethnic" over "race" by proposing that an *Ethnic* Impact Statement be issued "with the promulgation of every Government policy and program" due to the "ethnic cleavages existent in our society," and "the political dissatisfaction [that] arises out of perceived ethnic discrimination in this area."[54]

POLITICALLY MOTIVATED RHETORIC

What could be the reason behind this shift in emphasis from "race" to "ethnicity"? It is this author's perception that the shift in rhetoric is in keeping with providing an alternative language and devising a political strategy to approach the ethnic/racial climate of Guyana. This is in line with Dev's proposal for crafting the Center Force that is to provide a counterweight to the PPP and the PNC. During the 2006 elections this strategy is an attempt to shift the focus from issues of "race" to those of "ethnicity" and culture. What is unique about the approach is a structure and discourse that for the first time tries to be different from the old formula heretofore existent. What is the Centre Force about?

Ravi Dev himself has articulated the notion of Centre Force, which according to him occupies the political, cultural, and social middle ground between the PPP and the PNC and calls on all the other marginalized parties (WPA, GAP, JFAP) to join forces to counter the ineffectiveness of influence on policy-making as it currently stands. It is an attempt to create a "conglomeration of smaller political parties working together" to "break the deadlock on governance."[55] It was clear from the last 2001 elections that the PPP-PNC stronghold was a difficult one to dislodge despite attempts by smaller parties such as the WPA and GAP to form an alliance (see Table 2). Therefore, the Centre Force, as envisioned by Ravi Dev would be a confederacy of parties with a common program that expresses diversity but is unified against the "behemoths" the PPP and the PNC.[56] He has been received with some skepticism by those who believe that Ravi Dev's strategy is to dupe marginalized minority parties to install an ultranationalist regime.

TABLE 2

NATIONAL ASSEMBLY 19 March 2001(89.1 %)		% VOTES	SEATS
People's Progressive Party/Civic (socialist)	PPP/C	53.1	34
People's National Congress/Reform (socialist populist)	PNC/R	41.7	27
GAP/WPA - Guyana Action Party (socialist) - Working People's Alliance (social-democratic)	GAP/WPA	2.4	2
Rise Organise and Rebuild Guyana	ROAR	0.9	1
The United Force (conservative)	TUF	0.7	1
Justice for All Party	JFAP	0.7	-
GDP	GDP	0.4	-
National Front Alliance	NFA	0.1	-

Sources: electionworld.org; http://www.nationmaster.com/country/gy/Democracy

An erudite man with excellent communication skills, Ravi Dev has mastered the use of the media (both print and online), which in Guyana's tightly constrained political circle is his main avenue, as well as the floor of the National Assembly, for spreading his ideas about identity and state politics. His voluble writings include not only the Guyanese news media such as *Stabroek News* but also online political commentaries that quote from the writings of philosophers from Hegel and Marx to Mill and Foucault. He is known to be an ardent devotee of the Hindu scriptures, especially the *Ramcharitmanas* that informs his daily practice. Not only can he chant the traditional values and norms of Hinduism, but he can turn cosmopolitan, and cleverly articulate a middle path in the form of the Centre Force—an attempt to provide the vehicle for other minority parties—and managed to persuade the secular WPA-GAP parties (that have represented the Amerindian and other minorities) to follow this strategy for the 2006 elections. Such a leader cannot be easily dismissed from the ethno-political scene of Guyana that certainly includes more than the two main ethno-political groups, not excluding the indigenous peoples. The next section will explore the role of Amerindians through the WPA-GAP parties and their role in the nation/state dilemma.

Amerindians and Party Politics[57]

> The evidence suggests that the separate communities have been driven so far apart that talk of ... intercommunal cooperation and fellowship at the grassroots is viewed with great skepticism.[58]

These words of Premdas from 1978 continue to be strikingly true to this day. The bitter ethnic rivalries that have defined Guyana's politics and that have extensively shape its distribution of resources have mostly ignored or excluded Amerindians, who together comprise the third largest ethnic group among Guyana's "Six Peoples." In an atmosphere of severe ethnic polarization, Amerindian groups are too small to mount much of a political challenge. Historically, and to a large extent today, what happens in Guyana's capital, Georgetown has very little to do with "Guyana's first people," the Amerindians who dwell almost exclusively in the hinterlands, a world away from the nation's seat of power. For their part, Guyana's indigenous groups have been generally content to be left in peace inland, out of the sometime violent political tug of war between the Afro- and Indo-Guyanese on the coast.

Geographically, the Amerindians are scattered throughout Guyana but are concentrated mostly in the hinterlands. They are broadly classified into two categories, the "Coastal Amerindians" (the Carib, Arawak, and Warao) and the "Interior Amerindians" (Akawaio, Arekuna, Barama, River Carib, Macushi, Patamona, Waiwai, and Wapishiana).[59] Too often it is overlooked that the Amerindian people are not a monolith and still lack an Amerindian ethnic or racial identity that would override tribal identities. They seem disposed to unite politically against threats from the national government or transnational corporations regarding land rights and resource use, or against the perceived meddling of Georgetown into their cultural affairs, yet that may never be enough to solidify them into an effective voting bloc. Even on seemingly common issues such as Amerindian land titles and land use, there are levels of complexities: for e.g. different tribal views regarding individual versus communal leadership and disputed territorial rights between groups.[60] Regarding the land demarcation process already under way, Minister of Amerindian Affairs, Carolyn Rodrigues, explains that some Amerindians are making individual claims to lands already claimed communally, and she presents the example of an individual holder selling title to his land to a coast Lander, which "may well lead to the break up of the fabric of that community."[61]

The identity of Amerindian groups remains largely tribal. Perhaps this is the main reason that they have tended to ally themselves with whatever party is preaching ethnic unity over those that emphasize race and ethnicity. They speak several distinct languages and promote their own customs.[62] Their own histories of inter-tribal rivalries and antagonisms fuel cultural stereotypes of one another.[63] "Forest people" and "savannah people" each have their own stories that commonly draw superior distinctions between them.[64] For example, Forte describes how the "Arawak-speaking Wapishana, often warring with the Carib-speaking Makushi until the twentieth century, refer to their neighbors as lazy and imbue them with black magic, so that the two groups can still 'regard each other with suspicion and distrust'."[65] The Wapishana allow their women to become wives for the Wai-Wai forest tribes but feel slighted that the Wai-Wai do not reciprocate in kind. In the village of Achiwuib, those that have intermarried with the descendants of a black ancestor who have migrated from St. Vincent were accepted as Wapishana, but were referred to as "smokes" and were segregated physically from the "pure" Wapishana. Moreover, the author's personal experiences with the Makushi of the North Rupununi in 2002 confirms that Amerindians can also operate under stereotypes that distance them from suspicious "coast Landers" or people of other racial groups (for example, Indo-Guyanese are more honest and hardworking than Afro-Guyanese, who tend to be lazy; the Makushi express much less tolerance for intermarriage with the darker Afro-Guyanese).

Also to consider are the physical distances between widely scattered groups that still largely lack adequate communication technologies and other resources—either to stay informed or to create a common ethnic dialogue.[66] The extension phase of land demarcation has been severely hampered in some regions because of a lack of communications over long distances. The important work of the SDNP which is sponsored by the United Nations Development Project to modernize communications in Guyana is a start, but Amerindian villages generally have yet to establish (reliable) sources of electricity.[67] Many communities who have expressed desire for land titles have yet to submit requests and their claims may conflict with those who have already filed.[68]

Even though the reigning party governments have sought alignments with Amerindians to provide a more secure majority, these alliances have hardly translated into shared governance or the significant advancement of Amerindian causes (e.g. self-sufficiency, self-determination, social and cultural stability, control over land use, sustainable development practices and ecotourism). Voting for ideology rather than race during the 1960s, Amerindians bolstered the showing of the old United Force, since it was voicing a priority for racial harmony and unification) perhaps not in small part because it stood to gain more power from such a message). In the United Force, a right wing party of mostly affluent Euro-Guyanese, Amerindian causes were seemingly not the focus of their campaigns nation-wide.[69] The Amerindian vote became aligned in the 1970s with the WPA (the Working People's Alliance), the party that began to be identified with the visionary Walter Rodney when he joined it in 1974.

The WPA was co-founded in 1974 by the historian, scholar, radical activist, pan-Africanist, and one of the fathers of the black consciousness movement, Walter Rodney. The WPA too had its roots in an interest group (just as the PPP had two decades ago and more recently the ROAR Guyana party) and eventually consolidated four other such groups over the following years while going across race lines to also include Afro- and Indo-Guyanese members. Interestingly, Rodney's WPA stands for "the genuine multiracial power of the working people."[70] When the WPA chose to sit out the 1980 elections in protest of wholesale fraud by Forbes Burnham's PNC, Amerindians were left without hope of sympathetic representation in the legislature. In June 1980 when Walter Rodney was assassinated by a parcel bomb, the Amerindians along with their fellow WPA members lost a formidable leader.[71] Though not an Amerindian by birth, Rodney's charisma and words spilled beyond black African consciousness and included all those who were disenfranchised by class and race by the political and economic elites. Then, with but one seat gained by the WPA in 1985, little changed. A paragraph from the WPA web page is illustrative:

> The PPP, which, for many years while in opposition, heaped scorn on the PNC for putting square pegs in round holes, has been setting new records in this regard... reflect[ing] two chronic weaknesses of the PPP: their refusal to look beyond their own political backyard and their elevation of party loyalty over professional qualifications, preferring to reward activists and supporters rather than appoint people of quality who would represent Guyana with distinction.[72]

In 1992, in what were probably the first free and fair elections since Independence, the WPA won less than 2% of the national vote, limiting them to a disappointing 2 legislative seats. Yet, the lack of a comfortable working majority for the PPP/C gave minority opposition parties some leverage, even if it required an uncomfortable arrangement with the new United Front, which itself had gained one seat. Referring to Amerindian regions, a WPA statement on these 1992 elections reads: "This meant that the PPP/Civic was able to send representatives from the RDCs of Regions 8 and 9 to build up its regional component in the Parliament, thereby achieving a working majority."[73] Yet, in the following two elections, the PPP has solidified its grip on national power, making unnecessary even the lip service it paid to the priorities of Amerindian voters.

It has sometimes been expressed that an Amerindian bloc might prove to be a swing vote in national elections closely contested by the PPP and PNC, putting them in the position of a kingmaker. If this has been the hope of indigenous or-

ganizers, it has never materialized. The primary response so far has been organizing politically to influence national policy in favor of Amerindian interests.

The Guyana Action Party (GAP) and the Amerindian People's Association
(APA) were organized largely because efforts to advance Amerindian causes
within the existing political process were getting nowhere. As put bluntly in an
APA website, "The APA was formed in 1991 at a conference *for Amerindian
leaders in Georgetown... to discuss various problems affecting their communities for which they were not finding solutions.*"[74] The GAP (or the "Amerindian
Party") and the APA, also an advocacy group, have helped organize and define
these interests. The encouragement of local *Touchous* (or tribal leaders) and
other decision-making bodies press Amerindians to become ever more engaged
in national politics. But, years of skilful organization and coalition building (e.g.
with the WPA in the 2001 national elections) have yielded very limited and disappointing results (arguably, for all practical purposes, this may always be the
case, at least in the near future). Albeit a necessary step to present a clear voice
for Amerindian demands, political organization and engagement is far from sufficient to deliver the desired results. One glance at the proceedings and resolu-
tions of the GAP-WPA is sufficient to understand the wide gap between the
Guyanese government and Amerindian interests.

In their January 30 (2001) press release, the GAP-WPA hint that the alliance gave Amerindians a vital presence in and around Georgetown by proclaiming, "over ninety percent of the peoples of the hinterland are among the poor and
powerless. In taking this step GAP did not try to separate the hinterland from the
coast. Rather it has joined with that party of coastal origin with the best record
of genuine concern for the dignity of the working people of Guyana."[75] It continues by expressing a common sentiment that the WPA was the hero and chal-
lenger of the bi-party system dominating Guyana yet "What the WPA's records
at the polls in 1992 and 1997 had shown is that despite its brave record of resistance to the Burnham dictatorship, the people were not yet ready for a party that
explicitly shunned ethnicity." Ironically, Amerindian support for "unity" helped
usher in the PNC and the Burnham era and further solidified ethnic-racial polarization. Though the Janet Jagan administration was supportive of numerous
Amerindian exhibitions and cultural demands, APA spokesperson, Jean LaRose,
was expressing Amerindian frustration with Georgetown over land demarcation
and politics: "They are not consulting with us."[76]

Just before the 2001 elections, an article about the GAP and Amerindian
representation in the Regions revealed that,

> Indeed, given present demographics and the new element of geo-
> graphical representation in the electoral system, any party that did
> manage to capture the bulk of the Amerindian vote could obtain six
> or seven seats and could become the kingmaker in a new govern-
> ment.[77]

Of course, GAP did join forces with the WPA to form a coalition whose expressed aim was to take advantage of the parliamentary seats won in the elections to articulate Guyana's needs that included an end to divisive ethnic politics. Even if Amerindians were able achieve a more united front at the polls, the solidification of power by the PPP/C over the last three elections and its thorough support by the international community (and the US particularly) makes the swing vote scenario even more unlikely in the foreseeable future. It is more likely that an organized Amerindian political movement will remain confined to alliances with other small minority parties (e.g. the WPA) in hopes to retain maybe one or two seats, as they did in the 1997 and 2001 elections. While the PPP/C has expanded its platform to reach out to the Georgetown business elite (who are not aligned with the PNC) and to the Amerindians in the interior, their power base remains among those invested in agricultural exports—particularly rice and sugar. Besides, as during the tenure of Desmond Hoyte, in the last PNC administration from 1985-1992, the PPP/C has had its mind on "rescuing the economy" from problems of crisis proportions, by "promoting and developing the interior"—effectively drawing concerned cries from the indigenous homelands of the Amerindians.

Amerindian tribal groups can no longer count on being left in relative isolation. Important aspects of globalization have begun to change all that. Another reason that the causes of the interior are unlikely to move Georgetown revolve around structures placed on the national government by the international lending agencies such as the IMF or other international actors—the surest sign that Georgetown is no longer in control of what happens in Guyana on the coast or the interior. Despite snappy growth rates during the early to mid-1990s, Guyana remains one of the poorest countries in the Western hemisphere, and its recovery had already begun to flatten out the end of the millennium.[78] Guyana, in the mid-1990s, saw "the advance of what was characterized as a 'buoyant economy' slowing to 5.1% in 1995 because of a devastating cyanide waste spill at the Omai gold mine."[79] There are two things to note: (a) the new PPP government in 1992 led by a "reformed" Cheddi Jagan that reassured foreign capitalists; and (b) the *foreign* control of the Omai enterprise. To get an idea of just how quickly things become different, foreign direct investments went from $8 million in 1990 to $74 million in 1995, and then $93 million in 1996.[80] With the blessings of Georgetown—itself under international pressure to open its resources to foreign investments—new transnational corporations are gaining access to Amerindian ancestral lands for extracting bauxite, gold, and timber, with their young men often serving as the cheap source of labor. Renewed boundary disputes with Venezuela and Surinam include much of the same land representing some of the world's most unspoiled wilderness, rich with a wide array of tropical plants and animals. New roads to promote trade crisscross their lands and there are plans for more. New technologies put the world on their doorsteps. Ecotourism is the mantra of the day. These changes strike deep at the cultural roots of the Amerindians, and thus those of Guyana's ethnic crosscurrents. K.R. Hope attempts to draw our attention to the linkage between ethnicity and economic resources thus:

> As ethnicity becomes increasingly salient, every political decision favors one community and hinders others. That is, the distribution of goods and services which result from political decisions become the preserve of the advantaged ethnic community. Such is the realm of ethnic political participation in Guyana.[81]

In the face of such common challenges, Amerindian groups recognize that self- preservation and self-determination will require a painfully aggressive, proactive, and united effort—one that must include a more active involvement in politics. Hopeless though the above words may sound, the GAP and the WPA, in preparation for the 2006 elections have laid the ground work through various initiatives. Rupert Roopnaraine, the co-leader of the GAP-WPA alliance, acknowledged (in an address in March 2003) that ethnic politics continue to rule the day even in the recent PPP/C era: "executive power-sharing is out because there is not enough trust and all of this."[82] In line with Amerindian preferences for greater community rule, Roopnaraine is proposing that the ineffective Neighborhood Democratic Councils (NDC) be revamped so that their membership is balanced between the governing party and opposition parties—a concept of local *shared governance* that has met with little enthusiasm in Georgetown.[83]

Ironically, the secular Roopnaraine's 2003 call for the NDC to be composed of the silenced and marginalized peoples finds its echo in the Centre Force (articulated by Ravi Dev in January 2005, as a political force that will bring together these same disenfranchised constituencies for shared governance in the National Assembly). In the absence of large-scale national support for Roopnaraine's localized power-sharing scheme, it is yet to be seen if WPA and the GAP will tow the ROAR line and if it would indeed lead to a bargaining power for the Amerindians. As discussed, there are reasons to believe that by offering such support they would have ended up catching the tiger (or the Jaguar, the animal identified with ROAR) by its tail.

Conclusion

The term "ethnic group" says Steve Fenton, "suggests a concreteness of 'membership' in which ethnicity is summative and totalizing, and this is a condition which is rarely met.... The analytical task is to identify why and how actors choose to act according to the prompts of ethnic allegiance."[84] National elections in Guyana bring to the front-burner this "ethnic allegiance" highlighted by the Afro-Guyanese, descended from African slave and indentured labor lineage and the Indo-Guyanese, who emerged as contractual laborers from East India (which began in 1838). The Amerindians in the meantime, served alongside the African slaves during the period of colonization (though some Afro-

Caribbeans counter that the Amerindians sometimes served as plantation policemen who rounded up escaped African slaves).[85] Thus has the divide-and-rule
policy begun by the colonial powers, particularly Britain, reverberate in the cor-
ridors of power in post-independent Guyana. In an age of globalization, as local
and state economies get ingrained in global economic networks, it is worthwhile
to recall Mimi Scheller's words comparing modern neo-liberalism to nineteenth-
century liberalism in its "claims to provide a level playing field, even though
restrictions, controls and exclusions continue to hold down the weakest participants. And race continues to be a key determinant of who wins and who loses in
the global marketplace."[86]

Ethnic identities become a significant political classification when immigrant groups and indigenous populations are brought into "direct political and
economic competition;" viz., after independence, in a society that has not
learned to be a civic society and a cohesive one at that.[87] The implication here is
that it is not so much strong ethnic identities that shake nation-state integration,
but rather that weak state structures create situations for certain individuals and
groups to shape the discourse under lines of politico-ethnic identity. Fenton de-
clares a three-fold typology of conditions for ethnicity to have a social currency:
(a) *corporate condition* where individuals are "enclosed within the group" in a
primordial fashion; (b) *formal condition* that provides ethnic groups certain constitutional rights; and (c) the inevitable *cultural condition* where respective ethnic groups imagine themselves as "the bearers of cultural difference."[88]

How would Guyana fit under such a three-fold classification? The foregoing
sections reveal the following: First, even the indigenous Amerindian groups
though classified as Amerindians do not "purely" belong to their respective
tribal categories due to intermarriage (both between and outside their respective
tribal groups). Though the Amerindians are larger in numbers in the hinterland,
their group identity is not restricted to their segregated space. Amerindians are
present on the coast and in Georgetown. Indeed, as their participation in the
WPA-GAP alliance and party politics show, they desire more attention from the
central government for reasons of economic development and modernization. In
the decades since independence, there has been no recent call for segregation by
the Amerindians that may result in such a *corporate condition* of ethnicity. As
for the Afro-Guyanese (including the PNC), contemporary demands have included a greater share in government employment, scholarships and contracts;
but not a separate homeland. Ravi Dev and ROAR, however, have expressed
indirectly, through the concept of "Integrative Federalism" and the division of
Guyana into administrative units composed of specific ethnic majorities, a desire
for such a *corporate* classification, which until 2005 was articulated along lines
of race (rather than ethnicity).

The second ethnic value of *formal condition* is explicitly enjoyed by the
Amerindians through constitutional protection and legislative decrees. Yet, in
2000, the UN Human Rights Committee criticized the Guyanese government for
not presenting a report to the UN in keeping with the International Covenant on

Civil and Political Rights, and for "the delay in amending the Amerindian Act... [where] members of indigenous Amerindian minority did not enjoy fully the right to equality before law."[89] Rights to forests, vegetation, timber, land and other such common goods are anything but clear, and neither are the responsibilities for faithfully maintaining them. Other racial-ethnic groups in Guyana are already questioning the size of Amerindian land demarcations and their expressed wishes to limit more traditional economic activities in the interior. Indigenous land rights are no laughing matter for the status quo. Given the current trend towards ecotourism as a development strategy, not only will Amerindians own or control the lands tourists most want to see, they may be in a position to limit traditional extractive industries. They are also the most logical people to be employed as guides, cooks and skilled craftspeople. There is no economic reason however, to imagine ecotourism as a zero sum—an essential role for Amerindians does not preclude the roles of or benefits to others. Instead, everyone benefits from good ecotourism—local, national, and international players alike. The control over the hinterlands for economic gain by exclusion is a strategy that answers to the logic of politico-ethnicism.

In the third variety of the *cultural condition* demarcating ethnicity, ROAR and Ravi Dev with ultranationalist fervor expressly come to mind. Ravi Dev's call for an Indian cultural revival especially in the school curricula against his perceived focus on African cultural expressions, only serve to further exacerbate the racial polemics in an already violent Guyana. Moreover, this "call" to Indian culture actually mirrors Dev's own criticism of Afro-Guyanese emphasis in the guise of multiculturalism and a "unitary" culture. In contrast, the GAP's chair, Edwin Glenn suggested to the visiting Conflict Transformation Consultant (Roelf Meyer) that the best way to solve the problem of ethnicity is to encourage intermarriages, along with the Guyana National Service which would increase youth interaction in the "cultural melting pot" that was Guyana.[90]

The 5 main questions, posed in the Introduction to this chapter, may be answered this way, beginning with the first: *Is ethnic identity culture bound?* Ethnic identity is culture-bound but only *along with* other conditions that lend expression and credence to such an identity. In other words, ethnic identity asserted through culture is not fixed nor a natural evolution; indeed, with changing demographic contours of the nation-state, culture will be constructed as an amalgamation of various influences until re-expressed externally (as in the case of Ravi Dev and "Indian" culture). In the case of Guyana, Amerindian ethnicity is not only cultural but is solidified through spatial values and linked to land rights in addition to their indigenous culture (both of which undergoes transformations); thus, their ethnicity is further emphasized through formal constitutionality.

The mainstay of this chapter has been the bipolar ethnic/racial politics between the Indo-Guyanese and the Afro-Guyanese—politics that have resulted in ongoing criminal violence and brutal deaths—in an attempt to answer the remaining questions that are inter-related: How is ethnic conflict expressed in

Guyana today different from previous times? Is the devastating or recurring conflict ethno-political or primordial, something ancient and/or pre-social? When
does the interface between ethnic issues and potential conflict situations result in
violence and why? What is the linkage between ethnic violence and ethnic issues—above all, is violence a necessary or inevitable form of collective social
action? Ethnic conflict in Guyana today is exacerbated by political conditions
and is not cultural, as witnessed by the increase in the scale of the same in the
aftermath of national elections when defeated political leaders swear to undermine the state and the victorious party's administration. This recurring tension is
not ancient and primordial among the Afro- and the Indo-Guyanese since they
are both transplanted populations who emerged under colonial times and
through different conditions of migration (as slaves and indentured labor respectively).

The class status, as a legacy of British Guiana of colonial times, deepens the
divide between the two groups much more than a pre-social or primordial cultural ethnicity; even though the discourse is framed along the lines of the latter
variable. Violence has become inevitable as a form of collective social action
due to lack of national cohesiveness or perceived alternatives, but is not a natural or a pre-destined outcome. Ethnic violence is manufactured through mistrust
between the various ethno-political groups who have not learned about shared
governance and the complexities of parliamentary politics. Instead, in a history
of mistrust where race/ethnicity is readily used by one group to force power over
another, guns and crime appear as instantly gratifying solutions. There seems a
need for a "Third Force" or "Centre Force" after all; but one without the under-
pinnings of distinct ethnicities—one that is truly inclusive. This remains the
main challenge of the Guyanese people—all of them.

Notes

1. A previous version of this paper (co-authored with Dr. B. Bullock) was presented
at the Caribbean studies association meeting in Belize (2003). I would like to thank Dr.
Bullock, without whose able assistance this paper would not be completed, the Mednick
fellowship, and Ariel Myers for procuring my research materials for me. All inaccuracies
are entirely mine.

2. The interim report originated from the UN Special Rapporteur (for Contemporary
Racism, Discrimination, Xenophobia and Related Intolerance) to the UN General As-
sembly (2003), cited in Amnesty International Report, *Guyana: Human Rights and Crime
Control – Not Mutually Exclusive*, AI Index: AMR 35/003/2003. (Emphasis added).

3. Bert Wilkinson, "Opposition Leaders Deny Government Claims They Incite Violence in Guyana," *Associated Press*, 29 August 2003. The article also notes that in the
years prior to 2002 the death rate related to such violence was less than 50.

4. *The Economist*, "A Small Riot in Guyana: Guyana's Post-Election Riots," 14
April 2001: 5; *The Economist*, "Tinderbox: Politics in Guyana (Fears of Racial Violence
in Guyana" (7 September 2002). For a gender analyses of ethnic violence in Guyana see,

Alissa Trotz, "Between Despair and Hope: Women and Violence in Contemporary Guyana," *Small Axe*, no. 15 <http://iupjournals.org/smallaxe/sm15.html>.

5. *The Economist*, "Policing the Cops: Guyana Worries about a Death Squad" (22 May 2004); Michael Smith, "Indo-Guyanese are Being Targeted for Crimes in their Country, Group Claims," *Associated Press* (7 January 2004).

6. *BBC Monitoring Americas*, "Guyana Human Rights Group Wants Unity in Fight Against Crime" (3 September 2004).

7. *Stabroek News*, "Race Relations Body to Check Complaints of Delayed Public Service Promotions," (1 April 2005), <www.stabroeknews.com/index.pl/article?id=15332275; *Stabroek News*, "Gajraj Reinstatement," (16 April, 2005), <www.stabroeknews.com/index.pl/article?id=16906970>; "People Still Want to Know Why Their Sons Died: Fresh Calls for Death Squad Inquiry" (17 April 2005), <www.stabroeknews.com/index.pl/article?id=16980364>.

8. UNDP, *Human Development Report 2004*, <http://hDr.undp.org/2004/>. The Human Development Index is a measure of educational achievement, life expectancy and aggregate income. Norway enjoys first place in the HDI and the United States is ranked 8th according to the 2004 HDI Report. Guyana's ranking dropped from the previous year's where it enjoyed the 92nd position among 175 countries (HDR 2003)—See *Economist Intelligence Unit*, "Guyana: Population" No. 301, September 22, 2003.

9. Emphasis mine. Judaman Seecoomar, *Contributions Towards the Resolution of Conflict in Guyana* (Leeds, UK: Peepal Tree Press, 2002), 63. Seecoomar's words reflect contemporary reality born out of history, politics and economics that arose from Dutch colonial rule in 1613 that was followed by British rule from 1815–1966, which led to a conglomeration of racial ethnicities as well as religious cleavages that have been inherited by the modern nation-state of Guyana. His statement underscores the friction between the Afro and the Indo-Guyanese groups through party politics and struggle for control of national resources, but fails to capture the urgent needs of another non-negligible minority in Guyana, the Amerindians.

10. US State Department, *World Factbook: Country Report, Guyana* (last updated, April 21, 2005) <www.cia.gov/cia/publications/factbook/geos/gy.html>. The demographic statistic is sometimes projected differently—the Afro-Guyanese are denoted as 33% of the population and Indo-Guyanese as constituting 48 percent of a national population estimated in 2001 as 774,800 by *The Economist Intelligence Unit: Number 301 Country Background*, "Guyana: Population," September 22, 2003. Religious cleavages crosscut the ethno-racial divide—50% Christian (primarily Afro-Guyanese), 35% Hindu (mostly Indo-Guyanese), 10% Muslim and other religions (5%) compose distinct ethnoreligious categories—*Library of Congress Country Studies: Guyana*, <http://memory.loc.gov/frd/cs/gytoc.html>.

11. Kemp Ronald Hope, *Guyana: Politics and Development in an Emergent Socialist State* (New York: Mosaic Press, 1986), 13.

12. P. Mars, "Political Violence in Guyana," *Guyana Election Reports*, Mars traces the decline in third-party support from 28% of the popular vote in 1957 to only 16% in 1961, falling further to 12 % in 1964 and 7% in 1968. "In the meantime," he writes, "support for the two major parties consistently increased over the years... The introduction of Proportional Representation as a new electoral system did not automatically produce the multiplicity of smaller parties which were expected to cut across the racially polarized lines." (91); see also Hope, *Guyana*.

13. US State Department, *The World Factbook: Guyana*, <www.cia.gov/cia/publications/factbook/geos/gy.html> (21 April 2005), 2; and Baz Dreisinger, "In Radical Matrimony: Thunder in Guyana," *The Nation* 280, no. 9 (March 7, 2005): 25.

14. Wilkinson, "Opposition Leaders Deny Government Claims," *Associated Press*, (29 August 2003).

15. Roy Arthur Glasgow, *Guyana: Race and Politics Among Africans and East Indians* (The Hague: Martinus Nijhoff, 1970), 100–101.

16. For an excellent account of personality politics of Burnham and Jagan see, Linden Lewis, "Forbes Burnham (1923–1985): Unraveling the Paradox of Postcolonial Charismatic Leadership in Guyana," in *Caribbean Charisma: Reflections on Leadership, Legitimacy and Populist Politics*, ed. Anton Allahar (Kingston: Ian Randle Publishers/ Boulder: Lynne Rienner, 2001), 92–120; Percy Hintzen, "Cheddi Jagan (1918–1997): Charisma and Guyana's Challenge to Western Capitalism," *Caribbean Charisma*, ed. Anton Allahar, 121–154.

17. Glasgow, *Guyana*, 103.

18. Priya Vishnu "Ethnicity and Politics: East Indians in the Political Process of Guyana and Trinidad," *India Quarterly* (2004): 106. On the recommendation of the British Waddington Commission, in 1953, based on universal adult suffrage, limited self-government was to transform Guiana from a Crown colony. This constitution was suspended, 133 days after elections on grounds that the PPP was "planning to institute a one party Marxist State," and a "Soviet leaning communist republic which would become a center for organising communist activity throughout Central and South America"—see J. Seecoomar, *Conflicts in Guyana*, 86.

19. L. Lewis, "Forbes Burnham," 101. Lewis accurately does not credit any one of the two prominent leaders as the sole catalyst for the racial tensions; indeed he claims that both together were responsible for the ethnic divide.

20. V. P. Vatuk, *British Guiana* (New York: Monthly Review Press, 1963), 8, cited in Glasgow, *Guyana: Race and Politics,* 99–100.

21. Kean Gibson, *The Cycle of Racial Oppression in Guyana* (Lanham, New York: University Press of America, 2003), 29. It is to be noted that in the racially sensitive climate of Guyana, there has been numerous calls on Guyanese websites for the banning of Gibson's work due to its explicit anti-Indian stance. On the same page, Gibson asserts this point by stating: "It was the appeal to the caste of race (a group that would include Hindus, East Indian Muslims and Christians) by Jagan and his colleagues, referred to as 'Apan Jaat' that swept the Jagan faction to victory in 1957."

22. Arthur Schlesinger, *A Thousand Days: John F. Kennedy in the White House* (Cambridge: Riverside Press, 1965), 779, cited in L. Lewis, "Forbes Burnham," 101.

23. Hintzen, "Cheddi Jagan," in *Caribbean Charisma*, Allahar, 138.

24. The PPP secured 20 seats while the PNC won 11, and the party of the White upper class, the United Front (UF), had the 4 remaining spots.

25. Gibson, *Racial Oppression in Guyana*, 30.

26. Vishnu, "Ethnicity and Politics," 108.

27. Seecoomar, *Conflicts in Guyana*, 88.

28. David Hinds, "Guyana's Dominant Political Culture: An Overview," in *Modern Political Culture in the Caribbean*, ed. Holger Henke and Fred Reno (Kingston, Jamaica: University of West Indies Press, 2003), 356; Vishnu, "Ethnicity and Politics," 107–108. Unlike these two authors, J. Seecoomar unequivocally blames the CIA for the machina-

tions of the ethnic violence, *Conflicts in Guyana*, 89–90. For casualty figures of the post-election violence, see Gibson, *Racial Oppression in Guyana*, 33.

29. Dale Bisnauth, *The Settlement of Indians in Guyana 1890–1930* (Leeds, England: Peepal Tree Press, 2000); Gibson, *Racial Oppression in Guyana*; Glasgow, *Guyana*, Priya Vishnu, "Ethnicity and Politics," to cite a few.

30. Perry Mars, "Political Violence and Ethnic Polarization in Guyana, 1947–1960," in *Selected Issues in Guyanese Politics I* (Georgetown, Guyana: University of Georgetown Press, 1976), 91.

31. Joan R. Mars, *Deadly Force, Colonialism, and the Rule of Law: Police Violence in Guyana, Contributions in Comparative Colonial Studies* (Westport, CT: Greenwood Publishing Group, 2002), 28.

32. Dutch colonial rule in Guiana (as it was then called) began in 1613 and British colonial rule ended in 1966. Mars, *Deadly Force*, 28.

33. Seecoomar, *Resolution of Conflict in Guyana*.

34. See Cheddi Jagan, "The Role of the CIA in Guyana and its Activities Throughout the World," in <http://www.jagan.org/articles2m.htm#CIA%20Controls%20The %20Trade%20Unions> and Jagan, *The West on Trial: My Fight for Guyana's Freedom*, <http://www.jagan.org/biograph6.htm>.

35. It is intriguing to read that while the CIA reports that agents of President Burnham are now widely believed to be responsible for the assassination of racial unification activist and WPA founder Walter Rodney in 1980, there is understandably no mention of the CIA's documented role in that assassination.

36. Bert Wilkinson, "Guyana Opposition Returns to Parliament," *New York Amsterdam News* (8 May 2003), 14.

37. Emphasis mine. R. Narine, "Is History Repeating Itself?" *Stabroek News*, Thursday (18 March 2004) <www.stabroeknews.com/index.pl/article?id=4828127>.

38. There is as yet no book or scholarly article that examines the politics and personality of the charismatic leader of ROAR. This section has been constructed through the synthesis of political commentaries and news items from a variety of news media and Guyanese websites (including guyanacaribbeanpolitics.com, *Guyana Chronicle*, and most importantly *Stabroek News*.

39. Ravi Dev, "Rodney: On Organising" (24 May 2005), <www.guyanacaribbeanpolitics.com/commentary/dev.html>; for information on GIFT see Jyotirmoy Datta, "Guyana Activist Here in Push for Equal Rights of Indians," in *India in New York* 3, no. 26 (December 24, 1999): 6.

40. *The Voice, London*, "Guyanese Indians Fight for Rights," Issue 818 (10 August 1998), 12.

41. The BJP's international wing, the Vishwa Hindu Parishad (VHP or the World Hindu Council), has a mission aimed towards consolidating the Indian diaspora with its global mission of unifying them even while soliciting the financial support from expatriate Hindu Indians.

42. *India Abroad*, "GOPIO Conference Focuses on Diaspora's Human Rights" (9 April 2004) 34, no. 28, C4.

43. Datta, "Guyana Activist Here," 6.

44. Wilkinson, "Guyana's Controversial Government Recognized," *Philadelphia Tribune* 114, no. 13, 7–A. It was not until the private sector and the CARICOM decided to hold a fact-finding international election audit, that President Clinton recognized the Jagan government.

45 The controversy stemmed from the PNC's Desmond Hoyte and other opposition parties' refusal to accept the election results on charges of widespread voter fraud and rigging that involved the Elections Commissioner and the Judiciary Chancellor. The two officials were accused by the opposition parties of guaranteeing "that the 77-year old [Janet] Jagan succeeds her late husband," through a secretly contrived swearing in ceremony just prior to a PNC-led court that may have prohibited her from her Presidential duties unless all legal challenges to electoral conduct had been heard. See Wilkinson, "Guyana's Controversial Government Recognized." Wilkinson notes in the same article that Janet Jagan, soon after being sworn in, was served with the court papers challenging the PNC's alleged fraud in the elections, and in light of her victory she "promptly tossed them away."

46. Datta, "Guyana Activist Here," 6.

47. Paul Gilroy uses the term "ethnic insiderism" in the context of black nationalism among the African diaspora in the Caribbean, Paul Gilroy, *The Black Atlantic* (Cambridge: Harvard University Press, 1993), 119, cited in Simboonath Singh, "Imagined Communities: Articulating a Return to Mythical Homelands in the African and Indian Diaspora," in *Modern Political Culture in the Caribbean*, ed. Henke and Reno, 218.

48. Datta, "Guyana Activist Here," 6.

49. For an excellent analyses of Guyana's military defense system, read I. W. Griffith, "The Military and Politics of Change in Guyana," *Journal of Interamerican Studies and World Affairs* 33, no. 2 (Summer 1991): 146.

50. Ravi Dev, "ROAR Advocates Integrative Federalism not Balkanisation," *Stabroek News*, Letter to the editor, 11 May 2005; R. Dev, "Revisiting First Principles," *Guyana Caribbean Politics Homepage* (Commentary), 20 May 2005, <www.guyanacaribbeanpolitics.com/commentary/dev.html>.

51. Ravi Dev, "Guyanese" *Guyana Caribbean Politics,* Commentary, (15 December 2004) <www.guyanacaribbeanpolitics.com/commentary/dev.html>.

52. Miranda La Rose, "Centre Force Can Lead to one Voice on National Programmes in *Stabroek News*, Ravi Dev (24 February 2005), <http://www.stabroeknews.com/index.pl/article?id=12052252>.

53. Ravi Dev, "The Rule of Law is the Line between Civilisation and the Jungle," *Stabroek News*, Op-Ed Section (17 March 2004) <http://www.stabroeknews.com/index.pl/article?id=4770663>. Even in addressing the People's Movement for Democracy in May 2004 Dev did not shy away from the word "race" however, later in the year the word almost disappears from his lexicon and is replaced by the word "ethnic"—See "Speech (PMJ) Rally 1763 Monument. May 22nd, 2004," <www.guyanacaribbeanpolitics.com/commentary/dev.html> (9 June 2004).

54. Ravi Dev, "Budget 2005: Stagnation," Commentary, 7 March 2005, <www.guyanacaribbeanpolitics.com/commentary/dev.html>.

55. M.L. Rose, "Centre Force -Ravi Dev," <www.stabroeknews.com/index.pl/article?id=12052252>.

56. Ravi Dev, "Centre Force," 10 January 2005, <www.guyanacaribbeanpolitics.com/commentary/dev.html>; and Ravi Dev, "ROAR is prepared to work in a New Centre Force," *Stabroek News*, Letter to the Editor (13 January 2005).

57. This section (on Amerindians) is borrowed heavily from B. Bullock's research (which serves as the primary source) from a co-authored work by B. Bullock and S. Manian, "Ecotourism and Ethnopolitics in Guyana" (paper presented at the Caribbean Studies meeting in Belize, 2003).

58. Ralph G. Premdas, "Guyana: Socialist Reconstruction or Political Opportunism?" *Journal of Interamerican Studies & World Affairs* 20, no. 2 (May 1978): 134.

59. Edwards, W. and K. Gibson, "An Ethnohistory of Amerindians in Guyana," *Ethnohistory* 26, no. 2 (Spring, 1979): 162; and *U.S. Library of Congress Country Studies: Guyana* <http://countrystudies.us/guyana/>.

60. *Encyclopedia of World Cultures* (Farmington Hills, Mich.: Thomson Gale/McMillan Reference USA, 2001) 7.

61. *GINA*, 23 May 2003.

62. National Development Strategy (NDS) <www.guyana.org>.

63. George Mentore contends that such rivalries both define and interpret tribal identity, as when the Wai-Wai still speak of the need to protect their community from Taruma rivals who they perceive are merely hiding, even though the latter group has been officially extinct for many years! George Mentore, "Anger in the Forest, Death by Documentation: Cultural Imaginings of the Taruma," *JASO* 30, no. 3 (1999): 261-287.

64. G. Mentore, *The Relevance of Myth* (Georgetown, Guyana: Department of Culture, 1988).

65. Janette Forte, *The Material Culture of the Wapishana People of the South Rupununi Savannahs in 1989* (Amerindian Research Unit, University of Guyana, 1992, 54).

66. *The Report on Amerindian Policies Within the NDS*, "Amerindian Policies," Chapter 22 <www.guyana.org/NDS/chapt22.htm>.

67. Forte et al, in their study of the Wapishana in Region 9 stress that the lack of transportation, radio communications, and reliable statistics was a "microcosm of a national situation. The information office at Letham did not seem to keep records...." *The Report on Amerindian Policies Within the NDS*, "Amerindian Policies," Chapter 22: 20 <www.guyana.org/NDS/chapt22.htm>.

68. *GINA*, 23 May 2003.

69. *Stabroek News*, "The Guyana Action Party (GAP) and Rise, Organise and Rebuild," in Editorial, 25 June 2001 <www.jaiag.com.roar/roar4.html>.

70. Working People's Alliance (History hyperlink) <www.guyanacaribbeanpolitics.com/wpa/wpa.html>.

71. *The New York Times*, "Leftist opponent of premier killed in Guyanese bombing: Walter Rodney," 15 June 1980: 6; and Helen William, "Murder? That's a laugh: Man accused of Rodney Bomb Blast Can't Believe It," in *The Voice, London* (25 June 1996) no. 708: 14.

72. WPA, "Overseas Embassies and High Commission," <http://saxakali.com/wpa/previous.htm>.

73. "Analysis of the WPA's Previous Participation in Elections," July 1997 <http://saxakali.com/wpa/previous.htm>.

74. Emphasis added. SDNP Guyana <www.sdnp.gy.org>.

75. <www.guyanacaribbeanpolitics.com>

76. Jean LaRose, "In Guyana, Indigenous People Fight to Join Conservation Efforts," *Cultural Survival Quarterly* 28, no. 1 (March 2004), <http://209.200.101.189/publications/csq/csq-article.cfm?id=1741>.

77. JAIAG Homepage Commentary <www.jaiag.com> (25 January 2001).

78. UNCTAD, *Statistical Yearbook 2002*. Even though there was a 6.1% increase in GDP in 1991—the first gain since 1984—these economic problems certainly had something to do with the margin of PNC defeat in 1992. See Arthur Banks, William

Overstreet, and Thomas Muller, *Political Handbook of the World 1999* (Washington D.C.: Congressional Quarterly Press, 1999).

79. Banks, *Political Handbook of the World 1999*, 408.

80. UNCTAD, *Statistical Yearbook, 2002*, Table 6.2.

81. Hope, *Guyana: Politics and Development*, 43.

82. At the Georgetown Rotary Club's Annual World Understanding Day Dinner on March 10, 2003, Rupert Roopnaraine's quote from, "Roopnaraine Proposes Shared Governance at NDC Level," *Commentary*, <www.guyanacaribbeanpolitics.com/commentary/roopnaraine.html>.

83. To put an exclamation point on his idea, Roopnaraine referred to the prophetic words of national poet Martin Carter following the 1962 racial upheavals: "None of the groups in Guyanese society is prepared to have another group ruling it. Not until each group is confident that no other group will rule will there be real peace in this country." Ibid.

84. Steve Fenton, "Beyond Ethnicity: The Global Comparative Analysis of Ethnic Conflict," in *International Journal of Comparative Sociology* 45, no. 3 (July–September 2004): 180.

85. *Stabroek News Editorial*, "Amerindians in Colonial History" (2 September 2001).

86. Mimi Sheller, "Citizenship and the making of Caribbean Freedom," *Report on Race Part 2, NACLA Report on the Americas* 38(4), 33. She notes how such racial and ethnic tension divides the various groups to an extent whereby their solidarity in the form of labor unions remains unrealized in the economic sector.

87. Fenton, "Beyond Ethnicity," 185, 186.

88. Fenton, "Beyond Ethnicity," 190.

89. *APA Newsletter*, "UN Human Rights Committee Criticises Guyana about Amerindian Human Rights" <www.sdnp.org.gy/apa/un_criticises_guyana.htm> (April 2000).

90. *Stabroek News*, "More Intermarriage Would East Ethnic Tensions," <www.Stabroeknews.com/inex.pl/article?id=17292202> (20 April 2005).

Chapter 8

Sudan's Identity Wars and Democratic Route to Peace

Rita Kiki Edozie

This chapter addresses important dimensions of Sudanese politics on the interrelated topics of conflict, multi-nationality, globalization and democratization, presenting a dual research objective that confronts the dilemma of dealing with emerging perspectives on ethnicity and nationalism on the one hand, and of themes around global democratic development on the other. This analysis of ethnic conflict in the Sudan examines the factors that have contributed to the emergence and persistence of the country's forty-nine year civil war and its expansion to Darfur in 2004. Recognizing the modern Sudanese state as a democratic state, which cannot be founded on religious, racial or even cultural homogeneity, by way of formal, non-formal and militant democratic struggle, the chapter illustrates ways in which diverse Sudanese constituencies have used ethnic and identity politics to posit democratic solutions to achieve peace. I would recommend a constructivist usage of "ethnic politics" and "democracy" as a public policy solution to the "Sudan crisis." Such a model seeks to utilize mechanisms of ethical discourse and expression to extend cultural pluralism into an active and constructive process of identity formation and reconciliation as the means to achieve what SPLM, southern resistance fighter and the late Sudanese

Vice-President John Garang's original goal of the 'New Sudan' was to be: a Sudan that is united, multi-national, multi-racial, and democratic.

The Machakos' Protocols (Sudan Peace Agreement) and the Darfur Spoiler

"Ethnicity," the concept Horowitz has dubbed 'Africa's boogey man' continues to appear as the dominant causation variable that explains a range of political patterns and processes across the Continent.[1] In the Sudan, for example, as late as December 2003, the international media reported the signing of an historic peace agreement whose objective sought to end Africa's longest civil war between the Sudan's acclaimed northern "Arab Islamic" regime and the country's southern "African Christian" "rebel" movement. Less than six months later, however, on the heels of this internationally supervised and celebrated signing of the Machakos Peace Agreement in April 2004, the media reported a second impending 'genocide' in Africa, approximating the magnitude of Rwanda— this time in the Darfur region of the Sudan. Thus, since the post-Cold War period, becoming the second African country to have been sanctioned by the international community for inflicting 'genocide' on its peoples and having prosecuted the longest civil war in the Continent's history, the mere symbol of the Sudan suggests that primordial sentiments appear to underscore much of this country's contemporary politics.

Much recent discussion of international affairs has been based on the misleading assumption that the world is fraught with primordial ethnic conflict.[2] But primordial, instrumentalist and constructivist theories of 'ethnicity' have more recently combined to construct new theoretical frameworks for examining ethnic conflict in Africa. In the contemporary global environment, more than referring to elements of language, religion, common origin, and codes of kinship ethnicity is in actuality manifested as a, 'cultural politics of representation.'[3] In this vein, ethnicity involves social processes of cultural 'identification' and 'formation' by groups in civil society and by disciplinary agencies such as the state and its institutions.[4] Thus, while acknowledging the validity of primal and political convictions regarding cultural difference, a constructivist 'moral life-world' paradigm addresses the reality of engaging the ethnic question in Africa by linking ethnic claims to critical dimensions of democratic politics. This is achieved by locating ethnicity in the context of a dynamic and syncretic understanding of nationhood and democratization. .

By employing this constructivist usage of 'ethnicity' that recognizes in a democratic state the importance of an individual's membership in a vital and respected cultural group with its own norms, values and traditions. This usage further uses liberal democratic mechanisms of ethical discourse and expression to extend 'ethnic politics' into an active and constructive process that serves to foster mutual learning among diverse groups and forge societal priorities and national democratic goals. With respect to conflict, the aforementioned analysis equates 'war and peace' with 'democratic struggle and consensus.' Conflict is democratic struggle for equitable inclusion; peace is the consideration of a democratic political system valued for its constructivist role in which diverse social constituencies and identities work out their differences.

Consistent with this way of examining democracy, the Sudan People's Liberation Movement (SPLM) has often declared as its reason for engaging in war as a struggle by regional political groupings for the attainment of rights for Sudan's backward areas, a political and military struggle defined by the masses of Sudanese for democracy, human dignity, progress, equal opportunity and justice.[5] Notably, SPLM leader John Garang's original concept of a 'New Sudan' envisioned a country that was to be secular, democratic and united in diversity.[6] In Darfur also, lack of political power and an unfair share of national resources for this region is the main reason that the Darfur Sudanese Liberation Movement (SLA) and the Justice and Equality Movement (JEM) have taken up arms to struggle for democracy.[7] Since the establishment of the liberal democratic state at independence, 'struggles' for identity, equal citizenship, and democracy that have been guided by the anticipation of a democratic political order have been the norm in the Sudan. Sudanese constituencies have since independence been engaged in a struggle to win, defend and protect rights of cultures for self-organization and participation in the state process.

Sudan's deeply divided country has persisted with 'a surprising instinct for democratic forms.'[8] Recognizing the modern Sudanese state as a democratic state, which cannot be founded on religious, racial or even cultural homogeneity, by way of formal, non-formal and militant democratic struggle, diverse and deeply divided Sudanese constituencies have posited as their platforms several democratic solutions to achieve peace. This is as true for constituencies pursuing democracy through formal means illustrated by the cyclical civil-military relations in the North as well as those pursuing democratic struggles through informal means mostly southerners and resistance movements in Darfur, Beja and the north (National Democratic Alliance). The democratic struggles and processes of the SPLM, the NIF, the Republican Brothers, Anya Nya, the NDA, the Justice and Equality Movement of Darfur (JEM), and the Sudanese Liberation Army (SLA) will all be examined in a framework of democratic theory.

While this struggle is significantly a domestic struggle, the internationalization of the Sudan's various conflicts cannot be minimized in an era of globalization. The post-Cold War transformations in global security relations have produced a new kind of internationalization of civil wars in which the framework for international intervention has changed. For example, the rhetoric of 'global democratization' has been incorporated into the sphere of global and US' foreign defense policy. New theories on 'collective global security' argue that by stabilizing less developed states through the transfer of democratic practices and

capacity building expertise, advanced democracies have less to fear from volatile Third World states. [9]

In societies like the Sudan, coming out of conflict, international conflict
resolution models of this sort have designed a post-conflict democratic transition
mechanism for reconstructing "collapsed states."[10] A product of new global
governance initiatives, this framework is symbolically illustrated by US-UN
efforts to rebuild Afghanistan and Iraq as democracies, an international political
process of remodeling 'failed' states around core features that include the holding of immediate elections, the formal recognition of liberal cultural pluralism
such as gender empowerment, secularism and multi-ethnicity through power-
sharing; and the dependence on international tutelage from international NGOs
working in specialized areas ranging from humanitarian aid to election monitoring.[11] The 2005 Sudan Peace Agreement adopted the democratic reconstruction
model as a key element of achieving a comprehensive Sudan peace. In this respect, in a post 9-11 environment, which placed the Sudan on the US State Department's terrorist list, the Bush Administration's War on Terror foreign policy
enlisted former US Senator John Danforth to end the country's civil war and
begin a process of reconstructing the Sudanese state.[12]

My goal is to both explore the deeper structural dynamics and features of
what has so commonly come to be known as "Sudan's War of Visions"[13] by
examining the factors that have contributed to the emergence and persistence of
the country's forty-nine year civil war and its expansion to Darfur in 2004, as
well as to reveal the underlying principles of the 1990s international conflict
resolution mechanisms. Embodied in the Machakos Protocols/Sudan Peace
Agreement and its prospect as a model to resolve the Darfur war are four general
democratic platforms for the achievement of peace proposed by the constituencies aforementioned: (a) the one-state liberal democratic state solution, including
the socialist genre and al-Turabi's Islamic democracy model; (b) the consociational power sharing democratic solution (1973 Addis Ababa and 2005
Machakos Agreements; and more recently proposed federalist proposals); (c) the
two-state solution implied in the self-determination referendum clause in the
2003 Agreement; and (d) the radical pluralist democratic solution. While the
Sudan has previously tried solutions (a) and (b) and the current peace process
(2005) recommends option (c), after six years of negotiations, my conclusion
will explore option (d), the radical pluralist democratic option as a yet truly un-
tested but important peace and democratic prospect for the foundations of long
term peace, self-determination and democracy in the Sudan.

Theories of Cultural Difference and the Vision of a
Postmodern Pluralist Democracy

In a post-Cold War environment, nation-states that are largely on the defensive against globalizing threats to their social, economic, geographical, and local

political boundaries, together with the rising cognizance of local cultural particularities, provide a newly animated politics of 'identity' expressed in ethno-nationalisms. To the surprise of modernization scholars, who had wishfully theorized that adherence to "ethnicity" would wither away with the attainment of economic resources, education, and national integration by the millennium, social practice in developing and transitional societies continued to be pursued as if ethnicity held the key to the structures of inequality. Both the protectionism of the dominant and the responses of the dominated alike served to reproduce an ethnically ordered world.[14]

Indeed, since the 1990s, the vision of civic nationalism or nation-statism began to give way to alternative identities usually ethnic in nature.[15] Especially in Africa, however, identity politics has always been characterized in "the national question dilemma," a political phenomenon engendered by the continent's legacy of late colonialism. The underlying factor driving African conflicts into the 1990s emerged as a result of this core feature of the continent's politics that veteran scholar Ali Mazrui has traced to the Continent's "inverted pyramid" a continent with two permanent racio-cultural complexes, three religious systems, four dominant languages, five external hegemonic systems competing for influence of profit in an Africa comprising over 50 countries with some 850 ethnic and linguistic groups.[16] In this respect, Africa's "national question" can be described as a problem that arises as a result of the continuous process of vertical and horizontal integration and development of the various nationalities, which made up the new African nation-state at independence.[17] In many African countries "the national question" has become a code name for all the controversies, doubts and experimentation that surround the countries' search for stability, legitimacy and development. The concept is concerned with the fundamental basis of African countries' political existence, power sharing and management of resources in terms of access, control and distribution. In more recent global arenas the "national question" in Africa is conveyed through the mobilization of collective rights among diverse peoples as well as calls for greater redistribution, greater equality, and poverty alleviation.[18]

The persistence of "ethnic" politics in Africa and the phenomena's global proliferation has fostered constructivist analyses of ethnicity that no longer dismiss psychological and cultural dimensions of ethnic politics by reducing them to traditional life-worlds that will transcend with modernization.[19] Previous analyses of ethnicity of this kind notably primordialism and instrumentalism, viewed ethnicity as regrettable false consciousness, to be trivialized, dismissed, disparaged and disappeared. Alternatively, constructivist scholars of ethnicity engage ethically and practically with the diverse political claims made in ethnicity's name. In this respect, ethnicity is examined as an array of political idioms referring to dimensions of "history", "tradition", "descent" and "virtue."[20] Constructivist scholars thereby privilege 'subjective' factors of ethnicity that examine the process of ethnic identification in social practice as a meaningful place of belonging for its participants.[21] To do so, constructivists have re-invoked primordial aspects of ethnicity in order to explore the psychological and cultural dimensions necessary to grasp the intensities that surround ethnic conflict. The constructivists have been successful in capturing ethnicity's capacity to arouse deep fears, anxieties and insecurities, and its ability to trigger collective aggression inexplicable in terms of simple instrumentalist versions that privilege an ethnic group's material pursuit of interest.

The constructivist model brings this subjective and cultural dimension back into the forefront of analysis, understanding the powerful emotional charge, the sense of emotional security, belongingness and self-esteem that embodies group identity. This account of ethnicity underscores the context of the historical genesis and social practice by which various state structures and particular social groups have invested cultural and political identities with nationally symbolic meaning. However, on its own terms, the existence of ethnicity is not the determining factor for conflict in much of Africa and the developing world. Rather, what causes political tensions and conflict is the fact that ethnicity exists in plural contexts especially where different cultural/ethnic groups are compelled to develop modern nation-states in the context of multi-nationalism as opposed to the homogeneous civic nationalist trajectory experienced in Western modern development.

When race, religion and language inform the basis of cultural difference in state formation and re-configuration (third world democratization), there tends to be a resistance of the homogenizing class-based rights discourse of classic liberalism. Instead in such state-society contexts cultural rights discourse is mobilized and informs the basis of political agitation and is expressed as the rights of competitive sub-nations, nationalities, national groups and ethnic minorities rather than the liberalized issue-orientated bases of citizenship politics that emerged to forge western liberal democracies. However, culturally plural societies may exist in political cooperation and consensus or in competition and conflict. The majority of developing world and African pluralistic states has existed in the latter; though, an important goal for political development in post-colonial developing states has been the capacity to accommodate multi-nationality or cultural pluralism via modern institutional forms. India is one developing world model that has been able to accommodate complex cultural pluralism by way of democratic means.[22] Nigeria has also developed institutionalized channeling and resolution of ethnic demands in its post-colonial development, a situation that has caused the attenuation, though certainly not the elimination of ethnic conflict and violence more successfully than the Sudan.

Significantly, constructivist "identity politics" engages the "multi-national" question by linking ethnic claims to the aforementioned critical dimensions of democratic politics. Moral ethnicity constructivist theorists, for example, examine ethnicity from the perspective of a moral debate about a culturally contested political community, about cultural rights and obligations and about ethnic citizenship.[23] In this respect, moral ethnicity constructivists analyze multi-ethnic claims by way of a post-structuralist discourse that examines conditions for imagining alternative political spaces. For example, in the early 1990s, South Africa faced the democratic peace challenge in the context of deep pluralism and identity politics. Proposing a constructivist democratic option for the deeply divided country instead of classic liberal and consociational conflict resolution mechanisms ethnicity scholar Arletta Norval warned of the need to distinguish between democratic solutions to national conflict that arose from validating the legitimacy of cultural difference and those resting on coercive unity.[24] Norval proposed the former alternative notion of democracy and cultural difference as a radical pluralist democratic option whose objective sought to move beyond the mere reification and acknowledgement of multi-nationality as existing models do. Norval's constructivist model of democracy and ethnic conflict resolution alternatively seeks to address contradictions that emerge from the social differentiation of the human community including cultural identity differences.[25] In so doing, a democratic politics that recognizes cultural difference avoids the problem of coercive unity insofar as identity claims are inserted into a democratic context in which cultural difference is open to continuous challenge, negotiation and renewal.

Understood this way, democratic politics increases the likelihood that the affirmation of differences in cultural identity will find expression in public life fostering a deepening of democratic spaces though avoiding the assimilation tendencies of modern liberalism as well as consociational mechanisms that tend to reify cultural identities and force them to become exclusionary and self-enclosed. Radical democratic politics uses liberal democratic mechanisms of ethical discourse and expression to extend pluralism and to turn its appreciation of established diversity into an active and constructive process that serves to foster mutual learning among diverse groups and help in forging societal priorities and national democratic goals.[26]

The challenge of reconciling deep cultural divisions and identity claims, as well as accommodating decades of democratic struggle in a united democratic Sudan may do well to heed Norval's prescription for dealing with the 'national question' in South Africa. Such a conflict resolution model in the context of the country's deeply divided ethno-religious terrain may suggest the need for much more profound democratic principles and initiatives than the liberal democratic conflict resolution framework endorsed by the North-South 2005 Sudan Peace Agreement and the Government of Sudan/Darfur: SLA-JEM[27] ceasefire agreements have put forth.

Deng's Clash of Visions and Salih's Authoritarian Circus: Identity Wars

Southern Sudanese scholar Francis Deng appropriately characterized the conflict in the Sudan as a "war of visions" seen as a situation in which identity wars between the Sudanese North incarnated in the Sudanese state as an

Arabized, Islamic north, is resisted by a non-Arabized, non-Muslim southern region resisting "northern" assimilation and decrying discrimination, subordination and marginalization of their own identity. And in the western region of Darfur, the identity conflict has less to do with cultural and language differences, but rather with regional exclusion and disparities based on lineage and heritage. These identity wars in the Sudan have as their principal cause the fundamentally opposing views of what it means to be a Sudanese otherwise defined by a crisis of the national question.[28] However, a failure of politics also explains the Sudan's identity wars. Northern Sudanese scholar Muahmmed Salih has described Sudanese politics since independence as an "authoritarian circus,"[29] where successive authoritarian state regimes—military and civilian alike—have associated the politics of history and exclusivist cultural identity with state power. Not only has the Sudanese state maintained a high level of militarism, illustrated by the reality of having waged a war against a segment of its citizens for almost fifty years of its existence,[30] the state became increasingly culturally authoritarian by constructing national identity upon hegemonic terms to the exclusion of the vast majority of its citizens. This has been responsible for the prolonged and expansive political violence that erupted in the Sudan on the heels of independence. The starting point for understanding the constitution of Sudan's cultural pluralism is the regional dimension not the racial or the religious per se.[31] The complexity of the challenges represented by the country's racial, ethnic, cultural and religious composition is best understood by the Sudan's unique location as a microcosm of Africa and a crossroads between the Continent and the Middle East. Understood in the context of a Sahelian North-South dichotomy prominent in other countries in the horn and northern West African region, including Chad, Mauritania, Ethiopia, and Mali, as the region known as the 'Land of the Blacks' (Bilad al Sudan), the territory documents a long history of attempts of conquest and assimilation of indigenous African cultures by Arab traders. Especially with the advent of Islam in the seventh century, the Arabs and Turks from Egypt invaded the region known as the Sudan and in the seventh and ninth centuries concluded peace accords with the Nubians and the peoples of Beja. Natural barriers, difficult living conditions, and resistance by the Nilotic peoples discouraged Arab migration and settlement in the deeper south. In 1820, the northern regions of the Sudan were used as a base for slave raid incursions into the South. This fostered a united resistance effort from the northern (especially the Dar Fur) and southern groups under the leadership of Ahmed al-Mahdi from 1881-1885. However, less than fifteen years later in 1899, the Sudan was to be reconquered by the British thereby beginning a period of colonization in the guise of the Anglo-Egyptian condominium (1899–1955). The Sudan subsequently gained independence as a modern nation state in 1956, at which time Africa's largest country in terms of territory constituted one of the continent's most diverse peoples.

The North is two-thirds of the country and constitutes six provinces consisting of indigenous African ethnic groups variably intermarried with Arab traders to produce a genetically mixed African-Arab racially cultural hybrid who Mansour Khalidi has referred to as the "Arabized African" not the "Arab".[32] A 1955–56 national census documented 39% of people of the Sudan as identifying as Arab by language, claimed genealogy and assumed racial identity[33] despite the fact that many of these people are indeed Arabized Nubiyin who over the last four centuries have adopted Arabic language, culture and Islam.[34] Also in the northern region (including the peoples of southern Korfordan and Darfur) are the indigenous ethnic groups that while have not been genetically mixed by Arab peoples, have been assimilated by their conversion to Islam (no different from much of West Africa) and the adoption of the Arab language. Many of these groups, the Baggara, for example, have intermarried with the Nilotic groups in the South and retain African racial and cultural characteristics.

One-third of the Sudan, three provinces and thirty percent of the population, constitutes the South consisting of several indigenous Nilotic ethnic groups including the most dominant the Dinka, the Nuer, the Shilluk and the Azande. Due to centuries of Southern resistance to northern incursions, groups in the South tend to loosely unite under an ethno-racial element known as "Africanism,"— though perhaps misleadingly constructed as "blackness"—due to a geographical affiliation with the cultural and linguistic groups in Eastern Africa. However, such "racial" constructs appear problematic when considering the northern peoples of the Southern Funj, the Blue Nile province, many of the inhabitants of Darfur, and the Nuba Mountains of Kordofan. All of these peoples neither professed Islam nor spoke Arabic until the Turko—Egyptian conquest of 1820.[35] Moreover, these ethnic regions tend to currently maintain their indigenous cultures, which are closely related to Dinka and other Nilotics.[36]

As a result of the Sudan's complex plural historical constitution, like most of Africa's ethnically heterogeneous nation—states, the Sudanese national identity entered a crisis of legitimacy as soon as the country was constituted at independence. Identity conflict and war became symbols of Sudanese political instability for most of the new democratic constituencies, as the nation that emerged at independence seemed an alien entity just as it had been perceived of during the colonial era. However, the source of the escalation of political violence in the country to date laid not so much in the existence of differences per se, but in the degree to which differences in the Sudan have failed to be mutually accommodating and compatible. This speaks to the failure of politics in the Sudan. The country's inability to reconcile ethnic and religious diversity is cognizant in the country's failure with liberal democratic politics despite its early establishment in 1956. The failure of the northern Sudan nationalist politicians to share power with other groups reinforced feelings of alienation and a belief that the North was a colonial successor to Britain. The peoples of the southern Sudan and most of those in western and eastern Sudan had little access to the benefits, which the state bestowed.[37] The attempt to coerce the South into the northern fold through forced integration Arabization and Islamization sowed the seeds for full-scale civil war by 1958.[38]

Dominated by the northern elite and heavily inclined toward just three core northern Arabic speaking groups, the Sudanese state has failed to share political power with political elites from the South and to distribute equitable resources to the rest of the country especially in Darfur, the country's poorest region. In fact, the Sudanese political elite have too many times missed crucial opportunities to establish democratic regimes that are people-dominated and inclusive of the rights and self-determination of all Sudanese people. This failure has resulted in the current social bases of the government's socio-political relations to consist of these northern Islamic Arabic-speaking elite whose ideological manifestation had crystallized by the 1990s in the select, orthodox and fundamentalist principles of the Muslim Brotherhood's National Islamic Front and People's National Congress regime currently led by President Omar Bashir. Significantly, the incarnation of the Sudanese state in these social bases negatively earned the country the status of a pariah terrorist state in the international global community by the 1990s,[39] a course of events that has had important implications for the current status of war and peace in the country.

The authoritarianism and racialist exclusivity of the contemporary Sudanese state traces its roots back to the British colonial state. While the first to give meaning to a united Sudan as a formal administrative unit, the British colonial regime administered ambivalent and contradictory policies that fostered and reified cultural cleavages especially between North and South. When the British came to the Sudan, they reproduced radicalized identities and ideology of the nineteenth century: that the South was inferior to the North; and that Muslim people were civilized, while non-Muslim were not.[40] Consequently, the Sudan was divided into two regions; 'Arab' North and 'African' South.

Consistent with the colonial state's radicalization of the modern bureaucratic state, the British developed a southern policy whose primary aim was to prevent economic integration of the regions in order to curtail the north's Arabic and Islamic influence in the south.[41] Southerners especially complain that because the British saw a distinct south as a buffer that could develop and preserve English values and beliefs through the introduction of Christianity, the British policy to keep the South "traditional" inhibited their social development especially vis-à-vis Northerners whose educational achievement and income levels had by pre-independence affected their ability to control the nationalist movement. Especially egregious is the lack of appropriate structural integration provided for the Southern region into the Sudanese polity during pre-independence preparations and the British's political pandering to Northern and Egyptian interests, which prejudiced the South during the de-colonization process and the transfer of power at independence.

Sudan's post-colonial state continued the British colonial state policies in the sense that at independence, for example, the northern elite-dominated liberal democratic regime led by Prime Minister Ismail al-Azhari merely replaced British officials with northern Sudanese nationals. For instance, in response to Southern dissatisfaction with the region's exclusion from independence national politics, riots and a bloody resistance broke out in the South (Torit mutiny). Backed by the departing British regime, the new "internally-self-governing" embryonic Sudanese state chose to crush southern resistance with a brutal militaristic act, thereby sowing the seeds of future political violence in the country.[42] Also, in building democratic institutions, the new northern nationalists immediately began a politics of exclusion. Out of forty-six members of the 1956 legislative assembly convened to draft the country's first constitution, the only three southerners were hopelessly defeated in their proposal for a federal constitution that would foster southern democratic ideals.

Formal authoritarian rule set in just two years after Sudanese independence when in November 1958 Sudan's liberal democratic state was deposed in the country's first military coup led by General Aboud; Aboud's first acts were to suppress political opposition and civil society within the core North. The political militarism of the Aboud regime extended to the South with an acceleration of forced southern integration through Islamization and a viscous military campaign against the southern resistance movement Anya Nya initiating the first southern refugee crisis into the Congo and Uganda. In 1969, demonstrating the growing political instability within the Sudanese state, another historical coup was conducted by General Jaafar al-Nimeiri, an event, which launched the Sudan as a Cold War state battleground.[43] However, despite al-Nimeiri's "communist" rhetoric, his regime actively courted the Soviet Union and relied on Moscow for financing aid armaments to wage the war in the South.

Whereas the al-Nimeiri regime presided over the 1973 Addis Ababa Agreement, which temporarily ended the war with the South by moving to grant the South regional autonomy and power sharing in the army; however, dominant northern interests bent on forced southern integration through hegemonic centralization policies forced the regime to renege on the ten year peace agreement. This happened when in 1977 a coalition of northern opposition parties demanded that the socialist Head of State review the Addis Ababa Agreement on provisions of security, border trade, language, culture and religion.[44] Following this political pressure, on June 5, 1983, the regime unilaterally without consultation with the southern region abrogated the Addis Agreement and restored southern regional powers to the central government, and in the same year decreed that Sharia laws were to be the sole guiding force behind the law of the Sudan. Indeed, in the 1980s, illustrating the degenerated Sudanese state-society relations and the regime's destructive ideological new allegiance to orthodox Islamic hegemony, the Nimeiri regime convicted and publicly executed liberal Islamist Mahmoud Taha on charges of religious heresy, for opposing the application of Islamic law and for re-establishing a banned political party.

In 1989, the Sudanese state underwent a third symbolic advancement toward authoritarianism when a coup organized by the most extreme elements of the country's Islamic sectarian politicians, the Muslim Brotherhood/NIF, and the military led by General Omar Hassan al-Bashir ousted a pro-democratic interim government that would have initiated a Third Wave democratic transition for the country. Through the coup, the Bashir regime acted quickly to consolidate power and destroy the political opposition by imposing a state of emergency, revoking the transitional constitution (TMC), abolishing parliament, banning political parties and leaders, closing newspapers, and reinforcing Sharia law. Significantly, underscoring the regime's extremism, acting as premier and defense minister, Bashir addressed the war in the south by providing new resources for the military and declaring northern soldiers as martyrs for the imposition of God's law.[45]

Supported by the Islamists, the Sudanese military state "reconfigured"[46] its authoritarianism into an "electoral democracy" in a 1996 election, an event that formally consolidated the regime's autocracy conveyed in the new ruling party, the People's National Congress. Due to the prominent platform given to the transformed National Islamic Front, especially with the leadership of Islamic cleric and intellectual Dr. Hassan al-Turabi, as attorney general and senate leader, "political Islam" established Khartoum as a base for Islamic internationalism, and the Sudanese state achieved its most symbolic label as a pariah terror state. Having invited Osama bin Laden to reside in the Sudan for five years where the infamous terrorist leader established a solid operating base for al-Queda[47], the Sudan had become internationally isolated for harboring terrorists, thereby causing the imposition of UN sanctions in 1996. Moreover, in the millennium, after 9/11, emboldened by the Bush Administration's support for the Sudanese government as an ally in the fight against terrorism, the Bashir regime sought to forcibly crack down on Darfur resistance guerillas who had initiated fighting for economic equality and political and democratic inclusion.[48] Arming former enemies, nomad Arabs, Khartoum collaborated with *Janjaweed* militias in bombing Darfur villages and proceeded to arrest and detain Darfur political activists for attempting to dispatch food to the region.[49]

Sudan's Democratic Prospects and Failures: Liberal, Social and Islamic

It is no wonder then that in view of the country's cultural wars and failed authoritarian (rather than democratic) attempts to address ethnic diversity that the Sudan's progress with democracy in 2004 is a disappointing failure despite the country's extensive periods of democratic regimes of the culturalist, socialist, consociationalist, and liberal orientations, and despite the long-standing and deep-seated democratic struggles for inclusion by marginalized groups. Freedom House classifies the Sudan as one of the few remaining authoritarian "not free" states in Africa,[50] a situation that has precipitated the imposition of an externally imposed democratic solution for the "Sudanese Wars."

Like most developing world and African states, modern democracy in the Sudan was forged as a result of a transfer of power from British colonialism to independence during the de-colonization era.[51] Given the adoption of liberal democratic institutions of constitutionalism, elections and multi-partyism, the new liberal democracy required that the Sudanese state recognize "citizenship", meaning a certain reciprocity consisting of rights against and duties toward the political community. Yet, like much of Africa during the period of post-independence, liberal democracy's "majoritarian" and "individualized citizenship" principles created many challenges for the deeply-divided and unevenly developed societies. Africa's liberal democracies tended to be "nationalist" democracies constituted by a small crop of urban elite who themselves struggled with many socio-economic circumstances associated with rapid modernization, as well as with the challenges of "nation-building." Few post-independence liberal democratic regimes successfully overcame the liberal democracy dilemma; the Sudanese regime failed woefully. The sectarian basis (Ansar and Ashigga Islamic sects/Umma and NUP-DUP parties) of party politics, northern dominance of party politics, and the absence of any sense of direction for the country's "national identity" crisis resulted in the Sudan's failure to establish liberal democratic rule, a condition that continues to present.

Rejecting liberal democracy many African and developing world post-colonial states adopted the concept of a "one party democracy", sometimes distinguished from the liberal genre as a social democracy. In post-colonial Africa, social democracies were preferred to non-liberal democratic systems due to their means of fostering greater nationalism in highly plural, underdeveloped societies. Between 1969–83, the Nimeiri regime established a Marxist-Leninist platform with a single party under the guidance of the Sudanese Socialist Union (SSU), a one party state union of working peoples whose goals sought to eliminate the influence of sectarianism stripping sectional parties of their tribal and religious base and establishing a secular socialist national identity over the entire country.

However, failure to resolve identity politics contributed to the failure of the socialist democracy experiment in the Sudan. The exclusion of the South in an equal and united status within the SSU conveyed the one party's inability to incorporate the idea of "cultural" determination in a broader notion of democratic equality. Instead, through the 1972 Addis Ababa Agreement, the South was variably maneuvered into unequal representation and finally settled with regional autonomy confining it to a status similar to the concept of 'separate but not equal'. Moreover, the principle of a socialist democracy was definitively subverted when in a "national reconciliation" agreement signed in 1977 between the northern Islamist dominated National Front and the Nimeiri regime, the SSU dropped its social democratic ideology and egregiously re-invoked religious-sectarian influence and dominance in Sudanese politics. At the behest of the restored northern sectarian parties, especially the Muslim Brotherhood, the Nimeiri regime unilaterally abrogated the southern regional autonomy arrangement and later announced the introduction of Sharia Laws for the entire country; this event caused the South to resume its war against the Sudanese state in 1983.

The Sudan has also had little success in establishing a multi-national democracy of the consociational kind commonly utilized and pioneered in Nigeria. Consociational institutions have combined with liberal democracy in Africa to adopt policies and principles for accommodating cultural pluralism. The consociational liberal state guarantees liberties in a state where no one culture holds a dominant place and a state that ensures the fullest security for the preservation of local custom and cultural communities. African democracies have often employed consociational mechanisms within a liberal democracy to ensure that all significant cultural groups are incorporated into government without being frozen out by a crude majoritarianism.[52] The country's 1990s state-led democratic transition had the fullest opportunity to achieve a multi-national democracy of this genre; however, instead the incumbent NIF/Bashir regime merely sought to "democratize political Islam" by deferring to rhetorical notions of cultural power-sharing while the regime's 1998 Constitution written by Islamic cleric al-Turabi developed a perversion of the liberal consociationalist democracy—the "ethnocracy". The ethnocracy represented a democratic regime, which has placed the Arab/Islamic culture as the dominant national Sudanese identity on the grounds of a cultural majority while minimally permitting protections for the country's ethnic minorities—especially in the South.

Celebrating the democratic principles of Islam, al-Turabi's vision for the Sudanese nation, reflected the Sudan's fullest attempt to build a modern Islamic state and society within a liberal democracy. However, the country's vision of an "Islamic democracy" also failed because of the contested notion of 'ethno-religion' in the Sudan, which tends to be an observation characteristic of the manifestation of Islamic politics in sub-Saharan Africa and Asia. Ironically, the contestation against Islamic dominance in democratic politics came not just from the non-Islamic southern region, but also from within the heterogeneity of Islamic practice in the North. The fact that there have always been two competing approaches to Islamization in the Sudan underscores the orthodoxy of al-Turabi and the NIF's brushings with Islamism represented in the current regime.

A fundamentalist ideology of the Muslim Brothers, the incumbent ideological faction of Muslims who have captured the Sudanese state embraced the traditional Sharia, the orthodox law of Islam and Islamic revivalism.[53] To the disappointment of many, including secular members of the northern Sudanese Muslims, it is the Muslim Brothers' fundamentalist brand of *Salafi* Islam—going back to the pious forebears—that dominates the national politics of contemporary Sudan reflected in the hard-line Islamist positions taken by the government during the 2004 peace negotiations. Upon coming to power, the National Islamic Front for example declared that the new Islamist state in the Sudan would not tolerate either those Arabs whose interpretation of the Quran remains unacceptable to the Muslim Brothers nor do those Africans who refuse to accept the political, economic, and social suzerainty of the Islamists.[54]

The alternative approach to Islam, a more liberal version, is reflected in the ideology of the Republican Brothers especially articulated in the writings of the movement's leader Mahmoud Muhammad Taha who, in 1985, was executed by the Nimeiri regime for religious apostasy. Adopting a modernist approach to Islam, the Republican Brothers argued that the ideals of Islam included democratic values, religious tolerance, fundamental freedoms, and equality between the sexes.[55] Thus, while Taha and the Republican Brothers advocated democracy, socialism and pluralism, the Muslim Brothers and Turabi politicized Islam using it as an instrument of power and control. Another lost opportunity thus for Sudanese democracy was the failure by the Sudanese elite to adopt Taha's Islamic principles conducive to the equality of peoples and democratic principles which would have encouraged a vision for the nation respected by both Northerners and Southerners.[56]

Democracy and Self-Determination: The Case of the Sudan

Self-determination, sovereignty, consociationalism, power sharing, autonomy, regionalism and federalism are all concepts that are of crucial importance for the theoretical and political importance for examining the prospects of democracy. In a deeply divided society such as the Sudan political organization, these aspects of democracy affect the degree to which inhabitants accept the domain and scope of a territorial unit as an appropriate entity to make legitimate decisions about the polity's possible future restructuring. In this context, democratic legitimacy nevertheless rests on the notion that the more the population of a territory of the sate is composed of pluri-national, lingual, religious or cultural societies, the more complex politics becomes because an agreement on the fundamentals of a democracy will be more difficult.[57] The Sudan is increasingly faced with this challenge.

Indeed, in this respect, one of the most important compromises on the side of the Sudanese government in the 2005 Sudan Peace Agreement is the regime's acceptance of a self-determination referendum for the southern Sudan that offers an option of secession after a six-year interim period. The self-determination referendum provides an opportunity for the Southern Sudanese to choose to remain as an integral nationality within a united Sudan—the unity option—or to officially secede from the nation to form an independent national territory of its own—the independence option. Support by the government for the self-determination referendum was surprising given the regime's previous displeasure at anything that might compromise the "unity" of Sudan.[58] However, agreement to the self-determination clause was an even bigger surprise for the Southern party in the negotiations—constituted politically as the SPLM—whose original was conceived of as a "united" Sudan in justice and mutual respect for all of the Sudanese provinces including the north, south, west, central and east configuration of a "New Sudan," rather than SPLM's current confinement to a few Southern regions: Equatoria, Barh-el Ghazal and Upper Nile, the Nuba Mountains, and Southern Blue Nile and Abyei.

For the Sudanese South, represented by the standpoint of the Anya Nya[59] the South's first resistance movement, the struggle for self-determination defined as a collective right for the equality of all peoples and nations began at independence. At that time, southern resistance fought against the rigidity of the North's assimilation policies and the forceful ruthlessness of its implementation. The Anya Nya viewed self-determination as a complete secession from the Northern Sudan—a two-state solution to the country's national identity crisis. Despite concerns over the viability of an independent Sudanese state—it would be landlocked and ethnically divided—with an area of some 250,000 square miles and a population of about six million people, the vision of an independent "Southern" state (once named Azania) was violently fought for as an important means of achieving peace and democracy. However, in 1973, the Anya Nya abandoned its self-determination independence claim in exchange for regional autonomy as a means of achieving peace and democratic freedom within a united Sudan. Nevertheless, when the regional arrangement was unilaterally abrogated in 1983 Anya Nya II, in going back to war distinguished itself significantly from the later SPLM in fighting for southern sovereignty as opposed to Sudanese unity, the latter being the central position of the SPLM.

While distinguishing itself as a foremost movement engaged in democratic struggle for a united Sudan respectful of equal citizenship and multi-nationality has been the hallmark of leader John Garang and the SPLM's movement ideology since the resistance organization's establishment,[60] by the time of the signing of the Sudan Peace Agreement of 2005, the movement's vision of a united 'New Sudan' was to be dramatically reversed to accept regional autonomy and sovereignty as had its predecessor. Deferring to crucially damaging ideological and ethnic factionalism (Dinka dominance) within the SPLM, the Unity vision succumbed to the self-determination and independence standpoints of Any Nya II loyalists and SPLM breakaway factions such as the Sudanese Democratic Salvation Front (SDSF) led by Riek Machar, a Nuer, and Lam Akol, a Shilluk. In what Collins calls a Byzantinian objective to end the brutal consequences of a forty year civil war on both sides, the inter factional war fostered the "compromise" of the 2005 Sudan Peace Agreement. The agreement was hurried into by the SPLM to reconcile elements of self-determination for the SDSF with its own (SPLM/Garang) consistent, though contrary, commitment to a secular democratic united Sudan.[61]

Thus, while holding out for the possibility for an independent republic for the Southern Sudan in six years of signing the agreement, at the same time, in the interim, peace and democracy—conveyed through the agreement—represents for the SPLM a bifurcated "federalist" notion of the "New Sudan", one that stands for genuine autonomous regional government. During the interim arrangement, the power-sharing settlement attempts to ensure that central power in the government of the Sudan is equally representative between North and South with a President from the North and a First Vice President from the

South who will preside over the exclusive regional authority of the South as well as have powers within the Federal government.[62]

Because the peace agreement is bilateral between the Sudanese government and the SPLM, its major shortfall is its inability to expand the practice of self-determination through territorial and fiscal federalism to other marginalized regions of the country, including in eastern Beja, western Darfur and southern Kordofan provinces which have politically agitated for some kind of power-sharing arrangements for a democratic Sudan since independence.[63] The idea that the agreement has the potential of being duplicated as a conflict resolution mechanism for Darfur especially was taken up by Ruud Lubbers, the head of the UN High Commission for Refugees (UNHCR), in a proposition for a federalist model of power-sharing between the government and the Darfur Province. [64]

The government has also begun to float the idea that Sudan Peace Agreement contains guiding principles for the idea of establishing a federal government with broader powers for the states, similar to the powers given to the south of Sudan, and has proclaimed its commitment to share power and resources in Darfur by developing a genuine federalism.[65] Introduced as a self-determination proposal, as early as 1956, by the provinces of the South, Darfur, the Beja and Korfordan, the notion of a federal democracy is certainly not new for the Sudan. Moreover, in the 1970s as then OAU Chairman and Sudan peace-broker, and currently, the Nigerian head of state, General Olusegun Obasanjo, commenting on the structural "identity" similarities between the two countries, attempted to persuade Sudanese leaders on the federalist option especially illustrating ways in which the federal commitment to state's rights had enabled the development of a political tradition in Nigeria where the separation of powers between the nation-state and its regions had become a cornerstone in stabilizing ethno-nationalist tensions in the country since the end of the civil war.

International Approaches

Internationalized approaches to the Sudanese civil wars have been circumspect to date, achieving little by way of bringing sustainable peace to the sorely conflicted deeply divided nation. This is evident by the fact that on the most recent question on Darfur, both the US and the UN have vacillated on the 'genocidal' classification, preferring to characterize this new spate of political violence in the Sudan as the mere extension of the wider, recurrent cycles of violence, collapsing governance and increased humanitarian disasters that have engulfed Africa since the decade of the 1990s. The US, while on the face appearing to collaborate with the international community (and its own domestic human rights lobby) in promoting a peaceful resolution of Sudan's wars, in reality is guided by its own state department's 'Bush Doctrine Policies' defined by the 'war on global terrorism' since 2001. Thus, while leading a UN resolution to impose strict sanctions on the Sudanese government,[66] the US also initiated steps to remove the Sudan from its 'axis of evil' terror states list.[67]

Meanwhile, the UN as well has vacillated on characterizing the Darfur crisis as "genocide" and yet tends to describe the conflict in a 'complex humanitarian emergencies assistance' paradigm.[68] Furthermore, the influential IGO reappointed the Sudan to its human rights commission despite the Darfur human rights atrocities.[69] Most significant to the obfuscation and divergent responses by the international community to the Sudanese conflict is the fact that Africa's regional response to the Darfur crisis especially counters the dominant US-UN internationalist persuasion. The African Union (AU), avoiding the terms 'genocide' and 'humanitarian crises' classified the Darfur crisis as "political".[70] And Nigeria's President Olusegun Obasanjo, also 2004 African Union chairman has been seeking an "African solution" to the crisis.

Most significantly absent, however, from the "global" analysis of the Darfur conflict was the connection and the contradiction raised by the fact that while violence of presumed "genocidal" proportions was erupting in one part of the country, a sub-regional and US-sponsored "international" peace agreement was being negotiated in another part. Nor has the international community produced a compelling argument supporting the assertion that the Darfur war was indeed 'genocide' as the concept has been defined by the UN's Convention on the Prevention and Punishment of the Crime of Genocide—acts committed with intent to destroy, in whole or in part, a national, ethnical, racial or religious group.[71] Most ironic is the fact that six months after the public pronouncements of the Darfur crisis as "genocide" by the US Congress, the US State Department and the UN's human rights community, besides the provision of humanitarian relief, little formal penalization of the magnitude against Nazi Germany's genocide under the Hitler regime has been discussed or deliberated to be undertaken against the perpetrators of the genocide to save its victims.

As a peace agreement based on the internationalized, post-conflict model, the Sudan Peace Agreement also suffers from shortcomings derived from external imposition. To its prejudice, "democracy" and "ethnicity" in this arrangement has been criticized for formulating notions of "peace and democracy" around simplistic rebel/government bilateral Arab-Muslim/Black-Christian power-sharing and resource-mobilization mechanisms.[72] Representing what Norval describes as a "coerced unity," the failure of the peace agreement to address the long-term historical and substantive questions of the country's national identity crisis led to northern and southern constituencies alike to dismiss the peace process as a "compromised" peace rather than a "just" peace. The agreement's superficial liberal conflict resolution mechanisms has caused its inability to be comprehensive and grass-roots induced thereby holding few prospects for becoming a viable option for addressing the country's "national question." Senator Darnforth's original agreement template while identifying peace as the prerequisite for achieving democracy, however, narrowed the protagonists of the conflict to the Government of Sudan (GoS) and the SPLM while egregiously sidelining the National Democratic Alliance (NDA)—the country's domestic pro-democracy movement. As a result, the lack of the national comprehensiveness of the agreement led the Darfur resistance fighters, the Sudanese Liberation Movement (SLA) and the Justice and Equality Movement (JEM) to take up arms to struggle for democracy on the grounds that the Sudanese Peace Agreement did not include them.[73]

Conclusion

The consequences of the dominance of internationalized conflict resolution measures to solve Africa's conflict has led to limitations in the emergence of a substantive democratic state and lasting peace for affected countries such as the Sudan. Alternatively, privileging a domestic, endogenous, nationally derived state-society approach to the resolution of Sudan's north-south conflict, in 1994, well before the much celebrated signing of the contemporary peace protocols, the horn of Africa's sub-regional body of northeast African countries, the Intergovernmental Authority on Development (IGAD), supported by the then Organization of African Union (OAU) proposed a conflict resolution solution for a "New Sudan" on the basis of the country's domestic democratic initiatives that had been ratified in the 1986 Koka Dam Declaration. The core animus of Koka Dam consisted of a national democratic alliance (NDA) of groups from the north, south, east and west engaged in democratic struggle. Presenting their views regarding the terms for a settlement of the "Sudan Problem" based on this internal pro-democracy struggle, IGAD condemned the ideology and policies of the current regime's Islamic Front. While recognizing the "unity" of the Sudan as a fundamental principle of the AU, IGAD's Declaration of Principles (DOP) set forth the proposals for the achievement of peace and unity on the basis of Africa's "national democratic question:" self-determination, recognition of racial, ethnic, cultural and religious diversity, legal, political and social equality, a secular and democratic state, freedom of belief and worship, independence from the judiciary and recognition of human rights.[74]

Conceived of as an idea as early as March 1986, the Sudanese liberal democratic regime, the SPLM, and all major political parties and civil organizations in the form of the National Democratic Alliance (NDA)[75] produced the Koka Dam Declaration, which called for a Sudan, 'free from racism, tribalism, sectarianism and all causes of discrimination and disparity.'[76] The declaration demanded the repeal of Islamic Sharia laws and the convening of a National Constitutional Conference to further deliberate the restructuring of a democratic Sudan. The Koka Dam Declaration and the call by all of the country's diverse democratic constituent forces for a National Constitutional Conference to deliberate upon the "problem of the Sudan" and posit a solution by way of a national democratic dialogue represented an internally driven opportunity by a wide ar-

ray of diverse Sudanese constituencies to dialogue the future of peace and democracy in the country.

The Koka Dam declaration produced the three-year liberal democratic government of Al Sadig Al Mahdi of the Democratic Unionist Party (DUP), who
headed a government in coalition with the National Islamic Front and four
southern political parties; however, the National Constitutional Conference was
never held. The restoration instead of liberal democratic status quo politics
rather than the prospects for a radical pluralist dialogue for a New Sudan based
on a comprehensive Sudanese multi-nationalism and all-inclusive democracy
bred the factionalism, exclusion and elitist politics that precipitated the 1989
military coup led by the most extreme religious sectarian forces in the NIF. Despite peace agreements between the GoS/SPLM, GoS/Darfur, and a separate
Egyptian-Libyan initiative between the now exiled NDA and the GoS, these
various movements continue to struggle for a pluralistic, united Sudan based on
the Koka Dam principles. Significantly, fifteen years later in exile in Egypt, the
Sudanese pro-democracy movement, the National Democratic Alliance, still
calls on the government of Bashir to step down and hand over power to a transitional government, which would convene a constitutional conference to organize
truly democratic elections. [77]

If unity is the choice for a future multi-national Sudanese state, then considerable political crafting of democratic norms, practices and institutions must
take place to accommodate diversity in the country. This would be the goal of a
National Constitutional Conference, which has previously through the Koka
Dam Declaration identified peace, justice, equality and democracy as primary
objectives for the country. Over the course of the Sudan's many years of democratic struggle, Koka Dam constituents have already identified key items that the
Sudan needs to deliberate nationally: the nationalities question, the religious
question, basic human rights, system of rule, development, underdevelopment,
and natural resource production and distribution.[78] The Declaration and the need
for a national constitutional conference self-defined by internal actors, sought to
trigger these fundamental changes in Sudanese national politics, and thereby it is
this event that continues to represent a watershed for the realization of a lasting
peace and democracy for the country.

Acknowledgment: As this book goes to press, the death of John Garang in a
helicopter crash has just been announced. In light of this tragic news, I'd like to
dedicate this chapter to Dr. Garang's memory and legacy in achieving a democratic peace in the Sudan.

Notes

1. Horowitz, Donald. *A Democratic South Africa? Constitutional Engineering in a Divided Society* (Berkeley: University of California Press, 1992).

2. John R. Bowen, "The Myth of Global Ethnic Conflict," in *Journal of Democracy* 7.4 (1996): 3–14.

3. Ali Rattansi, "Cultural Politics of Representation," in *Social Postmodernism: Beyond Identity Politics*, ed. Linda Nicholson and Steven Seidman (Cambridge University Press, 1995).

4. Nicholson, *Social Postmodernism*.

5. John Garang and Khalid Mansour, *The Call for Democracy in Sudan: John Garang* (London: Kegan Paul International, 1992).

6. Garang, *Call for Democracy*.

7. Anonymous, *The Black Book of Sudan* (Khartoum: privately published, 2000).

8. Ali A. Mazrui, *The African Condition: A Political Diagnosis* (London: Cambridge University Press, 1980).

9. Tarak Barkawi and Mark Laffey, *Democracy, Liberalism and War* (Boulder, Colo.: Lynne Rienner Publishers, 2001).

10. Larry Diamond, *Developing Democracy: Toward Consolidation* (Baltimore: John Hopkins University Press, 1999). Diamond illustrates that one way of understanding the Third Wave of Democracy is through the "US-UN Power Diffusion Global Democracy model," which promotes "electoral democracy" to the developing world in order to conform to a new global democratic order.

11. Marina Ottaway and Anatol Lieven, "Rebuilding Afghanistan," *Current History* (March 2002).

12. Alex de Waal, *Islamism and Its Enemies in the Horn of Africa* (Bloomington: Indian University Press, 2004).

13. Franics Deng, *War of Visions* (Washington, D.C.: Brookings Institute, 1995).

14. Edwin N. Wilson and Patrick McAllister, eds., *The Politics of Difference: Ethnic Premises in a Word of Power* (Chicago, IL: University of Chicago Press, 1996).

15. Crawford Young, "The Dialectics of Cultural Pluralism: Concept and Reality,"in *The Rising Tide of cultural Pluralism: The Nation-State at Bay*, ed. Crawford Young, (Madison, WI: University of Wisconsin Press, 1993).

16. Mazrui, *African Condition*.

17. Richard Akinleye, "Power-sharing and Conflict Management in Africa: Nigeria, Sudan and Rwanda," in *African Development* XXV, nos.3 & 4 (2000).

18. Michael Neocosmos, "Democracy, Rights, Discourse, National Healing and State Formation," *Ashgate Policy Paper Series* (Ashgate, U.K.: 2000).

19. Young, "The Dialectics of Cultural Pluralism."

20. Paris Yeros, *Ethnicity and Nationalism in Africa: Constructivist Reflections and Contemporary Politics* (New York: St. Martin's Press, 1999).

21. Arletta Norval, "Rethinking Ethnicity: Identification, Hybridity and Democracy," in *Ethnicity and Nationalism in Africa: Constructivist Reflections and Contemporary Politics*, ed. Paris Yeros (New York: St. Martins Press, 1999).

22. Atul Kohli, *The Success of India's Democracy* (Cambridge: Cambridge University Press, 2001).

23. John Lonsdale, "Globalization, Ethnicity, and Democracy: A View from the Hopeless Continent," in *Globalization in World History*, ed. A. G. Hopkins (London: Random House, 2000 London): 194–219.

24. Norval, "Rethinking Ethnicity."

25. Wamba dia Wamba, "Democracy, Multi-partyism and Emancipative Politics in Africa," *CODESRIA* (Dakar, Senegal: 1994).

26. Amartya Sen, "Democracy as a Universal Value," in *The Global Resurgence of Democracy* ed. Larry Diamond and Marc Plattner (Baltimore: Johns Hopkins University Press, 2001).

27. Ceasefire Agreement between GOS and SLA/JEM, July 2004.

28. Deng, *War of Visions*, 34.

29. M.A Salih, "An Authoritarian Circus: Sudan from NIF to Multi-party Democracy?" in *African Democracies and African Politics*, M.A. Salih (London: Pluto Books, 2001).

30. Edgar Balance, *Sudan, Civil War and Terrorism 1956–1999* (New York: St. Martins Press, 2000).

31. In characterizing the country's complex pluralism, in the current Darfur conflict-especially where the international community seems to want to apply the concept of 'genocide'—my own approach attempts to avoid the simplistic racio-religious labels used to simplistically describe the political violence as a war between Arab Muslims and Black Muslims. Along these lines, for years the Sudan's civil war has been characterized simplistically as a war between northern Islamic Arabs and southern 'black' Christian Africans.

32. Khalidi, *The Government They Deserve*, p. 67.

33. Deng, *War of Visions*, 67.

34. Mazrui, *The African Condition*, 56.

35. Khalidi, *The Government*, 90.

36. Deng, *War of Visions*, 60.

37. Tim Niblock, *Class and Power in the Sudan* (Albany: State University of New York Press, 1987).

38. Wai, *The African Arab*, 112.

39. The UN imposed sanctions on the Sudan in 1996 for harboring terrorism: the sanctions were lifted in 2001 because it was believed that the GOS was cooperating with the US in arresting terrorist suspects and driving out Al-Queda cells in the country (<terrorismfiles.org>, "State-Sponsored Terrorism Sudan," 2000).

40. According to J. Winder, a British officer, "The north possesses ethical foundations of a society, and the south does not," in *The Condominium Remembered* ed. Deborah Lavin (Center for Middle Eastern and Islamic Studies, University of Durham, 1991), 34.

41. Robert Collins, *Shadows in the Grass: Britain and the Southern Sudan, 1918–1959* (Yale University Press 1983)

42. Douglas Johnson, *The Root Causes of Sudan's Civil Wars* (Bloomington: Indiana University Press, 2003)

43. John Markakis, *National and Class Conflict in the Horn of Africa* (Cambridge University Press, 1987).

44. Ahel Alier, *Too Many Agreements Dishonored* (Exeter Press, 1990).

45. Justice Africa "Briefings: Prospects for Peace in the Sudan," *Review of African Political Economy* 28 (June 2001).

46. Catherine Boone, "Empirical Statehood and Re-configurations of Political Order" in *The African State at a Critical Juncture*, ed. Leanardo A. Villalon and Phillip A. Huxtable (Boulder: Lynne Rienner, 1998). See Boone's democratization thesis, "recon-

figuring states"—third world democratic transitions are not transitioning to liberal democracies but to neo-authoritarian states.

47. *International Crisis Group Africa Report* 39 (2002).

48. Abdalla Osman El Tom and M.A. Mohammed Salih, "Review of The Black Book of Sudan," in *Review of African Political Economy* 97, 2003: 511–530.

49. Dr. Mudawwi Ibrahim Adam, head of Sudan Social Development Organization picked up and tried for treason and Salih Mohammed Osman, human rights lawyer in Nyala Darfur was detained (*New African*, June 2004).

50. *Freedom in the World Country and Territory Ratings: The Sudan* (Freedom House, 2004). Classified as a military dominated presidential-parliamentary polity, for the past ten years, the Sudan has maintained the IGO's worst democracy ratings with a 'Not Free' 7.7 political rights and civil liberties rating.

51. Sudan's "first wave of democracy" appeared between 1941 when the first Sudanese parties began to emerge and contest for power and ended in 1958 when due to excessive inter-party factionalism caused by sectarianism, the country experienced its first military coup under the leadership of General Ibrahim Aboud. In the typical vanguardist style of civil-military relations in Africa (Edozie, Rita Kiki, *People Power and Democracy: the Popular Movement Against Military Despotism in Nigeria, 1989–1999* (Africa World Press, 2002)), democratic protestations among the northern civil society forced the Aboud military regime to organize a democratic transition which in 1965–1968 established a second liberal democratic regime with Mahjoub winning the seat of Prime Minister in 1965, Al Sadig Al Mahdi in 1966 and Mahjoub's return in 1967. A second coup in 1969 led by Colonel Jaafar Nimeiri cancelled the second liberal experiment in the country for almost two decades.

52. David Apter, *The Political Kingdom of Uganda: A Study of Bureaucratic Nationalism* (Princeton University Press, 1961); David Apter, *The Politics of Modernization* (Chicago University Press, 1965).

53. Abdullahi Ahmed An-Na'im, "The Elusive Islamic Constitution: The Sudanese Experience," in *ORIENT* 26, no3 (Sept. 1985).

54. Robin Collins, "Africans, Arabs and Islamists: from the conference tables to the battlefields in the Sudan," *African Studies Review* 42, no. 2 (September 1999).

55. Khalid Duran, "The Centrifugal Forces of Religion in Sudanese Politics," in *ORIENT* 26, no. 4 (December 1985).

56. Deng, *War of Visions*.

57. Linz, Juan J. and Alfred Stepan, *Problems of Democratic Transition and Consolidation: Southern Europe, South America, and post-communist Europe* (Johns Hopkins University Press, 1996).

58. ICG Report, "Sudan's Best Chance for Peace: How Not to Lose It," September 2002.

59. Anya Nya began as a 'guerrilla army' in 1955, transforming into a Land Freedom Army (LFA) in 1963 and adopted the name 'poisonous insect' or Anya Nya in 1964 and established a platform for secession and independence for the Southern Sudan provinces. Edgar Balance, *Sudan, Civil War and Terrorism 1956–1999* (New York, St. Martin's Press, 2000).

60. See Garang, *Call for Democracy*, for an elaborate discussion on the political goals of the SPLM and southern struggle

61. Robert Collins, "Africans, Arabs and Islamists: From the Conference Ttables to the Battlefields in the Sudan," *African Studies Review* 42, no. 2 (September 1999).

62. Reporter, "Sudan: Prospects for Peace," *ROAPE* (July 2003).

63. In the Black Book of Sudan, an anonymous book published in western Sudan exposing the gross economic inequality in the country skewed toward the core Arabized North, suspected to have been written by the Darfur resistance, the publication unveils the level of injustice practiced by successive northern governments to the special detriment of eastern, western and central regions and thus establishes a call to violent struggle on the basis of a united economically equal Sudan ("Book Review of the Black Book of Sudan," Abdalla Osman El tom and Mohammed Salih, *Review of African Political Economy* 30 (December 2003)).

64. "My gut feeling is the best would be that Sudan finds itself in a way where it accepts relative autonomies of regions.... It is a question of sharing power up to a certain point. It doesn't amount to putting the territorial integrity of the Sudan at risk.... This country is engaged in negotiating a power-sharing deal with rebels in the south.... There are many big countries which have evolved by sharing power between the capital and the regions" (John Ashworth, "A View from the Sudan: Monthly Briefing," *Sudan Focal Point*, 29 September 2004).

65. Quoted by Sudanese Information Minister Al-Zhawi Ibrahim Malik. Mohammed Zeinelabdin, "A View from the Sudan Monthly Briefing 09–04," *Sudan Focal Point*, 29 September 2004.

66. The US-drafted resolution demands that Sudan make good on promises it made on 3 July to rein in the fighters. It calls for UN Secretary General Kofi Annan to issue a report in 30 days on the progress made. *BBC News World Update*, "Sudan's army says the UN resolution on the conflict in Darfur is 'a declaration of war' and threatens to fight any foreign intervention." 2 August 2004.

67. In 2003, US Department of State officials began to take steps to remove Sudan from its list of "terror countries," where it was placed in 1997 by the Clinton administration. An Egyptian official who was asked about the surprising change in American policy said: "In the post-Iraq War reality, it is important for the U.S. to improve relationships with Sudan and to assist Egypt in her campaign against militants operating from Sudan and to counter the danger of Wahabi activities from that country," Joseph Farah, "US to Forgive Sudan for 2 Million Deaths?" *WorldNetDaily.com* <http://www.worldnetdaily. com/news/article) (2 June 2003).

68. Supported by the new multi-lateralism of the 1990s- a growing consensus within the United Nations adopted largely by international NGOs and the human rights' interests of powerful states' foreign policies- the humanitarian assistance model sought from the international community legitimation for intervention into a country's sovereign relations to save the victims of complex, humanitarian emergencies.

69. John-Claude Buhrer, *UN Commission on Human Rights Loses All Credibility: Reporters Without Borders* <http://www.rsf.org/IMG/pdf/Report_ONU_gb.pdf> (July 2003).

70. "The problem with Darfur is political, its solution is political, hence the necessity for the parties to quickly begin political negotiations...." Alpha Oumar Konare, AU President ("Talks on Sudan Crisis to Begin on July 15: AU Chief" *AFP*, July 2004)

71. Kenneth Campbell, *Genocide and the Global Village* (New York: Palgrave Press, 2001).

72. Editorial, "Sudan's Best Chance for Peace: How Not to Lose it," *ICG Report* (September 2002).

73. Sali Makki, "Darfur More than a Conflict" *New African*, May 2004.

74. Robert Collins, "Africans, Arabs, and Islamists: From the Conference Tables to the Battlefields in the Sudan," *African Studies Review* 42, no. 2 (September 1999).

75. With the exception of the National Islamic Front and the Democratic Unionist Party which constitutes the core of the current rightist Government of the Sudan.

76. Mohammed A. Salih, African *Democracies and African Politics* (Pluto Books, 2001).

77. <www.ndasudan.org/English/doc/vision.htm>.

78. Garang, *Call for Democracy.*

Chapter 9

Ethnic Conflict in Mexico: The Zapatistas

Michael R. Hall

On 1 January 1994, the Zapatista Army of National Liberation (EZLN) launched a surprise attack on several towns and an army barracks in Chiapas, the southernmost state in Mexico. The EZLN was a phenomenon of both Indian revivalism and armed struggle against neoliberalism, globalization, and political oppression. The Zapatistas, whose name, methods, and rhetoric invoked the spirit of Emiliano Zapata, a hero of the Mexican revolution, chose to launch their revolution on the day that the North American Free Trade Agreement (NAFTA) went into effect. Strategically, the Zapatistas hoped that their surprise attack would be facilitated by a weak response from Mexican soldiers recovering from heavy New Year's Eve drinking activities. The Zapatista uprising was also part of the long history of Indian resistance against repression, forced assimilation, exploitation, and poverty.[1] As the first major outbreak of revolutionary activity in Latin America since the demise of the Cold War, the Zapatista movement gained immediate national and international attention.

In the post-Cold War period, ethnicity replaced ideology as the force most likely to provoke violence and regional instability. During the Cold War, the two superpowers–the United States and the Soviet Union–were reluctant to openly confront each other in a nuclear war. At the end of World War II, the world was divided into two hostile camps based on competing ideologies: democracy and communism. The two superpowers and their respective European allies were engaged in a contest to win the hearts and minds of the people of the Third

World. Dozens of wars were fought in the Third World by proxy armies of the superpowers. The re-emergence of religious and ethnic conflicts, especially where such friction previously had been subordinated by ideological conflict, has become the norm in the post-Cold War period.

With globalization and the spread of modern transportation and communication services, ethnic conflict has the potential to achieve a global impact. The Internet can easily transform a local ethnic conflict into a global issue. Unlike traditional forms of media diffusion, the Internet allows not only for the sharing of information, but also for the ability to immediately react to the provided information. The Internet, therefore, is a place where ethnicity can play an important role.[2] The Internet was used by both Zapatista sympathizers to gain support for the EZLN and by critics of the Zapatistas to condemn the movement.[3]

The Roots of Indian Oppression

Underlying the Zapatista uprising is the status of Indians in Chiapas, who make up over thirty percent of the state's population of three million people. In the early sixteenth century, after the Spanish conquistadores conquered Mexico, millions of Indians died from newly introduced European diseases and the remaining Indians were converted to Catholicism and relegated to a marginal social existence as agrarian laborers. While most Mexican states flourished because of their agricultural potential or mineral wealth, Chiapas languished in poverty and neglect. Unlike most of Mexico, which underwent an ethnic blending known as *mestizaje* [racial mixing] over the last five centuries, Indians and non-Indians have remained isolated from each other in Chiapas.[4] As a result, the identity of the Chiapas Indians, while altered, did not achieve the levels of cultural assimilation found in other parts of Mexico. Thus, while Indians in other parts of Mexico witnessed the cultural demise of Indian groups, in Chiapas the Indians have been able to maintain many of their ancient cultures, customs, and traditions.

The Spanish colonial government introduced the *encomienda*, a system whereby land and Indians labor were granted to the Spanish conquerors. In return, the Indians received protection and salvation through religious indoctrination. The *encomienda* system virtually reduced the Indian population to slavery and bondage. A group of Mayan-speaking Indians in Chiapas, the Tzeltales, who fiercely resented the colonial government's assimilation efforts and bi-annual tribute collections, launched the Rebellion of the Tzeltales in 1712. Although the revolt was ultimately crushed by the colonial authorities, it was a concerted attempt by a contingent of Indians in Chiapas to eradicate the whites and mestizos who had been exploiting them in Chiapas. Essentially, the Indians "tried to somehow reverse the conquest."[5] As such, the Indians in Chiapas fought the only major ethnic war in colonial Mexico. By the eighteenth century, Indian birth rates had recovered to their pre-conquest levels. Nevertheless, the acceleration of the *mestizaje* process excluded the possibility that the Indians would ever comprise a numerical majority in Mexican society.

After independence in 1821, the Liberal and Conservative elites, who vehemently disputed the path of political and economic development that the newly independent nation should follow, fought amongst themselves. Political and economic chaos contributed to U.S. military intervention during the 1840s, which resulted in the loss of almost half of Mexico's national territory, and French military intervention during the 1860s, which resulted in a monarchy led by a naive Austrian prince placed on the throne of Mexico by Napoleon III, the French emperor. In 1867, a group of Mayan-speaking Indians in Chiapas, disgruntled by constant humiliation and exploitation at the hands of the whites and mestizos, launched the War of the Tzotziles. Although the rebellion had been brutally suppressed by 1872, the Indians had once again launched an ethnic war in Chiapas.

During the rule of Porfirio Díaz (1876–1910), commonly known as the Porfiriato, Mexico's Liberal elites, who were able to co-opt the Conservative elites, established a viable political and economic system based on the principles of Social Darwinism and Positivism. Positivism, as first explained by French philosopher Auguste Comte in *The Positive Philosophy* (1835), held that technology and science offered mankind the tools to build a utopian society of prosperity. This utopia, however, would only be possible if the political atmosphere was conducive. Thus, elite solidarity and control of the unruly masses was essential if prosperity was to be achieved. Social Darwinism, based on the writings of English philosopher Herbert Spencer, who had expanded upon the ideas of Charles Darwin, was a philosophy used by Latin America's elites to explain Latin America's relative underdevelopment to Europe. According to the Latin American elites, the non-white people of Latin America were responsible for Latin America's economic and social woes. To rectify the situation, the Latin American elites encouraged immigration of white Europeans to Latin America, the continuation of the *mestizaje* process of cultural and racial assimilation, and the marginalization of the Indians.

Díaz implemented a centralized political state based on a concept known as *pan ó palo* [bread or bludgeon]. Those who cooperated with the regime were rewarded, while those who resisted the regime were severely punished. The Mexican government implemented the Liberal, export-led economy, opened the nation to massive infusions of foreign investment, initiated the rapid development of the nation's infrastructure (especially railroad building), and encouraged the development of large agricultural and mining operations.[6] The Porfiriato established the basis of Mexico's modern economic system and the integration of the Mexican economy into the global capitalist system. Although a period of great economic prosperity, it was economic prosperity for relatively few people. The Porfiriato enhanced the inequitable distribution of wealth and land in Mexico. This inequality was especially noticeable in the rural areas. The peasants, many of whom were Indians, worked under horrific conditions on the semifeudal estates known as *haciendas*. Almost seventy-five percent of Mexico's people, and virtually the entire Indian population, worked in this rural agricultural system at the beginning of the twentieth century. In 1910, over ninety-six percent of the people living in rural Mexico were landless.[7] The discontent of these agricultural workers contributed to revolutionary activities that resulted in the Mexican Revolution of 1910.

Zapata and the Mexican Revolution

When Francisco Madero issued the Plan de San Luis in 1910, his primary goal was to end the Díaz dictatorship. Although not a sweeping statement of proposed social reforms, Madero promised that all land illegally confiscated from the *campesinos* [rural peasants] by the *hacienda* owners would be returned. This promise earned him the support of Emiliano Zapata, a young mestizo who had achieved fame as an able horse trainer. Zapata was able to mobilize oppressed agricultural workers with his rallying cry of *Tierra y Libertad* [Land and Liberty]. Although a leader of peasants, Zapata himself was a member of the middle class who had never worked as an agricultural laborer. Zapata's Liberating Army of the Center and South added to the strength of the revolutionary movement that convinced Díaz to flee the country in 1911.[8] Although he had initially supported Madero, by late 1911 Zapata had become disillusioned with Madero's lack of interest in agrarian reform.

Claiming that Madero had betrayed the revolutionary cause, Zapata joined forces with Otilio Montaño to compose the Plan de Ayala in November 1911. The Plan de Ayala articulated his agrarian reform agenda, demanded land and water rights for peasants, called for the expropriation of land from large estates, and demanded that anyone opposed to the plan should have all of their land expropriated.[9] Madero sent troops against Zapata in 1911 when he refused to lay down his arms. Madero, however, was overthrown and killed by Porfirian General Victoriano Huerta in 1913. After Huerta was overthrown in 1914, the revolution finally came to Chiapas. Venustiano Carranza, who led the revolution against Huerta, abolished debt servitude, which freed thousands of indentured Indians from the western coffee plantations and cattle ranches and allowed them to go back to the highlands. By September 1914, however, Zapata had withdrawn his support of Carranza's leadership of the revolution. In late 1914, at the Convention of Aguascalientes, Zapata joined forces with Francisco "Pancho" Villa against Carranza. In December 1914, Zapata and Villa took control of Mexico City, albeit briefly, and were memorialized in a revolutionary photograph that featured Villa in the presidential chair and Zapata next to him with a giant sombrero.[10] Villa's forces were subsequently crushed by pro-Carranza General Alvaro Obregón in early 1915, which placed Carranza at the head of the revolutionary movement once again.

In 1917, Carranza called a constitutional convention in Querétaro, the site of Emperor Maximilian von Hapsburg's execution by firing squad in 1867. Although the 1917 constitution did not specifically recognize Indian rights, it did incorporate the spirit of Zapata's Plan de Ayala into Article 27 of the Constitution, which provided for the establishment of *ejidos* [communal-held peasant land].[11] Meanwhile, *hacienda* owners in Chiapas had launched a counter-revolution after Huerta's overthrow. The estate owners employed *mapaches* [racoons], armed thugs who kept the Indian population docile and working for the wealthy land owners. In 1919, revolutionary leader Alvaro Obregón, who was plotting to overthrow Carranza, made a deal with *mapache* leader Tiburcio Fernández Ruiz. In return for supporting his coup against Carranza, Obregón agreed to support *mapache* activities and made Fernández Ruiz governor of Chiapas when he became president in 1920.[12] While Obregón was plotting the overthrow of Carranza, Carranza's supporters ambushed and murdered Zapata at Chinameca on 10 April 1919. Ironically, Zapata's supporters, who saw Carranza as a greater threat than Obregón, supported Obregón's forces who killed Carranza in 1920.

Obregón, who became president in 1920, used the Ministry of Public Education (SEP) to build Mexican nationalism and solidify the revolution. Obregón's Education Minister, José Vasconcelos, was in charge of a national program to disseminate the revolution's nationalistic philosophy of a unified, mestizo, Mexico. In his book, *La Raza Cosmica*, Vasconcelos argued that the Mexican people were a distinct race. Although he glorified the Indian past and promoted *indigenisimo*, which held that the Indians had made a valuable contribution to Mexico, the future of Mexico was based on cultural assimilation. In an effort to co-opt the revolutionary image of Zapata, Vasconcelos hired artist Diego Rivera to paint a huge mural in the SEP building. In the mural, titled the "Court of Fiestas," Zapata appeared as a "martyred saint."[13] Lázaro Cárdenas (1934–1940) expanded on Zapata's ideas and implemented the most extensive land reforms of the twentieth century in Mexico. Nevertheless, although the Institutional Revolutionary Party (PRI) had distributed over 100 million hectares of land by 1988, it never lived up to the ideals of the Mexican Revolution that celebrated the right to land for all people.[14] The Indians remained poor, especially when compared to the *hacienda* owners, who, although their estates had diminished in size, were still able to generate huge profits.

The PRI's ability to maintain a functional corporatist state was first questioned on a national level in the aftermath of the 1968 Tlatelolco incident. While the Mexicans were preparing to host the Olympic Games, university students staged a protest at the Plaza of the Three Cultures in the Mexican capital. The Mexican military fired on the unarmed students, killing and wounding hundreds, which led to increased criticism of the PRI. Economic disruptions during the 1970s and 1980s further inhibited the ability of the PRI to dominate the Mexican political economy. During the 1980s, the corporatist pillars that had supported the PRI since its inception in 1929 began to crumble. No longer did business, labor, and the rural poor support the PRI wholeheartedly. In what many observers considered to be Mexico's most fraudulent presidential election, PRI candidate Carlos Salinas defeated Lázaro Cárdenas's son Cuauhtémoc in 1988.

Salinas and Neo-Liberalism

In an attempt to revive the Mexican economy, Salinas expanded the neo-liberal economic reforms begun under the administration of Miguel de la Madrid (1982–1988). In 1983, the de la Madrid administration initiated constitutional reforms of Articles 25, 26, and 28 of the Mexican Constitution. The most significant changes affected Article 28, which held that the Mexican state would control oil, petrochemicals, electric power, minting money, railroads, satellite communications, and the postal service. In certain sectors, specifically mining, banking, the media, and transportation, the government would allow domestic, but not foreign, investors to obtain a majority share of control. In less important sectors, such as textiles, foreign companies could obtain a majority share of control. The petroleum industry, however, was one industry that would remain under state control.[15] By 1983, Salinas had privatized a number of state-owned enterprises originally considered strategic sub-sectors of the economy, such as banking, steel, mining, telecommunications, the railroads, and basic petrochemicals.[16] Noticeably absent from the list of corporations to be privatized was PEMEX, the state-owned oil company that had been nationalized in 1938 by Lázaro Cárdenas.

The lynchpin in Salinas's economic plan was Mexican membership in the North American Free Trade Association (NAFTA), which was designed to promote free trade between Canada, the United States of America, and Mexico. In 1991, in order to fulfill Mexican obligations under the agreement, the Salinas administration revised Article 27 of the Mexican Constitution. The revisions facilitated the buying and selling of any parcel of land, including *ejido* land.[17] Although this ruling might result in the reestablishment of large landed estates, the decision to sell *ejido* land was placed in the hands of the members of the *ejido*. Thus, it allowed for, but did not demand, the privatization of *ejido* land. The revisions ended the Mexican government's obligation to redistribute land to landless Indians who had organized to form an *ejido* and allowed foreign companies to buy, lease, or rent land.

The Procuraduría Agraria, the Agrarian Attorney General's Office, sent hundreds of government bureaucrats into the *ejidos* to explain the implications of the revisions to Article 27.[18] If individuals wished to obtain title to an individual parcel of land, the Procuraduría Agraria agents would facilitate the process. Individuals would receive certificates to individual plots of land, which could serve as the basis of a land title if the person decided to sell his land. Many *ejido* residents supported the plan and demanded their certificates. In Chiapas, almost half of the three million inhabitants lived on about 2,000 *eji-*

dos.[19] The Zapatistas feared that the peasants would sell their land out of economic despair, thus worsening the economic hardship of the rural poor. Not all of the *ejido* members, however, wanted to privatize their holdings. Many young Indians were convinced that their chances of ever obtaining land had ended with the revisions to Article 27. In 1992, during the celebration of the five-hundredth anniversary of Christopher Columbus's discovery of the New World, Indians in San Cristóbal de las Casas, the colonial capital of Chiapas, demonstrated against what they believed to be the government's disregard of their dignity and rights. Armed with traditional weapons, thousands of peasants entered the city and destroyed the statue in the main plaza of Spanish conquistador Diego de Mazariegos.[20] For many Indians, violence was the perceived path to achieve their demands and Zapatista leaders were able to harness this high level of Indian anger in Chiapas.

The Emergence of the Zapatistas

The EZLN, established in the Lacandona jungle at Camp Pesadillas on 17 November 1983, had been preparing its revolt for over a decade. The first members were three mestizos and three Indians. Rafael Sebastián Guillén Vicente, a mestizo, became the primary spokesperson, although he repeatedly claimed that he was not in charge of the movement. Technically, decisions were left to the Indigenous Revolutionary Clandestine Committee (CCRI). Known as Subcomandante Marcos, Guillén Vicente has never appeared in public without his black *balaclava* [ski mask] and bandolier of red shotgun cartridges over a waterproof jacket.[21] The ski masks hide the identity of the Indian soldiers, who fear government reprisals, and add mystery and intrigue to their identity.[22] It took the Zapatistas eleven years to assemble a fighting force of 3,000 and convince a significant number of Indians in Chiapas that armed struggle was the only alternative to poverty and exploitation.

In December 1993, the Zapatistas issued the Declaration of the Lacandona Jungle, in which the EZLN declared war on the Mexican government. Although the Zapatistas would eventually use the Internet to convince the world of their peaceful intentions, their initial aim was a violent revolution to rectify what they perceived as injustices against the Indians and unlawful rule by the PRI. The declaration of war concluded:

> We, honest, free men and women, believe that the war we are declaring is our last hope and that it is just and necessary. For many years, dictators have been engaged in an undeclared genocidal war against our people. For this reason, we ask for your participation and support in our struggle for jobs, land, housing, food, health, education, independence, liberty, democracy, and justice and peace. We will not stop fighting until these basic demands are met and a free and democratic government rules in Mexico.[23]

The Zapatistas launched their revolution against the Mexican government at the moment that the PRI was at its weakest and had lost much of its revolutionary legitimacy in the eyes of many Mexicans. Although the government knew of the Zapatistas before the 1 January attack, it was hesitant to take military action for fear of complicating the ratification of NAFTA in the US Congress, which eventually took place on 17 November 1993. Salinas hoped that *Solidaridad* [Solidarity], his government-funded program that offered development funds directly to the peasants, would lure the Indians away from the Zapatistas.

On the morning of 1 January 1994, the EZLN surprised the world by capturing San Cristóbal de las Casas, Altamirano, Ocosingo, Las Margaritas, and several small communities in the highlands of Chiapas. The EZLN claimed that "armed struggle" was the only route available to them.[24] On 2 January, the rebels moved to attack the military garrison in Rancho Nuevo. By 6 January, the military had forced the Zapatistas to retreat back into the Lacandona jungle. Casualty estimates vary. Historian John Womack claims that 13 Mexican soldiers, 38 local police, more than 70 EZLN rebels and from 19 to 275 civilians died during the first two weeks of January. The National Commission for Human Rights (CNDH), a Mexican government agency, reported that the twelve-day armed conflict resulted in the death of 16 army soldiers, 38 policemen, 67 civilians, and 38 others. Other NGOs and the Zapatistas themselves place the number of Zapatista dead at a much higher figure[25]. This was the first time that the Mexican army had to take up arms against Mexican citizens since the 1968 Tlatelolco massacre. Although international human rights groups were quick to point out the alleged abuses of the Mexican army against the Zapatistas and the Indians in Chiapas, it was noticeably silent on the issue of human rights abuses committed by the Zapatistas.

Marcos' unrealistic expectations of marching on Mexico City and removing Salinas from power had been dispelled. Meanwhile, thousands of workers and peasants throughout the country had taken to the streets to protest the government's counterattack on the Zapatistas. These protests convinced Salinas to end his policy of direct military confrontation against the Zapatistas and implement a unilateral cease-fire. Salinas appointed Manuel Camacho Solís to negotiate with the Zapatistas. On 20 January, the Mexican Congress passed an amnesty decree that cleared the way to begin negotiations with the Zapatistas. At the same time, the Mexican government increased social welfare spending in Chiapas to dilute the support for the Zapatistas. Although the Zapatistas had been defeated militarily, they won an important public relations battle. During the first few months of 1994, Marcos became a popular media celebrity. Marcos was able to project a positive image to many–that of a "Robin Hood defending the rights of the down-trodden against an unjust, repressive government."[26] He placed the demand for Indian rights within the context of criticism of neo-liberal economic policies and support of democracy, liberty, and justice. Marcos used Web sites and electronic mailing lists to disseminate information about the Zapatista rebellion. His short stories, especially those involving a beetle named Durito who fought against neo-liberalism, were very popular[27]. As such, the Zapatistas were the first virtual global resistance movement.[28]

The Zapatista Agenda

Marcos and the Zapatistas were able to generate a significant following among the poor Indians and mestizos of the highlands of Chiapas. Notwithstanding massive infusions of capital in the *Solidaridad* program and an economic boom throughout much of Mexico during the early 1990s, the rural poor, especially the Indians, in Chiapas experienced an economic depression.[29] Many Indians believed that the situation would only get worse once the NAFTA accords went into effect in 1994. Numerous factors concerning access to land, all of which were exacerbated by Salinas's alteration of Article 27 and a high birthrate in the state, contributed to the pessimistic outlook held by the rural poor in Chiapas.

First, cattle ranching, which needed huge tracts of land, had expanded from two million head of cattle in 1970 to four million head of cattle in 1983[30]. In the fertile Grijalva valley, 6,000 families controlled over three million hectares of cattle grazing land. As the acreage devoted to cattle raising increased, the amount of land available to the peasants decreased[31]. Since cattle ranching require fewer employees than growing corn, more peasants found themselves without a job. In addition, the construction of hydro-electric dams resulted in tens of thousands of hectares of farmland being flooded by lakes and reservoirs. Although the elites of the Grijalva valley had ceded land to the Indian *ejidos*, they had ceded their marginal land and kept the best land for themselves.

Second, for those peasants who continued to grow corn on their land, they found their income severely reduced. Chiapas was the third largest producer of corn in Mexico. Corn growing was an important economic activity for many Indian families in Chiapas until the NAFTA regulations went into effect. Both Mexico and the United States were major producers of corn. In southern and central Mexico, peasants grew hundreds of varieties of corn on small plots of land. In the United States, commercial farmers grew fewer varieties of corn[32]. In 1994, the Mexican government ended corn subsidies paid to farmers in Chiapas and lowered tariffs on U.S. corn. Under NAFTA rules, therefore, cheap corn from the U.S. flooded the local markets and drove the producers of the more expensive Chiapas corn out of business. Since corn and coffee were the main products of the *ejidos* in La Margarita, Altamiano, and Ocosingo, direct exposure to world market forces, as unleashed by NAFTA, had a negative impact on the Indians who were unable to compete with U.S. farmers who still received corn subsidies and utilized more cost-effective methods of production.[33]

Third, in 1989 the price for coffee on the international market collapsed. This was particularly devastating in Chiapas, Mexico's largest coffee exporter. Farmers who had invested their entire savings in planting coffee trees found themselves destitute. When Salinas deregulated coffee prices and withdrew government price supports the price of Mexican coffee declined by fifty percent[34]. To make the situation more problematic, farmers intensified their slash and burn activities in the Lacandona forest, one of the few surviving rain forests in the Americas, which threatened the bio-diversity of the region.

On 22 February, the Bishop of San Cristóbal de las Casas, Samuel Ruiz, a supporter of Liberation Theology and Indian rights, hosted a series of negotiations in the cathedral in San Cristobal between Camacho Solís and the Zapatistas. The meetings, known as Meetings of Peace and Reconciliation, were attended by Marcos and nineteen EZLN Indians in black ski masks. Three human rings around the cathedral, composed of 300 Non-Governmental Organization (NGO) workers, 500 military police, and 400 Red Cross workers, provided security for the event. After ten days, both sides reached a tentative agreement. Significantly, fifteen of the thirty-four demands made by the Zapatistas were explicitly for the Indians[35]. The Zapatista communities, however, rejected the government's response to their demands.[36]

In an attempt to each portray itself as the legitimate defender of the Mexican Revolution, both the EZLN and the Salinas administration claimed that it was continuing the legacy of Zapata. In April, to celebrate the seventy-fifth anniversary of Zapata's death, the Procuraduría Agraria distributed thousands of *ejido* parcel certificates in Zapata's home state of Morelos[37]. Salinas announced that the reforms to the constitution were part of the PRI's "seventy-five years of commitment and work carried out for the good of the Mexican peasants."[38] The CCRI frequently joined Zapata's name with the Tzeltal name Vo'tan to personify a force supporting and directing the Zapatista cause. The CCRI introduced Vo'tan Zapata to its followers in a press release on 10 April 1994, the seventy-fifth anniversary of Zapata's death. The press release stated:

> Brothers and sisters, we want you to know who is behind us, who directs us, who walks in our feet, who dominates out heart, who rides in our words, who lives in our deaths. . . . From the first hour of this long night on which we die, say our most distant grandparents, there was someone who gathered together our pain and our forgetting. There was a man who, his word traveling from far away came to our mountain and spoke with the tongue of true men and women. His step was and was not of these lands; in the mountains of our dead, in the voices of the old wise ones his word traveled from him to our heart. . . . It was, and is, his name in the named things. His tender word stops and starts inside our pain. He is and is not in these lands; Vo'tan Zapata, guardian and heart of the people. . . .He took his name from those who have no name, his face from those with no face; he is sky on the mountain. Vo'tan, guardian and heart of the people. And our road, unnameable and faceless, took its name in us: Zapatista Army of National Liberation.[39]

The name Vo'tan Zapata combines two powerful images: the Tzeltal legend who was the first man sent by God to give land to the Indians and the hero of the Mexican revolution who fought to get land for the Mexican peasants. In addition, during the first four months of 1994, Indians, supporting their actions with Zapatista rhetoric, invaded large estates in Chiapas and claimed over 50,000 hectares of land.

The Zapatistas, who argued that the 1917 constitution was no longer valid, held the Democratic National Convention (CND) in the Lacandona jungle from 6–9 August 1994. The EZLN constructed a new town and convention center to host the convention. The site was called Aguascalientes, in honor of the site where Villa and Zapata supporters met in 1914 to hold a similar convention. In addition to the more than 6,000 Mexican delegates invited, Marcos invited internationally known writers such as Carlos Fuentes, Carlos Monsiváis, Noam Chomsky, Eduardo Galeano, Ryzward Kapuscinsky, and Elena Poniatowska to attend the Democratic National Convention[40]. The convention, which tried to recreate the radical atmosphere of the 1914 convention, hosted five round table discussions that concerned the following themes: the illegitimacy of the PRI, peaceful routes to democratic transition, constructing a new nation based on the Declaration from the Lancandona Jungle, a transitional government, and a new constitution[41]. Although the media devoted a great deal of attention to the conference, the main media event at the time was the presidential election won by the PRI's Ernesto Zedillo.[42]

The Zapatista Struggle for Indian Rights

By the beginning of December 1994, over 20,000 Mexican troops had contained 3,000 EZLN insurgents in the Lacandona jungle. It seemed as though the only possible escape route for the Zapatistas was the Guatemalan frontier. Nevertheless, on 19 December, Marcos announced that the Zapatistas had left their jungle refuge and captured thirty-eight towns in Chiapas[43]. Although Marcos was lying, it caused an economic panic. Foreign investors fled, the peso was devaluated, and only a $50 billion aid package orchestrated by the Clinton administration saved the Zedillo government from economic ruin. In response, on 9 February 1995, the federal government issued arrest warrants for the leadership of the EZLN and launched a military offensive against the EZLN. On 11 March 1995, realizing that the military offensive against the leadership of the EZLN was ineffectual, the Mexican Congress unveiled the Law for Dialogue, Reconciliation, and a Just Peace in Chiapas, which suspended military actions against the EZLN and suspended the arrest warrants against the EZLN leadership. On 20 April, representatives of the Mexican government and the EZLN met in San Andrés, a Tzotzil Indian community in Chiapas, to begin discussions of a permanent peace between the government and the EZLN. One of the major themes discussed at the peace talks concerned Indian rights.

Although defeated militarily, the Zapatistas formed a political wing of the EZLN in January 1996. The Zapatista Front for National Liberation (FZLN) emphasized four major themes: Indian rights, anti-neoliberalism, women's rights, and reinvigorated democracy. The Zapatistas, however, have demonstrated certain ambivalence towards participatory democracy. At times, the Zapatista leadership has instructed Indians not to participate in municipal elections. As a result, support that could have been given to Cárdenas' Democratic Revolutionary Party (PRD), which supported many of the same platforms as the Zapatistas, was denied, and this facilitated the election of PRI candidates[44]. In February 1996, the EZLN and the Zedillo government signed the first San Andrés Agreement on Indigenous Rights and Culture, which laid the groundwork for a possible solution to the Indians' demands. The peace accords dealt primarily with the issue of self-determination and autonomy for the Indian communities, and not with issues about land distribution and agrarian reform[45]. Nevertheless, on 19 March, Zedillo agreed to purchase 80,000 hectares of private property in Chiapas that was being illegally occupied by Indian peasants and sell the land to the Indians at a greatly discounted price[46]. Meanwhile, to draw attention to their cause, the Zapatistas hosted the First Intergalactic Encounter for Humanity and Against Neo-Liberalism. Thousands of activists, feminists, environmentalists, homosexuals, artists, Marxists, and liberals from dozens of countries converged on five Zapatista communities at the end of July 1996. In December 1996, however, Zedillo, who was afraid that the Indian's demands would result in the balkanization of Mexico, failed to support legislation that would have made the substance of the San Jose Accords law.[47]

Tension between Zapatista supporters and opponents increased, especially in the highlands of Chiapas and the Lacandona jungle. One such incident, an attack by paramilitary forces against Zapatista supporters in Acteal on 22 December 1997, resulted in the death of forty-five Tzotzile Indians[48]. The forty-five dead Indians–nine men, twenty-one women, and fifteen children–were members of a Roman Catholic peasant organization called Las Abejas [The Bees]. Most of the seventy-four peasants jailed for the massacre were Evangelical Christians.

Conclusion

Although the Zapatista conflict has earned a great deal of media attention, the internal struggle between contentious Indian groups within Chiapas has not. For example, Marcos claimed that the death of the 45 Indians in Acteal was a form of ethnocide committed against the Indians of Chiapas by death squads supported by the Mexican government. The Zedillo administration, however, asserted that the death of the Indians in Acteal was the result of a group of Indians disgruntled over the fact that a community of pro-Zapatista Indians had established an autonomous municipality and taken over complete control of a local gravel quarry.[49]

In 2000, for the first time in over seven decades, the PRI lost a presidential election. National Action Party (PAN) candidate Vicente Fox, who won the election, held out an olive branch to the Zapatistas. In 2001, a Zapatista bus trip from Chiapas to Mexico City to champion Indian rights was a public relations success for both Fox and the Zapatistas[50]. Fox appeared to have restored a level of stability in Mexico, while simultaneously acceding too many Zapatista demands, including the removal of federal troops from Indian communities in the EZLN zone and the release of many Zapatista prisoners. In April 2001, the Mexican Congress passed an Indian rights law that, although it did not go as far as the San Andrés Accords of 1996, did provide a level of autonomy to the nation's Indians. Five regions in Chiapas—Oventik, Morelia, La Garrucha, Roberto Barrios, La Realidad—have since declared themselves multi-ethnic autonomous regions.

Although the pro-Zapatista Indians have achieved local autonomy, their economic plight continues. Many Zapatista Indians have renounced government aid, which further complicates their living conditions[51]. Although the EZLN no longer has the support of the majority of the Indians in Chiapas, it has placed the issue of Indian rights at the center of Mexican politics.

The Zapatista conflict has captured the attention of government officials, human rights activists, Mexican citizens, and foreigners. In many ways, the Zapatista conflict is unique. It is the first major ethnic conflict to be globalized by the Internet. Many have referred to the conflict as the first post-modern revolution after the collapse of the Soviet Union. The Zapatista struggle, however, is similar to previous revolutionary struggles in Latin America. The Zapatistas, who wish to redistribute limited land and resources, are challenging a society dominated by the socio-economic elite. The Zapatista struggle for Indian rights is yet another manifestation of the struggle of the dispossessed in Latin America.

Notes

1. Where there is ethnic conflict there is usually economic disparity. Chiapas, one of the poorest states in Mexico, is a prime example. Historian John Womack has referred to Chiapas as "Mexico's Mississippi." Ranked among Mexico's states, Chiapas has the highest illiteracy rate of people over age 15 (30 percent). Whereas 30 percent of Mexico's people live in rural areas, 60 percent of the people in Chiapas live in rural areas. Over two-thirds of the people in Chiapas live below Mexico's official poverty line. John Womack, Jr., *Rebellion in Chiapas: An Historical Reader* (New York: New Press, 1999), 4.

2. Unfortunately, the virtual absence of regulation and quality control on the internet can lead to distortion and manipulation of information.

3. If one searches the internet for on the Zapatistas, it becomes immediately apparent that the overwhelming majority of sites support the Zapatista movement. One can access sites that sell Zapatista dolls, masks, coffee, mugs, videos, books, and other

items, which, when purchased, supposedly provide revenue for the Indian families living in Chiapas and help to alleviate their economic hardship. Unfortunately, most of these sites are extremely biased and present an unhistorical view of the Zapatistas and their movement.

4. Although Mexico is predominantly a nation of mestizos, in 2000 there were still 10 million Indians (about 8 percent of the national population). In 1910, at the outbreak of the Mexican Revolution, one-third of Mexico's 15 million inhabitants were Indians. Enrique Krauze, *Mexico Biography of Power: A History of Modern Mexico, 1810–1996* (New York: Harper Collins, 1997), 31.

5. Krauze, *Mexico Biography*, 780. Although calling for the expropriation of land from haciendas, it did not call for the eradication of the *hacienda* system.

6. James Francis Rochlin, *Vanguard Revolutionaries in Latin America: Peru, Colombia, Mexico* (Boulder: Lynne Rienner Publishers, 2003), 173. Railroads represented one of the fundamental signs of modernity at the end of the nineteenth century. Mexico had about 1,000 kilometers of railway in 1880. The only major line connected Veracruz to Mexico City. By 1910, Mexico had almost 20,000 kilometers of railway. Four major lines connected Mexico to the United States at Nogales, El Paso, Corpus Christi, and Eagle Pass. The railways facilitated the extraction of raw materials as well as served to connect culturally diverse parts of the country. The majority of Mexican railways were owned by US investors.

7. James Cockcroft, *Mexico: Class Formation, Capital Accumulation and the State* (New York: Monthly Review Press, 1983), 91.

8. Ironically, Zapata used the premier emblem of capitalism at the time, railroads, to transport his troops from battle to battle.

9. Krauze, *Mexico Biography of Power*, 288.

10. When the Zapatistas held their version of the Aguascalientes conference in 1994, they covered Mexico City with posters of the famous photograph. Using their already well-hewed propaganda and public relations tactics, the Zapatistas inserted, in place of Zapata's face, the face of Subcomandante Marcos "wearing his signature ski mask, but also with the sombrero. Beside him, supplanting Villa, was social activist and professional wrestler Superbarrio Gómez, in his customary wrestling garb." Samuel Brunk, "Remembering Emiliano Zapata: Three Memories in the Posthumous Career of Chinameca," *Hispanic American Historical Review* 78, no. 3 (August 1998): 459.

11. Unlike the US Constitution, the Mexican Constitution is not a statement of rules, but rather a statement of ideals to be strived for. The Zapatistas argue that Mexico needed a new constitution. Article 27 of the Mexican Constitution of 1917 establishes the state's ownership over all land and water resources, forests, and mineral deposits. It gives the state the power to limit private ownership and break up existing large estates. This was the basis of Mexico's agrarian reform program and the *ejido* system.

12. Philip L. Russell, *The Chiapas Rebellion* (Austin, TX: Mexico Resource Center, 1995), 4. Fernández Ruiz was a cattle rancher. According to historian José Casahonda Castillo, Fernández Ruiz was "opposed to land reform and kept his land until his death, the same land that his parents and his grandparents had cherished before him. He was the backbone, the core, the true leader of the *mapache* movement. Thanks to him and his men, the social reforms in Chiapas were postponed." Although estates were limited to 8,000 hectares, these limitations were infrequently enforced.

13. Lynn Stephen, *Zapata Lives: Histories and Cultural Politics in Southern Mexico* (Berkeley: University of California Press, 2002), 42.

14. Rochlin, *Vanguard Revolutionaries in Latin America,* 178. Although the PRI distributed a sizeable amount of land, PRI land distributions were often sporadic. Almost half of the land was distributed during the presidencies of Lázaro Cárdenas (1934–1940) and Gustavo Díaz Ordaz (1964–1970).

15. Melissa H. Birch and Jerry Haar, eds., *The Impact of Privatization in the Americas* (Miami, FL: North-South Center Press at the University of Miami, 2000), 56.

16. Birch and Haar, *Impact of Privatization,* 58. Most passenger service was discontinued as soon as private investors purchased the railroads. One notable exception was the continuation of the scenic ride through the Copper Canyon from Chihuahua to Los Mochis.

17. *Ejidos* are the agrarian reform communities granted land confiscated from large landowners. Although the impetus for the land distributions was the Mexican Revolution, most of the land was dispersed during the administration of Lázaro Cárdenas (1934–1940). The land is held corporately by the members of the *ejido,* who are primarily Indians. Initially, the government retained property rights to the land, while members of the *ejido* were allowed to use allocated parcels of land. Although the peasants could not sell or rent their allocated parcel of land, they could pass on their allocated rights to their descendants. See Lynn Stephen, "Pro-Zapatista and Pro-PRI: Resolving the Contradictions of Zapatismo in Rural Oaxaca," *Latin American Research Review* 32, no. 2 (1997).

18. Programa de Certificación de Derechos Ejidales y Titulación de Solares Urbanos (Program for the Certification of Ejidal Land Rights and the Titling of Urban House Lots), or PROCEDE sent agents to over 27,000 ejidos in Mexico. Stephen, *Zapata Lives,* 63.

19. Programa de Certificación, xxviii.

20. Stephen J. Wager and Donald E. Schulz, "Civil-Military Relations in Mexico: The Zapatista Revolt and its Implications," *Journal of Interamerican Studies and World Affairs* 37, no. 1 (1995): 8.

21. Marcos is an acronym, with each letter signifying the first letter of one of the six towns–Margaritas, Altamirano, La Realidad, Chanal, Ocosingo, and San Cristóbal–attacked by the Zapatistas on 1 January 1994. Although he did not confirm his identity, Guillén Vicente was a member of a well-to-do family in Tampico who graduated from the Universidad Autónoma de México (UNAM) in 1980. He also served as a volunteer worker in Sandinista Nicaragua.

22. Mexican intellectual Octavio Paz was fascinated by the different "masks" that Mexicans wear. In his discussion of Mexican identity, Paz states: "his face is a mask and so is his smile." Octavio Paz, *The Labyrinth of Solitude* (New York, NY: Grove Press, 1961), 29. The masks can also represent the faceless people of the world excluded from the important decision making processes that determine the direction of the neo-liberal political economies.

23. Russell, *The Chiapas Rebellion,* 38. This declaration of war was circulated both nationally and internationally. The clear, simple message was enthusiastically received by liberals around the world because of moral and ethical tone.

24. Frank Bardacke, et. al., eds., *Shadows of Tender Fury: The Letters and Communiqués of Subcomandante Marcos and the Zapatista Army of National Liberation* (New York, NY: Monthly Review Press, 1995), 55.

25. Russell, *The Chiapas Rebellion,* 23. The Zapatistas reported more than 500 dead, 300 disappeared, 370 taken prisoner, and 50 wounded. Although the Zapatistas and

their supporters were predisposed to inflate the number of their losses, they frequently omitted mention of the number of government troops and policemen killed by their revolutionary activity. Womack, *Rebellion in Chiapas*, 44.

26. Mexicans were buying flattering dolls of the masked Marcos at the same time that street venders in Mexico City were selling dolls of a bald President Salinas with the body of a bat. Marcos was becoming as much of a legend as Zapata. Wager and Schulz, "Civil-Military Relations in Mexico," 9.

27. Marcos, *Zapatista Stories* (London: Katabasis, 2001). Don Durito de la Lacandona is a beetle reminiscent of Don Quixote de la Mancha. He rides into battle against the forces of neo-liberalism on a turtle. Like Marcos, Durito also smokes a pipe.

28. Rochlin calls them "the planet's premier online guerrilla group." Rochlin, *Vanguard Revolutionaries in Latin America*, 171.

29. Birch and Haar, *Impact of Privatization*, 59. Much of the funding for the *Solidaridad* program came from the sale of state-owned industries. Critics of *Solidaridad* argued that the program was more political that economic. They contended that the program was merely a ploy to placate marginalized groups, such as the Indians in Chiapas, adversely affected by the neo-liberal reforms initiated by Salinas.

30. Roger Burbach, *Globalization and Postmodern Politics: From Zapatistas to High-Tech Robber Barons* (London: Pluto Press, 2001), 121.

31. Wager and Schulz, "Civil-Military Relations in Mexico," 3.

32. James K. Boyce, "Green and Brown? Globalization and the Environment." *Oxford Review of Economic Policy* 20, no. 1 (2004): 106. This change in production also threatens to have an important environmental impact. Since far fewer varieties of corn are produced in the United States, US corn suffers from genetic vulnerability. The cessation of corn farming by thousands of *campesinos* in Chiapas, which has traditionally been one of Mexico's largest corn producers, threatens Mexico's rich biological diversity in corn.

33. Boyce, "Green and Brown?" 113. Before the NAFTA regulations went into effect, one ton of US corn sold for $110 per ton, whereas one ton of Mexican corn sold for $240 per ton. US corn was cheaper because of better soil, more regular rainfall, and a killing frost that reduces insect problems in the United States. In addition, the generous farm subsidies paid to corn growers by the US government gave US corn producers a decisive advantage over Chiapas corn producers.

34. Wager and Schulz, "Civil-Military Relations in Mexico," 6.

35. Womack, *Rebellion in Chiapas*, 268. Four of the demands concerned Indian autonomy.

36. Russell, *The Chiapas Rebellion*, 64–68.

37. Stephen, "Pro-Zapatista and Pro-PRI," 52. Zapata is a central figure in Zapatista press releases.

38. Stephen, "Pro-Zapatista and Pro-PRI," 53.

39. Stephen, "Pro-Zapatista and Pro-PRI," 59–60. This CCRI communiqué was dated 10 April 1994. Whether or not Vo'tan was the creation of EZLN intellectuals or actually part of Tzeltal myth is debated.

40. Bardacke, *Shadows of Tender Fury*, 55.

41. Lynn Stephen, "The Zapatista Army of National Liberation and the National Democratic Convention," *Latin American Perspectives* 22, no. 4 (1995): 92.

42. Zedillo was not the first PRI candidate. PRI candidate Luis Donaldo Colosio was assassinated on 23 March 1994. Zedillo took office as president on 1 December 1994.

43. In reality, what had happened was that pro-Zapatista civilians had declared themselves the municipal heads of 38 municipalities.

44. Tom Hayden, ed., *The Zapatista Reader* (New York: Thunder's Mouth Press, 2002), 398.

45. Womack, *Rebellion in Chiapas*, 304–315. Womack provides the Acuerdos de San Andrés in their entirety. Henceforth, Mexico would be known as a multi-cultural nation rather than a mestizo nation.

46. Womack, *Rebellion in Chiapas*, 319.

47. Stephen, *Zapata Lives*, 331. Zedillo did not think Indians should have special rights, but rather the same rights as everyone else.

48. Womack, *Rebellion in Chiapas*, 56. The 45 Indians who died in the assault were killed by Tzotzil Indians who belonged to a group known as the Red Mask.

49. Hayden, *The Zapatista Reader*, 399.

50. Ironically, the Zapatista caravan was protected by the Mexican army.

51. The Zapatistas opposed Fox's Plan Puebla-Panama, a free-trade zone incorporating southern Mexico and Central America. Fox's plan to economically revive southern Mexico called for dozens of hydro-electric dams, highways, platforms for petroleum extraction, and mines.

Chapter 10

Kurdish Ethnonationalism: A Concise Overview

Mir Zohair Husain and Stephen Shumock

The Kurds—a people located mainly in Turkey, Iraq, and Iran—are the largest ethnic minority without a land of its own. Their struggles for autonomy in their respective countries since the fall of the Ottoman Empire in 1918 have been both diplomatic and military. However, as a people divided by both political borders and terrain features, their struggles have had disappointing results. A comparison between Kurds and Palestinians highlights the difficulties in establishing a recognizable Kurdish identity and putting a face on the Kurdish struggle, and an examination of the plight of Native Americans in North America underscores the differences between the Kurds and other ethnic groups who have attained some degree of autonomy in otherwise dominant nation states. In the current geopolitical climate, Kurds might do well to prioritize their demands as they deal with various nation states, which have marginalized, persecuted, and murdered them in the decades since World War I.

Who Are the Kurds?

The Kurds are mainly located in Turkey, Iraq, and Iran, but are also found in much smaller numbers in Syria, Armenia, Georgia, and Azerbaijan. Conventionally, people are identified by their country of origin or citizenship. However, despite their large numbers and historical presence in the same geographical locations over long periods, the Kurds do not have an independent state of their own, and many people are unaware of them. One of the latest breakdowns of the population distribution of Kurds lists the number of Kurds residing in Turkey as 12.5 to 15 million, in Iraq as 3.5 to 4 million, in Iran as 6 to 7 million, and in Syria as about 1.5 million.[1] The Kurdish population is estimated between 20 and 30 million. The disparity in numbers occurs because host governments often manipulate the population statistics and marginalize Kurdish identity in domestic and international politics. Conversely, Kurds inflate their estimates to attract world attention. Consequently, the figure of 25 million Kurds will be used as a working estimate.

The Kurd-occupied regions, sharing a common language, heritage, and culture, are often referred to as Kurdistan (literally meaning "land of the Kurds"). Since Kurdistan is not a state, it lacks the official boundaries that normally characterize a country. Instead, Kurdistan's borders are loosely defined "in the North by the Aras river in eastern Turkey and on the Iran-USSR border; in the West by the Kara-Su and upper Euphrates rivers in Turkey and Iraq, in the south by the border between mountain country and undulating plains in Iraq, approximately along a Mosul-Kirkuk-Khanaqin line; in the east by a line drawn from Hamadan to Lake Rezaiyeh (Urmia) and Maku, in Iran. The area of Kurdistan thus defined would be c. 135,000 square miles (350,000 square kilometers)." Kurdish residencies are concentrated mainly in the eastern parts of Turkey and Syria as well as in northern Iraq and western Iran.

The Kurds are united by three additional elements: a shared history, a language (Kurdish), and a religion (Sunni Islam). Some historians trace the long, rich, and distinctive lineage of the Kurds either to the Kuti in Sumeria (3000 BCE) or to the Medes of Iran (900 BCE). Most scholars trace them to at least as far back as 612 BCE, and see a hardy and resilient people who have weathered both the Ottoman and Persian empires. Kurdish, a language of Indo-European origins related to the Iranian language of Farsi, is the mother tongue of the Kurds. There are three major Kurdish dialects: *Kurmanji,* the dialect of most Kurds, is the most developed and is spoken in Turkey and the former Soviet Union; *Kurdi* is spoken mainly in Kermanshah in Iran and by some Kurds in Iraq; and *Zaza* is spoken by some Kurds in Iran and Turkey.[2] Additionally, most Kurds share a common religion, since they adopted Sunni Islam with the Arab conquests of their areas in the seventh century.

The largest ethnic minority without a land of its own, most of the world's Kurds live within the confines of Kurdistan, which can be generally defined in geographic terms; nonetheless, the Kurds have been unable to achieve the political currency necessary to realize their state potential. Because they are spread out in several countries, the substantial Kurd population constitutes only large minorities in each of these four states. As a result, the divided Kurds lack not only a state of their own, but also the political influence needed to prevent discrimination against their people.

The Kurds were masters of their own territory until the fall of the Ottoman Empire, when their lands were divided between the newly formed nation-states of Turkey, Iraq, Iran, and Syria. Kurdish loyalties lie first with their families and tribes, rather than a national government, religious affiliation, or any other form of ideology that is usually the unifying factor within a group of people.[3] Due to their loyalties and lack of unifying ideologies, they were left behind by the rising tides of nationalism that so many other peoples used to create independent states.

Today, the Kurds seek recognition as a nation of people with the right to claim a land of their own and the privileges shared by other nations throughout the world. However, they face many obstacles.

Broken Dreams

At the conclusion of World War I and with the collapse of the Turkish Ottoman Empire, the Allied Powers were in a position to return the sovereignty of Kurdistan to the Kurds. In fact, when Great Britain and France were dividing the old Ottoman Empire into new states, they attempted to establish a new Kurdistan under the terms of the Treaty of Sevres, signed on August 10, 1920. The new Kurdistan was to be founded in western Antatolia and the province of Mossul.

However, the treaty was never ratified because of both Turkish nationalism and the Great Powers' interest in the oil reserves of the Middle East. As a consequence of the rebellion and victory of Mustapha Kemal in 1923, the Treaty of Lausanne replaced the Treaty of Sevres. The new treaty abandoned the promise of re-establishing Kurdistan, and instead provided for the establishment of the Republic of Turkey. The Kurds were initially supposed to have a role in the Turkish government; however, they were denied their rights. Then Britain and the League of Nations decided that Kurds would be given a limited amount of autonomy in the newly-formed Iraq, but the other sides did not hold up their end of the deal, and the Kurds were left "homeless" and politically powerless.

Tired of relying on foreign entities to keep their promises, the Kurds took matters into their own hands. They attempted several revolts, most prominently in Turkey, where the largest concentration of Kurds resided. In 1925, 1930, and 1937, they tried to gain their autonomy, only to be brutally beaten back. The countries where the Kurds resided—Afghanistan, Iran, Iraq, and Turkey—decided to form the Saadabad Pact to coordinate their efforts against any Kurdish efforts to undermine their authority and sovereignty.

Finally, the Allied Powers—this time the USSR—granted the Kurds their own territory. In January 1946, following World War II during which Iraq and Iran had been under the Allied Powers' control, the Kurdish Republic of Mahabad was established in Iran with the support of the USSR. However, with the USSR's withdrawal of its troops, the Iranian military brought the Kurdish Republic to an end in December of the same year.

Throughout this period many groups of Kurds in their respective countries attempted to claim their autonomy, if not their own state, by violent revolts rather than relying solely on anyone else to establish Kurdistan for them. From the failure of the Mahabad Republic through contemporary times, host countries have made efforts to oppress the Kurds, and groups of Kurds have in turn attempted numerous revolts in each of these countries.

Turkey

Turkey covers the largest single share of the former Kurdistan and hosts the largest number of Kurds. Turkey is also the most developed of the top five countries with Kurdish inhabitants. These factors have brought Turkey to the forefront of the discussion over the treatment and rights of Kurds. The intertwined history of the Turks and the Kurds reveals much friction between the two parties.

From its creation, Turkish political leaders set out to establish one unified Turkey, with one language, one culture, and one nation. Non-Turkish elements would ideally be absorbed into a dominant Turkish culture. Unfortunately for the Kurds, this meant the exclusion of the Kurdish language from schools and from print media. Turkish residents were not allowed to speak about Kurds as a distinct ethnic people or their oppression under penalty of law. Kurds came to be referred to as "mountain Turks" as the very concept of Kurdish identity and Kurdistan were outlawed and erased from public awareness. While Turkey stopped short of taking the physical lives of the Kurds, they stripped them of everything else that constituted the Kurdish nation's existence.

Additionally, the Turkish nationalists instituted the replacement of the treaty of Sevres with the treaty of Lausanne. These same Turkish nationalists saw to it that all mention of Kurdish autonomy or a Kurdish state was removed from the treaty by barring Kurdish representatives from attending the Lausanne treaty negotiations with the League of Nations Council in 1923.

The Kurds, aware that Turkey would not afford their people the same rights and privileges given to other minority groups, united to strike back against Turkish discrimination with the "Sheikh Said Uprising," which began in February 1925 with the collision between a group led by Sheikh Said and the Turkish forces in the village of Piran. This conflict set off a massive Kurd uprising against the much larger force of Turks. Using the element of surprise, the Kurds drove Turkish officials from the nearby villages and took control of approximately a third of the former lands of Kurdistan within Turkey's borders. They proclaimed the city of Diyarbekir as the capital of the forming "Kurdistan."

However, the advantage of surprise was temporary, and Turkey possessed superior numbers and firepower. Under newly declared martial law, Turkey sent a force of 50,000 into these provinces to re-establish Turkish control. Diyarbekir fell and Sheikh Said was defeated in March of 1925.

Turkish officials attempted to send a clear message to Kurds in an effort to deter any further struggles against Turkish sovereignty. Sheikh Said and 52 of his supporters were publicly hanged in Diyarbekir; villages were destroyed and many of their inhabitants were massacred. In the bloody aftermath, tens of thousands of Kurds were murdered or driven completely into exile. However, despite the hopes of Turkish officials, this was not the end of Kurdish struggles.

A new policy in 1934 precluded the recognition of Kurdish tribes and their officials and authorized Turkey to abolish non-Turkish-speaking villages and transplant their residents to Turkish-speaking ones. In August 1937, Turkish forces attempted to uproot the population and demolish villages in Dersim. The Kurds attempted to fight back; however, their struggles ended a year later in failure with the utter destruction of Dersim and the deaths of approximately 40,000 Kurds. Kurdish uprisings would be greatly deterred for several decades.

In 1978, a group of students at Ankara University established the PKK (*Partiya Karkeren Kurdistan* or Worker's Party of Kurdistan). Despite its name, the PKK was concerned less with Kurdish workers than with launching an independent Kurdistan for Kurds residing in Turkey. Initially, the PKK was characterized by Marxist-Leninist tendencies such as advocating freedom from colonialism and class divisions, but its focus changed as it began to take more violent actions to attain its goal of freeing Kurdistan.

The PKK did not really stand out from various other Kurdish nationalist movements until 1980, when a military coup took place in Turkey. In its aftermath, the PKK was the only organization to endure the fierce crackdowns of the Turkish government. Even then, the PKK was fighting for its own survival. Its leader, Öcalan, had managed to flee to Syria, where he was able to salvage the PKK and recover its potency. With the aid of Palestinians and Syrians, Öcalan trained PKK members in guerilla warfare.

When the PKK was ready to strike again, it began initiating strategic raids from Iraq on military targets in Turkey. Again Turkey sought to disrupt the PKK and organized Kurdish resistance. Turkey conducted air raids and various operations into Iraq to attack PKK camps. Undeterred, PKK continued its operations in Turkey. In response, Turkey's government gathered an armed militia of 65,000—an army of Kurds, not Turks. Neither Turkey nor the PKK would accept disloyalty to their nationalist causes. As a result, tens of thousands of Kurds lost their lives for choosing to support neither the PKK nor Turkey.

In the 1990s, the PKK began shifting its involvement from violence to politics to appeal to a wider audience; it abandoned its Marxist-Leninist doctrines and became more welcoming to Muslims. In an even larger reform, the PKK altered its aim from a sovereign Kurdistan to settling for more autonomy over Kurdish areas. The PKK even attempted to improve its public image and bring international attention to the plight of Kurds in hope that mighty and influential Europe would step in and assist Kurds in securing civil and human rights.

However, this transition took several steps back when the PKK gave up hope of a diplomatic solution with Turkey. The PKK had repeatedly attempted to enter into negotiations with Turkish officials, but Öcalan remained a wanted man for his role in PKK incursions into Turkey. Thus, Öcalan was Turkey's primary concern, and Turkey pressured Syria to expel him. Following his expulsion, Öcalan managed to find temporary havens in several other countries before Turkish operatives finally captured him.

At his trial in Turkey, Öcalan called for PKK members to cease guerilla activities. Some members obeyed, while others, feeling betrayed, ignored the order. Öcalan was found guilty and sentenced to death in 1999, but in 2002 his sentence was commuted to life imprisonment. The PKK was dissolved and Öcalan was elected president of the newly formed Congress for Freedom and Democracy in Kurdistan (KADEK). KADEK aims to assist and protect Kurds through democratic and non-violent channels. However, the organization still has several thousand armed members residing in the Kurdistan portion of Iraq.

Today, Turkey has lifted some of its worst restrictions on Turkish Kurds, due in part to its desire to enter the European Union (EU). The EU frowns upon the Turkish government's treatment of the Kurds, and has made it clear to Turkey that if it truly wants admission, it will have to clean up any human rights issues.

Signs of progress over the last decade include the 1991 repeal of Turkey's law prohibiting public use of Kurdish and the 2002 lifting of prohibitions against the use of Kurdish in television broadcasts. And the concessions have not been all one-sided. Kurds are permitted to hold a wide variety of positions in Turkey's government as long as they identify themselves as Turks, and not by their Kurdish ethnicity. "'Millions of Kurds are totally assimilated into Turkish society.' And, despite an overwhelming desire for greater cultural expression, when asked, many Kurds stop short of seeking independence."[4]

Iraq

Following the Allied Powers failure to establish a new Kurdistan for the Kurds, Britain allocated a large portion of the carved Kurdistan, the province of Mosul, during the creation of the new state of Iraq in December of 1925, making the Kurds an ethnic minority in another country. However, the situation grew much more complicated in 1927 when oil was discovered near Kirkuk in the Mosul province.

The beginnings of the Iraqi-Kurd relations were somewhat foggy. While there were several Kurdish uprisings in the 1920s and 1930s, there were also signs of cooperation. Typically, the Iraqi government included several Kurdish

Ministers and entered into several agreements aimed at giving the Kurds a limited degree of local autonomy. However, such agreements never fully satisfied either of the two parties and were never carried out.

With the Qassem coup of the ruling monarchy in Iraq in 1958, Kurds held out hope for greater autonomy. The new Qassem regime included Kurds in the state's first constitution, thereby guaranteeing their rights. Unlike their counterparts in Turkey, Kurds in Iraq were able to use the Kurdish language in the media and even in educational institutions in predominantly Kurdish-speaking areas. Moreover, a Kurdish leader, Mulla Mustafa Barzani, was permitted to return from his previous exile and allowed to play a role in aiding Qassem in deflecting attempts to overthrow the new regime by Nasserists and Communists.

Barzani had been a leader of the Kurdish struggle in the late 1930s, which led to his imprisonment and exile. He returned briefly in 1943 to lead a new Kurdish rebellion, but returned to Iran around 1946 and was the commander of the short-lived Kurdish Republic of Mahabad's army.

But progress towards greater autonomy for Kurds evaporated and with it, their hopes that had rested with the new regime. By 1960, amidst great unrest, Kurds had been stripped of their constitutional rights and Barzani had fled Baghdad for the Kurdish mountains in preparation for a new wave of Kurdish rebellion that would begin in 1961.

Iraq tried to stop the rebellion, but the Kurds possessed ample resources and were receiving outside assistance from Iran. Military tactics proving unsuccessful, leaders made diplomatic attempts to end the bloodshed. In June 1966, Prime Minister al-Bazzaz laid out a proposal for Kurds. It would provide the Kurds a greater role in Iraqi affairs and a certain level of autonomy in Kurdish provinces, among other concessions. However, Iraqi politics caused the negotiations to be broken off. By 1968, the Kurdish rebellion was back in full swing.

By March 1970, it seemed all the Kurdish hardships were on the verge of paying dividends. The leader of the Ba'th Party, Saddam Hussein, was now in power, and the two sides agreed on a new and even more favorable proposal than that of 1966. The new agreement would give Kurds recognition as members of one of two nations comprising Iraq, as well as greater local authority, unrestricted use of the Kurdish language, a Kurdish region in Northern Iraq, a Kurdish vice-president, and proportional Kurdish representation in the Iraqi government.

While many of the agreed terms were implemented, the Kurdish leader nominated for Vice-President was rejected, and progress was lacking in implementing semi-autonomous rule in Kurdish majority areas. Moreover, there was much disagreement about the terrain to be incorporated under a Kurdish Region, especially in the Mosul and Kirkuk areas. It had been unofficially agreed that majority Kurdish districts in Kirkuk would be decided via census. However, Kurds claimed Iraq was stalling the census in order to take Kurds out and replace them with Arabs. This was a pivotal issue as the proportion of revenue that the Kurdish Region was to receive was being hotly contested, and a majority of Iraq's revenue was directly derived from the oil in the Kurdish Region.

Barzani and his supporters, suspicious of government promises, believed Iraq was intentionally not fulfilling its end of the agreement. At the March 1974 deadline, Iraq began unilaterally fulfilling its part of the agreement. Some of the Kurdish leadership held a benign attitude towards Iraq's actions, though many Kurds who had attained higher authoritative positions in Iraqi government resigned. Once again Kurdish rebellion ignited.

However, there were also those Kurds who tried harder to make the agreement work—including those that were anti-Barzani. With the assistance of these Kurds, a Kurdish Region was established, a Kurdish Vice-President was appointed in April 1974, and by the 1980 and 1984 elections, Kurds held many positions in the Iraqi government, though less than a proportional amount. Those Kurds associated with the rebellion were mercilessly suppressed.

Meanwhile in 1974, the Kurdish rebellion was in stalemate with Iraqi military forces. Following the withdrawal of the Shah of Iran's support to the rebellion as part of an agreement between Iran and Iraq, the Kurdish rebellion finally collapsed. In the wake of the rebellion's defeat, its leader, Barzani, fled to America, where he died in 1979. Approximately 200,000 other refugees fled to Iran. They were eventually granted amnesty and allowed to return to Iraq, but they were forced to reside in majority Arab areas in the southern part of the Kurdish region.

Barzani's sons made several efforts to revive the rebellion in the latter part of the 1970's without much success. However, outside countries bolstered Kurdish rebels in Iraq for their own interests. Syria was rumored to have provided assistance, and with the beginning of the Iran-Iraq War in September of 1980, Iran (led by Khomeini) resumed the assistance it had given to Kurdish rebels in the past. These events served to unify the Kurdish resistance in Iraq. Several previously disagreeing Kurdish factions were able to come to an agreement and the Iraqi-Kurdistan front was established in 1987. The front was comprised of the Kurdish Democratic Party (KDP), the Patriotic Union (PUK), the Kurdistan Popular Democratic Party (KPDP), the Socialist Party of Kurdistan in Iraq, and several other smaller Kurdish organizations. The front set three main goals: (1) defeat the Ba'th regime in Iraq, (2) establish democracy in Iraq, and (3) gain national recognition of Kurds in Iraq.

Iraq sought to quell the uprising in the Kurdish regions in Northern Iraq with numerous military assaults on the Kurds, in which chemical weapons were sometimes employed. The attack on Halabje alone resulted in the deaths of approximately 5,000 Kurds. In consequence of the attacks in 1988, there was another massive fleeing of Kurds, this time into neighboring Turkey. In that same year, Iraq and Iran agreed to a cease-fire, dashing any hopes of a successful Kurdish rebellion in Iraq.

The failure of Iraq's invasion of Kuwait set the stage for another Kurdish uprising. Against the background of American President George Bush's call for

Iraqis to rise up and overthrow Saddam Hussein's Ba'thist regime and Iraqi Shi'as, Kurds made another push to secure their independence in March of 1991. However, following the initial Kurdish successes in gaining control over most of the Kurdish region's major cities, Iraq quickly squashed the Shi'a uprising in southern Iraq and concentrated its forces against the Kurds. The United States decided to abstain from invading Iraq in an effort to avoid entanglement in a civil war and possible diplomatic consequences. Iraq had regained control of the cities it had lost in the Kurdish region by April of 1991.

Consequently, approximately 500,000 Kurdish refugees took flight towards the lands near Turkey's borders, where thousands died due to exposure in the mountainous environment. In a move to prevent the situation from growing even worse—both of Kurdish oppression from Iraq and from the instability such a massive influx of Kurds might create in Turkey—the "no-fly zone" beyond the thirty-sixth parallel was established. The zone, enforced by the United States, Britain, and France, barred any Iraqi aircraft from traversing this line. Further, as part of these rescue efforts, known as Operation Provide Comfort, a large contingent of military personnel and fifty nongovernmental organizations furnished assistance and relief to try to curb the death toll of the refugees.

Military actions having failed, the Kurds turned once again to diplomatic channels. They requested that Iraq's government permit Kurdish autonomy over the Kurdish regions of Iraq. However, negotiations between the two parties quickly fell apart. Iraqi officials asked for much more in concessions than the Kurds were willing to give, such as the disbanding of the Kurdish military forces and forfeiture of all Kurd-controlled radio stations.

Also of concern was the return of friction between the two main parties of the Kurdish government two years after the establishment of a Kurdish government in 1992. In addition to the traditional differences of the two parties, the PUK's leader, Talabani, held ties with Iran and Syria, while the KDP's leader, Barzani, held ties with Iraq and Turkey. A number of conflicts and cease-fires ensued. In the end, Barzani, fearful of losing political influence to the PUK, enlisted Iraq's government and military in efforts to gain control of key Kurdish cities. Talabani fought back and regained most of the cities.

A more effective cease-fire was attained in October of 1996 due in large part to Turkey, the United States, and Britain facilitating negotiations between the parties, though this agreement did not resolve all the issues separating the two parties or lead to their re-unification. However, the Iraqi Kurds as a people have managed to make significant strides despite the apparent schism between political leaders.

The Kurdish Regional Government (KRG) was able to use its 13 percent share of revenue from Iraq's "Oil for Food" program to vastly improve the infrastructure the Iraqi regime had ignored. The results have been astounding. Between 1996 and 2002, infant mortality decreased, 2,600 of the 4,000 villages that were destroyed were rebuilt, and in just Dohuk and Erbil, "410 new schools, 145 health clinics, 3,600 kilometers of new roads…and 90 kilometers of new sewers" have been constructed.[5] However, Iraq's polices of repression have continued with the number of displaced Kurds at almost 1 million in 1999—up from 640,000 five years earlier.[6]

Following the 2004 overthrow of Saddam Hussein's Ba'athist regime and subsequent democratic elections in Iraq, Iraqi Kurds are seeing new possibilities and opportunities. And while the long-term future of this new Iraqi political system is uncertain, Kurds have already begun to make full use of the situation. Kurds in Iraq are making a strong case that if the new Iraq cannot hold together, the Kurdish region in Iraq can. The Kurds are building on their recent success, continuing to strengthen their infrastructure, evaluating the environmental impact of businesses, addressing gender equality issues, and boasting the highest educational standards of any neighboring countries.

Moreover, there is no clear political majority in Iraq. Both Sunni and Shi'a Iraqis comprise very large minorities, but are at odds with each other. Therefore, the door is wide open for the Kurds to use their leverage to be the swing voting bloc in Iraqi policy-making. Hence, over the last ten years, the future has grown ever brighter, though Kurdish optimism remains guarded.

Iran

The experiences of the Kurds in Iran, who comprise about 10 percent of Iran's population, are very symbolic to the overall Kurd struggle for autonomy.[7] The greatest triumph for Kurdish autonomy came in Iran in the form of the short-lived Republic of Mahabad, though efforts for autonomy by Iranian Kurds predate Mahabad. Between 1920 and 1924, for example, the chief of the Shakkak Kurdish tribe, Ismail Agha Simko, took part in the first official Kurdish rebellion, and the tribe was able to overwhelm its neighboring tribe to gain authority of much of the Kurdistan land in Iran. Simko's brief tenure came to an end when the Iranian leader Reza Khan reduced Simko's ranks from 10,000 to about 1,000 by 1924.

Following his surrender, Simko was pardoned and pledged his loyalty to Reza Khan, who had taken the name Reza Shah and become the monarch of Iran. Simko's loyalty lasted until 1926, when he took up another Kurdish rebellion against the Iranian government. This time Simko was imprisoned. Following his subsequent release, Simko was killed in June of 1930, though reports conflict as to whether he died in battle or was assassinated by Iranian forces.

Simko's defeat was the first in many steps by Iran's Reza Shah in repressing Iranian Kurd tribes and their tribal leaders, as well as Iran's other ethnic minorities. Following a model similar to Turkey's, Reza Shah sought to establish a national unity by imposing a singular Persian consciousness on all Iranians. In addition to suppressing all non-Persian identity characteristics, his policies included banning the use of other languages in the media, forbidding other languages in schools, attempting to purge all non-Persian terminology from the Persian vocabulary, and using the term "mountain Iranians" to refer to Kurds.

And while Reza Shah did not go so far as to deny the very existence of Kurds, he did ignore their economic needs by failing to develop their infrastructure. Moreover, Reza Shah used government subsidies to allow his tobacco products to dominate the market, which crippled the Kurds economically as tobacco was their main cash crop.

World War II brought new hope to Iranian Kurds. It was the invasion of Iran by English and Soviet forces on August 25, 1941 that led to the flight of Reza Shah and the establishment of rule in Iran by England and the Soviet Union. This change of events was a welcome opportunity for the repressed Kurds. With Soviet assistance, the autonomous Kurd Republic of Mahabad was founded in 1945.

Kurds were able to make progress in other areas prior to the founding of the Republic of Mahabad. On September 16, 1942, Kurds in Mahabad founded Komala, a committee of Kurds formed to advance the Kurdish self-determination movement. The goal was to establish autonomy of Iranian Kurdistan and ultimately re-found an autonomous Kurdistan with regions in Kurdistan regions [rephrase] in neighboring countries. Komala was successful in gaining support in other key cities beyond Mahabad, such as Sanandaj. Komala's efforts ultimately led to a pact between Turkish, Iraqi, and Iranian Kurds entitled *Peman e Se Senur* (Pact of the Three Borders), perhaps the greatest demonstration of Kurdish unity ever displayed.

Komala was also evolving as an organization. First, in October of 1944, the Sunni religious leader whose father had ties to Simko, Qazi Mohammad, was invited to join in an effort to transcend tribal rivalries. Then in early 1945, Komala attempted to obtain military assistance from the Soviets, who suggested that the Kurds needed a more disciplined political party. In their desire to obtain Soviet assistance, they formed the Kurdish Democratic Party (KDP) in September of 1945.

The decision-making structures of Komala and the KDP were at odds with one another, however. While Komala represented the Kurds' ideal of a democratic organization, the KDP was perceived as an authoritarian organization with Qazi Mohammad as its leader. However, in the end, Kurds fell in line behind the beliefs of Qazi Mohammad, and KDP was one of the principal actors in the establishment of the Republic of Mahabad on January 22, 1946. Qazi Mohammad was elected as its president and many other top leaders of the KDP were its cabinet members.

But the Mahabad was short-lived. The Soviet Union and the Iranian governments began an open dialogue to remedy the rift in their relations. As of May 9th, 1946, Soviet forces had withdrawn from Iran and taken with them the support that kept the Iranian government from actions against the Republic of Mahabad. Iranian forces entered Mahabad on December 17, 1946. Following its downfall, many Mahabad leaders, including Qazi Mohammad, were hanged. Iranian repression returned, barring Kurds from being employed and ruining Kurdish economic infrastructures. The KDP was outlawed. The demolition of

Mahabad and return of Iranian government sovereignty coincided with the return of Reza Shah's power, authority, and policies, including the renewed repression of Iranian tribes and marginalization of non-Persian ethnic minorities. Other forces were also at work in the Iranian political structure. A new organization formed in 1949 known as the National Front was pushing for "the establishment of a strong central government that guaranteed basic freedoms to all Iranians, irrespective of their ethnic or linguistic background."[8] The National Front (NF) was instrumental in the monarch Reza Shah's appointment of Dr. Mohammad Mosaddegh, a leader in the NF and a strong advocate of democratic, free elections, as Iran's prime minister in 1951. Because of his emphasis on democratic rule, many Kurds supported Dr. Mosaddegh.

In 1952, the first elections subsequent to the fall of Mahabad were held, and many of the outlawed KDP's candidates won elections in majority Kurd provinces. However, Reza Shah, with the backing of Iran's military, rejected the election's results and inserted his own people into office in their stead. Moreover, many Kurdish rebellions were taking place in Iran against both the Iranian government and feudal landlords, who were Kurds themselves. Hence it was that Kurdish landlords and the Iranian government teamed up and quelled these rebellions together.

These events led to widespread Kurdish support for Iranian Prime Minister Mosaddegh, but Kurd hopes tied to Dr. Mosaddegh would not last. On August 19, 1953, a U.S.-British sponsored coup resulted in his overthrow. Several Kurd rebellions erupted periodically in the following years, but none were successful, possibly as a result of a perception of greater Kurd inclusion in the Iranian government. The Shah allocated high-level positions in local governments to some Kurdish tribal leaders, and Kurds in the Iranian military attained high-level positions there as well.

This was not the standard of living enjoyed by most Kurds, however, who continued to suffer, especially with higher taxes on Kurd-grown tobacco. The Shah continued to bar non-Persian languages in schools and the media. Thus, while a few of the more elite Kurds were better off under the Shah and apparently gave their allegiance to him, the majority of Kurds were suffering.

Moreover, Reza Shah had been giving assistance to Mullah Mostofa's peshmergas (a Kurdish guerilla group) in their efforts to combat Iraq's Ba'athist party. In 1966, the Shah threatened to cut off support to Mostofa's group unless Kurdish militants in Iran ceased attacking the Iranian government. Weighing this option, Mostofa decided that Iranian Kurds would have to sacrifice their own interests for what seemed like a better opportunity for the Kurds in Iraq. This resulted in major rift between Iraqi and Iranian Kurds, demonstrating the Shah's ability to divide and neutralize Kurdish threats.

Thus, it was between 1978 and 1979 that the biggest event in Iran since World War II occurred—the Iranian Revolution. The majority of Kurds welcomed this change and actively participated in it. Their optimism quickly died with the realization that Iran's new strong, centralized Islamic republic led by

Ayatollah Khomeini would not bring Kurds any closer to their dream of autonomy. Khomeini viewed all Iranians in terms of religion (Muslims) rather than ethnic nationalities (such as Kurds, Arabs, Persians, etc.), so he saw politically autonomous divisions on the grounds of ethnic identity as counterproductive if not totally irrelevant.

Notwithstanding, Iranian Kurds did receive better treatment under the new political system. The country's new constitution kept Persian as the official language of Iran, but other languages were no longer banned from education or the media as long as they were used in some conjunction with Persian. Furthermore, the religious demographic paradigm now being employed meant that Kurds were just as much a part of Iran as any other Muslims.

This was still a far cry from the long-sought Kurdish autonomy. Additionally, new concerns arose among Sunni Kurds. They were worried the Ayatollah would replace Sunni Kurds with Shi'a leaders to further entrench his vision of Iran's Islamic Republic. Tensions mounted quickly between leaders on both sides. One of these Kurdish leaders was Dr. Abdul Rahman Ghassemlou, who returned from exile at the start of the Iranian Revolution to revive the Kurdish Democrat Party in Iran (KDPI) and shape it into the dominant Kurdish political organization. Another, was the Kurdish Sunni leader, Shaikh Ezzedin Husseini. Both sought to secure Kurdish autonomy as an ethnic group within the context of Iran. On the Iranian side, there was Ayatollah Khomeini himself. Moreover, as a result of Husseini's ever-growing influence over Iranian Kurds, the Shi'a leadership in Qom decided to promote Ahmad Moftizadeh, a Kurdish Shi'a cleric, as the authentic Iranian representative for Iranian Kurds.

It was against this backdrop that affiliates of the KDPI won elections in several cities. These affiliates were also supported by anti-Khomeini Kurdish organizations such as the Fadaiyan-e-Klaq (People's Sacrificers), a Marxist-Leninist group that was involved in military conflicts against the new Iranian regime. Khomeini rejected the elections' results and decided that the neo-Marxist Dr. Ghassemlou and the socialist Husseini were trying to undermine the Islamic Republic of Iran. Both were declared to be *mofsid-e fil arz* (corrupters of the earth) and the KDPI was banned.

Several events surrounding the new Iran's Prime Minister, Mehdi Bazargan, further illustrate the contrast between simultaneous Kurdish gains and setbacks under the new political system. His first cabinet included two prominent Kurds. The first, Dr. Karim Sanjabi, was a leader of the National Front and was appointed as foreign minister. The second, Dariush Foruhar, was another well-respected Kurd and was given the labor portfolio. Furthermore, on February 14th, 1979, Bazargan sent a delegation spear-headed by Foruhar to commence a dialogue with Kurd officials over Kurdish demands for autonomy.

However, being only the prime minister of Iran, Bazargan could not assure delivery on any promises, and Kurds were not given any specific details on what an autonomous Kurdish government would entail. These events led to an increase in conflicts between the Iranian forces (*pasdarans*—Iran's new military group, the Revolutionary Guards) and KDPI forces (*peshmergas*—a Kurdish guerilla group of militants). Following the victory of Iranian forces, Shaikh Sadeq Khalkhali presided over the trials of Kurdish militants and KDPI sympathizers. "The hanging judge," as Khalkhali became known, ordered the execution of hundreds of Kurds.

Finally, a highly respected Iranian religious leader and advocate of civil rights, Ayatollah Taleghani, stepped forward to act as an intermediary between Kurds and the Iranian government. On March 24th, 1979, his intervention facilitated an agreement whereby Kurds would be given limited autonomy. Under this agreement, both Kurdish and Persian would be taught in educational institutions, Kurdish officials would have authority over local government and economical issues, and Kurds would participate in drafting the new constitution for Iran. The Iranian government was to receive Kurdish support for an Islamic state and Kurdish participation in the upcoming referendum on Iran's constitution. However, as more extreme individuals began to pressure the KDPI and doubt Iran's sincerity in their part of the agreement, the agreement fell apart and conflict re-erupted.

The fighting would not persist, however. By early September 1979, Iranian forces had gained control over all the major cities in Kurdish regions from Kurdish insurgents. Yet the *peshmergas* were able to survive with the assistance of Saddam Hussein near the Iraqi border. These events culminated in another attempted negotiation between both sides on August 26th, 1979. The Kurds asked for the removal of Shaikh Sadeq Khalkhali from Kurdish regions, the cessation of Kurd executions, the replacement of non-Kurdish *pasadarans* with Kurds in Kurdish regions, a cease-fire, and another discussion of Kurdish autonomy within the context of a sovereign Iran.

Ayatollah Khomeini refused to accept any such demands as long as armed Kurdish resistance continued against his Iranian regime. So, on September 3rd, 1979, Prime Minister Bazargan tried to step in and offer concessions contingent on Kurdish compliances and an end to armed conflict. But, once again, being only the Prime Minister of Iran, Bazargan lacked the power necessary to broker a peaceful settlement with the Kurds. In the end, Ayatollah Khomeini rejected any demands made by the Kurds.

In February 1980, Ghassemlou approached the newly elected Bani-Sadr with another Kurdish autonomy proposal. President Bani-Sadr seemed to be open to Kurdish demands, but he made the stipulation that no settlement would be brokered until Kurds disarmed. Ghassemlou reiterated that the Kurds would disarm, but only after a settlement had been reached. Hence, conflict between both sides renewed.

Another long-standing hurdle for the Kurds has been their difficulty in explaining what Kurdish autonomy actually entailed. Part of the problem was one of definition. In the Persian language, the word for autonomy entails the total independence that can only be attained outside of another independent state (that is, a group would have to secede from Iran to be autonomous under this definition). However, the Kurds always insisted on not desiring secession, though their continued use of the word "autonomy" was a source of confusion.

Thus, the Iranian government viewed Kurdish actions following the Iraqi invasion of Iran in September of 1980 with suspicion. The KDPI sought military assistance from invading Iraq, consequently leading Iran to conclude that previous Kurdish declarations of autonomy within the context of a sovereign Iran were attempts to be misleading.

The KDPI would take another hit with the assassination of Dr. Ghassemlou on July 13th, 1989. His death contributed to the decline of the KDPI and the emergence of Komala as the dominant Kurdish political organization in Iran. However, Komala has not been very effective militarily or politically, in part because of continuing conflicts between their and the KDPI's *peshmergas*. Moreover, Komala's vision of Kurdish autonomy is viewed as unrealistic and utopian. Therefore, even though Komala was able to dominate KDPI in the area of membership, it has not been an effective vehicle for Kurdish interests.

Today, Kurds continue to participate in Iran's Majlis, or national legislative body, but Kurdish government representatives continue to be undermined. "The Council of Guardians, for example, regularly prohibits the candidacy of ethnic Kurdish representatives who seek to use the political system to address local concerns. Other Kurdish politicians are eliminated based upon the alleged activities of their relatives. In March 2002, all six Majlis deputies from Kurdistan province resigned in protest of 'discrimination against Kurd and Sunni minorities.'"[9] Hence, Iranian Kurds are still being marginalized and repressed, despite a promise of "political participation."

Syria

Kurds in Syria comprise approximately eight percent of its total population. Most Kurds are geographically located in the northeast Jazira region of the country along the Turkish and Iraqi borders.[10] Their presence in Syria is largely due to a failed Kurdish revolt in Turkey in 1925.

Following the example of Iraqi Kurds, Syrian Kurds established their own Kurdish Democratic Party (KDP) in 1957. Like other Kurdish organizations, the KDP's mission was to attain national recognition of Kurds as a distinct ethnic group with its own unique culture. However, the KDP faced an uphill climb from the start. Beginning in 1958, the government repressed the KDP and banned the publication of any materials in Kurdish. In 1962, a census of the Jazira region stripped 120,000 Kurds of their Syrian national affiliation.

Then in 1963, when the Ba'ath Party came to power through a coup d'etat, Kurds faced increased discrimination. Many Kurds were expelled and thousands more were stripped of their Syrian national affiliation. Moreover, Syria's and Iraq's Ba'ath parties joined together in an effort to neutralize any potential threat from the Kurds. So when oil was discovered in the Jazira region, Syria accelerated its policy of Arabization (transplanting Kurds from predominantly Kurdish populated areas to Arab populated ones, and replacing them with Arab Syrians). By 1971, approximately 30,000 Kurds had been transplanted from the Jazira region.

Syria has differed from Iraq in one important regard. While both Ba'ath parties were of Arab nationalist orientation and had little tolerance for non-Arabs, Syria was dominated by a religious minority, the Alawites. However, this has not brought about the restoration of citizenship to those Kurds who had it stripped away during the 1962 census. Consequently, nearly a quarter million in number now, Syrian Kurds have for the last four decades been "prohibited from owning land, legally marrying, receiving an education...[and] cannot even enter a public hospital..."[11]

Overall, compared to Kurds in Turkey, Iraq, or Iran, Syrian Kurds have been less influential and sparked far fewer secessionist movements, so more concentration is placed on the situations in Turkey, Iraq, and Iran.

The Kurds, Palestinians, and Native Americans Compared

With as many as five thousand ethnic groups in today's world and 261 minority groups facing discrimination, it is natural for one to compare the plight and goals of the Kurds to other ethnic groups in similar situations.[12] Two such groups are the Palestinians and Native American Indians. The Palestinians reside in the same global region as the Kurds (the Middle East), are an ethnic minority in their country of residence (Israel), are in the midst of often violent conflicts with the government and people of their country of residence (Israel and Israelis), and are struggling to regain their historical homeland (Palestine) over which they no longer have sovereignty. Also, while the Palestinians do have relatively more autonomy than the Kurds, they are constantly pursuing total autonomy. On the other hand, the Native American Indians are an ethnic minority in their country of residence (the United States), were in many often violent conflicts with the government and people of their country of residence (the United States and Americans), and struggled to regain their historic homelands (America) over which they no longer have sovereignty. However, in this ethnic conflict, the Native Americans gained that which Kurds desire most (autonomy), and they have been able to maintain it.

As has already been illustrated, the Kurds face both internal and external barriers to total autonomy and the re-founding of a Kurdistan for modern Kurds. Similarly, the Palestinians have also had to face numerous such obstacles. Therefore, two major questions arise: (1) Why has the plight of the Palestinians garnered so much more international sympathy and attention than that of the Kurds? (2) Why have the Palestinians seemingly been more successful in their pursuit of an autonomous land? The answer to both questions is essentially a matter of the different levels of unity between the two groups. On the whole, the Palestinians have been able to unite more successfully and form strong bonds among themselves throughout their turbulent confrontations with Israel. This united front allowed Yasir Arafat to become the human face of the struggles of his people, which helped them to garner sympathy from the world. Moreover, their unity has allowed all Palestinians to rally behind one common goal—the re-establishment of Palestine. Thus other peoples can clearly understand who the Palestinians are, what their plight is, and what it is specifically that they desire.

This clarity has typically been lacking in the case of the Kurds. The unique internal and external problems they face have precluded the world from understanding the key elements of their struggle. The Kurds' struggle is not tied to one nation, border, oppressor, or even political history, and Kurds as a people are harder for the world to identify for all the reasons discussed previously. There is no single Kurdish political representative, and therefore no face for people to associate with the Kurds. Certainly, then, there is a much clearer and simpler understanding of Palestinian identity.

The world knows the Palestinians want their homeland, and they know exactly where it is located and with whom the Palestinians are struggling to gain control over it. The Kurd's Kurdistan, however, is loosely defined and is spread over at least six countries. Unlike the Palestinians, Kurds cannot point to one person or nation as being the "culprit" responsible for barring them from their homeland. For this reason, it is difficult for the world to put a face on their adversary, whereas the Palestinians have a face not only for themselves but also for their opponents. Thus, for the Kurds, there are many generalities and complexities resulting in an extremely difficult story for people to become emotionally invested in.

As with the answer to the first question, the reason for the greater Palestinian success in their pursuit of a land of their own has a lot to do with unity—in this case, the common vision that maintains a united Palestinian people. While it is true that the Kurds, like the Palestinians, share a common vision of an autonomous ethnic homeland, the bonds shared by Palestinians go much further. Conversely, the differences between Kurds outweigh what they have in common. Hence, the Kurds fail to attain the overall unity that is a characteristic of the Palestinians. Internally, with the three main forms of the Kurdish language all being different, Kurds face a barrier that makes just communicating with all parties difficult, whereas most Palestinians speak Arabic. Kurds feel greater allegiance to their tribes and families than to the ideology of a united Kurdish ethnic group, and the cultural barriers between different tribes within and between countries facilitate divergent interests that preclude all Kurds uniting to lay claim to Kurdistan. Conversely, Palestinians and their families remain firmly united behind the shared ideology of their beloved Palestine.

Palestinians not only have a common language and vision, but also possess allegiance first and foremost to the plight of their people as a whole. Hence, while 10 million Palestinians spread all over the world do not have the numbers that the Kurds have, they have had the ability to overcome any differences they

if something! / someone could rally the Kurds, it would be hard to fight them.

may have had between themselves, thus presenting the world with a united and more forceful front.

Externally, even tougher, if not insurmountable, barriers challenge the Kurds. To begin with, they must overcome the geographic borders of the sovereign states in which they reside. Overcoming one such border dispute with a single country (such as the Palestinians must do with Israel) is an arduous enough task, but having to overcome several (such as the Kurds must do with Turkey, Iraq, Iran, and Syria) just does not seem reasonable. Such actions would entail individual Kurdish struggles for independence occurring simultaneously in all their different countries of residence. So, while the Kurds may have a large population size overall, the Kurds are too divided to succeed in all the struggles necessary to geographically reunite their historic homeland of Kurdistan. Also, Kurds face different types of discrimination in each country in which they reside. As a result, while the Kurds do have inequality and discrimination in common, the efficacy of using them as rallying points in enjoining Kurdish unity is diluted.

In contrast, the Palestinians are all in the same country, even if it is in different sections of Israel, and Israel itself is much smaller geographically than any one of the countries Kurds reside in, much less all of them together. Moreover, Palestinians do not have mountainous terrain to deal with. Finally, all Palestinians suffer from the same discriminatory policies at the hands of a common government and people, so they all have the same objectives and adversaries to unify their people. Hence, the above problems facing the Kurds differ from those of the Palestinians, and while these Kurdish problems serve only to hinder any hope of the re-establishment of Kurdistan, at least Palestinian problems can serve as a force for keeping their unity intact. It should also be remembered that Kurdish differences amongst themselves are so profound that during the time of an obvious threat from Saddam Hussein, and while under the protection of the "no-fly zone," Kurds were not able to avoid falling into an internal civil war.[13]

Kurds have often promoted the solution of Kurdish autonomy within the regions of the countries where they reside. One such example of an ethnic minority that has successfully gained autonomy within a nation is the American Indians (also referred to as Native Americans), who live on reservations in the United States. At first glance, it would seem that both situations are very similar, and one may perhaps mistakenly believe a similar autonomous solution could also work for the Kurds. After all, both the Kurds and Indians were heavily suppressed and in many cases were moved off their land when it was seen as valuable to the government (or people) in power. Both were promised land only to have those promises broken. Moreover, there were violent conflicts in which many of these ethnic minorities were killed over the historic lands they felt should remain theirs. But despite the argument that an autonomous ethnic group and a sovereign country can co-exist, Kurdish autonomy is not a realistic solution, at least not in the foreseeable future.

There are key differences between the situations of the Kurds and the American Indians. The Indians were moved every time it was discovered that the land they were on had valuable resources, so that, in the end, their reservations were located on undesirable land. But in Iraq and Syria, the land the Kurds call their home contains great natural resources, especially oil, that the respective governments will not give up. Therefore, the regions where they are now located would not be permitted to be autonomous Kurdish "reservations." But, since the Kurds do not want to give up these resources, they do not want to move. Another difference is that the Indians did not get their reservations until there was public sympathy for the many wrongs that had been visited upon them, and even then, as previously noted, they were not given the best lands for their reservations. There is no such public sentiment, displayed or otherwise, for the Kurds in any of their countries of residence. So, these countries have no motivation to concede autonomy to the Kurds on such a basis. One other difference of note is that when the reservations were established, the Indians were relatively poor, so the United States had very little to lose in the way of tax revenues. In contrast, the Kurds' host countries rely heavily on their tax revenues. In fact, it is a point of contention with Kurds that they are often taxed more heavily than other citizens of the same country, and/or receive less in expenditures derived from taxes in proportion to other, non-Kurdish, regions. So, for these three reasons alone, it can reasonably be argued that the Indian reservation model for autonomy within a state maintaining national sovereignty will not work in the case of the Kurds.

Certainly, there are many other comparisons that could be made, but the main point is that the difficulties facing the Kurds are unique. One may be able to draw similarities with others; however, the key differences drawn out with the two comparisons above demonstrate that the Kurds' situation requires unique courses of action. While certain policies and programs may assist more than one group of Kurds, each group in its respective country will probably find resolution of the ills it faces through different means.

Outlook

Given the unique situation of the Kurds as a people, any potential solutions to their problems and persecutions will involve difficulties. As previously illustrated, the Kurds face both internal and external obstacles to total autonomy and the re-founding of a modern Kurdistan. These obstacles may be too numerous to overcome. Therefore, more moderate solutions within the framework of existing nation-states, aiming to decrease the number of violent and non-violent conflicts involving the Kurds, are probably the best option, though even these would take time to phase in. At this point, any notion of an overnight solution to end all such conflicts would be unrealistic.

The outcome Kurds would probably most hope for is the re-establishment of their historic Kurdistan. However, because of the difficulties elaborated above in the comparison with the Palestinians, the Kurds must abandon, at least for the moment, their dream of the old Kurdistan as a homeland for all Kurds, with its previous boundaries and Kurdish sovereignty. This dream fails to take into account the reality of their situation as a divided people, as well as the status of state sovereignty in today's global and geopolitical environment.

Another welcome outcome may be just as impossible, and this is the hope that foreign countries or organizations might intervene on their behalf for full citizenship. While it is true that Operation Provide Comfort's "no-fly zone" was enforced by foreign countries in an attempt to offer some relief to the Kurds in Iraq, this effort was not totally successful, and was a humanitarian mission mainly intended to provide sustenance to the Kurds, rather than to promote their advancement as a people. It is true that some acts taken against Kurds in Iraq and Iran may qualify as genocide. However, as in Rwanda and Bosnia, foreign countries and organizations are wary of intervening in such cases, so Kurds should not rely on these entities to come to their rescue. Moreover, foreign countries and organizations have failed at every historical opportunity to be successful in this regard. There have been key moments in history (such as the time following World War I) when foreign powers could have provided the Kurds with autonomy and a homeland of their own. However, it seems now that any real and viable solution will require much of the "heavy lifting" to be done by the Kurds themselves, and will involve patience with smaller changes over a relatively longer period of time.

Then again, employing violence has historically not gotten the Kurds any closer to their goal of autonomy. Sporadically, and with the aid of diplomatic negotiations, they have made progress by gaining promises of greater self-rule, but these gains slipped away with time. Furthermore, what all Kurds ultimately want is the right to continue their way of life and to flourish in it; however, they cannot achieve this end under the threat of military action and government-initiated discriminatory policies. The most important step in attaining the former is to best secure against the latter—thus, acquiring the same recognition and rights of other national citizens is a prerequisite to achieving any Kurdish goals. After all, even if the Kurds were somehow able to secede and establish their Kurdistan, in order to be an economically, politically, and militarily viable state, Kurds would need their neighbors (the states they just seceded from) to recognize them with the same respect and dignity as their own citizens. Therefore, attaining equal recognition prior to secession must be the priority.

Today, the Kurds have good opportunities to make gains in Turkey, Iraq, and Iran; they simply need to identify and seize them. Turkish-Kurds are presented with the strong desire of Turkey to join the European Union (EU); Iraqi-Kurds are presented with the two other major factions in Iraq, Sunnis and Shi'as, not having the majority necessary to impose their policies without the assistance of the Kurds; and despite such significant developments in Iran, Iranian-Kurds have plenty in common with Iranian-Arabs. Each Kurd situation will have both shared and unique parts in their paths to conflict resolution.

Kurds, especially in Iraq and Iran, have been able to bring the governments of their respective countries to the bargaining table, although they often doubt the sincerity of the concessions they have received. This skepticism is understandable given the history of broken promises experienced by the Kurds as a people. However, in order for real negotiations to take place, the parties involved will have to trust each other. Hence, early concessions should be small. Historically, negotiations involved discussions to end the entire conflict between the respective parties in a single, broad agreement. The results have been disappointing at best. Smaller and less significant agreements should be used as springboards to building the essential trust for the larger concessions sought by all parties involved.

First, Turkey's urgent desire to join the EU is a great advantage to Turkish-Kurds. To gain entry into the EU, Turkey needs to change its reputation among EU members for suppressing Kurds, and clearly Kurds need that suppression to stop. However, Turkey has remained almost blindly preoccupied with forging a single Turkish identity, while the Kurds have been struggling to save their own identity.

This is precisely where a compromise is necessary; however, it may not be as major as both sides make it out to be. If Kurds want the same rights and treatment as other Turkish citizens, then they should accept their nationality as Turkish. This is not a major concession, since nationality and ethnicity are not the same, although they are sometimes misconstrued. For instance, in the United States, many employ the ethnic term "black" and the nationalistic term "African-American" interchangeably. However, this is not an entirely correct usage, since a person may be a "black" in America and not be from Africa, and conversely, a person may be in America and from Africa, but not be "black." Hence, if Kurds live in Turkey and enjoy Turkish citizenship, then by definition (operationally and contextually), they are Turkish in nationality. At the same time, Kurds would be permitted to keep their ethnic identity and language. This premise is not any more contradictory than the concept of federalism. Under federalism, the local and federal governments do not always agree, but the national one speaks for the state as a whole, while the local government makes some of its own decisions tailored for that local community.

Although not a perfect solution for either side, this compromise would improve the situation of both. Certainly, Turkey will not be completely satisfied without a homogenous identity, and Kurds will not be completely satisfied without autonomy However, each side must make hard choices about its priorities. In this scenario, both sides make concessions to gain something they really crave. The question that each side must answer is what it desires more: Does Turkey desire a completely homogenous identity more than entry into the EU? Do Kurds desire complete autonomy more than an end to the suppression of their ethnic identity?

Second, in Iraq, with no Shi'a or Sunni majority, the Kurds suddenly find themselves in the position of having the political swing voting bloc desired by both parties. However, given the past treatment of Kurds by Sunni-dominated regimes, Kurds will probably side much more often with Shi'as. However, a majority of Kurds are Sunni; therefore, political affiliations of today will not necessarily be maintained in the long run.

Third, in Iran, there is not the same kind of "new" opportunity that has been developed. However, more so than in other countries, Iranian-Kurds have plenty in common with Iranian-Arabs. Iranian-Arabs are the descendants of Persians, while Kurdish is a cousin of the Persian language. Moreover, there has not been the level of secessionist tendencies by Kurds in Iran compared to their neighboring brethren. This is because Kurds have been relatively more integrated into Iran than have Kurds in Turkey and Iraq. Also, many Iranian-Kurds in the Kermanshah region are Shi'a Muslims like most other Iranians, not Sunni-Muslims. Additionally, on more than one occasion, there have been officials (albeit often without the power to close such a deal) in Iran who have demonstrated the willingness to negotiate with Iranian Kurds and give the concessions sought. One of the largest sticking points has been on the issue of Kurdish autonomy, which is why this should not be considered as the first step in negotiations or part of an "all or nothing" bargaining ploy.

These are just the more obvious examples of how Kurds in all three of these states have opportunities to make gains, but both sides might need to give up on hard-line stances to make such gains. Two areas where both sides in these states will need to work to make real long-term progress in decreasing conflict are in emphasizing integration over assimilation and de-emphasizing marginalization and replacing it with societal incorporation. Both issues are major points of tension. However, in order to decrease conflicts, it is essential to remove those sources of conflict. As Dr. Nader Entessar points out in *Kurdish Ethnonationalism,* the removal of assimilationist policies and disproportional representation would actually be in the long-term benefit of both parties.

Overall, while assimilation has been a cause of resistance, integration efforts may not have the same outcome. In fact, it is possible for these states to not only influence the Kurds, but also to integrate them into their societal fabrics. One needs to look no further than Iran for evidence. In the Kermanshah region of Iran, where a majority of Muslims are of the Shi'a sect, a majority of the normally Sunni Kurds are in fact Shi'a. Furthermore, Kurds have traditionally utilized a tribal governing structure. And while that structure does still have substantial influence, Kurds who have been able to participate in government structures of their countries of residence have adapted to working as successfully in those systems as the parties in power have allowed them to be. The same is true economically as well.

The key is that the country must attempt to integrate rather than assimilate Kurds. Both seek to unify the people of a country; however, while assimilation does so through much more destructive means and tries to force change all at once, integration moves at a much slower pace. Moreover, integration works by allowing the "foreign" culture to find its own niche within the dominant one, a subtler and less destructive approach.

Another change that could improve the situation and decrease conflict in all three of these countries is decreasing or eliminating disproportional representation. However, proportional representation by itself is not sufficient. It must be done in the context of a larger state policy of societal incorporation whereby Kurds are integrated into the society as a whole. This would ease tensions in two very significant ways. First, it would assist in relieving the sense of deprivation pervasive throughout the Kurd population. Second, it would make Kurds feel more included, help them realize they have a stake in the country's national interests, and encourage greater loyalty to the states that they reside in.[14]

However, proportional representation by itself is insufficient. Without societal integration, eventually Kurds would realize that their daily life and the treatment they receive have not really changed. The reason is that Kurds are an ethnic minority in every country they reside in, so any political representation based on numbers will be unable to change the political, economical, or social systems of an entire nation. For example, under Reza Shah in Iran, even if Kurds had control over local economic and political policies, the subsidies to the Shah's own tobacco and the increased taxation of the Kurds' would still have resulted in poor economic conditions. In Turkey, Kurds would have a voice, but it would be the voice of a "mountain Turk" and not a Kurd. So, proportional representation means nothing without real changes in the treatment of Kurds.

Proportional representation does not solve the real root problem faced by Kurds, as their representatives are still not in a position to fix the underlying problem of inequality. All that proportional representation fixes, is disproportional representation—one of many forms of inequality. Therefore, as alluded to earlier, there is only one authentic solution to the problems faced by Kurds and that is recognition, respect, and rights afforded equally with the other citizens of each respective country. This does not necessarily entail the state guaranteeing cultural rights and freedoms. What it does entail is if a state says all their people are the same in the eyes of the state (all Turks, all Muslims, all Iraqis, etc.) then the state cannot discriminate against an ethnic group without violating its own ideology.

Kurds in each country must start with small changes, and those changes will not necessarily be the same in each country. So, demanding wholesale affirmative action is unrealistic. Rather, Kurds should begin by asking for decreases in discrimination and repression, one part of which would be proportional representation.

Therefore, the real battle here is to convince these regimes in power that it is in their best national interest to provide proportional representation and otherwise incorporate Kurds into the fabric of their societies. Aside from the benefits just listed, these countries need to realize the benefit in reduced expenditures for maintaining this marginalization and countering the conflicts that periodi-

cally erupt between themselves and the Kurds. Moreover, such domestic instability hurts economic development prospects hinging on greater foreign direct
investment of companies. These continuing ethnic conflicts are also detrimental
to the national interests of the state. So at best, in their efforts to protect their
national interests, such states are really only attaining one national security
agenda item at the cost of others.

Moreover, the worst fear of all the states in question comes in the form of a
"Kurdish snowball effect." These states fear that if any one of the groups of
Kurds in another country succeeds in seceding from their respective country of
residence, other Kurds in their countries may attempt to follow suit. This was
the case in Turkey prior to the United States initiative of regime change in Iraq
in 2004. Turkey was concerned that, with the collapse of Saddam Hussein's
Ba'athist regime, Kurds in Turkey and Iraq might attempt to unite and form their
own independent and autonomous "Kurdistan." Therefore, it would seem that
the states in question should recognize it as in their best national interests to
seize an opportunity to preclude this threat through compromise.

These are the reasons that programs such as proportional representation and
participation seem like such a win-win scenario for all the parties involved. Both
sides need to be able to look beyond their immediate personal/national interests.
Kurds must abandon their long-standing demand for immediate and complete
self-determination. The countries must abandon their tactics of marginalization
and discrimination. If both sides are able to look at their long-term per-
sonal/national interests, then they will also need to be willing to compromise at
their respective bargaining tables. They must abandon their hard-line stances
and learn compromise.

Despite their understandable lack of trust in governmental promises, Kurds
need to take initiative and use any amount of leverage they have while they still
have it. After all, their experience tells them no one else is going to do it for
them. And, although they have historically been proud warriors, the Kurds must
allow the state to "save face" for the sake of diplomacy. The Kurds should convince their states that their inclusion serves to further the national interests and
does not hinder or detract from them. First, though, they must build a consensus
among the traditionally disagreeing tribes.

The first step would be to find something the tribal and political leaders can
agree on, such as how they believe Kurds should be treated by their national and
local governments. This would facilitate an agreement on a minimum standard
even if they were still unable to agree on an overall goal or direction. Such a
consensus and actions taken on that consensus would at least plant the seed for
cooperation among the tribes and leaders in the future.

In conclusion, Iraq and Turkey clearly represent the best opportunities for
Kurdish improvements, with Iran also on the horizon. Moreover, even if the two
sides in each country are able to find a solution to the current conflict, changes
should be implemented over an extended time period. For, while both sides
would like a quick resolution to these matters, moving slowly would give the

people time to adjust to a changing environment and allow any missteps made along the way to be corrected without necessarily having to go all the way back to square one. The Kurds are people of a rich and lengthy history. Therefore, it seems almost appropriate that they have such significant roles in so many different countries.

Notes

1. "Rebellion in the Mountains," *Canada and the World Backgrounder* 69, no. i.2 (October 2003): S18–22.

2. Nader Entessar, *Kurdish Ethnonationalism* (Lynne Rienner Publishers: Boulder & London, 1992), 4–5.

3. "25 Million in Search of a Home," *Swiss News,* January 2003.

4. Michael Rubin, "Are Kurds a Pariah Minority?" *Social Research* 70, no. i.1 (Spring 2003), 295–231.

5. Rubin. "Are Kurds a Pariah Minority?"

6. Rubin. "Are Kurds a Pariah Minority?"

7. "Rebellion in the Mountains."

8. Entessar,*Kurdish Ethnonationalism*, 25.

9. Rubin. "Are Kurds a Pariah Minority?"

10. Michael Collins Dunn, "The Kurdish 'Question:' Is There an Answer?" A Historical Overview," *Middle East Policy* 4, no. 1–2 (September 1995): 72–86.

11. Rubin. "Are Kurds a Pariah Minority?"

12. Entessar,*Kurdish Ethnonationalism*, 161.

13. Dunn, "The Kurdish 'Question's There an Answer?"

14. Dunn, "The Kurdish 'Question's There an Answer?," 169.

Chapter 11

The Roots of Contemporary Ethnic Conflict and Violence in Burundi

Johnson W. Makoba and Elavie Ndura

Though understudied and overshadowed by the genocide that occurred in neighboring Rwanda in 1994, ethnic conflict and violence in Burundi (which began soon after independence in 1962) has claimed thousands of lives and is currently threatening to unleash genocide. Burundi's colonial, post-colonial and contemporary experiences are characterized by a legacy of Tutsi-Hutu hatred and violence. There are three ethnic groups in Burundi-Hutu (85 percent), Tutsi (14 percent) and Twa (1 percent). However, the most powerful ethnic groups and the focus of this chapter are Tutsi and Hutu. In this chapter, we explore the historical and socio-cultural roots of the ethnic conflict that has locked the Hutu and Tutsi into an endless and destructive cycle of violence. Furthermore, we analyze the socio-political and socio-cultural patterns that characterize the Hutu-Tutsi coexistence throughout the pre-colonial, colonial, post colonial and contemporary eras in order to develop greater understanding of the complex Hutu-Tutsi discord. This perspective is enhanced with one of the co-authors' personal anecdotes drawn from real life experiences as a Burundian native who was born, raised, and educated in Burundi. Three major questions drive the discussion in this chapter. How did the Hutu and Tutsi ethnic identifications develop in Burundi? What have been the long-lasting consequences of the ethnicized discourse in Burundi and the Great Lakes region of Africa? And, what are the prospects for ending ethnic conflict and violence in Burundi?

The colonial, postcolonial and contemporary history of Burundi has been characterized by a legacy of Tutsi-Hutu hatred, violence and selective genocide. From independence in 1962 to the present, the political history of Burundi has been characterized by ethnic conflict and violence with a great potential for genocide. Although the contemporary ethnic violence in Burundi is traced to 1993, when the first popularly elected Hutu President was assassinated in a Tutsi-led coup d'état, we argue that the Tutsi-Hutu conflict dates back to the colonial period and has intensified ever since. The continuing ethnic conflict is fueled by a power struggle between the Tutsi and Hutu for the control of political power and access to economic resources and privileges. Tutsi-Hutu dominant-subordinate relations engender resentment by the Hutu majority who feel both excluded or deprived and repressed. It is argued that the Tutsi-Hutu conflict is political rather than ethnic. The failure of several peace-initiatives (both from within and outside Burundi) over the years underscores the complexity of the conflict as well as the widespread and deep-rooted distrust or suspicion of Hutus and Tutsis toward each other. And efforts aimed at seeking a political compromise under such suspicious circumstances are doomed to fail as they are often perceived as betrayal by either side.

The Pre-Colonial Era

The pre-colonial Burundian people are considered to have been a peaceful people. According to Ndura, "Burundi's peaceful history is reflected in the culture of sharing and self-help that has molded the strong family and community bonds that characterize the Burundian way of life across ethnic groups."[1] Historically, the Tutsi and Hutu in Burundi have intermarried and coexisted peacefully. Due to the intermarriages and other cross-cutting ties, ordinary Tutsi and Hutu were largely on equal social footing. This rendered Tutsi-Hutu distinctions on the basis of ethnicity, feudal power relations, or socioeconomic status difficult to make.

Tutsi ruled the Hutus for nearly four hundred years.[2] Over this period, there was considerable conflict, even warfare—especially, due to competition or power struggle within the ruling Tutsi/Ganwa Clan (i.e. between King and minor nobility). Overall, traditional Burundian Society (though characterized by feudal Tutsi-Hutu power relations) was free of social tension or conflict. However, when potential for ethnic violence in the society emerged it was often directed against external enemies or was quickly resolved by the *Ganwa* political (ruling) class. The role of the *Ganwa* ruling class in Burundi as the intermediary between Hutu and Tutsi continued throughout much of the colonial era. It is noted that "unlike the situation in Rwanda... the potential for conflict between Hutu and Tutsi was contained by the existence of *Ganwa*, an intermediate princely class between the Mwami (King) and the population."[3] In addition to being farmers, "... the Hutus did menial jobs in the traditional [European] feudal-type structure of Lord and Serf."[4] On the other hand, Tutsis were pastoralists and firmly established themselves as the dominant minority group or ruling elite. In particular, the minority Tutsi elite regarded themselves as "an elite... ruling the Hutus—politically, socially, and economically—in a firm, stratified society."[5] The Tutsi who were in control of political power during the pre-colonial era remained in power during the colonial and postcolonial periods. As noted previously, Tutsi hegemony in Burundi throughout the pre-colonial era never contributed to ethnic violence between Tutsi and Hutu. However, racist Belgian colonial policies and practices prepared ground for ethnic violence in Burundi and Rwanda during and after colonial rule to the present.

The Colonial Era

Initially, German and later, Belgian colonial governments used "indirect rule" to govern what was then called Rwanda-Urundi. Both colonial governments, recognizing the feudal structure in place decided to govern Rwanda-Urundi through the existing traditional political structures of authority controlled by the minority Tutsi elites. Use of colonial indirect rule did nothing to erode or diminish minority Tutsi hegemony over the majority Hutus. Colonial rule which lasted 68 years (1894–1962) bolstered/reinforced minority Tutsi dominance over the majority Hutu in both Rwanda and Burundi. Through indirect rule, the Belgian colonial government enabled the Tutsi minority in Burundi to retain control over political power and to enjoy great access to economic resources and opportunities. Sons of Tutsi aristocrats benefited extensively from the European-type educational opportunities made available through Catholic missionary schools. Once educated, the Tutsi elite filled in the top and middle level administrative positions in the Belgian colonial government. As a result, the Tutsi elite who were already dominant in the colonial administration were favored and promoted over the Hutus. Towards the end of their administration in the 1960s, the Belgians called for the creation of a representative plural society, which inevitably benefited the already well entrenched and advantaged Tutsi minority elite.

Racist Belgian colonial policies and practices reshaped and transformed Tutsi and Hutu ethnic identities into highly politicized racial identities with great potential for violent conflict. During the Belgian colonial rule in Rwanda-Urundi, Tutsi-Hutu ethnic identities were transformed into bipolar racial identities with profound social and political consequences. The Tutsi minority were constructed into an alien superior (ruling) Hamitic race, while the Hutu majority were constructed into an indigenous Bantu race, ruled by the Tutsi elite. Mamdani argues that:

... after the Belgian colonial reform(s) of 1926–36 [regarding
Rwanda-Urundi Customary Law and Native Authorities], Hutu were
not ruled by their own chiefs, but by Tutsi chiefs. The same reforms
constructed the Tutsi into a different race: the Hamitic race.... The
bulk of the colonized population... were made into a single mass—
the Hutu, said to be indigenous Bantu – who cut across all Native Authorities. [And] this Bantu majority was not ruled through their own
chiefs but through those constructed as racially different and superior,
the Hamites.[6]

The Tutsi in Rwanda and Burundi were constructed as an alien superior
race as opposed to a local ethnic group. The notion of Tutsi as an alien superior
race and different from the local or indigenous population of Hutus originated
with the colonial rule. Rival European colonists such as Germans, English,
Dutch or French shared the so-called Hamitic hypothesis. This was the notion
that whenever in Africa there was evidence of organized life or progress, the
ruling groups must have come from elsewhere, outside of Africa. Africans were
not expected to be so organized or advanced, especially in the art of governance!
    According to Ndura, European colonial observers and scholars who con-
structed and framed Tutsis as superior to Hutus were motivated by their own
racist ideology.[7] Mamdani contends that the colonial view of Tutsi and Hutu as
racial or political identities (rather than ethnic or cultural ones) helped to emphasize the power-subject relationship of both groups in Rwanda and Burundi.[8] Being Tutsi was construed as being in power, near power or identified with power
and privilege. In contrast, being Hutu was synonymous with being deprived and
powerless, or being a subject. This implies that the feudal (i.e. Lord-Serf) relationship that characterized the Tutsi and Hutu during the pre-colonial period was
amplified or intensified during the colonial era. As a result, racialization of
Tutsi-Hutu ethnic identities accomplished through institutional reforms that the
racist ideology inspired became potentially more volatile or explosive during
colonial rule. The colonial racialization of Tutsi and Hutu identities in Rwanda
and Burundi was both ideological and institutional. Such racialization "was the
creation of a joint enterprise between the colonial state and the Catholic
church."[9] The Catholic missionaries considered Tutsis to be "superb humans,"
as they supposedly combined both Aryan and Semitic traits.[10] Indeed, some missionaries went to the extraordinary extent of calling Tutsis "European(s) under
[a] black skin."[11]
    The colonial government relied on Catholic missionary knowledge of Tutsis
and Hutus to develop, refine and implement race-based policies between 1925 to
1936. It is said that "race policy" became such a preoccupation with the colonial
power that from 1925 on, annual colonial administration reports included an
extensive description of the "races" in a chapter called "race policy."[12] The Belgian colonial power used the Hamitic racial ideology as the basis of making
changes in political, social and cultural institutions in the decade from 1925 to
1936. As indicated below, the two-tiered colonial educational system was fo-

cused on educating the sons of Tutsi aristocrats for leadership and administrative positions in the colonial government, while preparing Hutu children for manual labor. Mamdani observes that:

> The tendency was to restrict admission mainly to Tutsi, especially to the upper schools. But where both Tutsi and Hutu children were admitted, there was a clear differentiation in the education meted to each. The Tutsi were given a "superior" education, taught in French in a separate stream.... In contrast, the Hutu were given an education considered "inferior," since they were taught in a different stream, one where the medium of instruction was Kiswahili.[13]

The introduction of "ethnic" identity cards by the Belgian colonial government in 1926 gave way to segregation in Hutu and Tutsi access to resources and opportunities in Burundi. In particular, Hutus were severely discriminated against in the school system and local administration. As noted previously, the colonial education system run by Catholic missionaries had two tiers: one for Tutsi sons of aristocrats and the other for Hutu children. Hence, the educational system in colonial Burundi separated pupils the same way the apartheid system in South Africa did.

According to Mamdani, key institutions—starting with education then state administration, taxation, and finally the church—were organized (or reorganized...) around all active knowledge of these identities. The reform was capped with a census that classified the entire population as Tutsi, Hutu, or Twa, and issued each person with a card proclaiming his or her official identity.[14]

Discrimination against Hutu children went beyond the poor quality of education or inferior curriculum to include eating poor meals or feeding on an inferior diet within the school system.

Scherrer points out that:

> The Tutsi [children] were given milk and meat-based meals [while] the Hutu children had to eat maize porridge and beans. The Catholic missionaries justified and reinforced the Tutsi feeling of superiority, both in terms of curriculum and diet.[15]

The separatist education system prepared Tutsis exclusively for public service and higher education, while relegating Hutu to hard labor for "public works" ordered by the colonial administration. Tutsi supremacy in local administration was strengthened by reforms initiated by the colonial government from 1926 to 1936. In the 1926 local government reform, powers of chiefs were streamlined and redefined. More importantly, the reform removed the traditional balance of forces that existed between Tutsi and Hutu chiefs. It abolished the traditional trinity of three chiefs (chief of the pastures always a Tutsi, the chief of the land often a Hutu, and the chief of the men usually a Tutsi) and concentrated the authority into the hands of a single powerful Tutsi chief. The new

powerful Tutsi chiefs were products of colonial schools designated for sons of
the Tutsi aristocracy. Finally, the introduction of Native Tribunals in 1936
headed by a single Tutsi chief with centralized authority consolidated Tutsi hegemony over the local government. The reforms centralizing powers of chiefs
under the colonial administration in Burundi undermined the powers and authority of the *Mwami* (King) to appoint or dismiss chiefs. This provided the basis for
conflict between the monarchy and the colonial state.

Overall, colonialism brought a "deep rooted subjection and "reprogram-
ming" of the local people – what might be called a "colonization of the mind."[16]
As Scherrer points out:

> Before 1959 and in the pre-colonial age of the Kingdoms, there was
> never any outbreak of organized violence between the two social
> groups in either of the two countries [i.e. Rwanda and Burundi]. It
> was the rapidly increasing strength of ethnicization and polarization
> fostered by the colonialists and by the postcolonial policies of the
> ethno political power elites on either side that led to the demonization
> and dehumanization of the respective opposing group. In both
> [Rwanda and Burundi] there were repeated massacres that made any
> peaceful political solution difficult and ultimately impossible.[17]

The First Postcolonial Phase, 1962 to 1992

Since achieving political independence from Belgium in 1962, Burundi has
consistently experienced ethnic conflict and violence with an increasing potential for genocide, similar to what occurred in neighboring Rwanda in 1994. The
ethnic hatred between the minority Tutsi and majority Hutu that emerged during
the colonial era erupted in open conflict and violence in 1961, following the
assassination of Prince Louis Rwagasore, leader of the UPRONA (Union for
Nation Progress) nationalist and royalist political party.

The rift within the Burundian aristocracy over Burundi's independence
from Belgium occurred at the same time political parties were being created to
prepare the country for self-government in 1961.[18] UPRONA, the nationalist and
royalist party, led by Prince Rwagasore (son of King Mwambutsa IV) called for
Burundi's self-determination, before that of Congo. On the other hand, the
Common Front (Christian Democratic Party (PDC)) led by two brothers Jean-
Baptiste Ntindendereza and Joseph Birori (sons of Baranyanka, a powerful Tutsi
chief and rival of King Mwambutsa IV) and staunchly supported by the Belgian
colonial administration wanted to delay Burundi's independence for fear of undermining relations with Belgians. It is not, therefore, surprising that when
UPRONA led by Prince Rwagasore (King Mwambutsa's son) won a landslide
victory in the UN-supervised self-government elections in September 1961, he
was promptly assassinated a month later by an individual of Greek origin and
considered a henchman of the rival Baranyanka clan.[19]

Burundi became independent first as a monarchy in 1962 (same year as Rwanda) and was proclaimed a republic in 1966. Unlike in Rwanda where Hutus came to power after independence in 1962 (following the 1959 social revolution), in Burundi the Tutsi were in power before and after colonial rule. However, the Hutu revolution in Rwanda provided the nascent Hutu elites of Burundi with the 'model polity' they tried to emulate later. On the other hand, it gave the incumbent Tutsi grounds for their incipient fears of Hutu majority domination. Indeed, the Tutsi in Burundi controlled political power and the military. The initial split within the Burundian aristocracy and political tensions created during the politics of independence (between 1960 and 1962), did not lead to Tutsi-Hutu violence or massacres as was the case in Rwanda in 1959. However, the split within the Burundi aristocracy and political competition between UPRONA and PDC (caused by the Belgian colonial administrations' manipulations) gave rise to the early political conflict between Tutsi and Hutu in Burundi. Ndura points out that:

> Burundi's violent history began in 1961 with the creation of political parties to stimulate the western-type government. The assassination of Prince Louis Rwagasore, head of the winning UPRONA party in October 1961 crystallized ethnic relations and weakened the ground on which Burundi was to stand as an independent nation in 1962.[20]

Prince Rwagasore's death was the first tragic event that contributed to a sharp polarization of Tutsi-Hutu relations. However, the monarchy *(Mwami)* remained as the most important stabilizing element in the Tutsi-Hutu power equation. But by 1965, both Tutsi and Hutu elites saw the monarchy as the major problem rather than the solution. Hence, the monarchy lost both its legitimacy and neutrality. A weakened and vulnerable monarchy was overthrown in 1966 by the then captain Michel Micombero who proclaimed Burundi a republic with himself as president. The struggle for political power and economic resources between the Hutu and Tutsi intensified during the early years of independence (1962 to 1972). Dissatisfied with continued Tutsi political and military control and economic deprivation, Hutus attempted to overthrow the Tutsi dominated government in 1965, 1969 and 1972.

The first explosive violence against Hutus came in October 1965, when a group of Hutu military officers staged an unsuccessful coup d'état directed at the Tutsi-dominated government. The mutineers took a big gamble and lost. And the losses far exceeded the revenge Tutsis exacted upon the Hutu community. In addition to exterminating the entire first generation of Hutu military officers and political leaders, "an estimated 5000 Hutu civilians lost their lives in the capital (of Bujumbura) alone at the hands of local civilian defense groups organized under the supervision of the [Tutsi] army and governor."[21] The Burundi monarchy, once the rallying point for moderate Tutsis and Hutus, could no longer sustain the *status quo* or prevent the worsening relations between the two ethnic communities as its authority had been greatly eroded. As previously indicated, the weakened monarchy was overthrown in 1966 by then Prime Minister, Captain Michel Micombero, who proclaimed Burundi a republic with himself as president. From 1966 until 1972, President Micombero headed a new government proclaimed of 'Unity and Revolution'. Although Micombero's government included Hutu cabinet ministers, the government firmly remained in Tutsi hands, with Tutsi extremists holding key positions inside and outside the army.[22] For some Hutu elites, the consequences of the failed 1965 coup attempt were clear. They realized that they had no alternative but to start an armed rebellion against Tutsi control of both the government and army.

In 1969, the Hutu tried another insurrection against Tutsi hegemony, but it failed with deadly consequences for the mutineers. According to Melady, "in the 1969 troubles, 67 Hutu leaders were accused of trying to overthrow the government; they were tried, and 26 were executed by firing squad in December 1969."[23] Despite two failed attempted coups detat (in 1965 and 1969) with deadly consequences, "a majority Hutu uprising took place in 1972."[24] In contrast to the two previous rebellions, the 1972 uprising was organized on a much broader and more violent scale. The former U.S. Ambassador to Burundi (1969-1972), Thomas Melady, described the 1972 Tutsi-Hutu strife as "one of the worst bloodbaths of this century—and one of the least known."[25] According to the U.S. Ambassador, "The severity of the Tutsi response was probably rooted in the fear that such a plot would result in the wholesale killing or expulsion of Tutsis."[26] Indeed, it is reported that President Micombero and other Tutsi leaders felt there was a vast Hutu conspiracy to eliminate them once and for all.

Although the hatred and hostility on both sides was deep and personal, the "genocide by the Tutsi's against the Hutus in Burundi... exceeded in its horror the genocide by the Hutus against the Tutsis in Rwanda ten years earlier."[27] The massacres of Hutu by Tutsi were not only related to the immediate strife, but also to revenge motivated by deep-rooted hatred of Hutu.

Stavenhagen has described the horror of the Tutsi massacres of the Hutus in Burundi in 1972 this way:

> Within hours of its outbreak, a reign of terror was unleashed by Hutu upon the Tutsi, and then on an even more appalling scale by Tutsi upon Hutu. The killings went on unabated for several months. By then almost every educated Hutu element was either dead or in exile. Some conservative estimates put the total number of [Hutu] lives lost at 100,000, others at 200,000. Approximately 150,000 Hutu refugees fled to neighboring territories.[28]

The crises that occurred in Burundi between 1965 and 1972 were decisive in intensifying Tutsi-Hutu hatred and violence. The U.S. Ambassador characterized the hatred between Tutsi and Hutu in Burundi in the early 1970s this way:

> While the animosity between the Hutu and Tutsi communities [in Burundi] had been evident to me [Sic.] from the beginning, I had under-

estimated how deeply rooted it was, like a malignant growth, spreading through all their relationships.[29]

Between 1972 and 1987, "only Tutsi elements were qualified to gain access to power, influence and wealth."[30] In contrast, the Hutu were systematically excluded from the army, civil service, economy and higher education and were increasingly reduced to the hopeless status of a vast underclass. In 1976, a military coup d'état brought Colonel Jean-Baptiste Bagaza (from the same Southern Bururi Province as Michel Micombero) to power. Although President Bagaza proclaimed a government of "National Unity," he "did little to alter the stranglehold of Tutsi elements"[31] within the government and army.

From 1976 to 1979, Burundi "remained firmly under the control of a Supreme Military Council consisting of 30 officers, all of them Tutsi."[32] The UPRONA political party, once a moderate nationalist movement with its membership cutting across ethnic and regional lines, became a stronghold of Tutsi extremist interests. The regime of Bagaza fell in 1987 after yet another military coup d'état led by Major Pierre Buyoya, a young Tutsi military officer from the south of the country. In 1988, Buyoya was faced with a significant Hutu rebellion in northeast Burundi.[33] In the same year, a local incident of Tutsi abuse and impunity in a rural commune triggered an explosive Hutu violence directed at Tutsi supremacy. It inevitably provoked a confrontation with the Tutsi dominated army, with deadly consequences for the Hutu community. Stavenhagen observes that, "although the exact number of Hutu victims remains a matter of speculation... estimates suggest that 15,000 may not be too wide a mark."[34]

It is reported that soon after the 1988 massacre, the Buyoya regime introduced several constitutional and political reforms including increasing the number of Hutu cabinet ministers from six to twelve and naming a Hutu Prime Minister. However, because these reforms lacked Tutsi support or Hutu trust, they had no impact on the Tutsi-Hutu relations. To underscore the ineffectiveness of the reforms on Tutsi-Hutu relations, "renewed killings occurred in November 1991, with an estimated 3,000 Hutu killed by [Tutsi] government troops."[35]

For a period of thirty years after Burundi achieved political independence from Belgium (1962-1992), the minority Tutsi held political power and controlled the army. During the same period, Hutu were excluded from the control of power and reduced to a vast underclass. Repeated massacres over three decades led to thousands of Hutus killed or forced into neighboring countries as refugees. And educated Hutus in government, higher education or the military were either exterminated or exiled.

The Second Postcolonial Phase, 1993 to 2005

The current conflict in Burundi is linked to the violent ethnic confrontation of 1993 that followed a Hutu electoral victory. As a result of the first free and fair "elections in decades, held in June 1993, FRODEBU (Front for Democracy in Burundi) unseated the long ruling UPRONA government."[36] Following the elections, President Melchior Ndadaye, a Hutu, affirmed his desire to eliminate Burundi's "ethnic virus" and formed a government composed of one third Tutsi and a Tutsi Prime Minister. Despite these positive gestures, the Tutsi feared the democracy would help consolidate Hutu majority power and undermine their dominant and privileged positions in government and the army. A few months later, the Tutsi military staged an attempted coup d'état that led to the assassination of President Ndadaye, the speaker of the National Assembly and several senior Hutu members of the FRODEBU government. In addition, an estimated 100,000 unarmed Hutu civilians were killed by Tutsis. These massacres made national reconciliation and reconstruction in Burundi difficult "as each political-ethnic camp held to its positions...."[37] The 1993 coup attempt has been described as 'the most successful failed military take-over' in Africa's postcolonial history, as the President, Hutu cabinet ministers and the speaker were killed and the FRODEBU government was seriously weakened, "leading to significant concessions to militant Tutsi demands."[38] The concessions included distribution of offices and functions in the cabinet and so-called 'sensitive sectors' such as intelligence, information and police.

From 1993 to 1998, Burundi was involved in a series of ethnic massacres, including selective genocide. These killings took the lives of tens of thousands of mostly unarmed Hutu civilians and caused the displacement of hundreds of thousands more. Although the Burundian Society managed to wither the impact of the 1994 Rwanda genocide which claimed lives of about 800,000 Tutsis and moderate Hutus, the country was still "bogged down in an impasse born of a dormant civil war."[39] Extremists on both sides who were kept out of the 1994 UN brokered government of national unity negotiated between moderates from FRODEBU and UPRONA continued ethnic violence. It is reported, for example that both "ethnic cleansing" and "ethnic apartheid" prevailed in Bujumbura (the capital), "where the [Tutsi] militias laid down the law and the last "mixed" neighborhoods... were "purified" in March 1995."[40] In general, extremists on both sides have taken up arms and have radicalized and fragmented the Burundian political landscape. This has made power-sharing arrangements suspect and a negotiated political solution to ethnic violence almost impossible to achieve.

While regional negotiations among warring Tutsi-Hutu parties chaired by former President Nyerere of Tanzania were underway in Arusha, former President Buyoya retook power with Tutsi army support in July 1996. Buyoya had taken advantage of continued violence and erosion of government authority since the 1993 coup attempt to stage his own successful coup d'état three years later. However, regional governments in collaboration with the UN Security Council and the Organization of African Unity (OAU now African Union) reacted strongly and swiftly against the coup by imposing economic sanctions on Burundi which lasted from July 1996 until January 1999. Economic sanctions combined with diplomatic pressure forced Buyoya to form a transitional power-sharing government between moderates in UPRONA and FRODEBU in June 1998. Power-sharing provided for a Hutu President, a Tutsi Prime Minister and twenty-two ministerial portfolios that were evenly divided between UPRONA and FRODEBU. At the same time, issues of trust and the fight over the relative power of the President vis-à-vis the prime minister emerged, but still important reforms were started. Reforms initiated by the Buyoya regime included broader representation in the National Assembly, setting up a broad based National Conference as a permanent forum for all Burundian political parties and social forces at all levels, reforming the Tutsi dominated army, and the reestablishment of the traditional institution of arbitration (known as the *abashingantahe* similar to *gachacha* in Rwanda).

The internal peace process, which started in June 1998, prepared ground for the signing of the Arusha Peace Accord in August 2000. Though both events were considered major political breakthroughs, ethnic violence persisted and many issues remained unresolved. The Arusha Peace Accord was signed by nineteen political organizations and movements, but was boycotted by two Hutu-led armed groups, Forces for the Defense of Democracy (FDD) and Forces for the National Liberation Front (FNL). Even after the signing of the Arusha Peace Accord, the Burundi government in collaboration with regional governments and mediators continued to pursue peace talks with both armed groups.[41] However, the continued low-intensity violence waged by the armed groups excluded from both the internal peace process and external talks in Arusha halted the Burundi peace process until recently.

Observers of the Burundian political situation believed that smaller armed groups such as FDD and FNL wanted to demonstrate their resolve and capacity to strike at the capital, Bujumbura, so as to increase their bargaining power in the ongoing peace talks in the region. Such observers expected the armed rebel activity to continue in the midst of peace talks. Hence the rebel maxim of "talking peace while waging war" against the Burundi government seemed to hold true. However, as we discuss in the concluding remarks below, the Forces for the Defense of Democracy (FDD)—a former Hutu-led rebel group is expected to win both parliamentary (general) and presidential elections slated for the months of July and August 2005, respectively. According to the 2004 Kampala (Uganda) Plan, 40 percent of parliamentary seats would be reserved for Tutsi and 60 percent for the Hutu.[42]

Conclusion

The ethnic conflict and violence in Burundi is the result of decades of struggles between Tutsi and Hutu over political power and economic control. The struggles have occurred within the context of Tutsi dominance, political repression and economic deprivation of the Hutu majority. Hutu political repression and economic marginalization have been due to continued Tutsi minority control of both the government and the army.

The biggest problem facing Burundi since independence in 1962 has been "its failure to create a political system that would allow the Hutu majority to govern democratically and protect the rights of the Tutsi minority who have long occupied a privileged position within society."[43] Over the years, concerted efforts by internal and external actors to find a political solution to the ethnic problem in Burundi have been largely undermined by the deep rooted hatred and distrust compounded by the "dual fears" of annihilation on both sides of the conflict.[44] Such "double fear" is entrenched on both sides of the conflict and it is further exacerbated by "a culture of impunity or immunity" for the coup conspirators and human rights violators.

The two most important political approaches so far attempted to address the ethnic problem in Burundi are power-sharing and the implementation of democratic changes. At various times in the political history of Burundi, a consociational or power-sharing approach to ethnic conflict has been attempted. In 1994, for example, a power-sharing arrangement was concluded between UPRONA and FRODEBU. The arrangement provided for a Hutu president and a Tutsi prime minister. Soon the issue of the relative power of the president vis-à-vis the prime minister became a very contentious issue, leading to a Tutsi-led coup in 1996. A combination of economic sanctions imposed by regional governments and diplomatic pressure from the United Nations and the Organization of African Unity forced Buyoya to form a power-sharing government in June 1998. As in the 1994 power-sharing arrangement, the 1998 power-sharing agreement provided for a Hutu president and a Tutsi prime minister, with twenty-two cabinet positions evenly divided between UPRONA and FRODEBU. This government, like the previous one, was undermined by lack of trust and fights over the relative power of the Hutu president vis-à-vis the Tutsi prime minister.

Power-sharing by nature entails compromise. According to Forster, "... a compromise between the Tutsi and the Hutu view of the situation will lead to retention of at least some Tutsi privilege."[45] Above all, any system of power-sharing is subject to a continuous assessment of its fairness. Hence a lack of trust and concern about the fairness of the power-sharing arrangements have contributed to the ethnic bipolarization of Burundi's political landscape. Negotiated power-sharing arrangements have been hampered by actions of armed extremists on both sides. At the same time, the Tutsi- dominated army's unwillingness to support power-sharing arrangements has tended to destabilize or undermine such arrangements. In the final analysis, it is the same Tutsi-dominated army which has been deeply involved in Hutu-Tutsi power struggles that has to guarantee the success or failure of such power-sharing arrangements.

As previously stated, the first ever free and fair-elections held in Burundi in June 1993, brought FRODEBU, a Hutu-led political party to power. Even if President Melchior Ndadaye, a Hutu, formed a government of "national unity" composed of one-third Tutsi and a Tutsi prime minister, Tutsi feared democracy would undermine their dominant and privileged positions in government and the army. A few months later, President Ndadaye's government was overthrown by the Tutsi military who assassinated him along with the Speaker of the National Assembly and Hutu cabinet ministers. Twelve years after the 1993 massacre of Hutus, another Hutu-led political party, Forces for the Defense of Democracy (FDD), which abandoned its armed struggle in 2004 and joined the FRODEBU transitional government is expected to take power in Burundi on August 26, 2005.[46] Parliamentary elections were held on July 4, 2005 and Presidential elections are scheduled for August 19, 2005.

According to provisional parliamentary results announced recently by the National Election Commission, FDD won by taking 58.23 percent of the vote, followed by the ruling FRODEBU party with 22.33 percent of the vote and UPRONA Tutsi-stronghold with 7.3 percent, respectively.[47] Under the current Burundi constitution approved in a referendum in February 2005, "the new government will be formed by all parties that have won at least five percent of the votes cast in parliamentary elections."[48] In addition, the new FDD-led government is expected to have a 60-40 split in government positions between the majority Hutu and minority Tutsi. This arrangement is similar to the 60-40 percent split in parliamentary seats reserved for Hutu and Tutsi. The system of proportional representation to distribute seats in the national assembly and positions in government is aimed at addressing Tutsi concerns about Hutu majority rule. It has been argued that while most Hutus call for democracy or majority rule, most Tutsis wish to avoid majoritarian democratic rule at all cost.[49] This sentiment makes it difficult to establish a political system that permits Hutu majority rule, while safeguarding the minority Tutsi rights. Hence safeguards enshrined in the 2005 Burundi Constitution and inherent in a proportional representative government are intended to address minority Tutsi concerns about a democratic government dominated by the majority Hutu. This arrangement may also help to reduce the confusion between equating a "political majority" with an "ethnic majority." In other words, the Hutu can be an ethnic majority without being a political majority.

The inauguration of the FDD-led government on August 26, 2005 is expected to bring to an end the current FRODEBU-led transitional government and to "usher in a democratic political dispensation after 12 years of civil war, in which some 300,000 civilians [mostly Hutus] have died and hundreds of thousands of others displaced."[50] However, whether or not this Hutu-led coalition-style government survives another Tutsi-led military coup d'état similar to the one that occurred in 1993, remains to be seen. The greatest threat to Hutu-led democracy in Burundi remains the Tutsi dominated army. Efforts to reform the army began in 1998 have stalled. For example, plans developed under ousted President Ntibantunganya to recruit more Hutus did not materialize. Failure to sufficiently reform the army to include Hutu puts in grave jeopardy the future of democracy in Burundi. In the final analysis, it is the army, not the Hutu-led democracy that will guarantee Tutsi supremacy and privilege in the Burundian society. Hence, there is an urgent need to reform and de-ethnicize the Burundi army.

Extremists, not included in the peace process and not part of the expected FDD government pose a threat to the nascent democracy Burundi wants to nurture. In particular, although the FNL Forces led by Agathon Rwasa, a Hutu extremist, signed a ceasefire agreement on May 15, 2005 in Dar es Salaam, Tanzania, its armed groups continue to mount attacks, mostly in and around Bujumbura, the capital. FNL spokesman, Pasteur Habimana is said to have recently "told a local radio station... that his group had "deep concerns" about the Dar es Salaam agreement because [Burundi] government troops were attacking FNL positions."[51] Some political opposition elements have had "mixed" to "ambivalent" early reactions to the recent FDD parliamentary elections victory. For example, a representative of the party of former President Bagaza claimed the "elections were "peppered with fraud."[52] On the other hand, an FNL spokesman Habimana, is said to have expressed ambivalence about the elections saying; "we are accustomed to seeing parties win elections but not respecting the law...."[53]

The lack of a national and regional vision of societal reconstruction will continue to fuel the current ethnic conflict and violence in Burundi and the Great Lakes Region. The negotiations and political compromises upon which national decisions are made have so far failed to take into consideration the fractured social fiber of the country and the region, and instead focused on individual, even egotistical gains and benefits with little concern for the general population and the countless families that have been victimized by the decades long cycle of ethnic conflict and violence. For the new Burundi political system to be sustainable it must be grounded in a social system that affirms and validates all of its citizens' ethnic identities and other social roles, and be defined by a shared quest for justice, equity, and the common good.

Finally, without concerted regional peace initiatives to find a political solution to the ethnic conflict in Burundi from 1998 to the present, current elections would not have been possible. By the same token, until there is peace in the Great Lakes Region as a whole, neither Burundi nor neighboring Rwanda will ever be expected to be at peace internally or at peace with their larger and militarily more powerful neighbors. Hence curbing the never-ending cycle of violence in Burundi or Rwanda depends on achieving a comprehensive regional peace in the Great Lakes Region.

Notes

1. Elavie Ndura, "Peaceful Conflict Resolution: A Prerequisite for Social Reconstruction in Burundi, Africa," in *Conflict Resolution and Peace Education in Africa*, Ernest E. Uwazie, ed. (Lanham: Lexington Books, 2003), 151.

2. Thomas Patrick Melady, *Burundi: The Tragic Years* (Maryknoll and New York: Orbis Books, 1974), 71–72.

3. Filip Reyntjens, "Burundi: Breaking the Cycle of Violence," in *Minority Rights Group* (Manchester, United Kingdom: Manchester Free Press, 1995), 7.

4. Melady, *Burundi*, 41.

5. Melady, *Burundi*, 42.

6. Mahmood Mamdani, *When Victims Become Killers: Colonialism, Nativism, and the Genocide in Rwanda* (Princeton, New Jersey: Princeton University Press, 2001), 34–35.

7. Ndura, "Peaceful Conflict," 152–153; see also, Mamdani, *When Victims Become Killers*, 78–79—who says that even if the origin of European race doctrines about Africa lay in the trans-Atlantic slave trade, European racist ideology became more complex during the period of "discovery" and colonial conquest.

8. Mamdani, *When Victims Become Killers*, 74–75.

9. Mamdani, *When Victims Become Killers*, 87.

10. See also, Elavie Ndura, "Peaceful Conflict," 153.

11. Mamdani, *When Victims Become Killers*, 88.

12. Mamdani, *When Victims Become Killers*, 88.

13. Mamdani, *When Victims Become Killers*, 89–90.

14. Mamdani, *When Victims Become Killers*, 88.

15. Christian P. Scherrer, *Genocide and Crisis in Central Africa: Conflict Roots, Mass Violence and Regional War* (Westport, Connecticut and London: Praeger, 2002), 27.

16. Scherrer, *Genocide and Crisis in Central Africa*, 4.

17. Scherrer, *Genocide and Crisis in Central Africa*, 28.

18. In 1959, King Mwambutsa IV (Prince Louis Rwagasore's father, who had ascended to the throne at age two and had been king since 1915) called for Burundi's self-determination from Belgium, before that of Congo. The call for immediate self-determination caused a split within the Burundian aristocracy that was carried over into the period of political party formation and call for self-government. While Mwambutsa IV called for immediate self-government, the powerful chief of the Baranyanka Tutsi clan called for delayed independence. Twenty five political parties that federated into three major political blocs/coalitions that contested the 1961 elections for limited self-government are: UPRONA, The Common Front Centered on the Christian Democratic Party, and the Union of popular parties centered on the Peoples' Party.

19. Jean-Pierre Chretien, *The Great Lakes of Africa: Two Thousand Years of History* (New York: Zone Books, 2003), 311–12.

20. Ndura, "Peaceful Conflict," 152.

21. Rodolfo Stavenhagen, *Ethnic Conflicts and the Nation-State* (New York: St. Martin's Press, 1996), 118. Also see, Thomas Patrick Melady, op.cit. 48.

22. Consider Melady, *Burundi*, 51–52: who claims that President Micombero (1966–1972) was known as a man of moderation concerned with avoiding violence between the Tutsi's and Hutus; and that in spite of low level violence, there was more Hutu participation in the political process due to concessions he initiated; others, especially Micombero's critics, insist he promoted the new politics of revenge "at regional and national levels."

23. Melady, *Burundi*, 48.

24. Stavenhagen, *Ethnic Conflicts*, 119.

25. Melady, *Burundi*, 52.

26. Melady, *Burundi*, 12.

27. Melady, *Burundi*, 52.

28. Stavenhagen, *Ethnic Conflicts*, 119; Also see, Jean-Pierre Chretien, op.cit. 316.

29. Melady, *Burundi*, 21.

30. Stavenhagen, *Ethnic Conflicts*, 119.

31. Stavenhagen, *Ethnic Conflicts*, 119. Also, see Chretien, *Great Lakes of Africa*, 316.

32. Rodolfo Tavenhagen, op.cit. 119.

33. Chretien, *Great Lakes of Africa*, 317.

34. Stavenhagen, *Ethnic Conflicts*, 121.

35. Stavenhagen, *Ethnic Conflicts*, 121.

36. Stavenhagen, *Ethnic Conflicts*, 121.

37. Chretien, *Great Lakes of Africa*, 328.

38. Jos Havermans, "Peace-Initiatives Help Stem the Violence," in *Searching for Peace in Africa*, ed. Monique Mekenkamp, Paul van Tongeren, and Hans van de Veen (Utrecht, the Netherlands: European Platform for Conflict Prevention and Transformation, 1999), 198.

39. Chretien, *Great Lakes of Africa*, 338.

40. Chretien, *Great Lakes of Africa*, 339.

41. Scherrer, *Genocide and Crisis in Central Africa*, 243.

42. Television news broadcast in Kampala. Wavamuno Broadcasting Service (WBS), 5 July 2005.

43. Reyntjens, "Burundi: Breaking the Cycle of Violence," 5.

44. Ethnic conflict and selective genocide provide each side with an point of reference. See also Filip Reyntjens, "Burundi: Breaking the Cycle of Violence," 7; who argues that "for the Hutu, it is proof of the existence of an ongoing genocidal plan nurtured by extremist Tutsi; and for the Tutsi fear... that the majority will exterminate the minority...." As a result, both ethnic groups feel insecure and are at a "security impasse" or state of "mutually assured violence." For similar views, see also Melady, *Burundi*, 12.

45. Peter G. Forster, Michael Hitchcock and Francis F. Lyimo, *Race and Ethnicity in East Africa* (Macmillan Press, 2000), 117.

46. As of July 30, 2005, the National Electoral Commission, known as the CENI, had announced that the only Presidential Candidate to be elected by elected senators and assemblymen, (majority of whom were National Council for the Defense of Democracy (CNDD)-FDD members) was the leader of CNDD-FDD, Pierre Nkurunziza.

47. Ex-rebel group wins Burundi elections, <http://www.namibian.com.na/2005/July/World/05C16ACCD3.html>, 1.

48. <http://www.namibian.com.na/2005/ July/World/05C16ACCD3.html>, 2.

49. Stavenhagen, *Ethnic Conflicts*, 74.

50. Burundi: Elections calendar issued, <http://www.ivinnews.org/report.asp? Report ID=46787>, 7.

51. "Burundi: Winning the Legislature, Former Rebels Vow to Negotiate Peace," <http://www.ivinnew.org/report.asp? Report ID=47989> and Select Reg. 2.

52. "Burundi" <http://www.ivinnew.org/report.asp? Report ID=47989>.

53. "Burundi" <http://www.ivinnew.org/report.asp? Report ID=47989>.

Bibliography

Abbot, Freeland. *Islam and Pakistan*. Ithaca, NY: Cornell University Press, 1968.

Adedeji, Adebayo. *Comprehending and Mastering African Conflicts—The Search for Sustainable Peace and Good Governance*. London: Zed Books, 1999.

Adelman, Howard and Astri Suhrke. *The Path of a Genocide: The Rwanda Crisis from Uganda to Zaire*. New Brunswick Transaction Publishers, 1999.

Aditjondro, George. *Violence by the State Against Women in the East Timor: A Report to the UN Special Rapporteur on Violence Against Women, Including its Causes and Consequences*. Melbourne: East Timor Human Rights Centre (ETHRC), 7 November 1997.

Ahmed, Samina. "The Politics of Ethnicity in India." *Regional Studies* (Islamabad) IX, no. 4 (Autumn 1991).

Alagappa, Muthiah, ed. *Political Legitimacy in Southeast Asia: The Quest for Moral Authority*. Stanford, Calif.: Stanford University Press, 1995.

Allahar, Anton. *Caribbean Charisma: Reflections on Leadership, Legitimacy and Populist Politics*. Kingston: Ian Randle Publishers. Boulder, Colo.: Lynne Rienner, 2001.

Allen, Tim and Kate Hudson. *War, Ethnicity and the Media*. London: South Bank University, 1996.

Alpers, E. A. and P.M. Fontaine. *Walter Rodney: Revolutionary and Scholar, A Tribute*. Los Angeles: Center for Afro-American Studies and African Studies Center, 1982.

Amin, Shahid. *Pakistan's Foreign Policy: A Reappraisal*. Karachi, Pakistan: Oxford University Press, 2000.

Amnesty International Report, *Guyana: Human Rights and Crime Control—Not Mutually Exclusive.* AI Index: AMR 35/003/2003.

Anderson, Benedict R. O'G. *Imagined Communities: Reflections on the Origin and Spread of Nationalism.* London: Verso (Second revised edition), 1991.

Anderson, G. Norman. *Sudan in Crisis: the Failure of Democracy.* Gainesville: University Press of Florida, 1999.

Anthias, Floya and Nira Yuval-Davis. *Woman Nation State.* London: Macmillan, 1989.

Arendt, Hannah. *The Origins of Totalitarianism.* London: George Allen and Unwin, 1967.

Aung-Thwin, Michael A. "Myth of the 'Three Shan Brothers' and the Ava Period in Burmese History." *The Journal of Aisan Studies* 55, no. 1 (1996).

Awolowo, O. *Thoughts on Nigerian Constitution.* London: Faber, 1966.

Bardacke, Frank, et. al., eds. *Shadows of Tender Fury: The Letters and Communiqués of Subcomandante Marcos and the Zapatista Army of National Liberation.* New York, NY: Monthly Review Press, 1995.

Barth, Fredrik, "Ethnicity and the Concept of Culture." Paper presented at the Conference of Rethinking Culture in Harvard University, 23 February 1995.

Bates, Roberts H. *Ethnicity in Contemporary Africa: East African Studies VIV.* Syracuse, New York: Syracuse University, Maxwell School of Citizen and Public Affairs, 1973.

Bateson, Gregory. *Steps to an Ecology of Mind: Collected Essays in Anthropology, Psychiatry, Evolution, and Epistemology.* New York: Balantine, 1972.

Benjamin, Geoffrey. "The Unseen Presence: A Theory of a Nation-state and Its Mystifications," *Department of Sociology Working Paper Series,* no. 91. Singapore: Nanyang Technology University, 1988.

Berber, Mark T. "Romancing the Zapatistas: International Intellectuals and the Chiapas Rebellion." *Latin American Perspectives* 28, no. 2 (2001).

Berdún, Guibernau i and M. Montserrat (Maria Montserrat). *Nations Without states: Political Communities in a Global Age / Montserrat Guibernau.* Cambridge, UK; Malden, MA: Polity Press, 1999.

Berghe, Pierre Van der. *The Ethnic Phenomenon.* New York; Oxford: Elsevier, 1981.

Bhutto, Zulfiquar Ali. *The Myth of Independence.* London: Oxford University Press, 1969.

Billing, Michael. *Social Psychology and Intergroup Relations* (London: Academic Press, 1976).

Birch, Melissa H. and Jerry Haar, eds. *The Impact of Privatization in the Americas.* Miami, FL: North-South Center Press at the University of Miami, 2000.

Bisnauth, Dale. *The Settlement of Indians in Guyana 1890-1930.* Leeds, England: Peepal.

Boyce, James K. "Green and Brown? Globalization and the Environment." *Oxford Review of Economic Policy* 20, no. 1 (2004).

Brass, Paul R. *Language, Religion and Politics in Northern India.* London: Cambridge University Press, 1974.

———. *The Production of Hindu-Muslim Violence in Contemporary India.* Seattle: University of Washington Press, 2003.

Brown, Michael E. *Ethnic Conflict and Ethnic Security.* Princeton, NJ: Princeton University Press, 1994.

———. "International Conflict and International Action," in *The International Dimensions of Internal Conflict,* edited by Michael Brown. Cambridge, MA: MIT Press, 1996.

Brubaker, Rogers and David D. Laitin. "Ethnic and Nationalist Violence." *Annual Review of Sociology* 24 (1998).

Brunk, Samuel. "Remembering Emiliano Zapata: Three Memories in the Posthumous Career of Chinameca." *Hispanic American Historical Review* 78, no. 3 (August 1998).

Budiardjo, Carmel and Liem Soei Liong. *West Papua: The Obliteration of a People.* London: TAPOL, 1988.

Bunge, Mario. *Finding Philosophy in Social Science.* New Haven, CT: Yale University Press, 1996.

Burbach, Roger. *Globalization and Postmodern Politics: From Zapatistas to High-Tech Robber Barons.* London: Pluto Press, 2001.

Burton, J. *Dear Survivors.* Boulder, Colo.: Westview Press, 1986.

Cahoone, Lawrence E. *Civil Society: The Conservative Meaning of Liberal Politics.* London: Blackwell, 2002.

Campbell, Aidan. *Western Primitivism: African Ethnicity.* London: Cassell, 1997.

Campbell, Kenneth. *Genocide and the Global Village.* New York: Palgrave Press, 2001.

Carment, David and Patrick James. "Internal Constraints and Interstate Ethnic Conflict: Toward a Crisis-based Assessment of Irredentism." *Journal of Conflict Resolution* 39, no. 1 (1995).

Chadha, Maya. *Ethnicity, Separatism and Security.* Columbia, N.Y.: Columbia University Press, 1997.

Chambers, Iain and Lidia Curti. *The Post-Colonial Question: Common Skies, Divided Horizon.* London: Routledge, 1996.

Chandra, Bipan. *Indian National Movement, the Long Term Dynamics.* New Delhi: Vikas Publishing House, 1988.

Choudhury, G. W. *Pakistan's Relations with India, 1947-1966.* NY and Washington: Frederick A. Praeger Publishers, 1968.

Chretien, Jean Pierre. *sans frontieres Rewanda: les medias du genocide.* Karthala, Paris, 1995.

Cockcroft, James. *Mexico: Class Formation, Capital Accumulation and the State.* New York: Monthly Review Press, 1983.

Codere, Helen. *The Biography of an African Society, Rwanda 1900-1960 Based on Forty-Eight Rwandan Autobiographies*, Musee Royal de l'Afrique Centrale, Sciences Humaines, no. IN-8, Tervuren (Belgium), 1973.

Cohen, Stephen Phillip. "Identity, Survival and Security: Pakistan's Defense Policy." In *Perspectives on Pakistan's Foreign Policy* edited by Surendra Chopra. Amritsar, India: Guru Nanak Development University Press, 1983.

Collier, George Allen. *Basta!: Land and the Zapatista Rebellion in Chiapas.* Oakland, CA: Food First Books, 1999.

Collignon, Stephan. *The Burmese Economy and the Withdrawal of European Trade Preferences.* Brussels: European Institute for Asian Studies, March 1997.

Connor, Walker. *Ethnonationalism: The Quest for Understanding.* Princeton: Princeton University Press, 1994.

Conteh-Morgan, Earl. *Collective Political Violence: An Introduction to the Theories and Cases of Violent Conflicts.* New York: Routledge, 2004.

Cook, Edward M., Jr. "India Plays the Role of A Regional power: The Sri Lankan intervention." Unpublished research report submitted to the faculty for fulfillment of the curriculum requirement. Alabama: Air War College, Air University, Maxwell Air Force Base, 1996.

Cornell, Stephen and Douglas Hartmann. *Ethnicity and Race: Making Identities in a ChangingWorld.* Thousand Oaks, Calif.: Pine Forge Press, 1998.

Crawford, Berverly and Ronnie D. Lipschutz, eds. *The Myth of "Ethnic": Politics, Economics, and Cultural Violence.* Berkeley: University of California, International Area Studies, 1999.

Cribb, Robert. *Historical Atlas of Indonesia.* Honolulu: University of Hawaii Press, 2000).

Croaker, C.A., F.O. Hampson, and P. Aall. *Turbulent Peace: The Challenges of Managing International Conflict.* Washington, D.C., United States Institute of Peace, 2001.

Dark, K.R., ed. *Religion and International Relations.* New York: St. Martin's Press, 2000.

de Silva, K.M. and Peter May. "Are Middle East Conflicts More Religious?" *Middle East Quarterly* 8, no. 4 (2001).

Deng, Francis. *War of Visions.* Washington, D.C.: The Brookings Institution, 1995.

——— and I. William Zartman. *Governance as Conflict Management Politics and Violence in West Africa.* Washington, DC: The Brookings Institution Press, 1996.

Des Forges, Alison. *Leave None to Tell the Story: Genocide in Rwanda.* London: Human Rights Watch, 1999.

Diamond, Larry. "Issues in the Constitutional Design of a Third Nigerian Republic." *African Affairs* (1987).

Dube, S. C. *Modernization and Development: The Search for Alternative Paradigms.* London: Zed Books, 1988.

Dubois, R.D. and Li, Mew-Song. *Reducing Social Tension and Conflict Through the Group conversation Method.* New York: Association Press, 1971.

Dunn, Michael Collins. "The Kurdish Question: Is There an Answer?: A Historical Overview." *Middle East Policy* (September 1995).

Edozie, R. Kiki. *People Power and Democracy: the Popular Movement against Military Despotism in Nigeria, 1989-1999.* New York: Africa World Press, 2002.

Edwards, W. and Gibson, K. "An Ethnohistory of Amerindians in Guyana." *Ethnohistory* 26, no. 2 (Spring, 1979).

Eiser, Richard J. "Accentuation Revisited," in W. Peter Robinson (ed.), Social *Groups & Identities: Developing the Legacy of Henri Tajfel.* Oxford: Butterworth-Heinemann, 1996.

Eller, Jack David. *From Culture to Ethnicity to Conflict.* Ann Arbor: University of Michigan Press, 1999.

Engineer, Ashgar Ali. *Indian Muslims—A Study of Minority Problems in India.* Delhi: Ajanta Publications, 1986.

Entessar, Nader. *Kurdish Ethnonationalism.* Lynne Rienner Publishers: Boulder & London. 1992.

Fancher, Robert T. "Psychoanalysis as Culture," *Issues in Psychoanalytic Psychology* 15, no. 2 (1993).

Fenton, Steve. "Beyond Ethnicity: The Global Comparative Analysis of Ethnic Conflict." *International Journal of Comparative Sociology* 45, issue 3 (July-September 2004).

Feyide, M. O. *Oil in World Politics.* Lagos: University of Lagos Press, 1987.

Fisiy, Cyprien. "Of Journeys and Border Crossings: Return of Refugees, Identity and Reconstruction in Rwanda," *African Studies Review* 41, no. 1 (April 1998).

Forster, Peter G. Michael Hitchcock, and Francis F. Lyimo, *Race and Ethnicity in East Africa.* New York, St. Martin's Press, Inc., 2000.

Forte, Janette. *The Material Culture of the Wapishana People of the South Rupununi Savannahs in 1989.* Georgetown: Amerindian Research Unit, University of Guyana, 1992.

Fox, Jonathan. "Counting the Causes and Dynamics of Ethnoreligious Violence." *Totalitarian Movements & Political Religions* 4, issue 3 (Winter 2003).

Fox, Jonathan. "Is Islam More Conflict Prone than Other Religion? A Cross Sectional Study of Ethnoreligious Conflict." *Nationalism and Ethnic Politics* 6, no. 2 (2000).

Friedlander, Saul. *Nazi Germany and the Jews: the Years of Persecution 1933–39.* London: Weidenfeld and Nicolson, 1997.

Ganguly, Rajat. *Kin State Intervention in Ethnic Conflicts: Lessons from South Asia.* New Delhi: Sage Publications, 1968.

Ganguly, Sumit *The Origins of War in South Asia: Indo-Pakistani Conflicts since 1947.* Boulder, CO: Westview Press, 1986.

Gbadegesin, S. *The Politicization of Society During Nigeria's Second Republic, 1979-1983.* Lewiston, New York: The Edwin Mellen Press, 1991.

Ghosh, Partha S. *Conflict and Cooperation in South Asia.* New Delhi: Manohar, 1995.

Giannakos, S.A. (ed.). *Ethnic Conflict: Religion, Identity, and Politics.* Athens: Oxford University Press, 2002.

Gibson, Kean. *The Cycle of Racial Oppression in Guyana.* Lanham, New York: University Press of America, 2003.

Giddens, A. *Modernity and Self Identity. Self and Society in the Late Modern Age.* Cambridge: Polity, 1991.

Gilpin, Robert. *War and Change in World Politics.* Cambridge and NY: Cambridge University Press, 1981.

Glasgow, Roy Arthur. *Guyana: Race and Politics Among Africans and East Indians.* The Hague: Martinus Nijhoff, 1970.

Glaston, William. *Liberal Purposes: Goods, Virtues, and Diversity in the Liberal State.* Cambridge: Cambridge University Press, 1991.

Gold, Daniel "Organized Hinduisms: From Vedic Truth to Hindu Nation," in Martin E. Marty and R. Scott Appleby (eds.), *Fundamentalisms Observed* 1. Chicago: University of Chicago Press, 1991.

Gourevitch, Philip. *We Wish to Inform You That Tomorrow We Will Be Killed with Our Families.* New York: Farrar Straus and Giroux, 1998.

Gros, Jean-Germain. "Towards a Taxonomy of Failed States in the New World Order: Somalia, Liberia, Rwanda and Haiti." *Third World Quarterly* 17, no. 3, 1996.

Gunaratna, Rohan. *Indian Intervention in Sri Lanka.* Colombo, Sri Lanka: South Asian Network on Conflict Research, 1993.

Gurr, Ted G. *Minorities at Risk: A Global View of Ethnopolitical Conflicts.* Washington, D.C.: United States Institute of Peace Press, 1993.

Gutman, Roy and David Rieff. *Crimes of War.* New York: W.W. Norton, 1999.

Hardin, Russell. *One for All: The Logic of Group Conflict.* Princeton: Princeton University Press, 1995.

Harvey, Frank, eds. *Millennial Reflections on International Studies.* Ann Arbor, MI.: University of Michigan Press, 2002.

Harvey, Neil. *The Chiapas Rebellion: The Struggle for Land and Democracy.* Durham, NC: Duke University Press, 1988.

Held, David. *Democracy and the Global Order.* New York: Polity Press, 1995.

Heppner, K. "'My Gun was as Tall as Me': Child Soldiers in Burma." *Human Rights Watch.* 2002. <http://www.eldis.org/static/DOC11178.htm>.

Hinds, David. "Guyana's Dominant Political Culture: An Overview." In Holger Henke and Fred Reno. *Modern Political Culture in the Caribbean.* Kingston, Jamaica: University of West Indies Press, 2003.

Hintjens, Helen. "Explaining the 1994 Genocide in Rwanda." *Journal of Modern African Studies* 37, no.2 (1999).

Hobsbawm, Eric and Terence Ranger. *The Invention of Tradition.* Cambridge: Cambridge University Press, 1983.

Hope, Kemp Ronald. *Guyana: Politics and Development in an Emergent Socialist State.* New York: Mosaic Press, 1986.

Horowitz, Donald L. *The Deadly Ethnic Rio.* Berkeley: University of California Press, 2001.

———. *Ethnic Groups in* Conflict. Berkeley: University of California Press, 1985.

Huddy, Leonie. "From Social to Political Identity: A Critical Examination of Social Identity Theory," *Political Psychology* 22, no. 1 (2001).

Huntington, Samuel P. *Political Order in Changing Societies.* Connecticut: Yale University Press, 1975.

International Crisis Group. *God, Oil, and Country: Changing the Logic of War in Sudan. Africa Report No.39.* 2001.

Isaacs, Harold A. *Idols of the Tribe: Group Identity and Political Change.* New York: Harper and Row, 1975.

Jaffrelot, Christophe. "The Politics of Processions and Hindu-Muslim Riots." In Amrita Basu and Atul Kohli, eds. *Community Conflicts and the State in India.* Delhi: Oxford University Press, 1998.

James, Patrick. "Systemism in International Relations: Toward a Reassessment of Realism." In Michael Brecher and James, Patrick. *International Relations and Scientific Progress: Structural Realism Reconsidered.* Columbus, OH: Ohio State University Press, 2002.

Jetley, Nancy. "India: The Domestic Dimensions of Security." In *South Asian Insecurity and the Great Powers* edited by Barry Buzan and Gowher Rizvi. UK: Macmillan Press, 1986.

Johnson, Douglas. *The Root Causes of Sudan's Civil Wars.* Oxford: James Currey, 2003.

Judgment, *Akayesu* (ICTR-96-4-T), Trial Chamber I, 2 September 1998.

Juergensmeyer, Mark. *The New Cold War?* Berkeley: University of California Press, 1993.

Kadane, Kathy. "U.S. Officials' Lists Aided Indonesian Bloodbath in '60s'." *Washington Post,* 21 May 1990.

Kadian, Rajesh. *India's Sri Lanka Fiasco: Peacekeepers at War.* New Delhi: Vision Books, 1990.

———. *The Kashmir Tangle: Issues and Options.* New Delhi: Vision Books, 1992.

Kakar, Sudhir. *The Colors of Violence.* Chicago: University of Chicago Press, 1996.

———. *Culture and Psyche: Psychoanalysis and India.* New York: Psyche Press, 1997.

————. *The Essential Writings of Sudhir Kakar* (with an introduction by T.G. Vaidyanathan). Oxford: Oxford University Press, 2001.

Kaufman, Chaim. "Possible and Impossible Solutions to Ethnic Civil Wars." *International Security* (1996).

Kaufman, Stuart. "An 'International' Theory of Inter-Ethnic War." *Review of International Studies* (1996).

————. *Modern Hatreds: The Symbolic Politics of Ethnic War.* Ithaca, NY: Cornell University Press, 2001.

Kazdin, Alan E. (ed.), *Encyclopedia of Psychology.* New York: Oxford University Press, 2000.

Keane, Fergal. *Season of Blood: A Rwandan Journey.* Harmondsworth: Penguin, 1996.

Keddie, Nikki. "The New Religious Politics and Women World-wide: A Comparative Study," *Journal of Women's History* 10, no. 4 (2004).

Keeling, W. and M. Holman. "Nigerian Coup Attempt Defeated." *Financial Times* April 23, 1990.

————. "Religious Tension Behind Challenge to Babangida." *Financial Times* April 23, 1990.

Khalidi, Mansour. *The Government They Deserve.* London: Paul Kegan International. 1990.

Khan, Mohammad Ayub. *Friends Not Master.* London: Oxford University Press, 1966.

Khan, Sarah Ahmed. *Nigeria: The Political Economy of Oil.* Oxford: Oxford University Press, 1994.

Khong, Yuen Foong. *Analogies at War: Korea, Munich, Dien, Bien Phu and the Vietnam Decisions of 1965.* Princeton, NJ: Princeton University Press, 1992.

Kim, David Chanbonpin, "Historical Background," *Holding the United States Accountable for Environmental Damages Caused by the U.S. Military in the Philippines: A Plan for the Future.* Manoa: University of Hawaii, 2003.

Kodikara, Sheton U, ed. *The External Compulsions of South Asian Politics.* New Delhi: Sage Publications, 1993.

————. "Internationalization of Sri Lanka's Ethnic conflict: the Tamil Nadu Factor," in *Internationalization of Ethnic Conflict* edited by K.M. de Silva and R.J. May. New York: St Martin's Press, 1991.

Kohli, Atul. *Democracy and Discontent: India's Growing Crisis of Governability.* Cambridge: Cambridge University Press, 1990.

Krauze, Enrique. *Mexico Biography of Power: A History of Modern Mexico, 1810–1996.* New York, NY: Harper Collins, 1997.

Krishna, Sankaran. *Postcolonial Insecurities: India, Sri Lanka and the Question of Nationhood.* Minneapolis, MN: University of Minnesota Press, 1999.

Kristeva, Julia. *Nations without Nationalism.* New York: Columbia University Press, 1993.

Kurtz, Stanley N. *All Mothers are One: Hindu India and the Cultural Reshaping of Psychoanalysis*. New York: Columbia University Press, 1992.

Leach, Edmund. *Political Systems of Highland Burma. A Study of Kachin Social Structure*. Boston: Beacon, 1964.

Lemarchand, René. *Rwanda and Burundi*, London: Pall Mall Press, 1970.

Lemke, Douglas. *Regions of War and Peace*. Cambridge and NY: Cambridge University Press, 2002.

Lewis, Linden. "Forbes Burnham (1923-1985): Unraveling the Paradox of Postcolonial Charismatic Leadership in Guyana," in *Caribbean Charisma*, 2001.

Lijphart, Arend. *Democracy in Plural Societies: A Comparative Exploration*. New Haven: Conn.: Yale University Press, 1997.

Linden, Ian. *Church and Revolution in Rwanda*. Manchester: Manchester University Press, 1977.

Louis, Wm. Rogers. *Rwanda-Burundi, 1884–1919*. Oxford: Clarendon Press, 1963.

Macintosh, Anne. "The International Response: Escape from Genocide." In *Ethnic Hatred: Genocide in Rwanda*, edited by O. Igwara. London: ASEN. 1995.

Magnarella, Paul J. *Justice in Africa: Rwanda's Genocide, Its Courts, and the UN Criminal Tribunal*. Aldershot, England: Ashgate, 2000.

Malik, Y.K. and D.K. Vajpeyi, eds. (1988) *India: The Years of Indira Gandhi*. New York: E.J. Brill, 1988.

Mamdani, Mahmood. *When Victims Become Killers: Colonialism, Nativism, and the Genocide in Rwanda*. Princeton: Princeton University Press, 2001.

Mann, M. "The Dark Side of Democracy: The Modern Tradition of Ethnic and Political Cleansing," *New Left Review*, no. 235 (May-June 1999).

Maquet, Jacques J. *The Premise of Inequality in Rwanda: A Study of Political Relations in a Central African Kingdom*. London: Oxford University Press, 1961.

Marcos, B. *Zapata Stories*. London: Katabasis, 2001.

Marian Wilkinson, "Indonesia: Hidden Holocaust of 1965," *Sydney Morning Herald*, 10 July 1999.

Markakis, John. *National and Class Conflict in the Horn of Africa*. Cambridge: Cambridge University Press, 1987.

Mars, Perry. "Ethnic Politics, Mediation, and Conflict Resolution: The Guyana Experience," *Journal of Peace Research* 38, no. 3 (May 2001).

Mason, Philip. *Patterns of Dominance*. Oxford: Oxford University Press, 1970.

Massey, Douglas S. "A Brief History of Human Society: The Origin and Role of Emotion in Social Life," *ASA: American Sociological Review* 67. no. 1 (2002).

Maung, Mya. *The Burma Road to Poverty*. New York: Praeger, 1991.

Menon, UIsha. "Do Women Participate in Riots? Exploring the Notion of 'Militancy' among Hindu Women," *Nationalism & Ethnic Politics* 9, issue 1 (Spring 2003).

Mentore, George. *The Relevance of Myth.* Georgetown, Guyana: Department of Culture, 1988.

Miall, H., O. Ramsbotham, and T. Woodhouse. *Contemporary Conflict Resolution.* Cambridge, UK: Polity Press, 1999.

Migdal, Joel S. *Strong Societies and Weak States: State-Society Relations and the State Capabilities in the Third World.* New Jersey, Princeton University Press, 1988.

Miller, J.D.B. *Survey of Commonwealth Affairs: Problems of Expansion and Attrition 1953–69.* London: Oxford University Press, 1974.

Montagu, M.F. Ashley. *Man's Most Dangerous Myth: the Fallacy of Race.* New York: Harpers, 1953.

Mosse, George L. *Toward the Final Solution. A History of European Racism.* London: J.M. Dent & Sons, 1978.

Mukagasana, Yolande. *N'aie pas peur de savoir Rwanda: une rescapee tutsi raconte,* Ed. J'ai lu, Paris, 1999.

Muni, S.D. "Indo-Sri Lankan Relations and Sri Lanka's Ethnic Conflict." In *Internationalization of Ethnic Conflict* edited by K.M. de Silva and R.J. May. New York: St Martin's Press, 1991.

Muthiah Alagappa, ed. *Political Legitimacy in Southeast Asia: The Quest for Moral Authority.* Stanford, Calif.: Stanford University Press, 1995.

Nandy, Ashsis and Rajni Kothari, "Culture, State and the Recovery of Indian Politics," *Economic and Political Weekly* (December 8, 1984).

Narayan, Deepa, Raj Patel, Kai Schafft, Anne Rademacher and Sarah Koche-Schulte. *Voices of the Poor: Can Anyone Hear Us?* Oxford: World Bank/Oxford University Press, 2000.

Nash, June C. Mayan Visions: *The Quest for Autonomy in an Age of Globalization.* New York, NY: Routledge, 2001.

Ndura, E. *Western Education and African Cultural Iidentity in the Great Lakes Region of Africa: A Case of Failed Globalization.* Peace and Change. (forthcoming).

Newbury, Catherine. *The Cohesion of Oppression: Clientship and Ethnicity in Rwanda.* New York: Columbia University Press, 1988.

Nikki R. Keddie. "Secularism and the State: Towards Clarity and Global Comparison." *New Left Review* (November/December 1997).

Nyankanzi, Edward L. *Genocide: Rwanda and Burundi.* Rochester, VT: Schenkman, 1998.

Nzongola-Ntalaja, G. "The Congo Holocaust and the Rwanda Genocide," *CODESRIA Bulletin* 2 (1999).

Obeyesekere , Gananath. *The Work of Culture: The Symbolic Transformation in Psychoanalysis and Anthropology.* Chicago: University of Chicago Press, 1990.

Olson, Jr., Mancur. *The Logic of Collective Action: Public Goods and the Theory of Groups.* Cambridge, MA: Harvard University Press, 1965.

Olzaks, Susan and K. Tsutsui. Status in the World System and Ethnic Mobilization. *Journal of Conflict Resolution* (1998).

Omvedt, Gail. "Dalit Literature in Maharashtra." *South Asia Bulletin* 7, nos. 1 and 2 (Fall 1987).

Onishi, Norimitsu. "As Oil Riches Flow, Poor Village Cries Out." *New York Times* online. December 22, 2002.

Osborne, Robin. *Indonesia's Secret War: The Guerilla Struggle in Irian Jaya* (Sydney: Allen and Unwin, 1985).

Palmer, Norman D. *Pakistan: The Long Search for Foreign Policy.* Durham, NC: Duke University, Press, no. 43 (1977). Series published for the Duke University Center for Commonwealth and Comparative Studies.

Parekh, Bhikhu. *Rethinking Multiculturalism: Cultural Diversity and Political Theory.* London: Macmillan, 2000.

Parsons, Talcott and Robert Bales. *Family, Socialization and Interaction Process.* New York: The Free Press, 1955.

Persram, Nalini. "Guerrillas, Games and Governmentality," *Small Axe* 5. no. 2 (September 2001).

Pieterse, J. Nederveen. *White on Black: Images of Africa and Blacks in Western Culture*, New Haven, CT.: Yale University Press, 1992.

Pinkney, Robert. *Democracy in the Third World.* Boulder, Colo.: Lynne Reinner Publishers, 2003.

Posen, Barry. The Security Dilemma and Ethnic Conflict. *Survival* 35 (Spring 1993).

Posner, Daniel Nolan "The Institutional Origins of Ethnic Politics in Zambia," Ph.D. thesis, Department of Government, Harvard University, 1998.

Pottier, Johan. "Representations of Ethnicity in Post-Genocide Writings on Rwanda." In *Ethnic Hatred: Genocide in Rwanda*, edited by O. Igwara. London: ASEN, 1995.

Power, Samantha, *"A Problem from Hell": America and the Age of Genocide* (New York, NY: HarperCollins, 2002).

Premdas, Ralph R. "The Internationalization of Ethnic Conflict: Some Theoretical Explorations," in *Internationalization of Ethnic Conflict* edited by K.M. de Silva and R.J. May. New York: St Martin's Press, 1991.

Putnam, Robert. *Making Democracy Work.* Princeton, N.J.: Princeton University Press, 1993.

Rajah, Ananda. "A 'Nation of Intent' in Burma: Karen Ethno-Nationalism, Nationalism and Narrations of Nation." *The Pacific Review* 15, no. 4 (2002).

Ram, Mohan. *Sri Lanka: The Factured Island.* New Delhi: Penguin, 1989.

Ram-prasad, C. "Hindutva Ideology: Extracting the Fundamentals," *Contemporary South Asia*, vol. 2, no. 3 (1993).

Randrianja, Sofolo. "Nationalism, Ethnicity and Democracy," in Stephen Ellis, ed. *Africa Now: People, Policies & Institutions*. London: Heinemann, 1996.

Republic of Rwanda. *Recommendations of the Conference Held in Kigali from November 1st to5th, 1995 on "Genocide, Impunity and Accountability: Dialogue for a National and International Response."* Kigali: Office of the President, December, 1995.

Ress, D. *The Burundi Ethnic Massacres: 1988* (San Francisco: Mellen Research University Press, 1991).

Reyntjens, Filip. *Burundi: Breaking the Cycle of Violence*. Manchester, United Kingdom: Manchester Free Press, 1995.

Rizvi, Hasan-Askari. *Pakistan and the Geostrategic Environment: A Study of Foreign Policy*. UK and New York: St. Martin's Press, 1993.

Robinson, Geoffrey. "The Fruitless Search for a Smoking Gun: Tracing the Origins of Violence in East Timor." In *Roots of Violence in Indonesia*. Edited by Freek Colombijn and J. Thomas Lindblad. Leiden: KITLV Press, 2002.

Rodney, Walter. *A History of the Guyanese Working People, 1881-1905*. Baltimore: Johns Hopkins University Press, 1981.

Rosenau, James N. "Roles and Role Scenarios in Foreign Policy." In *Role Theory and Foreign Policy Analysis* edited by Stephen G. Walker. Durham, NC: Duke University Press, 1987.

Rotberg, Robert. "African Nationalism: Concept or Confusion?" *Journal of Modern African Studies* 4, no. 1 (1967).

Russett, Bruce M., and John R Oneal. *Triangulating Peace: Democracy, Interdependence, and International Organizations*. New York: W.W. Norton, 2001.

Rutinwa, Bonaventure. "Durable Solutions: An Appraisal of the New Proposals for Prevention and Solution of the Refugee Crisis in the Great Lakes Region," *Journal of Refugee Studies* 9, no. 3 (September 1996).

Salih, Mohammed. A. *African Democracies and African Politics*. London: Pluto Books, 2001.

Sandler, Todd. *Collective Action: Theory and Applications*. Ann Arbor, MI: University of Michigan Press, 1992.

Scherrer , Christian P. *Genocide and Crisis in Central Africa: Conflict Roots, Mass Violence, and Regional War*. Westport, Connecticut: Praeger, 2002.

Seecoomar, Judaman. *Contributions Towards the Resolution of Conflict in Guyana*. Leeds, UK: Peepal Tree Press, 2002.

Semujanga, J. *Origins of Rwandan Genocide*. Amherst, NY: Humanity Books, 2003.

Shils, E.A. "Primordial, Personal, Sacred, and Civil ties." *The British Journal of Sociology* 8 (1957).

Silverman. M. *Race, Discourse and Power in France*. Avebury: Aldershot, 1991.

Silverstein, Josef. *Burmese Politics: The Dilemma of National Unity.* New Brunswick: Rutgers University Press, 1980.

Simmel, Georg. 1955. *Conflict,* trans. by Kurt H. Wolf. Glencoe, Ill.: The Free Press, 1955.

Singer, J.D. Accounting for International War: The State of Discipline. *Journal of Peace* 98 (1981).

Singh, Sangat. *Pakistan's Foreign Policy: An Appraisal.* New York: Asia Publishing House, 1970.

Smith, M.G. *The Plural Society in the British West Indies.* Berkeley: University of California Press, 1966.

Solomon, Jay. "Mobil Sees Its Gas Plant Become Rallying Point for Indonesian Rebels." *Wall Street Journal,* 7 September 2000.

Somerville, Keith. *Foreign Military Intervention in Africa.* New York: St. Martin's Press, 1990.

Soyinka, Wole. *The Open Sore of a Continent: A Personal Narrative of the Nigerian Crisis.* New York: New York University Press, 1996.

Spencer, Jonathan. "Problems in the Analysis of Communal Violence." *Contributions to Indian Sociology* 26, no. 2 (1992).

Speth, James Gustave. The Plight of the Poor: The United States Must Increase Aid. *Foreign Affairs* 78 (May-June 1999).

Stavenhagen, Rodolfo. *Ethnic Conflicts and the Nation-State.* New York: St. Martin's Press, Inc., 1996.

Sten Widmalm. "The Rise and Fall of Democracy in Jammu and Kashmir, 1975-1989." In Amrita Basu and Atul Kohli. *Community Conflicts and the State in India.* Delhi: Oxford University Press, 1998.

Stephen, Lynn. "Pro-Zapatista and Pro-PRI: Resolving the Contradictions of Zapatismo in Rural Oaxaca." *Latin American Research Review* 32, no. 2 (1997).

———. "The Zapatista Army of National Liberation and the National Democratic Convention." *Latin American Perspectives* 22, no. 4 (1995).

———. *Zapata Lives: Histories and Cultural Politics in Southern Mexico.* Berkeley: University of California Press, 2002.

Suryadinata, L., Evi N. Arifin, and Aris Ananta. *Indonesia's Population: Ethnicity and Religion in a Changing Political Landscape Singapore.* Singapore: Institute of Southeast Asian Studies, 2002.

Taylor, Charles. *Multiculturalism and the Politics of Recognition* Princeton: Princeton University Press, 1992.

———. *Sources of the Self.* Cambridge, MA: Harvard University Press, 1989.

Taylor, Christopher C. *Sacrifice as Terror: The Rwandan Genocide of 1994.* Oxford: New York: Berg, 1999.

Than, Mya and Myat Thein, eds. *Financial Resources for Development in Myanmar: Lessons from Asia.* Singapore: Institute of Southeast Asian Studies, 2000.

Thompson. S.W. and K. M. Jensen. *Approaches to Peace*. Washington, D.C.: United States Institute of Peace, 1991.

Throup, D. *The Colonial Legacy*. In O. Furley (Ed.), *Conflict in Africa*. London: Tauris Academic Studies, 1995.

Tiryakian, E.A. and R. Rogowski. *New Nationalsims of the Developed West*. London: Allen & Unwin, 1985.

Turton, David, ed. *War and Ethnicity: Global Connections and Local Violence*. Rochester: University of Rochester Press, 1997.

Uvin, Peter. "Prejudice, Crisis and Genocide in Rwanda," *African Studies Review*, 40 (2) (1997).

Uwazie, Ernest E., ed. *Conflict Resolution and Peace Education in Africa*. Oxford, UK: Lexington Books, 2003.

Vaidyanathan, T.G. *The Essential Writings of Sudhir Kaka*. Oxford: Oxford University Press, 2001.

———. and Jeffrey J. Kripal, eds. *Vishnu on Freud's Desk: A Reader in Psychoanalysis and Hinduism*. Delhi: Oxford University Press, 1999.

Varshney, Ashutosh, "Ethnic Conflict and Civil Society: India and Beyond," *World Politics* 53, no. 3 (April 2001).

———. "Postmodernism, Civic Engagement, and Ethnic Conflict: A Passage to India," *Comparative Politics* 30, issue 1 (October 1997).

——— . "The Local Roots of India's Riots," *The Milli Gazette* 3. no. 7 (March 1, 2004).

Veltmeyer, Henry. "The Dynamics of Social Change and Mexico's EZLN." *Latin American Perspectives* 27, no. 5 (2000).

Venkateshwar, P. Rao. "Ethnic Conflict in Sri Lanka: India's Role and Perception." *Asian Survey* 28 (1988).

Volkan, Cyprus, Volkan. *War and Adaptation: A Psychoanalytic History of Two Ethnic Groups in Conflict*. Charlottesville: University Press of Virginia, 1979.

Wager, Stephen J. and Donald E. Schulz. "Civil-Military Relations in Mexico: The Zapatista Revolt and its Implications." *Journal of Interamerican Studies and World Affairs* 37, no. 1 (1995).

Walker, Stephen G. "Conclusion: Role theory and Foreign Policy Analysis: an Evaluation." In *Role Theory and Foreign Policy Analysis* edited by Stephen G. Walker. Durham, NC: Duke University Press. 1987.

Wallace, Paul. "Globalization of Civil-Military Relations: Democratization, Reform and Security." Paper presented at the International Political Studies Association, Bucharest, Romania, 27 June-3 July 2002.

Waller, David. *Rwanda: Which Way Now?* London: Oxfam Country Profile, 1993.

Wallerstein, Immanuel. *The Capitalist World Economy*. Cambridge: Cambridge University Press, 1979.

Waltz, Kenneth N. *Theory of International Politics*. Reading, Mass: Addison-Wesley Publishing Co., 1979.

Wee, Vivienne. "Social Fragmentation in Indonesia: A Crisis from Suharto's New Order," *Southeast Asia Research Centre Working Paper Series*, no. 31 (Hong Kong: City University of Hong Kong, September 2002).

———— and Kanishka Jayasuriya, "New Geographies and Temporalities of Power: Exploring the New Fault Lines of Southeast Asia," *The Pacific Review* 15, no. 4 (2002).

Weiner, Myron. "The Macedonian Syndrome." *World Politics* 23 (1971): 4.

Weller, Worth H. *Conflict in Chiapas: Understanding the Modern Mayan World*. North Manchester, IN: DeWitt Books, 2000.

Wilkinson, Marian. "Indonesia: Hidden Holocaust of 1965." *Sydney Morning Herald*, 10 July 1999.

Wilson, Alfred Jeyaratnam. *The Break-Up of Sri Lanka: The Sinhalese-Tamil Conflict*. London: Christopher Hurst and Co., 1988.

Winter, Roger. "Slaughter in Rwanda: It's More Politics than Tribalism." *Monday Development 12* (April 1994).

Wolters, Heine-Geldern. History, Culture, and Region in Southeast Asian Perspective. Ithaca: Southeast Asia Program Publications, Southeast Asia Program, Cornell University, 1999.

Womack, John, Jr. *Rebellion in Chiapas: An Historical Reader*. New York: New Press, 1999.

World Bank. *World Economic Indicators*. Washington, DC: World Bank Publications, 2003.

Wright, Jr., Theodore P. "The Muslim Minority Before and After Ayodhya." In Arvind Sharma, ed. *Hinduism and Secularism After Ayodhya*. New York: Palgrave, 2001.

Yeros, Paris. *Ethnicity and Nationalism in Africa: Constructivist Reflections and Contemporary Politics*. New York: St Martin's Press, 1999.

Yurick, S. "The Emerging Metastate Versus the Politics of Ethnonationalist Identity." In Nederveen Pieterse and B. Parekh. *TheDecolonization of Imagination: Culture Knowledge and Power*. London: Zed Books, 1995.

Ziring, Lawrence. *The Ayub Khan Era: Politics in Pakistan, 1958-69*. New York: Syracuse University Press, 1971.

Index

1962 Sino-Indian clash, 26
1963 Constitutional Conference in London, 204
1969 Land Use Act, 181
1980 elections, 212
1994 genocide, 116, 119
1994 post-genocide government, 115
2005 Burundi Constitution, 307
2005 Sudan Peace Agreement, 228, 239, 240, 244
9-11 environment, 228

Abacha administration, 179
absence of legitimacy, 52
Abyssinia, 114
Acehnese leaders, 63
Addis Agreement, 235
African cultural manifestations, 207
African Rights, 121, 128
African Union (AU), 242
Afro-Guyanese police, 198
agrarian and paternalistic values, 126

agrarian laborers, 252
agrarian reform, 254, 262
Agreement on Indigenous Rights and Culture, 262
Ali Bhutto, Zulfikar, 29
alienated Hindu child, 142
alienated parties, 184
Aligarh city, 142
Allied Powers, 271, 272, 274
al-Nimeiri, Jaafar, 235
al-Queda, 236
alternative approach to Islam, 238
al-Turabi's vision, 238
Amerindians, 197–199, 201, 205, 207, 208, 210–216
Amnesty International, 92, 218
Anglo-American mission, 28
Ansar, 237
anthropological literature, 48
anthropological proofs, 83
anticipated range of expectations, 20
Anti-Tamil riots in 1983, 31
Anya Nya, 227, 235, 240
Arab/Islamic culture, 238

Arabic, 61, 233, 234, 285
Arabized Nubiyin, 233
Arabs and Turks, 232
Armed Forces of Rwanda, 119
Arusha Accords, 119, 120, 121
Arusha Peace Accord, 123, 305
Aryan and Semitic traits, 298
ascriptive group identities, 49
ascriptive legitimacy, 53
Association of Southeast Asian
    Nations (ASEAN), 59
asylum advocacy, 87
authoritarian propaganda, 86
autonomy of Kashmir, 26
Azar, Edward, 174

Babangida, Ibrahim, 179
Babri mosque, 135, 140
Bagaza, Jean-Baptiste, 303
Bagchi, Amiya Kumar, 149
Bajrang Dal, 152
Balewa, Tafawa, 180
Bangladesh crisis, 37
Bangladesh War of 1971, 34
Bantu, 80, 87, 108, 297, 298
Bantu majority, 298
Bantu-speakers, 108
Bashir, Omar, 234
Bashir regime, 236, 238
Batutsi masters, 113
Bazargan, Mehdi, 281
Beja, 227, 232, 241
Belgian colonizers, 81
Belgium, 81, 113, 115, 300, 303
Biafran civilians, 178
Biafran Republic, 178
Biafran secession, 184
Biafran war, 181
bin Laden, Osama, 236
Birori, Joseph, 300
Brass, Paul, 136, 137, 144, 146,
    151, 159
British colonization, 55, 56
British North Borneo, 55

Bujumbura, 301, 304, 305, 308
Burma, 47, 49, 55–61, 63, 64, 67,
    68, 69
Burma Project, 59
Burman nation-making myths, 56
Burmese Way to Socialism, 57
Burnham, Forbes, 202, 212
Burundi, 95, 98, 111, 113, 116,
    117, 120, 121, 123, 127, 295–
    308
Burundi army, 120, 308
Burundi political system, 308
Butare, 123

Camp Pesadillas, 257
Caribbean Free Trade, 203
CARICOM (Caribbean
    Community), 203
caste stereotypes, 113
Catholic missionary schools, 297
Catholic seminary, 116
centralizing military rule, 68
Centre Force, 209, 210, 215, 218
charismatic authority, 51, 52
Chevron executives, 190
Chiapas, 251, 252–259, 261–263
Chiapas Indians, 252
Chomsky, Noam, 261
Christian Belgians, 114
Christian missionaries, 114, 178
Civic groups, 61
classification system, 90, 123
coalition of northern opposition,
    235
Codere, Helen, 110, 128
colonial ideologies, 84
Common Front, 300
community of murderers, 122
composite nationalism, 135
conflict generating, 194
conflict situations, 86, 134, 199,
    218
conflict-laden politics of race, 79
Congress Party, 32, 35

conservative elites, 253
construction of differences, 49
constructivist scholars, 229
Cooperative Republic of Guyana,
    203
counter-claims to resources, 53
counter-productions of time, 53
Court of Fiestas, 255
Cross River, 180
cultural affirmation, 151
cultural and racial assimilation, 253
cultural assimilation, 252, 255
cultural condition, 142, 216, 217
cultural demise of Indian groups,
    252
cultural fundamentalism, 85
cultural interpretation, 137
cultural markers, 61, 135
cultural particularities, 208, 229
culture of sharing and self-help,
    296
current territory of the state, 68

Dalits, 136, 152
Darfur, 225–228, 231–234, 236,
    241–244
Darfur Sudanese Liberation
    Movement, 227
Darfur villages, 236
Darul Islam (House of Islam), 62
Darwin,Charles, 253
De Gaulle, Charles, 184
decentralization of significant
    power, 193
deeply divided society, 239
defense of democracy, 305, 307
dehumanization of rival groups,
    177
Delta communities, 182, 190
Democratic National Convention
    (CND), 261
Democratic Republic of Congo, 78,
    93

Democratic Revolutionary Party
    (PRD), 262
Department of Petroleum
    Resources, 181
der Berghe, Van, 48, 69
desire for hegemony, 176
developmentalist future, 53
developmentalist project, 53, 68
diasporic nationalism, 99
differences between self and other,
    48
Dinka dominance, 240
discrimination against Tutsi, 111
divide-and-rule, 81, 204, 216
Dr. Mosaddegh, 280
Dravidian parties, 32
Dutch colonial government, 56
dynamics of primordial
    attachments, 174

East Indian, 198, 200, 202, 203,
    205, 207
East Timor, 49, 54, 60, 62–64, 69
East Timorese refugees, 64
economic sanctions, 58, 304, 306
ecotourism, 214
Edo State, 182
egalitarian ideology, 109
ejido land, 256
elite manipulation, 175
Eltringham, Nigel, 82
embryonic Sudanese state, 235
emerging sense of nationalism, 86
Equatoria, 239
ethnic affiliations, 22, 28, 160
ethnic apartheid, 304
ethnic brethren, 22, 23
ethnic cleansing, 82, 304
ethnic composition, 25
ethnic conflict and ethnic violence,
    49
ethnic constituency, 25, 37, 54
ethnic differentiation, 48, 54, 55,
    57

ethnic domination and diversity,
  24, 37
ethnic Hindu traditions, 137
ethnic imperatives, 38
ethnic insurgencies in Southeast
  Asia, 59
ethnic intervention in South Asia,
  25
ethnic nation, 37, 54, 59, 69, 281
ethnic policies, 50
ethnic spectrum, 136
ethnic violence in Burundi, 296,
  297
ethnicist, 86, 88, 100, 199, 200,
  206, 207
ethnicity as a social phenomenon,
  47
ethnocentric baggage, 138
ethnocentric orientation, 153
ethnocentrism, 137, 143, 151, 153,
  155, 161, 174
ethno-historical narratives, 61
ethnoreligious consideration, 18
ethnos of a nation, 136
Euro-Guyanese, 212
European Union (EU), 274, 288
Evangelical Christian, 262
external environment, 18, 19–24,
  26–28, 33, 34, 142
external manipulation, 87
externalization, 139
extraordinary virtuosity, 51

false information, 86
federal imbalance, 177
federalist option, 241
Federated Shan States, 56
feudal-type structure of Lord and
  Serf, 297
First and Second Republics, 90
First Republic (1960-1966), 177
Fox, Vincent, 263
fragmenting the Rwandan
  population, 86

Franco-British rivalry in Africa,
  184
Frederick, Duke, 111, 128
Free Aceh Movement (Gerakan
  Aceh), 63
Free Papua Movement, 63
French aid to Biafra, 184
French military intervention, 253
Freudian analysis, 156
functional prerequisite, 136
functional role of the state, 52

Gacaca, 90, 92
Galla tribes, 111
Gandhi, Indira, 33, 35, 37
Gandhi, Rajiv, 33, 35, 37
Ganwa political (ruling) class, 296
Garang, John, 226, 227, 240, 244,
  245
genealogical accounts of kinship,
  61
genocide, 77, 82, 100, 120, 123,
  128, 242
genocide suspects, 92, 95
geographical affiliation, 233
geo-political moments, 51
Georgetown, 197, 200, 205, 210,
  213–216
German East Africa, 113
global capitalist system, 253
global democratic development,
  225
Global Organization of People of
  Indian Origin (GOPIO), 206
globalization, 245
goal-rational authority, 51, 52
God Ganesh, 146
Gold, Daniel, 137, 151
golden age of perfection, 52
government hierarchy, 127
Great Lakes region, 77, 79, 80, 87,
  97–100, 296
group-binding functions, 175
Guerilla activities, 274

Guha, Ranajit, 146
Gujarat riots, 147
Guyana Indian Foundation, 205
Guyanese people, 218

Hamitic hypothesis, 124, 298
hamitic myth, 79, 114
hamitic people, 114
hamitic racial ideology, 298
hanging judge, 282
hardening of differentiation, 49
Hausa, 176, 177, 182
Hausa-Fulani, 177
hegemonic power, 23, 36
Hindu psyche, 154
Hindu tolerance, 152
Hindu-Muslim riots, 134, 135, 138,
    139, 144, 146, 147, 156, 161
Hindutva ideology, 135
historical analogies, 24, 29, 36
HIV/AIDS crises, 58
Hobbesian mission of the state, 67
Holy Quran and Sunna, 30
homeland, 84, 188, 189, 216, 284–
    286, 288
Horowitz, Donald, 69, 136, 141,
    142, 154
Hoyte, Desmond, 206, 214
hunger and malnutrition, 127
Hutu, 77, 78, 80–82, 86–91, 93,
    96–98, 107–127, 295–308
Hutu and Tutsi ancestry, 87
Hutu children, 299
Hutu citizens, 108, 120
Hutu farmers, 109, 116, 124
Hutu hoodlums, 120
Hutu majority domination, 301
Hutu Manifesto of 1957, 115
Hutu masses, 107, 127
Hutu political leaders, 113
Hutu Prime Minister, 303
Hutu refugees, 118, 121, 302
Hutu uprising, 302
Hutu-Tutsi coexistence, 295

Hutu-Tutsi discord, 295
Hutu-Tutsi divide, 99
hyper-nationalist, 199

ideational domain, 53
ideational engagement, 54
identity cleavages, 174
ideological conflict, 61, 62, 252
Ideology of genocide, 84
Ideology of separate races, 79
Igbo, 177, 180
Ijaw communities, 189
Imidugudu (villagisation), 95
Impuza-mugambi, 120
Indian ethnicity, 207
Indian involvement, 33
Indian islands, 55
Indian reservation model, 287
Indian rights, 255, 258, 260–263
indigenous Dayaks, 65
indigenous organizations, 176
Indigenous Revolutionary
    Clandestine Committee
    (CCRI), 257
individual human rights, 99
Indo-Guyanese factions, 202
Indonesia, 47, 49, 55, 56, 60–69
inequities in institutions, 54
institutional constraints, 24
institutional domain, 53
institutional innovations, 77, 90
institutionalized differences, 48
instrumentalist, 139, 161, 226, 230
instrumentalist and constructivist
    theories, 226
integrative federalism, 207, 216
Interahamwe, 120–122, 125
intercaste mobility, 109
international complicity, 99
international structure/hierarchy,
    21, 27, 33, 38
inter-tribal, 81, 211
intrinsic social and cultural
    differences, 50

inverted pyramid, 229
Iranian-Arabs, 289, 290
Iran-Iraq War, 276
Islamic Front, 243
Islamic history, 61
Islamic ideology, 29–31
Islamic party, 62
Itsekiri youths, 191

Jaffrelot, Christophe, 137, 151
Jagan, Cheddi, 200, 202, 214
Jagan, Janet, 200, 202, 206, 213
Jaguar Committee for Democracy, 205
Javanese-dominated military, 64
Jazira region, 283
Jehadist Islamic fundamentalism, 135
Jemaah Islamiya, 62
jihadists, 66
Jinnah, Mohammad Ali, 29
Justice and Equality Movement (JEM), 227, 243
Justice for All Party, 209
juvenile delinquency, 125

Kachin state, 57
Kagame, Alexis, 83
Kagame, Paul, 123
Kakar, Sudhir, 139, 142, 156, 159, 161
Karens and Shans, 59
karsevaks, 140
Kashmir, 17, 25–31, 38, 138, 154, 155, 157
Kashmir ethnic conflicts, 138
Kayibanda, Gregoire, 116
Khalidi, Mansour, 233
Khan, Ayub, 27, 29, 30
Khomeini, 276, 281, 282
Kigali regime, 78
Kigali, 78, 84, 89, 93, 97, 120, 121, 123, 125

King (mwami) Kigeri Rwabugiri, 109
King Kigri V, 116
Kinyarwanda, 98, 108, 115
Kirkuk, 270, 274, 275
Kohli, Atul, 146, 148, 245
Koka Dam Declaration, 243, 244
Kurd rebellions, 280
Kurdish autonomy, 272, 277, 278, 281–283, 286, 290
Kurdish Ethnonationalism, 269, 290, 293
Kurdish identity, 269, 270, 272
Kurdish landlord, 280
Kurdish optimism, 278
Kurdish political representative, 285
Kurdish population, 270
Kurdish Republic of Mahabad's army, 275
Kurdish-speaking areas, 275
Kurdish uprising, 273, 274, 276
Kurdistan, 270–274, 276, 278, 279, 283–288, 292
Kurds and Indians, 286

La Raza Cosmica, 255
Land of Six Peoples, 198, 200
Land of the Blacks, 232
Laskar, 65
leftist scholars, 135
legitimate state, 50, 54
lethal ethnic riots, 134
liberal democratic state, 227, 228, 235
liberal Islamist Mahmoud Taha, 235
Liberation Theology, 260
Low-priority prisoners, 91
LTTE, 33

Machakos Protocols, 228
macro-level sub-system, 24
mainstream Rwandan army, 91

major ethnic rebellions, 68
major ethnic war in colonial
    Mexico, 252
major structural flaw, 52
Malacca and Penang, 55
Malayam cultural stream, 155
Maldives, 28
Mamdani, 111, 114, 115, 148, 297–
    299
manipulative act, 146
Maquet, 109–111, 113, 128
marginalization of the Indians, 253
Marxism, 51
Marxist argument, 156
Marxist-Leninist tendencies, 273
mass murder, 86, 107, 108, 127,
    128
materialistic interpretation, 150,
    156
Mayan-speaking Indians, 252, 253
Mazrui, Ali, 229
Mexican Congress, 258, 261, 263
Mexican revolution, 251, 261
Mexican society, 253
micro-level variables, 18, 26
micro-micro linkages, 24
Middle Belt, 179, 180
MIG fighters, 183
Ministry of Petroleum Resources,
    181
modern Kurds, 284
Modi government, 149
Mohajirs, 30
Mohammad, Oazi, 279
Mombasa, 126
Mosul province, 274
Mulla Mustafa Barzani, 275
multiple hierarchy model, 23
Muslim League, 28, 29
Mwami (King), 297, 300

nation without a state, 54
National Action Party (PAN), 263

National Democratic Alliance, 227,
    243, 244
National Election Commission, 307
National Front, 209, 237, 280, 281
National Front Alliance, 209
National Islamic Front, 234, 236,
    238, 244
National language in Rwanda, 98
national leadership, 24, 29, 36
National League for Democracy
    (NLD), 58, 59
national role conceptions, 20
National Unity and Reconciliation
    Commission, 91
nation-of-intent, 53, 54, 64
nation-state, 50–56, 60, 62, 84,
    207, 216, 217, 228–230, 241,
    271, 287
Native Americans, 269, 284, 286
naturalization of ethnic difference,
    49
negative myths, 138
negotiated power-sharing, 306
Neo-Liberalism, 256, 262
Neo-traditional institutions, 92
Netherlands East Indies, 55, 60, 63
New Sudan, 226, 227, 239, 240,
    243, 244
Niger Delta communities, 186, 190,
    191, 192
Niger Delta Region, 180, 184, 185,
    188
Nigerian Federation, 178, 183, 184
Nigerian National Oil Company,
    181
Nigerian women, 173
Nilotic, 80, 87, 232, 233
Nilotic stock, 87
Nilotics, 233
Non-Turkish elements, 272
North American Free Trade
    Agreement (NAFTA), 251
Northern Region, 177

North-South 2005 Sudan Peace
    Agreement, 231

Obote, Milton, 118
Observable customs and habits, 61
Ogoni ethnic group, 187
Ogoni women, 188
Ogonis and Niger Delta
    Commission, 186
Ojukwu, Odumegwu, 178
oppressive identity, 99
ordinary Rwandans, 82, 87, 89, 93,
    98
Organization of African Union, 243
organization of ethnicity, 48
Organization of Islamic Conference
    (OIC), 179
organized systematic rape as a
    weapon of war, 49
organizers of the massacres, 122
Oromo, 109
Ottoman Empire, 269, 271

Pakistani politics, 30, 31
Palestinians, 269, 273, 284, 285,
    286, 288
Panglong Accord, 57, 58
PARMEHUTU, 116
Pathans, 31
pathological behavior, 117
pathological character, 140
Patriotic Union (PUK), 276
persecution campaign, 116
Persian vocabulary, 278
Philippines, 55
PKK camps, 273
PKK incursions into Turkey, 274
Plan de Ayala, 254, 255
Plan de San Luis in 1910, 254
political and military elite, 85
political identification, 90
political Islam, 60
political majority, 278, 307

political manipulation, 143, 149,
    150
Political Parties Act, 29
political project of
    developmentalism, 52
pollution of farms, 188
post-Cold War conflicts, 175
post-genocide, 90
post-genocide Rwanda, 86–89, 98
post-genocide strivings, 90
post-Suharto ethnic conflicts, 60,
    64
powerful truths, 86
powerful Tutsi, 110, 299, 300
PPP government, 206, 207, 214
pre-capitalist spatial structures, 52
pre-colonial Burundian people, 296
pre-colonial Rwanda, 87
pre-Colonial Rwandan Culture, 112
pre-cultural understandings, 136
preferred diets, 112
pre-modern states, 51
President Ali Hassan Mwinyi, 121
President Bani-Sadr, 282
President Jayawardene, 33
President Nyerere, 304
Presidential Guard, 117, 121
primal violence, 81
primordial perspective, 174, 175
primordial rationale, 52
problem of governability, 138
pro-natal policy, 127
protection and salvation, 252
proximate cause, 31, 107, 127, 128
psychological character of social
    control, 174

Quran, 61, 238

race labels, 79, 84
race politics, 77, 79–81, 205
racial enemy, 83
racialization, 298
Radio Milles Collines, 120, 121

Radio-Kigali, 120
Rashtriya Swayam Sevak Sangh
    (RSS), 135
rational-legal authority, 51, 52
rebellion of the Tzeltales, 252
reduction of the differentiation, 48
re-education camp, 91
regional organizations, 23, 34
regional peace, 308
religious and ethnic conflicts, 252
religious ideology, 126
religious majorities, 149
religious violence, 133, 134, 148
Republic of Pakistan, 30
Republic of Turkey, 271
Research and Analytical Wing
    (RAW), 36
revivalist communalism, 135
rights of traditional-law
    communities, 65
rigid class structure, 111
Rise Organize and Rally (ROAR),
    197, 199, 201, 205, 206, 208,
    209, 212, 215–217
Ritambhara, 140
River Boat Clinic, 192
Riverine people, 185–187
role expectation, 20–25, 27–30,
    33–38
role performance, 20, 24, 25, 27,
    35–38
role theory, 19
royal tribute, 109
rumors, 149
Rwanda and Burundi, 113, 128,
    297, 298, 300
Rwandan exiles, 87
Rwandan Patriotic Army (RPA),
    118
Rwandan peasants, 93
Rwandan politics, 80, 84, 99
Rwandan society, 80, 83, 87, 89,
    93, 96, 113

Rwanda-Urundi Customary Law
    and Native Authorities, 298
Rwanda-Urundi, 297, 298

Saadabad Pact, 271
SAARC, 23, 28, 34
Saddam Hussein, 275, 277, 278,
    282, 286, 292
Sakaria Commission, 148
Salafi Islam, 238
Salinas, Carlos, 256
Second Republic (1979-83), 180
secular nationalism, 60
selective genocide, 296, 304
self-determination, 30, 138, 211,
    215, 228, 234, 239, 240, 241,
    243, 262, 279, 292, 300
sense of social solidarity, 84, 86
separatist education system, 299
serious structural problems, 93
Shaikh Ezzedin Husseini, 281
Shan Democratic Union, 59
shared citizenship, 91
Sharia Laws, 237
Shari-ah, 179
Sheikh Abdullah, 26
Sheikh Said, 272, 273
Simmel, Georg, 175, 194
Singapura, 55
single-party dictatorship, 117
social categorization, 151
social comparison, 153
social conflict, 174
social conformism, 82
social Darwinism, 113, 253,
social Darwinism and Positivism,
    253
social differentiation, 48, 49, 231
social fragmentation, 54, 67
social identities, 151
Social Identity Theory, 151
social psychology, 134, 141
socialist-oriented government, 200
socially constructed, 48, 87, 140

soil erosion, 108
Solanki government, 148
solidaridad, 258, 259
solidarity camps, 91
South Asia, 17, 23, 28, 33, 34, 38,
     147, 162
South Sulawesi, 62
Southeast Asia, 47, 52, 55, 56, 67,
     69
Southeast Asian region, 52
Southwest villagesation, 95
Spanish colonial government, 252
specific hatreds, 83
Spencer, Herbert, 253
state legitimacy, 50
structural integration, 234
structural victimization, 174
subaltern classes, 54
Sub-altern historiography, 146
subjugated groups, 176
sub-national groups, 203
subsistence agriculture, 125
subsystem-level factors, 20
Sudanese state, 225, 227, 228, 231,
     234–238, 240, 244
Sudanese state-society relations,
     235
Sunni Islam, 270
supra-local cultural domain, 61
sustainable development, 192, 193
Suu Kyi, Aung San, 57–59
symmetrical type of violence, 53
Syrian national affiliation, 283
systemism, 18, 21

Tamil militancy, 31
Tamil Nadu, 31–33, 35, 155
Tamil secessionist conflict, 25
Tanzania, 95, 113, 119, 121, 123,
     304, 308
third-party intervention in ethnic
     conflicts, 17
Torit mutiny, 235
total social system, 175

totalitarian state, 84
transmigration Matters (1997), 66
Treaty of Sevres, 271
Turkish-Kurds, 288, 289
Tutsi as alien, 115
Tutsi compradors, 115
Tutsi hegemony, 297, 300, 302
Tutsi land and cattle, 117
Tutsi military regime, 117
Tutsi monarch (mwami), 113
Tutsi refugees, 116, 118, 125, 127
Tutsi royalty, 109, 116
Tutsi warriors, 110
Tutsi wives, 111, 112
Tutsi-dominated government, 116,
     301
Tutsi-Hutu conflicts, 110
Tutsi-Hutu hatred, 295, 296, 302
Twa, 77, 80, 81, 90, 98, 108–115,
     124, 295, 299
two main parties of the Kurdish
     government, 277

UN Human Rights Committee, 216
UN sanctions, 236
unilateral approach to global issues,
     21
unitary, 60, 151, 207, 217
United States Mutual Security Act,
     28
urban Rwandans, 99
utilizing systemism, 18
utopian society of prosperity, 253

Varshney, Ashutosh, 69, 136, 155,
     158, 162
Venustiano Carranza, 254
Villa and Zapata supporters, 261
Vishwa Hindu Parishad (VHP),
     135, 152

Warri, 182
Weberian state, 50
West Papua and Aceh, 49, 64

wholesale affirmative action, 291
win-win solution, 189
women of Aba, 188
WPA statement, 212
WPA-GAP parties, 210

Yoruba, 176, 177, 182

Zaire, 88, 89, 93, 95, 123, 127
Zapata, Emiliano, 251, 254

Zapatista Agenda, 259
Zapatista cause, 260
Zapatista conflict, 262, 263
Zapatista rebellion, 258
Zapatista rhetoric, 261
Zapatista uprising, 251, 252
Zapatistas, 251, 252, 257–259,
    260–263
Zedillo government, 261, 262

About the Contributors

Abdul Karim Bangura holds Ph.Ds in Political Science, Development Economics, Linguistics, and Computer Science, and is the author of 40 books and over 300 scholarly articles. He is currently a researcher-in-residence at the Center for Global Peace and a professor of International Relations in the School of International Service at American University in Washington, DC. He is the coordinator of the B.A. in International Studies—International Peace and Conflict Resolution (IPCR) focus, the coordinator of the Islamic Lecture Series, the coordinator of the National Conference on Undergraduate Research (NCUR), and the faculty advisor of the American University Undergraduate Research Association (AUURA), the International Peace and Conflict Resolution Association (IPCRA), the Student Organization for African Studies (SOFAS) and the Muslim Student Association (MSA) at American University, the United Nations Ambassador of the Association of Third World Studies (ATWS), and the director of The African Institution in Washington, D.C. From 1993 to 2000, Bangura taught Political Science and International Studies, served as Special Assistant to the President and Provost, founded and directed The Center for Success at Bowie State University of the University of Maryland System. He also has taught at Georgetown University, Howard University and Sojourner-Douglass College. He is Editor-In-Chief of both the *Journal of Research Methodology and African Studies* (JRMAS) and the *African Journal of Languages and Linguistics* (AJLL). He is a former President of the Association of Third World Studies (ATWS). Bangura's books include *United States Congress vs Apartheid* (in press), *Introduction to Islam: A Sociological Perspective* (in press), *Islamic Peace Paradigms* (in press), *Fettered–tions* (in press) *Surah Al-Fatihah: A Linguistic Exploration of Its Meanings* (2004), *Sweden vs. Apartheid: Putting Morality Ahead of Profit* (2004), *Islamic Sources of Peace* (2004), *The World of*

Islam: Country-by-Country Profiles (2004), *The Holy Qur'an and Contemporary Issues* (2003), *Washington, D.C. State of Affairs* (2003), *Law and Politics at the Grassroots: A Case Study of Prince George's County* (2003).

Rita Kiki Edozie (Ph.D. Political Science, The New School University, NY, 1999) is an Assistant Professor at James Madison College, Michigan State University, East Lansing. There, she specializes in Comparative Politics and International/African Affairs. Dr. Edozie has held appointments as the Deputy Director of the Institute of African Studies at Columbia University's School of International and Public Affairs (SIPA), and was a visiting assistant professor with the department of political science and international relations at the University of Delaware. Professor Edozie's current research interests include comparative democratization and developing world economic development. She is the author of "People Power and Democracy: the popular movement against military despotism in Nigeria, 1989-1999" (Africa World Press, 2002); and has recently published an article in "African and Asian Studies," entitled, "Promoting African Owned and Operated Development: Reflections on the New Partnership for African Development (NEPAD)", as well as in *Journal of Third World Studies* entitled, "Third World Democracies: South-South Learning from Each Other" (forthcoming). Dr. Edozie has contributed book chapters to several edited volumes, and is presently working on two book projects: a co-edited African politics volume with Dr. Peyi Soyinka-Airewele entitled, "Reframing African Politics: Politics, Culture and Society in a Global Era," and authored scholarly text on democracy in Africa, entitled, "Reconstructing Africa's Third Wave: a comparative analysis of democracy."

Gaurav Ghose graduated 1 from Missouri's journalism school, University of Missouri. There he did MA in political science. Ghose is a graduate of the University of Missouri-Columbia with a double master's in poltitcal science and journalism. Earlier he was Senior Editor of Politics with Oxford University Press-India. Presently he is a freelance journalist based in Tampa, FL.

Michael R. Hall is an associate professor of history at Armstrong Atlantic State University in Savannah, Georgia. He teaches U.S.-Latin American foreign relations and Latin American history. He earned an M.A. in History from Gettysburg College in 1983. He served in the Peace Corps in the Dominican Republic from 1984 to 1987. He earned his M.A. in International Studies from Ohio University in 1989. He earned his Ph.D. in History from Ohio University in 1996. He is the author of *Sugar and Power in the Dominican Republic* (2000). He taught at the Instituto Technologico de Santo Domingo (INTEC) and led study abroad programs in Brazil, Peru, Ecuador, and the Dominican Republic.

Helen M. Hintjens is Lecturer in International Development Studies and has published on post-colonial governance and human rights in International Development, including in Rwanda, Reunion island, and the French, British and Dutch Caribbean. She has published on asylum and immigration issues, gender, nationalism, new social movements, and activism. She has done intensive field studies in Rwandan genocides.

Mir Zohair Husain is an Associate Professor of Political Science at the University of South Alabama. He has written many articles and given numerous talk on Islam, Muslims, and the Muslim World. His popular book on Islamism, *Global Islamic Politics*, 2nd edition, was published by Longman Publishers in 2003. McGraw-Hill will be publishing his book *Global Studies: Islam and the Muslim World*, in December 2005.

Patrick James is the Frederick A. Middlebush Professor in the Department of Political Science at the University of Missouri Columbia (Ph.D., University of Maryland, College Park). James is the author of ten books and over a hundred articles and book chapters. Among his honors and awards are the Louise Dyer Peace Fellowship from the Hoover Institution at Stanford University, the Milton R. Merrill Chair from Political Science at Utah State University, the Lady Davis Professorship of the Hebrew University of Jerusalem, the Thomas Enders Professorship in Canadian Studies at the University of Calgary, the Senior Scholar award from the Canadian Embassy, Washington, DC, and the Eaton Lectureship at Queen's University in Belfast. He is a past president of the Midwest International Studies Association and the Iowa Conference of Political Scientists. James just completed a five-year term as Editor of *International Studies Quarterly*. At present he is Professor at the California Southern University in Los Angeles.

David Emmanuels Kiwuwa is a final year Doctoral candidate of Political Science and department teacher at the University of Nottingham. His thesis deals with Democratic Transition and Ethnicity in Rwanda. He has recently been to Rwanda for an extended research visit with The Unity and Reconciliation Commission, International Criminal Tribunal for Rwanda and the Centre for Conflict Management at the National University of Rwanda. His article, "Democratisation? The 2003 Rwanda Elections" is under active consideration for publication with the *Journal of Ethnopolitics*.

Graeme Stuart Lang is Associate Professor, Department of Applied Social Studies, and City University of Hong Kong where he teaches science, technology, religion, and society in Asia. His publications appeared in *Sociology of Religion*; *International Migration Review*; *Applied Sociology*; *Organization and Environment*; and other international journals. He has also coauthored a book on Chinese popular religion, *The Rise of a Refuge God: Hong Kong's Tai Sin*, with Lars Ragvald (New York: Oxford University Press, 1993). His current research includes a study of temples and temple reconstruction in China, and a comparative study of syncretistic sects in East and Southeast Asia.

Paul J. Magnarella holds the J.D. with Honors, University of Florida and the Ph.D., Harvard University. He is the Director of Peace Studies at Warren Wilson College, Asheville, N.C. He serves on the Editorial Boards of the *Journal of Social Justice*, and the *Journal of Third World Studies*. He has served as Expert-on-Mission with the United Nations Criminal Tribunal for the Former Yugoslavia and is Legal Counsel to the American Anthropological Association's Human Rights Committee and Special Counsel to the Association of Third World Studies (ATWS). He is Past President of the ATWS and recipient of ATWS's Presidential Award. His most recent book, *Justice in Africa: Rwanda's Genocide, Its National Courts, and the UN Criminal Tribunal* (2000) received the ATWS's Book of the Year Award and was nominated for the Raphael Lemkin Book Award.

Johnson W. Makoba is Associate Professor and Chair of the Department of Sociology at the University of Nevada, Reno. He received his Ph.D. from the University of California, Berkeley in 1990. Dr. Makoba, an African immigrant scholar who has spent nearly 25 years in the United States studying and teaching, has published several articles in the *International Journal of Sociology of Law, Scandinavian Journal of Development Alternatives, Austrian Journal of Development Studies, African Quarterly, Africa Development, Journal of Third World Studies, India Quarterly* and other scholarly journals. He has also published a book titled: *Government Policy and Public Enterprise Performance in Sub-Saharan Africa*. His areas of specialization include race and ethnic relations in the United States, South Africa and Brazil, organizations and bureaucracies, Third World development, and African Studies. He is currently engaged in research on role of the nongovernmental organization (NGO) sector in Third World development, political economy of reform in Sub-Saharan Africa and other issues in development studies.

Sabita Manian is Associate Professor of International Relations at Lynchburg College, Virginia, where she teaches Asian politics and international affairs. Her Ph.D. in Political Science is from Tulane University where she specialized in European Union politics. She has presented a variety of papers at academic conferences on ethnic-nationalism, China-Taiwan politics in the Caribbean, gender politics, and NATO to name a few and is currently working on a manuscript on the trafficking of women in Asia. Her publications include "*Israeli Party Politics: What is SHAS for the goose is not Sauce for the Gander,*" an article on Guyanese ethnic politics in this volume was made possible by the Mednick Fellowship awarded by the VFIC (Virginia Foundation of Independent Colleges) to conduct field research in Guyana.

Elavie Ndura, a Burundi native, is an Associate Professor of Educational Transformation in the Initiatives in Educational Transformation (IET) program, Graduate School of Education, George Mason University, Manassas, Virginia. She holds a doctorate in Curriculum and Instruction with emphasis in Bilingual and Multicultural Education from Northern Arizona University, USA; a master's degree in Teaching English for Specific Purposes from the University of Exeter, UK; and a bachelor's degree in English Language and Literature from the University of Burundi, Africa. Her research interests are in the areas of diversity and multicultural education, cultural identity development, immigrants' acculturation, students' academic achievement in culturally diverse educational settings, multicultural peace education, and peaceful conflict resolution. Dr. Ndura has contributed chapters to several books including *Suffer the Litter Children: National and International Dimensions of Child Poverty* (Elsevier, in press), *Teaching all of the Children in Your Classroom* (Guilford, 2004), *Multicultural and Multilingual Literacy and Language: Contexts and Practices* (Guilford, 2004), and *Conflict Resolution and Peace Education in Africa* (Lexington Books, 2003). Her scholarly articles have appeared in Peace and Change (in press); *Journal of Adult and Adolescent Literacy; Language, Culture and Curriculum; Multicultural Perspectives; Multicultural Education; American Secondary Education*, and other publications.

Santosh C. Saha is a History professor at Mount Union College in Ohio. He had previously taught Asian and African history in colleges and universities in India, Ethiopia, Zambia, Liberia, and the United States. Dr. Saha was Editor-in-Chief of the *Cuttington Research Journal* in Liberia. Currently he is on the editorial board of the *Indian Journal of Asian Affairs* and also edits *Mount Union Academic Journal.*

He is the author of twelve books including *Dictionary of Human Rights Advocacy Organizations in Africa* (Westport, Conn.: Greenwood Press, 1999), *Culture in Liberia: An Afrocentric View of the Cultural Interaction between the Indigenous Liberians and the Americo-Liberians* (Lewiston, N.Y.: Edwin Mellen Press, 1998), and *Indo-U.S. Relations, 1947–1989: A Guide to Information Sources* (New York: Peter Lang, 1990). His civil conflict related books are *Religious Fundamentalism in Developing Countries*, ed. with Thomas Carr (Greenwood, 2001); *Islamic, Hindu, and Christian Fundamentalism Compared – Public Policy in Global Perspectivesi*, ed. with Thomas Carr (Mellen, 2003); *Religious Fundamentalism in the Contemporary World* ed. (Rowman & Littlefield/Lexington Books, 2003). His articles have appeared in many journals including *International Journal of African Historical Studies; Journal of Negro History; Journal of Asian History; Pakistan Historical Journal; Indian Journal of Asian Affairs; Scandinavian Journal of Development Alternatives*, and *Canadian Journal of African Studies*.

Stephen Shumock graduated from the University of South Alabama in May 2005 with a B.A. in Philosophy and Political Science. He is currently employed as a Financial Support Worker with the Mobile County Department of Human Resources. He plans to attend graduate school to study Political Theory in the near future.

Mark Lewis Taylor is Maxwell M. Upson Professor of Theology and Culture, Princeton Theological Seminary, earned his Ph.D. in 1982 from The University of Chicago Divinity School. His most recent book is *Religion, Politics and the Christian Right: Post-9/11 Powers and American Empire* (2005), *Beyond Explanation: Religious Dimensions in Cultural Anthropology* (1985), *Paul Tillich: Theologian of the Boundaries* (1986), *Remembering Esperanza: A Cultural Political Theology for North American Praxis* (1990), and *The Executed God: The Way of the Cross in Lockdown America* (2001). His articles have appeared in many professional journals, including *Current Anthropology, The Journal of Religion,* and *Theology Today.* Dr. Taylor supervised the Mesoamerican Study Project at Princeton Seminary, 1989–1995, training and orienting students for travel and study in Mexico, Guatemala and Nicaragua.

Vivienne Wee is Associate Professor in the Department of Applied Social Studies and Programme Coordinator of the Southeast Asia Research Centre, City University of Hong Kong. She formerly taught at The Chinese University of Hong Kong and the National University of Singapore. She was also previously Executive Director of the Centre for Environment, Gender, and Development (ENGENDER)—a regional development organization. Trained as an anthropologist, she has wide-ranging interests in religion and ideology, nation-state evolution, ethnicity and ethnonationalism, gender and development. She has done field research in almost every country in Southeast Asia. Her special expertise is in the remaking of the Malay world in Riau, Indonesia. In the field of religion, she has done ethnographic research in Singapore, Malaysia, Indonesia, and Hong Kong on Buddhism, Chinese religion, Islam, and secularism. She has published extensively in international journals and books. She recently edited a special issue of *The Pacific Review* 15, no. 4: "Exploring the new fault-lines in Southeast Asia." She is currently editing a volume titled *Political Fragmentation in Southeast Asia: Alternative Nations in the Making* (New York: Routledge; City University of Hong Kong Southeast Asia Series, forthcoming).